THIS TIME, THIS PLACE

OTHER BOOKS BY JACK VALENTI

NONFICTION

The Bitter Taste of Glory
(1971)

A Very Human President
(1976)

Speak Up with Confidence
(1982)

Speak Up with Confidence
(revised edition, 2002)

FICTION

Protect and Defend
(1992)

THIS

 TIME,

THIS

 PLACE

JACK VALENTI

My Life

IN WAR, THE WHITE HOUSE, AND HOLLYWOOD

HARMONY BOOKS / NEW YORK

Library of Congress Cataloging-in-Publication Data
Valenti, Jack. This time, this place : my life in war, the White House, and
Hollywood / Jack Valenti.—1st ed.
1. Valenti, Jack. 2. Political consultants—United States—Biography.
3. Johnson, Lyndon B. (Lyndon Baines), 1908–1973—Friends and associates.
4. United States—Politics and government—1963–1969. 5. Executives—
United States—Biography. 6. Motion Picture Association of America—
Biography. 7. Motion picture industry—California—Los Angeles—History.
8. Air pilots, Military—United States—Biography. 9. United States. Army.
Air Corps—Biography. 10. Houston (Tex.)—Biography. I. Title.
E840.8.V35A3 2006
973.92092—dc22 [B] 2006028804

ISBN 978-0-307-34664-3

Printed in the United States of America

DESIGN BY BARBARA STURMAN

10 9 8 7 6 5 4 3 2 1

First Edition

This book is written for and dedicated to
my extraordinary wife, Mary Margaret,
Courtenay, my daughter, and her husband, Patrick Roberts,
and to my son, John, to my daughter Alexandra,
and to my wondrous grandchildren,
Wiley Roberts and Lola Lorraine Roberts,
who I pray one day will read this book and then pass it along
joyously to their children

CONTENTS

PREFACE

A Few Beginning Words

Publishers call this book a memoir. To me it is a collection of memories of triumphs and tumult, tragedies and adventures, in a life unplanned, full of unexpected turns. It's about several careers rounded by tasks and obligations that so many others could have handled if fate had intervened in their lives as it did in mine.

As a little boy growing up on Alamo Street in Houston, Texas, where few dared aspire to places so obviously beyond their reach. I dreamed, but even fantasies fell way short of what actually lay ahead of me.

How could I, as a small boy sitting on my daddy's shoulders to catch a glimpse of President Franklin Roosevelt standing on the back of a train in Houston, ever imagine that one day I would bear witness to the assassination of a gallant young president, or expect to fly to Washington aboard Air Force One with a new president, in my new role as his special assistant?

How could I, walking the aisles as a fifteen-year-old usher in the dingy second-run Iris Theater in Houston, popping corn and helping the janitor and the projectionist, ever conceive that someday two movie moguls would woo me for a leadership role in Hollywood?

As a very young man who had never been aboard an airplane,

how could I ever think that one day my courage and my very soul would be tested in combat as the pilot of a B-25 attack bomber in a brutal war, where a skilled enemy did his damnedest to kill me.

But I survived the war. And as I have recounted to my children, I was given opportunities to serve my country in war and at the highest levels of the federal government. Working in the White House was the summertime of my life. And then to be offered the gift of spending almost four decades in the dazzling world of Hollywood with its best of the creative breed—well, that is the stuff of dreams unrestrained by reality.

Why write this book? I have no idea how many, if any, will want to read this story of an unexpected life of adventure. But no matter, I wrote this book so that one day my very young grandchildren, Wiley and Lola Lorraine, will read what I have put to paper and learn something about their grandfather—his early beginnings, how he grew to manhood, what he did, and how he always tried to do what is right. I hope they will see how he dealt with life's challenges, with defeat and victory, with fear and success. I want them to understand how much he learned from his grandfather and his parents about this lovely land with its hard-bought freedoms and its encouragement of opportunity and hope.

I will have shuffled off to that "great screening room in the sky" long before my grandchildren will have formed their own families. But I dare to pray that one day they will pass this book onto their children who will read and hopefully say, "We wish we could have known our great-grandfather. He sounds like someone we would enjoy hanging out with."

This is what my longtime loving friend Kirk Douglas calls "immortality," passing onto succeeding generations the best of what has gone before. This is the tie that binds families together—immortality indeed! It is from that ageless, wondrous impulse to pass it on that this volume of memories comes to life.

PART I

REWIND

Chapter 1

THE LONGEST DAY

The swearing-in aboard Air Force One, November 22, 1963. That's my distraught face in the lower left-hand corner. Next is the late congressman Albert Thomas of Houston, Lady Bird Johnson, the new president, and Mrs. Kennedy. In the right-hand corner just above Mrs. Kennedy is then congressman Jack Brooks of Beaumont, Texas.

It was a scene unlike any ever recorded in the long history of this Republic. It was a scene that I pray we may never experience again. The day was November 22, 1963. Air Force One sat under heavy guard on a runway at Love Field in Dallas. Aboard the plane, Lyndon Johnson, former vice president of the United States, stood with Mrs. Jacqueline Kennedy on his left, his wife, Lady Bird, on his right, and his right hand upraised as federal judge Sarah T. Hughes administered the constitutional oath of office that formally confirmed him as the thirty-sixth president of the United States.

Only hours before, President John Fitzgerald Kennedy, in a senseless act of mindless malice, had been assassinated in the streets of Dallas. His lifeless body was now resting in a flag-draped coffin in the rear of the plane. Once the brief swearing-in ceremony was over, the new president said softly, "Let's get airborne." It was 2:45 p.m., Dallas time.

Even after all these years, that day comes back to me with all the terrible power of a recurring nightmare. But it was no nightmare. It was all too real. To bear personal witness to a motorcade gone berserk with fear and desperation, as a gallant young president lay mortally wounded in his open-top limousine, is to enter the cauldron of hell itself. How impossibly confusing to be standing bewildered and distraught a few feet from the new president on Air Force One as he swore to preserve, protect, and defend the Constitution of the United States.

An hour before, I had been an obscure co-owner of an advertising and political consulting agency in Houston. Now, because Lyndon Johnson had suddenly chosen me to become a key member of his White House staff, I would be anonymous no more but anointed with the special cachet that comes to anyone on whom presidential power has been visibly conferred.

What brought me here to this place and time? How did all this happen?

It began for me a month earlier, when I received a call from Vice President Johnson. He wasted no time on amenities. He said: "The president is about to cut a deal with John Connally [then the governor of Texas]. He's going to Texas sometime next month. I don't think this is a good idea, not right now. The Democratic Party there is in a mess; Ralph Yarborough [the liberal senior senator from Texas] and Connally hate each other. I had wanted to wait and clean that mess up, but the president wants to go, so the trip is on. He wants to get ready for the election next year. He wants to raise money in Texas, and he wants to win Texas. So do I. So I want this trip to go off without a hitch."

He went on: "Now I understand from Albert [Albert Thomas was the longtime congressman from Houston who ruled his House Appropriations Subcommittee on Independent Offices like a divine right monarch] that you're putting on a big dinner for him on the twenty-first of next month. Albert thinks it makes good sense for the president to be there. Of course I'll be there, too. You think this will go well?"

I nodded and said nothing, but I knew that his question was not merely academic. Texas had always been politically situated in the middle of the road, but lately the second largest state in the Union had been drifting to the right of center. The Democratic Party, weakened by bitter infighting between conservative and liberal Democrats, was losing ground to Republicans. The Belden poll, highly respected in Texas, had revealed a drop in President Kennedy's popularity in the Lone Star State.

It was the judgment of the Kennedy White House, according to LBJ, that a Texas visit would bear favorable fruit. The plan was a tour, beginning in heavily Catholic San Antonio, followed by Houston (the largest metropolitan area in the state), Fort Worth, Dallas, and finally Austin, where the trip would conclude with a huge fund-raising dinner. The visit's twin objectives were to lift JFK's sagging poll numbers and to help fill his campaign coffers with badly needed funds.

Governor John Connally was then at the height of his popularity. I counted Connally to be the most charismatic man in American public life. He was handsome, a spellbinding orator, and, when necessary, a ruthless, all-sharp-elbows player in the political game. He had first come to the attention of Lyndon Johnson as a young law student at the University of Texas. Both men were part of a special breed—intelligent, tremendously energetic, and shrewd to the point of prescience.

Governor Connally was currently embroiled in a particularly venomous dispute with senior Texas senator Ralph Yarborough. The antipathy that raged between these two men bordered on pathological hatred. Yarborough, a passionate but isolated figure in Texas politics, felt cornered by the growing reach of the bold, popular governor. Recently, Yarborough had flung aside all efforts to broker a truce for the good of the Democratic Party, even a temporary one. He brooded over what he considered slights, seeing them as indications of dark conspiracies aimed at unseating him. He stalked the state, moving relentlessly through as many Texas counties as he could navigate, taking stock of his allies, and searching out his enemies in unlighted passageways. Since the senator knew Lyndon Johnson to be Connally's mentor and longtime friend, it followed naturally (to Yarborough) that he should mistrust the vice president with the same intensity he lavished on the governor.

President Kennedy recognized that a reelection campaign visit to a state where two powerful Democrats were at each other's jugulars was not ideal. But he needed to not only win Texas, but raise money there. So he sought, through Kenny O'Donnell, his chief political aide, to mollify Yarborough and to enlist Connally to the larger cause. He pressed Johnson for an all-clear signal, an indication that the time was right.

But LBJ deferred to Connally. The brunt of the work for the Texas tour would fall to the governor and his staff. Connally hesitated. Not because he was uneasy about the volatile Yarborough, but because he wasn't sure how successful the Austin fund-raiser would be and how hospitably Kennedy would be received. Connally was reading the same tea leaves as LBJ, and like LBJ, he was not fond of failure. So Connally waited. Finally, in a private meeting with the president in Washington, Connally agreed to the trip. The signals were hoisted. The plans were sealed. And one of the calls Johnson made was to me, knowing that I was familiar with the Texas political landscape.

After a brief moment of silence, I spoke up: "It'll go well, Mr. Vice President. We'll have a great event in Houston and a strong turnout."

"How many you figure will attend?" he asked.

"With you and the president there, I reckon we could put twenty-five hundred people in the Sam Houston Coliseum, maybe more."

His voice was cool. "Good. I'll get back in touch. The president will be sending some advance people to Texas. I want this visit to be a big success, no foul-ups, you understand?"

"No foul-ups, Mr. Vice President, not from my end."

"We'll make an announcement soon. After that you and your agency can start working the press. I'll talk to you later." I heard the phone click. LBJ was off to the next task in his busy day.

That evening, I recounted that conversation to my wife, Mary Margaret, who had started working for Senator Johnson when she graduated from the University of Texas and rose steadily in the LBJ ranks. When we met, she was one of the vice president's chief lieutenants, in whom he placed great trust and full confidence. Mary Margaret was totally loyal to LBJ, who valued that loyalty as well as her keen political judgment. She fortified my own judgment that this would be a crucial, highly sensitive visit, particularly the dinner in Houston. She knew how much LBJ would have invested in the success of this trip. She, like me, wanted it to go extremely well—and to go extremely well according to the vice president's assessment.

I got on the phone the next day to Congressman Thomas, who confirmed having had his own conversation with LBJ. I had worked as the campaign manager for Albert Thomas in his last four runs for reelection—all of them successful. I had learned much in those campaigns. I had learned where the sources of money could be found (in those days of no regulations, cash was the legal tender of choice, and much of it didn't need to be reported). And I learned who the key players were in any congressional run in Harris County, or for that matter in any race in the state.

On the phone, Albert Thomas was cheerful. "We're going to have a fine old time, Jackson." (Albert never called me Jack; it was always "Jackson" or "podner.") "Everything going all right?"

"It is, Albert. Once the announcement is made, my staff will be on the job. We'll make this a night to remember."

"I'm counting on you, Jackson."

Soon after the White House released the news that the president and the vice president were coming to Texas, hordes of Secret Service agents and Kennedy advance people began flooding the state. Jerry Bruno, the top Kennedy advance man, arrived in Houston after calling me and arranging to meet at the Rice Hotel. Recently, JFK had praised Jerry publicly, making him a bit of a celebrity. He was a no-nonsense guy, self-assured, incessantly curious, and ready to dive into every nook and cranny of the planning. He also conveyed the distinct impression that he was the greatest advance man ever to arrive on the political landscape.

Since I had no national experience, I was willing to cede Jerry Bruno the reins and to listen and learn. He had brought with him Marty Underwood, a fellow I knew and liked. Self-effacing, generous with praise, and open to suggestions and ideas, Marty understood instinctively that if you don't establish a rapport with the locals, they could eat you alive. Many advance men don't grasp this essential fact. When LBJ became president, I dealt with a lot of the advance men and women serving him. I always admonished them, "Don't piss on the local guys. They know the streets and the alleys, and they know who to see and who to trust and who not to trust. Hold them close and let them know you care about their judgment." That's precisely the way Marty interacted with me, which is one reason I would later make sure that he remained a key advance man in the Johnson administration.

Jerry Bruno roamed the city for a day and a half and, seemingly satisfied with what he'd found, said to me: "Jack, this is your show, and I don't intend to tell you how to run it. I hear from everyone I talk to that you know your way around the town, so I'll leave you alone. I've asked Marty to stay on to give you whatever assistance you need; otherwise you are on your own. I'm going to do some checking on the Dallas portion of the trip and the Austin dinner." Well, that suited me just fine—and left me with the impression that Jerry Bruno's reputation might be well deserved.

The president's Texas tour began on November 21, 1963. After a stop in San Antonio, Air Force One, a sleek, silver-bellied Boeing 707, took to the air again, then eased down on Runway 90 at Houston International Airport. The big plane braked quickly and taxied to the open ramp area, where a crowd of about a thousand waited in anticipatory excitement. There it slowed and stopped, gleaming softly in the sun, the stately blue letters that spelled out "United States of America" visible just above the long blue striping that ran the full length of the plane, from nose tip to tail assembly.

Congressman Thomas and Senator Yarborough were already aboard Air Force One and would disembark with President Kennedy. The vice president and Mrs. Johnson had arrived from San Antonio only minutes earlier, in Air Force Two. I checked in with security police and made a last-minute reconnaissance of the area to ensure that the motorcade cars were in their proper position and ready to go. I nodded to the police captain standing beside the open convertible that would transport the president, Mrs. Kennedy, and their party to downtown Houston's Rice Hotel, where they would rest before dinner that evening.

As we waited for the president and his entourage, I chatted briefly with the vice president. He seemed calm, although his political position had seemed fragile in recent days. Columnists had been dropping vague, disquieting hints that Johnson would be dumped from the ticket in 1964. At a recent press conference, President Kennedy had answered that question head-on by making it clear that LBJ would be on the ticket with him. But the rumors had been slow to fade away.

Yet the vice president never allowed his self-discipline to give way. To my knowledge, LBJ never uttered a single word of criticism of the president. Indeed, I was present at the Johnson ranch in early 1963 at a small dinner attended by five hugely wealthy Texans who were among the few oil industry titans who supported LBJ. In the middle of dinner, one of the oilmen began to rant about President

Kennedy, coarsely conveying the low regard in which he held JFK. I saw Johnson's lidded eyes narrow as he faced this outpouring of venom from his guest. Suddenly he pounded the table, sending glasses and plates clattering.

"Let me make this clear," said LBJ, his tone low and menacing. "At my table no one, I mean no one, demeans the president. If you want to keep on talking, then you'll have to leave this room and this house." A heavy silence descended on the room as its guests looked at their half-eaten food and toyed with their glasses. The oilman glanced uneasily around at the others, who were as surprised as he was by the vice president's harsh words. These men were old friends of Johnson. More than once, they had put their prestige on the line in supporting him for the Senate and the vice presidency, and they had been more than generous in providing campaign funds. But they said nothing.

Finally the oilman gulped, swallowing hard. "I'm sorry, Lyndon, sorry as hell. Didn't know it meant that much to you."

"Well, it does. You are my friend. You've always been there for me, but you crossed a line tonight. Don't cross it again." LBJ turned back to his food, as did the others. Someone at the table made a comment on how well John Connally was doing as governor, breaking the tension, and dinner proceeded without further incident.

This was consistent with LBJ. In every moment where I was personal witness, he always referred to the president with respect and affection. LBJ was not so fortunate with his own treatment at the hands of Bobby Kennedy and those around the attorney general. Too often the vice president learned of rude jokes from Bobby's people that described LBJ as "cornpone" and unworthy to be the number two man in the Kennedy administration. It was hard for Johnson, who had been the most successful majority leader in Senate history, to now find himself becalmed in a windless sea. He understood clearly that the vice president had as much power—or as little—as the president chose to give him. He never gave voice to his inner feelings, but to all his intimates it was evident that he kept himself tightly harnessed. It was not easy. But he told me and Mary Margaret many times that President Kennedy and Mrs. Kennedy offered the Johnsons continuous affection and warmth, which is why, in my judgment, LBJ responded in kind.

Johnson and President Kennedy understood the rules of the game. They played by them, each doing what was required, each man measuring and keeping under control personal passions and emotions generated by what observers concluded was an unnatural arrangement. Johnson did his job the best he could, grateful that the president had turned over to him authority for the Office of Equal Opportunity and for NASA, the national space program. He was fully prepared to serve out his White House days in a modest role.

He once told me during those days that "no southerner will ever be nominated for president, much less elected, in my lifetime. When 1968 is over, I'm going home and that will be the end of it." It is true that LBJ was visited by gloominess from time to time (what Churchill called his "black dog"), and this may have been one of those moments, but I'm sure he meant what he said. I have no doubt that in 1963 the vice president was planning to support the president in his bid for a second term and serve in the event of a victory, but after that it would be back to Texas for him and retirement from political life.

Now the throng by the ramp came alive. The door of Air Force One swung open, the stairway was set in place, and all eyes focused on the dark opening. The president came into view. He was tanned, handsome, confident. He waved and the crowd went wild, some of his young admirers leaping in excitement. He smiled widely, thoroughly enjoying himself.

Then there she was. Jacqueline Kennedy appeared and screams of approval and applause greeted the First Lady. Mrs. Kennedy was mainly absent from campaign tours; she had chosen to make her first 1963 political appearance in this Texas setting. She waved hesitantly to the crowd, a whisper of a smile on her face that grew wider as the welcoming applause surged.

The president was now by her side. He took his wife's arm, guiding her down the steps. Mrs. Kennedy moved slowly, but with assurance and dignity, her left hand touching the rail. A pink pillbox hat sat back on her head. The wind at the airport rushed at her, but not once did she employ the brow-clearing touch of hand to forehead that was so much the mark of Jackie Kennedy.

I barked out orders to my group of aides. Get to the cars. Make sure the motorcade is ready to roll. Keep the ceremonial greeting line at attention. As security police circled the plane, the crowd began pressing against the barricades, so I dispatched two more aides to the crowd line.

The president moved down the receiving line. Mrs. Kennedy was first to shake hands, and he followed close on her heels. Governor and Mrs. Connally, Senator Yarborough, and Congressman Thomas followed the president. The vice president and Lady Bird Johnson greeted the Kennedys warmly.

I was so busy checking the motorcade that I did not shake hands with the president or Mrs. Kennedy. Over my shoulder, I could see the president reaching the edge of the crowd, which was now almost mad in its enthusiasm. So far, everything was working according to plan. Congressman Thomas was elated. He gripped my shoulder. "Great work, Jackson," was his happy greeting.

Then it happened: the first foul-up. Senator Yarborough refused to ride in the same car as the vice president. I couldn't believe what I was seeing. The police officer looked at me helplessly. I was furious at Yarborough's stupidity and the absurd rudeness of his action. I wanted to kick his fat ass. But I had no time to indulge my own feelings, although I could see that even the most partisan Yarborough supporters in attendance were shocked. We swiftly commandeered Congressman Thomas's car and shoveled Yarborough into it next to Thomas. Somehow, without too much delay, we got the vice president and Mrs. Johnson into their car, and the motorcade was under way.

As the motorcade began its slow movement toward the airport exit for the drive to downtown Houston, I clambered into a Ford and found myself riding with Kenneth O'Donnell, the president's chief political aide. Here, on the Gulf Freeway heading toward the city's center ten miles away, there was no place for crowds. They would come later, I devoutly hoped, as we made our entry into the outskirts of downtown Houston. O'Donnell was dour, silent, and unsmiling. Months later, when I found myself in the role Ken was playing that day, I fully understood how he was feeling. I was an unknown factor. How well did I know my job, and how well had I done it? Though he had sent Jerry Bruno and Marty Underwood ahead to supervise the advance planning, he knew the burden of success or failure really fell on the locals, who had been enlisted by the governor and the vice president.

I was praying all the elements would fall into place. If the results were disappointing, it would not be for lack of hard work. We had been toiling at an avalanche of details all month, frustrated by annoyances such as who was going to be seated in which car with whom and how far back that would be from the president. It was a petty drama that I would see played out a hundred times in other places, as public officials jockeyed for a position near the Sun King.

On the ride into the city, Ken O'Donnell became visibly nervous. I was surprised. I thought that a consummate political pro like O'Donnell would be a cool cat, but he wasn't. He was obviously fidgety. He wasn't sure of anything this day, and his manner betrayed his doubts. Perhaps there had been dissension within the Kennedy White House about the necessity for this trip.

Now we were off the freeway and within a mile or so from the Rice Hotel. To my enormous relief, the crowds were there. They were large, and they were noisy. We could hear their shouts as the presidential convertible passed them, and as the crowds grew thicker, louder, and more affectionate, the hard lines in O'Donnell's face seemed to soften. He peered out the window, first to one side and then to the other. "They're there, aren't they?" he said to no one in particular.

"They damn sure are," I responded with a clear inference that I had personally herded every one of them into place with specific instructions.

Finally we turned onto Main Street. On both sides of the wide thoroughfare, there was nothing to be seen but a great wave of human beings, three and four deep, clinging together, screaming, and waving signs supporting JFK. As the motorcade came to a halt in front of the Rice Hotel, there were fully five thousand people clogging the intersection and spilling over onto the side streets, screeching at everything and everybody.

"What's your estimate of the total?" asked O'Donnell, ever the political tactician.

"I'd say between three and four hundred thousand, give or take a dozen or so," I said.

"Be sure the newspapers and the TV guys get that number. Have the chief of police give it to them," he ordered.

I wanted to respond testily, but I didn't. Of course I would alert the chief. In fact, the chief and I had already agreed to compare our estimates and put forward the one we deemed most likely to be accepted by the press.

I leaped from the car, O'Donnell in my wake. The presidential party had already been taken up the elevators to the massive suite awaiting them. I had badgered the hotel general manager to make sure the president's accommodations were immaculate, complete with fresh flowers and fresh fruit. The hotel lobby was a roiling sea of confusion. I pushed myself through the crowd using a police officer to run interference and then squeezed into an elevator crowded with security personnel. O'Donnell was nowhere to be seen, but I figured he could make his way to the presidential suite; this kind of reception was nothing new to him. I went immediately to the suite of the vice president, where two Secret Service agents on duty let me in.

The vice president was in an expansive mood. "Fine reception, Jack," he said. "The president was mighty pleased."

I greeted Mrs. Johnson and Mary Margaret, who had arrived before me. The suite was thronged with friends of the vice president. I whispered to my wife, "It went well, it went very well."

She touched my shoulder. "I'm glad for you, Jack."

Some minutes later, the vice president beckoned to me and I followed him into a smallish room adjoining the living room of the suite. We sat and talked for a bit. I watched his face as he spoke, with its deep lines etched by long days in his beloved Texas hill country sun. He was, I thought, a truly imposing man, all the more impressive when he unfolded himself to his full height. He loomed over almost everyone, a massive presence that he used to intimidate when he could not persuade.

His pride and status were on the line this visit, as they would be in the Kennedy reelection campaign the next year. He knew with melancholy certainty that his association with the Kennedys had diminished his power in his home state, its hospitable embrace of the president this day notwithstanding. Metropolitan Houston was only one piece of the state demographic. This very day, the *Houston Chron-*

icle had run a story under the headline LBJ IMAGE TARNISHED IN TEXAS. The story said, in part: "In all areas except south Texas, Johnson is more disliked now than at any time in his long career in public office. The dislike is attributed directly to his having accepted the vice presidency, thereby identifying himself as part of the JFK team."

As we sat down together, the vice president made no mention of this to me, so I said nothing about it, either. Instead, he held up the program for the Austin dinner, which my agency had created and printed in record time. "This is excellent, Jack. You did it right, and you did it on time." He paused and then said, "Will we have any problems tonight?"

"No, sir, no problems. We're all set. Everything is ready. Your hall will be full. You saw the greeting you and the president got in the streets."

He nodded, got to his feet, and shrugged his shoulders into his jacket, and I followed him into the large living room, where Mrs. Johnson and Mary Margaret were sitting while dozens of others milled around. Abruptly, LBJ turned to me as I stood beside Mary Margaret and said, "Why don't you pack a bag and fly with me to Fort Worth tonight, and then tomorrow we'll go on to Dallas and Austin? We'll have a chance to talk." He smiled at Mary Margaret and continued, "You can be back home late tomorrow night or the next morning. That's not taking you away too long, is it?"

I was pleased. The vice president had divined my thoughts. I did want to go with him, but we both sensed that Mary Margaret felt otherwise. Our first child, Courtenay, was only three weeks old, and the prospect of my leaving town, even for only two nights, was difficult for her. She frowned slightly but remained silent in deference to the vice president.

Neither of us knew that when I boarded Air Force Two that evening, I would never again return to my life in Houston.

Soon it was time to go to the Sam Houston Coliseum for the Albert Thomas dinner. I bade a temporary good-bye to the Johnsons. Mary Margaret would accompany them and arrange for my clothes to be conveyed to the vice president's plane. I rushed to the coliseum to go over final details before the president and the vice president arrived. I knew we would have our crowd, but I had also hedged my bet. I had considered the potential disaster of empty seats, so I had told the press we would have 3,000 in attendance. Then, unbeknownst to anyone but my aides, I had instructed the hotel to set out tables and chairs for 2,500. We deliberately kept a wide aisle in the rear of the hall, and my floor managers were ready to set up the extra tables in that spacious aisle at a moment's notice.

At the rear of the large stage platform, shielded from view by a flowing, heavy curtain, we had constructed an enclosure with a carpeted floor, laid this very day, as well as comfortable chairs, tables, and a small refreshment bar. Here we would house the president, vice president, and their wives before the ceremonies began. Our head table guests, some fifty of them, were being corralled in a private room off the main hall, leaving the backstage enclosure strictly for our stars. A short set of stairs had been built from the backstage area to the head table platform so the president and his party would have to move no more than fifty feet to be visible to the audience.

The hall began to fill early. Almost ten minutes before my prearranged estimate, I gave the signal to start bringing in the extra tables. One of my operatives passed the word to the press that we were besieged with an overflow crowd. It was now clear that while we might still have problems, a shortage of guests was not going to be one of them.

Soon I received the message that the president and his party were arriving at the side entrance of the coliseum, where they would be escorted to the rear enclosure. I walked quickly around the dinner tables to the backstage area. A somber-faced man stopped me. "Sorry, sir," he said, "this is off-limits."

"But I'm in charge of these arrangements. For God's sake, let me in."

"Sorry," he repeated, unimpressed. "No further, and no exceptions."

I was beginning to boil. It was plain that this unsmiling Secret Service agent knew his duty and was going to do it. At that moment, another agent sauntered over. "He's okay," he said. "He's running the show, he's one of Albert Thomas's men."

I reached the private enclosure, hesitated, poked my head inside, and eased on in. The vice president caught my eye and beckoned me to his side. He held me around the shoulder and brought me over to John F. Kennedy. "Mr. President, this is Jack Valenti," he said. "I told you about him earlier."

President Kennedy turned to me with a wide, friendly smile and greeted me warmly. "Lyndon tells me I have you to thank for this terrific crowd in Houston. I ought to bring you with me to handle my other visits, particularly when I'm not sure what kind of reception I will get."

He grinned at the vice president, and they both savored their not-so-private joke. Close up, the president was more handsome than his pictures, his body more tightly knit. I could see signs of aging in his face, but he exuded a remarkable boyish grace and a sense of perpetual alertness. He reminded me of a Plantagenet royal, a wise, brave, splendid king who would save a lady in distress. Or a nation.

The president took my arm and introduced me to his wife, who was seated in a large, green wing chair commandeered for this occasion. Mrs. Kennedy murmured, "How do you do," and like so many Houston residents that day, I was enchanted by her beauty. I turned to embrace Mrs. Johnson, who was seated next to Mrs. Kennedy, and returned to the side of a very relaxed and jubilant vice president. JFK and LBJ talked easily about politics, Johnson slightly taller, leaning forward to emphasize a point. I withdrew quietly, for there was still work to be done before they climbed the newly constructed pine-wood stairs that would take them to the long head table where the ranking guests were now being seated.

It would strike me later that it was my lot to meet John Kennedy for the first time on the last night of his life. And it would be many years later that I would get to know Jacqueline Kennedy very well when she acquired a novel I wrote and became my editor. Odd indeed are the turns of fate.

When Congressman Albert Thomas introduced the president, the crowd went wild. They were on their feet, screaming, applauding, and whistling. I couldn't see the president's face, but I saw LBJ turning toward JFK, and he was beaming. That was good.

Then the president began to speak. Standing some six feet behind him in back of the dais, shielded from the audience by the height of the head table, I noticed his right hand on the rostrum. The hand was shaking! I was taken by surprise. How could this master of the TV screen, this glorious orator who had hypnotized countless audiences, be so obviously nervous? My eyes fastened on that hand. Even after it dropped to his side, the shaking was noticeable to me. Of course, the audience saw none of this. His speech, rather brief, was characteristically impressive and generated another stirring round of applause when he was done.

But it was the sight of that trembling hand that stayed with me. It fortified my own sense that it's good to be nervous when you are addressing an audience. The adrenaline keeps you sharp. Being too confident could leave you reaching for the right words, which is deadly. I felt vindicated in my own nervousness as a public speaker by seeing that same quality in the finest political speaker of the day—and one of the great orators of all time.

The vice president's plane landed in Fort Worth around midnight. I ran down the steps, located the vice president's car, a late-model Lincoln Continental, and stood quietly beside it while the lengthy welcoming ceremonies went forward. After concluding their final greetings, Vice President and Mrs. Johnson appeared ready to get in and begin the motorcade to the hotel where we would spend the night.

To my amazement, Senator Yarborough appeared with an aide, who whispered to me, "The senator will ride with the vice president." I must have looked stunned; I'm sure I couldn't disguise it. JFK or someone awfully close to the president must have had a long parental talk with Yarborough, for there was no sign of reluctance or pique now, only a beaming Yarborough who greeted LBJ and Mrs. Johnson. If so, it was quite marvelous what a good presidential spanking could achieve.

I sat in the front seat, with Mrs. Johnson in the middle in the rear, the vice president to her right, and Senator Yarborough to her left. The conversation could not be described as spirited, but words were exchanged, and the vice president filled in with funny anecdotes when the conversation flagged. I admired the ease with which LBJ handled Yarborough, and I was made aware, once again, of the vice president's many sides. He could be fierce when called for, but now he was full of good humor, graciously accepting Yarborough's presence as if completely unaffected by the bitter memory of a few hours before.

At the Hotel Texas, I joined aides Liz Carpenter and Cliff Carter in LBJ and Lady Bird's huge suite. Once everyone settled in, Mrs. Johnson said, "Didn't Mrs. Kennedy look pretty? And didn't she handle herself with such charm and dignity?"

I could have described Mrs. Johnson with those very same phrases. It was typical of Mrs. Johnson to be generous to others, particularly those for whom she had admiration and respect. In all my years of close contact with this remarkable, incredibly warm and loving lady, I never heard her utter an unkind word, not once. Invariably she conducted herself with integrity, with an inbred grace and unerring good taste, never succumbing to the intense pressures of public scrutiny to be anything other than who she was. She was a rare human being, an impossible target for enemies, and an inexhaustible pillar of strength to her husband.

Her political judgments were sound. She had definite opinions, and she expressed them lucidly, with a gentleness that took the edge off those moments when what she said was at variance with the opinions of everyone else in the room. From every encounter, she retrieved all the thorns. When it came to crunch time, LBJ valued her opinion more than those of any of his counselors, because he knew that, alone among his entourage, she delivered her views without any agenda of her own. She had stood by him through thirty years of rough political campaigning, and though she was always a lady, she was also a sturdy and shrewd political pro.

One has to be careful when describing Mrs. Johnson. There is the temptation to go overboard in heaping laurels on her. Yet the record supports that impulse. How she managed to combine the roles of wife, mother, adviser, environmental activist, and ceremonial White House partner while retaining her good humor is still not clear to me. She always did her job uncomplainingly. Years later, I remarked to an audience that without Mrs. Johnson, LBJ would have been crippled. I believed it then, and I believe it now. I remember years later, when she sought successfully to insert the beauty of wildflowers alongside the nation's highways. The legacy of her work was embodied in Lady Bird Johnson Park, on the banks of the Potomac in

Washington, D.C. Coming in from the airport, drivers passing that park in the springtime are enchanted by a wild profusion of color.

The late Charles Guggenheim, four-time winner of the Academy Award for Best Documentary, told me a story about filming Mrs. Johnson for a documentary to be exhibited at the LBJ Library in Austin. As they walked through the park that bore her name, he stopped filming for a moment. A young fellow in his mid-twenties, not yet born when LBJ was president, braked his bicycle to a stop and said, "Aren't you Mrs. Johnson?" She nodded pleasantly. He broke into a wide smile. "Oh, thank you, Mrs. Johnson, for this wonderful park. My friends and I are grateful to you every day." Then he smiled wider, got back on his bike, and pedaled off.

In Fort Worth the next morning, the president and the vice president and their wives breakfasted in the ballroom of the Texas Hotel with a mass of Democrats who had come to applaud their president. Mrs. Kennedy was there, cheerful and charming; more eyes were on her than on her husband, but he didn't seem to mind that in the least.

After breakfast, on a raised platform in front of the hotel, JFK, LBJ, Governor Connally, and Senator Yarborough spoke to roughly a thousand people who had come by to see the city's famous visitors. Soon we were aboard our planes again for the brief flight to Love Field in Dallas. There at the airport, we formed the motorcade. I found myself in a large car with Evelyn Lincoln, secretary to the president; Pamela Turnure, aide to Mrs. Kennedy; and the irrepressible Liz Carpenter, chief of staff to Mrs. Johnson. We were six cars back from the president's open convertible, where he and his wife sat in the back bench seat, with Governor and Nellie Connally in the seats just in front of them. The motorcade was under way.

The Longest Day had begun.

The crowds here in Dallas were as large as those in Houston. There was no trace of ill will, only thousands of cheering people four to five deep along the route, laughing, waving, and screaming their delight at being so close to the president of the United States and the First Lady.

We moved through an underpass, and the street curved as we passed by an undistinguished building later described to me as the Texas School Book Depository. We were on Dealey Plaza. Suddenly, without a trace of warning, the car in front of us accelerated from eight miles an hour to eighty. I saw a policeman wildly waving us ahead, and buildings began to blur as we raced to keep up. Then we lost the car in front of us as we swerved to avoid people running across our path.

The whole spectacle turned bizarre, like an arcade game run amok, as we drove madly toward or away from some unnamed terror. This was no sensible motorcade. What had happened? What was wrong? As if unwilling to know the answers, I found myself saying to our driver, "I think the president is late to his speech at the Dallas Trade Mart. Let's get over there as quickly as we can."

We caromed through the streets and wound up at the Trade Mart, the bulging cluster of buildings where the president was to speak. We drove to the back entrance to make inquiries. Surely someone could confirm what we eagerly wanted to hear, that the president had been a bit delayed by some security precautions but would soon make his speech. . . .

At the entrance, a distraught-looking man raced past us, his coat and tie flying, to a pay phone down the hall. He was holding a transistor radio, and through the crackle of static we could hear the announcer's voice: "The president and the governor have been shot . . . Parkland Hospital! . . ." I yelled at a man standing next to a dusty Chevrolet. He looked up, startled. I grabbed him by the arm and said, "I have President Kennedy's secretary with me. Can you take us to Parkland Hospital right now?"

He was a deputy sheriff, and he would take us. We emptied his rear seat of some tools and litter, and then we climbed in. We raced to Parkland, siren screaming. When we arrived at the hospital, its entrance was cluttered with cars parked helter-skelter and blocked by a swarm of uniformed police and plainclothesmen. Once I had identified my passengers, we were admitted through the front doors; I gently escorted Mrs. Lincoln, by this time in a state of nervous collapse, to the administrator's office, where I left her in the care of an understanding hospital staff assistant and nurse. I ran down the hall and down the steps to the basement, where I had been told the vice president could be found. The basement was a mass of people, their stunned faces a collage of anxiety and grief.

I recognized a cluster of Texas congressmen, and one of them pointed to a stainless steel door. "That's the emergency operating room. The president is in there." Was he alive? Was he dead? No one seemed to know.

Congressman Homer Thornberry was going to visit Mrs. Connally, so I joined him. She sat in a small room, her eyes red, her hands in her lap, her face drawn and pale with anxiety. Mrs. Johnson sat beside her.

"How is John?" I asked.

She looked up, tears filling her eyes. "We don't know, we just don't know." Mrs. Johnson embraced her.

I wandered out into the hall again. I must go check on Mrs. Lincoln, I thought. I must go see how she is faring. As I entered the stairwell to walk upstairs, I bumped into Cliff Carter, LBJ's aide.

"The vice president wants you, and he wants you now. I've been looking for you." Cliff Carter pulled at my arm, then he stopped and said softly, "The president is dead, you know."

I didn't know. Tears overcame me, and try as I might, I couldn't regain my self-control. Cliff stood silently for some seconds, and then very gently he said, "We must go now, Jack, the vice president is waiting for us. Compose yourself." I murmured something, wiped my eyes, and together we set off to find Lyndon Johnson.

A few moments later, we were in a small room on the basement floor where Cliff said the vice president would be waiting. The room was empty except for a Secret Service agent standing by the door. He was Lem Johns, later to become a trusted member of the White House Secret Service detail. Johns had clearly been waiting for us. "I'm to take both of you to Love Field. Mr. Valenti, the vice president wants you aboard Air Force One right now."

Lem Johns piled us into a police car, and with siren keening, we sped toward Love Field. I was puzzled. Why was I going to Air Force One? I needed to get back home to Houston. Mary Margaret would be expecting me. My thoughts were tumbling inside me, and I could barely make sense of them.

When we got to the airport, Air Force One had been moved to a remote corner of the field and was now guarded by a cordon of menacing, heavily armed men, their Uzi-type machine pistols at the ready. I clambered aboard the presidential plane, acutely aware of my own apprehension. This was new, unexplored territory. I had no idea what was in store for me.

The forward portion of the plane was fitted with three dozen seats for the press, staff, and visitors. The presidential office was just aft of the forward section of the plane. It was thickly packed with somber-faced officials and others. Aft of the presidential office was a narrow corridor leading to a starboard-side presidential bedroom, twin beds, shower, toilet, and closet, and aft of that was the galley.

I looked up as the huge figure of Lyndon Baines Johnson suddenly filled the narrow corridor. His face was grim, but beyond that he betrayed no emotion. Everyone seated in the now-crowded presidential office rose respectfully. He gave us all a slight wave and seated himself in the presidential chair.

He saw me and beckoned. I came quickly to his side. He murmured to me in a soft voice, "I want you on my staff. You'll fly back with me to Washington." That was it. Within seconds I became the first newly hired special assistant to the president.

Then I blurted out two questions that even now cause me to wince in embarrassment. "But, Mr. President," I said chokingly, "I don't have any clothes."

LBJ looked at me as if wondering, Who is this cretin I am bringing to my staff?, but not unkindly. "Well," he said, "we have phones on this plane. Call Mary Margaret and have her send some to you. Or you can buy whatever you need in Washington."

Then I hurled another one at him: Even now I wince when I think about it. I said to the new president, "But I don't have a place to live."

His answer was swift and decisive: "You can live with me until your family gets to Washington." And that was precisely what I did. I took up residence at the Johnsons' Spring Valley home for eleven days, until they moved into the White House.

The president then turned his attention to more pressing business. He was on the phone to Rose Kennedy, mother of JFK. He spoke softly to her: "Mrs. Kennedy, I wish to God there was something I could do for you." He listened for a moment and then said; "Please, Lady Bird wants to talk with you," and he passed the phone to Mrs. Johnson.

Mrs. Johnson said, "Oh, Mrs. Kennedy, the heart has been torn out of us today. Our love and our prayers are with you."

After that conversation ended, Johnson then called Nellie Connally, and he and Lady Bird chatted with her, their concern obvious. He then called McGeorge Bundy, national security adviser, and his own most trusted aide, Walter Jenkins. There were meetings to set up, critical meetings. Bundy and Jenkins received their instructions: "Reschedule the cabinet meeting for Saturday. Get hold of the congressional leaders. Tell them I want to meet with them as soon as I get to the White House."

Word was delivered to Andy Hatcher, deputy press secretary. Malcolm Kilduff, also deputy press secretary, was in charge of the press for President Kennedy's Texas visit since Pierre Salinger, JFK's press secretary, was on Secretary of State Dean Rusk's plane speeding to Tokyo with several cabinet officers on board. Kilduff asked Hatcher to alert the Washington press about our arrival and the meetings that the president had set up.

The president spoke several times with Secretary of Defense Robert McNamara, with Nicholas Katzenbach, deputy attorney general, and finally with Bobby Kennedy. While the rest of us on the plane were in varying degrees of hysteria, LBJ was preternaturally calm. Faced by the gravest challenge to America in that century, he had exercised phenomenal control over his galvanic moods. How do you deal with the assassination of the president of the United States when the nation is looking to you to act swiftly and decisively to calm its fears?

There were two pressing questions. First, should we get airborne now or should we wait for the body of the late president to be brought aboard? The Justice Department was urging swift departure, as was the Defense Department. Without hesitation, LBJ said flatly he would not depart Dallas until the coffin of President Kennedy was secure on the plane. He understood intuitively that he could not leave the body of President Kennedy alone in Dallas.

The other question was harder to answer. When should the new president be sworn in? McNamara and Katzenbach both recommended the president hold off. "It's a formality, Mr. President," said Katzenbach. "You are president now, you can be formally sworn in later." Secretary McNamara told Johnson that fighter planes had been scrambled from Barksdale Field in Shreveport and Bergstrom Field in Austin to escort Air Force One back to Washington. No one knew the extent of the danger posed by Kennedy's squalid assassination. There could be more threats lying in wait.

Johnson didn't question the logic put forward by McNamara and Katzenbach. He was simply seeing clearly what others didn't. The swearing-in ceremony wasn't essential to grant him presidential authority, but he saw that the entire world, not just the United States, was in a state of shock. LBJ judged it crucially important that he try to stanch the flow of fear before it spread too far too fast. Though I did not know it, LBJ had already summoned Judge Sarah T. Hughes, appointed to the federal bench by President Kennedy on the advice of her fellow Texan Lyndon Johnson, to swear him in as president.

What Johnson had also chosen to do was have his swearing-in photographed and to have that film developed as soon as the presidential plane landed at Andrews Air Force Base in Maryland. The photos would be flashed immediately to every country on earth, and to every chancellery on every continent. He meant to impress on this anxiety-ridden world that in the United States, the Constitution endured. For what the Constitution declares is, "The president is dead. The president lives. The nation goes on." He wanted his own citizens to confirm for themselves that the president was the custodian of the spirit of their great nation, the steward of its heritage, and the keeper of its national integrity. And the president always lived. A great leader had just been murdered, but the office of the president of the United States was greater than any one man. The nation that prized freedom above all else was resilient enough to absorb even this.

Johnson informed McNamara and Katzenbach that he would remain at Love Field until the coffin containing the body of President Kennedy was brought aboard and until the swearing-in ceremony was complete. He ordered the Tokyo-bound Boeing 707 carrying Secretary Rusk, press secretary Pierre Salinger, and a contingent of members of Congress to turn around and get back to Washington as quickly as possible.

At this moment, the Kennedy inner circle was in the after-portion of the plane, in the galley area. Kenny O'Donnell, Larry O'Brien, Mac Kilduff, and the others sat stone-faced, unable to fathom their loss. These men, intimate aides, trusted counselors, veterans of bare-knuckle campaign battles, were famous, feared, envied, and obeyed. They lived and worked at the highest level of American governance, alongside an urbane, witty, gallant president beloved by the world. And in a few seconds it had all come to an end. Gone. Finished. Forever.

Later chroniclers have described tension and antagonisms between the Johnson people and the Kennedy aides. I saw none of this. And on this day I saw only the sorrow and the pain, and the end of life as the Kennedy aides had lived it. If our positions had been reversed, I'm not sure I could have conducted myself with the courage and dignity that they did, and if reporters had seen what I saw, they would have known better than to posit frictions that never occurred. The one aberration was Major General Godfrey McHugh, military aide to President Kennedy, who was out of control. He flung himself into the pilot's cabin and screamed at the pilot, Colonel Swindal, to get airborne. The pilot told him calmly that he was awaiting orders from President Johnson, whereupon McHugh stormed down the aisle, threatening anyone who came near him. He leaned over me, his face contorted, to say he was ordering Air Force One to take off. Although I had no authority to countermand an order by a two-star general, I said that the president was going to be sworn in shortly and the plane could not take off until that ceremony was concluded. At that moment, a Secret Service agent interceded, and that was the last of my encounters with the agitated general.

A few weeks later, one of President Johnson's first decisions was to reduce the number of his military aides from three to one, army general Chester Clifton. I don't know if General McHugh's ravings on Air Force One influenced the president's decision. I certainly didn't tell him about them. But LBJ seemed to have knowledge of everything, to the point where I began to suspect him of mind reading, so possibly he knew this, too.

My first official duty aboard Air Force One was to phone Deputy

Attorney General Katzenbach, whom I had never met. I identified myself and said, "Mr. Katzenbach, we're in rather urgent need of the exact wording of the official oath of office. If you can dictate it to me, we'll type it up for use by Judge Hughes."

There was a moment's hesitation on the other end of the line. "Of course. Let me find it, and I'll get right back to you."

What I learned later was that Katzenbach, brilliant lawyer that he was, didn't know where to find the oath. I sure as hell didn't know. Some minutes later, he called back. "We have the oath. If you'll get someone on the line to take it down, I'm ready," he said.

"Fine," I said, "but can you tell me where you found it?"

I could almost hear Katzenbach smiling. "In the Constitution."

Of course.

Within seconds, Marie Fehmer, the vice president's unflappable and superbly efficient secretary, had the presidential oath of office typed cleanly on white paper and ready for Judge Hughes. We looked around for a Bible. None was to be found, but we did locate a Catholic missal in the presidential bedroom.

Judge Hughes was now aboard the plane. LBJ, when notified that she was ready to board, asked one of the Kennedy aides if Mrs. Kennedy would feel comfortable coming forward to stand next to him as he took the oath of office. She agreed to do so. I saw her emerge slowly from the rear of the plane, walking as if in a trance. Her pink blouse was liberally spotted with her husband's blood as well as fragments of his brain matter that had sprayed her when the assassin's bullet struck, but she had refused to change into another garment. While I marveled at her strength, she came to a stop at LBJ's side. Her eyes were open, but unseeing. I had read and heard of catatonic trances, but I had never confronted one until Mrs. Kennedy came forward to stand next to President Johnson.

The picture recorded by navy yeoman Cecil Stoughton's camera is arguably the most famous photograph of the twentieth century. There it is, in black and white: LBJ, his right hand upraised, with the top of Judge Hughes's head in the foreground, along with Mac Kilduff, JFK's assistant press secretary, holding a live mike. To Johnson's left is Mrs. Kennedy, and to his right stands his wife, Lady Bird. Next to her is the tall figure of the late congressman Albert Thomas. It was

Thomas who pulled me from my position behind him to his side for a better view of the most dramatic swearing-in of a president in the history of the nation, saying, "Come around here, Jackson, you have to see this up close." I had no idea that as a result, my face would be frozen forever in that famous photograph, but there I was in the lower left-hand corner of that picture, my face distraught, incomprehension in my eyes as I stared at Lyndon Johnson taking the oath of office with his right hand raised. I was transfixed. I was so caught up in the multiplying events of this emotional moment that it was not until later that I understood the grave and wondrous miracle that had unfolded before my eyes. For the new president had spoken the same words as George Washington had uttered 174 years earlier. Midship on Air Force One, LBJ had sworn the same oath that fifty-five men in Philadelphia had written down on a piece of parchment in 1787. The ritual was reenacted, as it had been for every president since the very first. It was indeed, in the words of Lord Macaulay, "a divine continuum."

Once Air Force One had lifted off and Mrs. Kennedy retired to the rear of the plane, the new president roamed the aircraft. At one point, he sat by a window across from the presidential chair. He motioned me to sit beside him, with Bill Moyers and Liz Carpenter in the facing seats. LBJ asked a steward for a glass of water. Why do I remember this? Because when the steward returned, LBJ reached past me to take the glass. His huge fingers were literally inches from my eyes. What I saw was astounding. The president's hand was absolutely steady. How could that be? I thought. Later on as I got to know LBJ intimately, I recalled a line Winston Churchill had written about Henry II of England: "It was said that he was always gentle and calm in times of urgent peril, but became bad-tempered and capricious when the pressure relaxed." Perhaps this didn't completely fit the man I would come to admire so much, but there were certainly times when it seemed a fair portrait of LBJ.

Then the president said, "I want you [meaning Moyers, Liz, and me] to put something down for me to say when we land at Andrews. Nothing long. Make it brief. We'll have plenty of time later to say more." When the president rose, the three of us began trying to create the brief statement the president wanted. Finally, we reached consensus. It certainly was short: fifty-seven words, to be precise. The president read over our draft once, then twice. He nodded, took out a pencil, and changed one line. Where we had crafted the last sentence to read, "I pray for God's help and yours," he had switched the emphasis: "I pray for your help and God's."

Not long afterward, Air Force One touched down in Washington. But before LBJ disembarked, one more strange moment would play out on this endless day. According to plan, once we landed the president would go immediately to the rear of the plane and depart the aircraft alongside Mrs. Kennedy and the coffin of President Kennedy. When Air Force One rolled to a stop at Andrews, LBJ and I were standing in the narrow corridor leading from the presidential bedroom to the galley area. Once JFK's coffin was forklifted off the plane, steps would roll up here, allowing Mrs. Kennedy to disembark, followed by President Johnson and the Kennedy aides.

At that moment, Bobby Kennedy, who had just boarded from the front of the plane, bolted through the passageway just inches from LBJ, pushing forward to get to the rear of the plane. LBJ stood impassively, his hands at his side. Bobby's face was stern, looking straight ahead, masking any emotions he was feeling. As he forced his way through the narrow corridor, pushing aside a Secret Service agent, he murmured, "Excuse me." The new president was literally trapped by Secret Service agents who moved to surround him. By the time LBJ got to the aft exit door, Mrs. Kennedy, Bobby, and the Kennedy aides had already followed the coffin to the tarmac.

LBJ was silent. He nodded to a Secret Service agent, then moved back to the forward section of the plane, with Mrs. Johnson by his side. They descended and stepped onto the brightly lit tarmac, where he was to deliver his statement.

The air was chilly as LBJ and Mrs. Johnson approached the cluster of microphones around a temporary lectern. Television lights stabbed the darkness. It seemed as if all of Washington officialdom stood in the large semicircle, along with every reporter in the area who had a press pass and transportation to Andrews Air Force Base. It was 6:10 p.m. eastern standard time when the president, his face somber, began his statement: "This is a sad time for all people. We have suffered a loss that cannot be weighed. For me it is a deep personal tragedy. I know the world shares the sorrow that Mrs. Kennedy and her family bears. I will do my very best. That is all I can do. I pray for your help and God's."

Once his brief speech was done, the president headed for the two helicopters sitting ready on the tarmac. He beckoned to me, and I climbed in after him, joining the Secret Service agents and others already on board. The other chopper filled up swiftly. We took off and several minutes later landed softly on the South Lawn of the White House. It was my first visit, and I had as my tour guide the new president of the United States.

We went inside the Diplomatic Reception Room, then walked through the basement to the portico of the West Wing. The president did not enter the Oval Office. Instead we strode across West Executive Avenue, a guarded private street for the use of government officials and special guests of the White House. We entered the Executive Office Building and took the elevator to LBJ's vice presidential suite of offices on the second floor.

McGeorge Bundy was waiting in the LBJ offices when we arrived. Bundy briefed him on all matters that demanded swift response. Governor Averell Harriman, now assistant secretary of state, and Senator Bill Fulbright, chairman of the Senate Foreign Relations Committee, were ushered in. The moment Harriman and Fulbright departed, the president got on the phone, calling first President Truman, then President Eisenhower, and then Sargent Shriver, brother-in-law to President Kennedy.

At 9:25 p.m., after various meetings and phone calls, President Johnson asked Bill Moyers, Cliff Carter, and me to join him in his limo, headed for his Spring Valley residence. There Rufus Youngblood, head of the new Secret Service detail, met us in the driveway.

"Mr. President," said Rufus, "we haven't had time to put in secure phones yet. So just remember when you talk, you're on AT&T, no security." The president nodded and even managed a smile.

When we all got inside, LBJ greeted and talked with several dozen close friends and colleagues who were already there, waiting for him. He sipped orange juice. Finally, as midnight neared, he prepared to go upstairs. He nodded to Bill, Cliff, and me, and we followed him to the second-floor master bedroom. He had now been president for a little more than eleven hours.

Mrs. Johnson had apparently gone to another bedroom, leaving LBJ with the three of us. He changed into pajamas and sat upright in his large bed, his back leaning against the headboard. I stirred fitfully in a chair to the left of the new president. Cliff Carter sat on a small chair on the other side of the bed, while Bill Moyers lounged on a chair near Carter. We watched the television set with morbid fascination. After the terrible events of the day were covered, television commentators worldwide gave careful scrutiny to this Texan who had been thrust so suddenly into a new role as leader of the free world.

We stared at the glowing screen while LBJ began to ruminate. He was not asking for our judgments or using us as a sounding board for his ideas. He was simply giving voice to the torrent of thoughts pouring through his mind.

"I'm going to pass that civil rights bill that's been tied up too damn long in the Senate. I'm going to get that bill passed by Congress, and I'm gonna do it before next year is done. And then I'm going to get a bill through that's gonna make sure that everybody has a right to vote. You give people a vote, and they damn sure have power to change their life for the better."

As I recall, Moyers, Carter, and I didn't offer any comments. If LBJ had said he was going to ride Pegasus to the nearest star, I would have bet on it.

Later on that evening, he pointed to the TV set when the commentator made some remark about Harry Truman. "By God, I intend to pass Harry Truman's medical insurance bill. He didn't do it, but we'll make it into law. Never again will a little old lady who's sick as a dog be turned away from a hospital because she doesn't have any money to pay for her treatment. It's a damn disgrace."

And he wasn't through yet. As we watched the TV screen, he spoke up again, forcefully: "We are going to do something about education. We're going to pass a bill that will give every young boy and girl in this country, no matter who they are, the right to get all the education they can take. And the government is going to pay for it." I was beginning to feel like an intimate observer to an unprecedented historic moment. As I scribbled notes on a pad of paper, it dawned on me that Moyers, Carter, and I were in a room with the person on whom the entire world's attention was now directed and whose presence in the days and years ahead would be relentlessly sought after and fanatically analyzed. But it wasn't until we began working on President Johnson's commencement speech at the University of Michigan in May 1964 that it hit me. Before he was president for a full day, LBJ had laid out for the three of us in his bedroom what later became the design for the Great Society! It was a stunning display of LBJ's gifts as a visionary, as well as the political instincts without which no leader ever achieves greatness.

Finally, sometime between 3:30 and 4:00 a.m., President Lyndon Johnson suggested that we try to get some rest. Strange, but even after the day's terrible events, and after going without sleep for almost twenty-four hours, I wasn't tired. As I lay and turned on a bed belonging to Lynda Bird Johnson, I knew I would never forget a moment of this day. And I wondered if the man who lay not thirty feet from me, the new president in the next room, would sleep at all.

Tomorrow I would begin a new life, performing on the largest proscenium stage in the world. My office would be in the West Wing right next door to the Oval Office. But what kind of America would the new president govern? How would we be changed by the murder of his predecessor, whose youthful ambitions had served to inspire us all? I tossed wearily and fitfully. What lay ahead of me? It was all so strange. Finally, sleep put a temporary end to my anxious musings.

The Longest Day was finally over.

Chapter 2

LYNDON BAINES JOHNSON

A very infrequent leisurely moment in the Oval Office, with the president and me chatting.

We must touch his weaknesses with a delicate hand. There are some faults so nearly allied to excellence, that we can scarce weed out the fault without eradicating the virtue.

—OLIVER GOLDSMITH, *The Good-Natur'd Man*

Lyndon Johnson was the most formidable political leader I will ever know. He was also arguably the most complex. His mind was honeycombed with contradictions. He was terrifying, kind, hyperenergetic, ruthless, loving; a lover of land, earth, water, and animals; patient, impatient, restless, caring, petty, clairvoyant, bullying, compassionate, tough, devious, generous, and full of humor and wit. I have often said that almost anything you could say about Lyndon Johnson, good or bad, had at least a hint of truth to it.

For years to come, historians, social scientists, and PhD candidates will study the grand design of the LBJ personality. To my way of thinking, LBJ was aptly described by David Halberstam when he wrote: "Lyndon Johnson was, perhaps, the twentieth century president most reeking of human juices." Of all the mythical characters I have read about, it was Achilles in Homer's *The Iliad* who most resembled LBJ: the courageous Achilles, the angry Achilles, the charismatic Achilles, the Achilles with all his skills, his pride, and his commanding presence.

There are already considerable volumes published about the Johnson presidency. More will surely come. No one of them can ever be definitive on the labors President Johnson performed, the deeds he accomplished, and the faults he exhibited, much less take an accurate or full measure of the man himself. To the press that examined his actions, and to the public that benefited from his leadership in the largest assaults ever made on the social, political, and economic ills that have infected this nation since the birth of the Republic, at least part of the fascination with Lyndon Johnson is due to the complexity of the man. Other than his wife, I do believe there is no single human being who will ever wholly grasp the design of a spirit so complicated that it was probably withheld from LBJ himself. But by any account, LBJ was an awesome engine of a man.

If you had asked Lyndon Baines Johnson what he was most proud of in his public life, he would have said, "First, the Voting Rights Act of 1965, and second, bringing electricity to the lamplit homes of the hill country." When LBJ was growing up in Texas, it was a common sight to see women walking long distances to the town well, then heading back to their homes burdened with poles balancing two large buckets of water, making the distance back to the house so much longer than the walk to the well. He knew life as it was in Lincoln's time: people reading by oil lamps and candles, warmed by wood-fired stoves, and stepping outside to answer nature's call. And all this in the twentieth century, when electricity was available to most Americans, but not those who lived in the hard-scrabble counties of Texas's hill country. In central Texas today, thanks to LBJ, there are dams and rural generators that have changed life for farmers and ranchers and their families, few of whom ever thought they would see the day when they could flick a switch and life and light would suddenly appear. Lyndon Johnson lit the lights that illuminated and energized his beloved hill country.

LBJ was a first-class storyteller, spinning tales that revolved around the land, animals, ranch country, and political environment. He was also a gifted mimic, capable of perfect-pitch renditions of Everett Dirksen, Hubert Humphrey, and almost every contemporary political figure of note. He loved to deal in parables. Sometimes they were earthy to make a point, or simply pressed home an idea, or illuminated a rule of behavior. His ambitions were not yet full-blown when Johnson was a congressman and a senator, although their stirrings made themselves felt when he was a young man. They grew as he began his long political climb. Everything that happened to LBJ in his earliest years, then later in his House and Senate tenure, was but a prologue to his performance as president. He learned from defeat and from mistakes made in unplanned moments. He vowed he would not make the same mistake twice. He read about past presidents, especially from Herbert Hoover and FDR on. He noted their slips and momentary setbacks, examining them with the concentrated engagement of a scientist surveying his microscope's revelations.

When he first came to Washington in 1931 at age twenty-three, as a fledgling congressional secretary to Texas congressman Richard Kleberg of King Ranch fame, Lyndon Johnson joined an organization called the Little Congress. It was populated by assistants to congressmen, a membership that could have had a substantive, and positive, effect on their bosses. But it was led listlessly by staffers who always seemed to have other fish to fry. It should come as no surprise that almost immediately upon arriving in Washington, LBJ would determine that the Little Congress could give a young, unknown aide heft and visibility. So with the unrelenting Johnsonian drive in full display for the first time, he prowled the corridors of the organization, getting to know the names (and foibles) of the other congressional aides. At the next election, Lyndon Johnson won his first important political triumph. He was elected Speaker of the Little Congress, the highest office in that group, celebrated by his young peers as the best among them. But LBJ had no intention of stopping there.

LBJ came to the attention of President Roosevelt's aides in 1935, when he was appointed by the president to head the National Youth Administration in Texas, one of the visible outgrowths of the New Deal. At age twenty-six, the seemingly inexhaustible Johnson inhaled his new duties. Within a year, the Texas NYA was held up as a model for other states to emulate and young LBJ as the prime example of how leadership could be developed to bring the NYA to its full potential. He brought to his side young, bright, ambitious, and loyal aides who stayed with him through his long career, among them John Connally, later governor of Texas and secretary of the Treasury; Jake Pickle, who would later be elected to Congress from LBJ's tenth Congressional District; and Robert Strauss, who would become chairman of the Democratic National Committee and ambassador to the Soviet Union. Bob Strauss once told me, "Jack, I've been around the biggest of the big in politics and business all over the world, but I swear the only man who totally intimidated me was Lyndon Johnson. Every time I came into his presence, I started sweating."

In 1937, Congressman James Buchanan from the hill country's Tenth Congressional District died in office. A dozen eager Democratic candidates vied for the seat, among them twenty-eight-year-old Lyndon B. Johnson. To everyone's surprise, the youngest man in the race won it. His platform? A full endorsement of FDR's policies. Now that the former Speaker of the Little Congress was a full-fledged Congressman, he swiftly became the first member of the House (and I daresay the last) to operate a twenty-four-hour-a-day office. This meant that a constituent could call Johnson's House office at any time of the day or night, and the phone call would be answered by a live human being, who would assure the caller that within a day their complaint or request would receive a response. And it did! Rumors persisted that on occasion LBJ himself would take some of these midnight calls.

Here a historian could observe how the congressional, senatorial, and presidential Johnson was taking shape. Attention to detail became his hallmark. His mania was perfection, for doing the job right the first time, along with a compulsion to know more about an issue or a meeting agenda point than anyone else at the table and to remember obscure statistics that would unsettle and frustrate those who opposed his views.

What was also ripening in Johnson was a compassion for the powerless, especially the Mexican Americans. It formed deep inside his gut, anchored by his past. One cannot grow up in the hill country of Texas, soil that only grudgingly gives up a living to those who work it each day, and not be affected by the ebb and flow of life that affects everyone alike. Rain, drought, grass, parched earth: The elements and what they bring become all-important. A hard-won education becomes a holy cause. Johnson felt completely at home with the tenant farmers, the Mexican Americans, the blacks—all those pressed to the wall by circumstances they could neither change nor control.

As a young man in his teens eager to earn some extra money, LBJ taught as a substitute teacher in a dingy little school in Cotulla, Texas, where his students were Mexican American children, the progeny of immigrants, poor beyond measure. These youngsters were struggling to learn an alien language and to try to fit into a strange, baffling, often inhospitable culture. They came to school in rags, barefoot and hungry, but they came. They wanted to learn. They idolized their teacher, who seemed to want to help them when few others did. The imprint of that time on Johnson's consciousness would never be erased. It became the source of stories to be recounted time and again. It was something he knew was wrong, terribly wrong, and had to be fixed. One day, he thought, when he had power, he would fix it. It is small wonder that in all his campaigns, the one group that always stood by him and believed in him were the immigrant Mexicans (and their progeny) who came to Texas to work and live and raise children as American citizens, the richest prize of all.

People without a voice attracted Johnson. He became close to the black citizenry of Texas. It is a piece of strange business that back east in Washington, this Johnson cadre of supporters that included Mexican Americans and blacks was little understood. The liberal Democratic inner leadership gauged LBJ to be right-wing, a hand-maiden of the oil barons, but they were sorely mistaken. The so-called oil establishment in Texas, and its financial advisers and investors in the East, viewed Johnson with suspicion. With few exceptions that establishment opposed him bitterly, from his campaign with Coke Stevenson in 1948 to his vice presidential candidacy in 1960, and never really made peace with him.

LBJ never heard of Richard Rumbold, who was hanged by the Stuart monarchy in the seventeenth century, but Rumbold's last words on the scaffold could have been Johnson's creed. Just before the noose tightened around his neck, Rumbold said: "None comes into this world with a saddle on his back, neither any booted and spurred to ride him." This is why the poor and the old, the black and the brown, the sick and the hopeless, trusted Johnson, followed him, and never deserted him.

One of LBJ's favorite stories tracked back to the time in Texas when he was a young congressman fighting the Texas electric utility companies. He was angry that they had denied his hill country constituents electric power on the pretense that it was too expensive to deliver. His old friend and mentor at the time was former state senator Alvin Wirtz. Senator Wirtz, as everyone called him, was attracted to the young congressman early on and counseled him frequently. Senator Wirtz finally set up a meeting with the top executives of several utility companies in his Austin law office. He had Congressman Johnson in tow as they arrived. As the meeting progressed, Johnson grew more combative, seeing that the utility magnates were not giving ground as swiftly as he wanted them to. Finally, in exasperation, LBJ stood up and bellowed, "You guys can go to hell. I'm leaving," and promptly departed the room. The meeting was over. Senator Wirtz followed Johnson out, corralling him before he could leave the building.

"Now, Lyndon, that was a damn stupid thing to do. I spent a lot of time trying to get this meeting on. We were making progress, and then you went and busted up the possibility of a deal. I hope this is a lesson to you. Just remember, you can tell a man to go to hell, but getting him to go there is another proposition."

Johnson told this story with great zest. The point was, don't bolt the room. Keep talking, keep the dialogue going, because sooner or later if what you push for has merit, you will be able to make the deal.

In his first term, Congressman Johnson came to the attention of FDR. He saw in Johnson a committed ally and acolyte. President Roosevelt also saw something else—that this young man had the potential to rise to the highest pinnacle to which a politician could aspire. So when LBJ importuned FDR and the leadership of the Congress to make things happen for Johnson's poorest constituents, the president supported him. And so it finally happened: Electricity came to the hill country. It was the most joyful moment of Lyndon Johnson's young life.

From the outset of his presidency, Johnson had one goal: to be the greatest American president doing the greatest good for all those who lived in this great free land, particularly those without any hope that tomorrow would be better than today. He also suffered one great tragedy: a war he did not start, a war he loathed, a war whose commitments he dared not cut and whose deadly spiral he could not break. He wanted most of all to leave this nation wiser, healthier, freer, and fairer than he had found it. To this objective, he committed all the energy, persuasive force, tenacity, and attention to detail residing in his oversize body and his sleepless mind. I believe he succeeded.

There is one overriding measure of LBJ that historians must take. Under terrible time pressure, Lyndon Johnson had to make a choice, one whose implications he understood with clear-eyed certainty. Should he push forward with his revolutionary agenda of civil rights and human justice, or should he deploy his considerable energies to fortifying the Democratic Party for the next election and possibly for a generation of elections? He didn't hesitate. No president in the twentieth century had ever mounted such an all-out attack not just on one or two barriers, but on every obstacle to social and political equality. He took on racism, discrimination, and bigotry, with an eye to writing freedom into law and revising civic conduct. LBJ recognized the political hazards of unleashing the agents of such radical change, no matter that his central goal was to set right what was so cruelly wrong. He knew that if he waged war on segregation in the only way he knew how—without fatigue, hesitancy, or doubt—it would tear the South apart. And it would drive a spear into the heart of the Democratic Party.

But he wasn't content to settle. He went to the barricades to fight the too narrow parameters of public education. He refused to allow the elderly to be turned away from hospitals because they had no money. He turned his wrath on those who fouled the air, water, and forests of the earth. He elevated the arts and founded public broadcasting. He launched his War on Poverty and gave birth to Head Start. He was everywhere, working tirelessly where no presidents save Lincoln and FDR had gone before.

As a southerner himself, Johnson understood the cultural fabric of the South. He knew well the motivations of powerful southerners who ruled the Senate and its standing committees. He could not forget that Senator Richard B. Russell of Georgia, the acknowledged political leader of the South, was a patron to whom he owed his very presidency. It was Russell's prestige and support that landed LBJ the post of Senate Democratic leader in 1953. At that time, Senator Ernest McFarland of Arizona, then Democratic leader, had been defeated in his home state. Senate Democrats urged Russell to take the post, but he demurred. He said, "Lyndon Johnson should be our leader." With such strong support from Russell, LBJ was elected

Senate minority leader. He was forty-four years old, in the fourth year of his first term. Never had a leader of either party been so young. More astonishing, never had a Senate leader of either party been elevated to the top leadership post so early in his tenure. And in two years he would be majority leader.

From that moment on, the Senate's tempo, command structure, and motives changed. Johnson expanded and kept expanding the power of the leader. It was the high-water mark of leadership in the Senate, never seen by any party before or since. He was by any gauge the greatest parliamentary commander in the Senate's history.

One morning, shortly after LBJ assumed the presidency, he told me to call Senator Russell and ask him to come over for a private visit. I did, and the senator agreed. I told the Secret Service agents at the Southwest Gate and in the Mansion that this was a private visit, so to take no note of the senator's arrival or his departure. I met him at the Diplomatic Reception Room just off the South Lawn, and together we took the private elevator to the second floor of the Mansion. There President Johnson was waiting for us. He embraced his old friend with obvious affection.

I sat next to Russell on the sofa in the West Hall. Behind us was a large window opening onto a broad view of the Rose Garden. LBJ was in a wing-backed chair, his knees and Russell's almost touching. Johnson leaned forward, put his hand on the senator's shoulder, one old comrade greeting another, and said softly: "Dick, I owe you, and I love you. If you hadn't made me leader, I would never have been vice president, and if I hadn't been vice president, I wouldn't be sitting here today. So, I owe you, Dick. I wanted to see you today to ask you not to get in my way on my civil rights bill. If you do, I will have to run you down." His voice was gentle and warm. There was no rancor and no hostility, only one old friend discussing a difficult matter with another.

Russell hunched his shoulders. He said in those rolling accents of his beloved Georgia countryside: "Well, Mr. President, you may well do that, but if you do, you'll not only lose this election, you will lose the South forever."

In all the years that followed, I was never prouder of Lyndon

Johnson than I was that morning. He put his hand on Russell's in a gesture of respectful affection and in a quiet voice said, "Dick, if that's the price I have to pay, I will gladly pay it."

Between these two men was a bond so tightly forged that no political confrontation could break it. Russell understood that Johnson wielded a new power that he himself had helped to create. LBJ understood that Russell was committed to a cause that he would not disavow. They both knew the battle lines were drawn, and as experienced professionals they had no illusions. It would be a hard, perhaps bitter, struggle. But as old and trusted friends, they would never turn on each other personally.

When the senator finally departed with a big hug from Johnson, I said: "Mr. President, he is a wonderful man, but he's wrong on both counts."

LBJ shook his head somberly. "No, Jack, not entirely. I'll win this election, but he's right about one thing. If I pass my civil rights bills, which I intend to do, the Democratic Party will have lost the South."

LBJ's estimate of Senator Russell's forecasts was eerily prescient. LBJ did win the election, but he was the last Democratic candidate for president to win a majority of white male voters in the South. From that election on, the South has moved steadily toward the Republican Party. Today, the Republican hold on the South is substantial and seemingly firm. Of course, nothing lasts in politics, neither victory nor defeat, but as of this moment, from North Carolina across Kentucky and Tennessee, from South Carolina around the rim of the Gulf through Texas, the color of the political map is Republican red.

Years later when I was in the movie industry, Anne d'Ornano, my dear friend, a beautiful, high-born Frenchwoman, absolutely fluent in English, then the mayor of Deauville in the Normandy countryside of France, suggested I visit the Banneville-Campagne military cemetery, about thirty kilometers east of Deauville and some ten kilometers west of Caen.

Anne said I should find a particular gravesite and read upon its tombstone an inscription that she found compelling. She said to me with some gravity, "I know your political background and I know what you did in the war, for which all of France is grateful. That is why you must see for yourself this gravestone. When you read it, you will know why I asked you to visit that cemetery."

So I made the trip. In the cemetery are some 2,175 graves mostly for soldiers from Britain, along with a sprinkling of Australian, New Zealander, Canadian, and Polish dead. Atop each grave sits a small rectangular slab of grayish white stone, about three feet high and some foot and a half wide. The top of each gravestone is beveled in a half circle. Beneath the stone slabs are beds of earth and flowers.

For the most part the men buried here were killed in the fighting from the first week in July 1944, when Caen was recaptured and Allied troops had gathered to advance beyond to attack Nazi forces. Each grave's stone has etched upon it the name of the soldier buried there. At the bottom of almost every slab are some few words put there by wives, children, and relatives that express their love for the fallen hero.

The grave I was looking for was in the center section of three. It was in the third group of the center section in the last line of graves in that section, nine graves from the right and sixteen graves from the left. I gazed down upon it. It read: "MAJOR SIR ARTHUR LINDSEY GRANT, THE GRENADIER GUARDS, JULY 18, 1944, AGED 32." (In the common book at the cemetery listing all the dead, one learns that Major Grant is the 11th Baronet of Monymusk, the son of the 10th Baron, Colonel Sir Archibald Grant, CBE, DSO).

But it is the additional inscription engraved in the stone at the bottom of the grave marker that Anne d'Ornano wanted me to see. I got down on one knee to read it close-up. This is what it said: LEADERSHIP IS WISDOM AND COURAGE AND A GREAT CARELESSNESS OF SELF.

I knew instantly why Anne had urged me to make this pilgrimage. As I read it, my mind reeled backward to that early meeting of LBJ with Senator Russell. What Major Sir Arthur Lindsey Grant's valedictory line meant was that there comes a time in a leader's life when he (or she) must be careless about his own personal ambitions and be ready to put to peril his political future, or his or her life, in order to do what he knows to be right in the long-term interest of the people he has by solemn oath sworn to serve. What distinguished

President Johnson in that meeting on the second floor of the Mansion was his willingness to do exactly that, to know so clearly what he was doing, even as he understood the terrible risks it unleashed.

When historians evaluate the Johnson presidency, they must choose what measure of worth to affix to a decision made with all the dangers of its downside plainly visible. I leave the final word to history itself, but what I know is, I was there to witness firsthand real leadership. To paraphrase Lord Macaulay, LBJ didn't seek glory in his choice to put civil rights at the top of his agenda, but he found glory because it lay in the plain path of his duty.

In late 2005, I was invited by Deborah Leff, director of the John F. Kennedy Presidential Library at the University of Massachusetts, to be on a panel whose subject was Lyndon Johnson. She told me that Robert Caro was to be one of the panelists and the guest speaker. Caro is an extraordinary biographer. He writes engagingly and combines masterful prose with tireless research. That night, seated next to Caro, I told him how unhappy I was with his first two volumes on LBJ, especially the second, which depicted LBJ as a satanic figure and Texas governor Coke Stevenson, his opponent in the 1948 Democratic primary election for the U.S. Senate, as full of righteous virtues. The real truth, I told Caro, was that Stevenson was bigoted in his views about race and religion and, in my opinion, not too smart.

Caro looked at me curiously, probably wondering why in the world he had allowed himself to be cornered on this panel with a rabid Johnson partisan. So he must have been at least a little relieved when I went on to praise his third volume, quoting one of Caro's eloquent lines about LBJ: "He was to be the President who, above all Presidents save Lincoln, codified compassion, the President who wrote mercy and justice into the statute books by which America was governed." When the evening came to an end, Robert Caro and I were driven back to the Charles Hotel in the same car. We sat at the bar having a drink together and chatted amiably for over an hour.

LBJ had little affection for critics, especially when they used personal invective to denigrate what he deemed to be worthy projects. When, after long negotiations to successfully build a consensus, he was subject to scathing denunciations of his final work, his rebuttal was, "Any jackass can kick a barn down, but it takes a damn good carpenter to build one." He had little patience with people who were ready to rush to battle stations without thinking of the consequences. His response was, "Remember what Sam Rayburn used to say. The three most important words in the English language are 'wait a minute.'"

He also used to quote Speaker Sam Rayburn about keeping straight what was important. Rayburn had had a brief tiff with President Roosevelt, so he asked a colleague in the House to go visit with FDR to find out if a reconciliation was imminent. When the colleague got back to Rayburn, he started off by saying, "I told the president—" Rayburn exploded. "I don't give a damn what you told Roosevelt. What I want to know is what Roosevelt told you." LBJ loved that story.

He made it clear to his aides that he wanted the "other side," meaning Republicans or anyone in his own party with whom he differed, to be treated with respect. He would say, "When you get into a political fight and you are on the verge of winning, always let your opponent depart the field with his dignity intact. Remember, your opponent today may well have to be your ally tomorrow. Never burn any personal bridges." Even after 1964, when he had majorities in both bodies of the Congress, he reached out to Republicans. Things are far different as of this writing, which is the worst time I remember for civil dialogue in Congress.

Today in Washington, the cords of collegiality that used to bind members of Congress to one another and to the president haven't just frayed, they've snapped. This descent into enmity isn't the fault of just one party. There is blame to distribute among all. But in my long years in and around the congressional scene, I have never borne witness to such rancor, such mean-spirited hostility, and such ideological rigidity as that which has torn our contemporary Congress into two hopelessly divided camps.

In this climate, it seems to me that understanding how President Johnson designed his relations with political leaders has a special relevance. Johnson had a clear sense of how to treat members on the other side of the aisle. His long years in the Senate and House had taught him that effective governance is built on listening to the other side. It also meant respecting the art of compromise. Compromise is not an ignoble word. It is what makes it possible for democratic institutions to function, to the long-term benefit of the country.

In 1964, the president deputized me to handle relations with key members of the leadership on both sides of the aisle, with special attention to the Republican leadership. It was my job to keep the door to the Oval Office open to Senator Everett Dirksen, Republican leader of the Senate, to Gerald Ford (who ten years later would ascend to the presidency), and to Charlie Halleck, the House Republican leader.

A typical encounter with Dirksen would go something like this:

The senator would call me, his majestic baritone rising up as if from fathoms deep, rumbling across the telephone line. "Jack, I'd like to see the boss today," he would say.

"Of course, Senator. How about coming by around six?" In the afternoon, Dirksen would rise on the Senate floor to flog the president and his policies, treating Nero and Caligula favorably in comparison to Johnson. It was a bravura performance.

Later, when Dirksen arrived at the White House, I'd walk with him, chatting amiably, to the family quarters on the second floor of the Mansion, where Johnson would be waiting. He'd greet Dirksen warmly and lead him to a green chintz sofa with an ample view of the Rose Garden. The president would drop himself into a large wing-backed chair next to the couch, very close to Dirksen. Johnson loved working at close quarters. I would sit next to Dirksen, whose rumpled suit and untamed wisps of hair masked a razor-edged wit and considerable wisdom.

LBJ, in one of his periodic fits of dieting, would order a Fresca from the kitchen. Dirksen, who was clearly hoping for something else, would hide a frown and, to be courteous, order one, too. Then the president, with the skill of an accomplished actor, would begin. "Ev, I wouldn't treat a cut dog the way you treated me on the floor today. It was just awful."

Dirksen, with a mock somber expression, would answer, "Mr. President, I have taken a vow to be faithful to the truth, so I had no choice in what I said."

LBJ would laugh. Touché. Dirksen, pleased with his retort, would rumble with laughter as well. They would trade stories and gossip.

Then the president would say something like "Ev, I need three Republican votes on my civil rights bill, and you can get them."

Dirksen would frown. Without answering, he would reach into his jacket and pull out a list of nominees to just about every regulatory commission in Washington. He would also suggest that the president relax his opposition to a bill the Republicans found congenial to their aims. The two men would ramble on, reminiscing and teasing each other. Johnson would say, "Ev, give that list of possible nominees to Jack. He'll check them out with Edgar Hoover to see if they are good citizens." When the Frescas were finished, Dirksen would depart. When he did, both men knew a deal had been struck. They didn't need a lawyer's summary of their conversation to seal their unspoken pledges. Their relationship was built on something that is sorely missing today: trust. Both men knew that plenty of quarrels would be played out on the Senate floor and on the campaign trail as well. They would not go easy on each other. But they also knew that once a commitment had been made, it would be kept. If they disagreed, they would keep talking. Every once in a while, LBJ would even test out a possible appointee on Dirksen before taking it any further.

Lyndon Johnson understood that the role of the opposition was to oppose. Dirksen (and Jerry Ford and Charlie Halleck) knew that opposing didn't mean you couldn't give a little here and there. Neither side surrendered core beliefs, but both knew that in politics nothing lasts for long. Mandates fade. Power passes. And majority, as sure as the seasons change, eventually becomes minority. The important thing is that the nation keeps moving forward.

As Senate leader and as president, LBJ used his immense physical presence as a weapon. In conversation with anyone he was trying to persuade, he would lean forward, getting right up close. For a man as tall as Johnson, his legs were shorter than they should have been, which meant his torso was unusually long. So when he leaned down from his six-foot-four-inch height, it was as if a huge dark cloud had blotted out the sun. As he continued to lean forward, you had no choice but to lean back while LBJ's face, massive and fearsomely weathered, his earlobes resembling some ominous winged creature, grew ever closer. It could be comic or intimidating—especially to someone whom LBJ had in his sights. There are some remarkable photographs of Johnson leaning toward Senator Theodore Francis Green of Rhode Island, a tiny man in his eighties, then chairman of the Senate Foreign Relations Committee. As this huge figure looms over him, Senator Green is leaning back like a willow in a high wind, trying desperately to keep from being swept away altogether.

Throughout his life, LBJ abhorred complexities. He always tried to sort out the complications of any issue, breaking down abstruse matters into simple, understandable language.

I remember with some glee a phone call I received from John Kenneth Galbraith, famed Harvard economist and elegant prose stylist. Ken called in a kind of frenzy: "Jack, the president has got to make an economics speech. He has not done that and it is needed. He has to talk to the people about monetary policy and trade deficits. I know it gets a little complicated, but I need to see him to convince him he has to make that speech."

Ken would have gone on, but I interrupted him. "Tell me when you're in Washington next and you can speak directly to the president."

The following Saturday, Ken and I entered the Oval Office, where Ken was greeted warmly by the president. Ken immediately launched into his litany of reasons why an economics speech was required. LBJ grinned and waved Ken off.

He said, "Ken, you have to understand that a president making an economics speech is like a fellow peeing down his leg. It makes him feel warm, but nobody else knows what the hell is going on."

Ken gasped. I damn near fell over laughing. In a moment the Harvard high priest of economics got a laugh out of it as well.

From the outset of his presidency, Johnson courted the Fortune 500 chieftains, the sultans of American business and industry. He embraced them on the phone, in private meetings, and in gatherings at the White House. This was unlike any seduction these financial heavy hitters had ever encountered in the Eisenhower or Kennedy administrations. On one particular evening several months before the 1964 election, Johnson was speaking to an East Room full of leviathans of American business. The chairmen of Ford and GM, of GE and U.S. Steel, were there, as well as the heads of Goldman

Sachs, Kuhn Loeb and Lehman Brothers, just to mention a few. Johnson stood before them with a lavaliere mike on his lapel as he strode back and forth.

"I want all of you to make as much profits as you can, stacking them up year after year higher and higher," he said as he moved near his audience.

The assembly liked that, and ripples of applause filled the room. He kept going. "I want to you to pile up profits and more profits. Then I am going to take a little bit of those profits and I am going to make taxpayers out of tax eaters, so they can buy more of what you are selling. And this country's economy will grow and grow and you'll make more and more profits."

Most of these longtime Republican supporters looked at one another warily, a bit puzzled. Why was this liberal Democrat talking like one of us? He's talking like the guys at the Union League Club. More profits? Taxpayers out of tax eaters? Buy more of what we sell? They had never heard anything like this, and from a Democratic president no less. They liked it.

Two months later, when LBJ began his campaign in Detroit, I got word that Henry Ford II wanted to come aboard Air Force One before the president disembarked. Fine, bring him aboard. The thickening figure of the grandson of the founder of the company was met by the president of the United States at the entrance to Air Force One, and then we all stepped into the president's office.

Henry Ford got down to business. With a wide smile, he said, "Mr. President, I am prepared to announce I will support you for election, if you would allow me to do so."

Well, LBJ sure wasn't going to turn that offer down. This big fish was a keeper. Nor was he going to give him a chance to slip off the hook. He grabbed Ford by the arm and said, "I'm mighty grateful, Henry. I say let's make this announcement right now and right here."

There was no room for Ford to change his mind. The press was assembled on the tarmac, and Air Force One was certainly a suitable backdrop. Minutes later, LBJ introduced Ford to the cameras with beaming good cheer. Ford would be the very first of America's most powerful business icons to endorse the president. This would have a ripple effect, as LBJ well knew.

The national press had a field day with Ford's announcement, which LBJ made certain to include in most of his speeches throughout Michigan. The Goldwater folks choked and fumed, but the dike had broken. The business community was now split. This usually reliable, traditional Republican bastion had been breached.

In truth, Johnson's blueprint for the success of American business was no mere political artifice. LBJ wasn't joking when he talked about taxpayers emerging from tax eaters. His whole plan as president was to build a Great Society on the rising incomes of business and industry, aided by increasing job opportunities, with a mixture of government programs and business investment to encourage an expanding economy. It made good political and fiscal sense to Johnson.

LBJ was a hard man when it came to measuring results from his key staff: Bill Moyers, Joe Califano, Harry McPherson, McGeorge Bundy, Larry O'Brien, Marvin Watson, Horace Busby, James Jones, Dick Goodwin, George Reedy, Douglass Cater, and me. To fulfill a task with a 99 percent finish rate was, to Johnson, a complete failure. It had to be 120 percent, no less. All of us at one time or another got the full "You have screwed up" LBJ treatment. We would rather have been attacked by wild boars.

Often, when LBJ's fury descended on me for not fully achieving the perfection he required, I would listen without reaction and then return to my office. The day would drag on and on, and around 9:00 p.m., the red phone button on my console would buzz and light up. This was the direct phone connection to the president. Each of his top assistants had one.

His voice would come over the wire in a conversational tone: "How about you calling Mary Margaret? Send a car for her and we'll have a bite in the family dining room."

I would call Mary Margaret, who sometimes found these late-night invitations less than irresistible. But she would agree and arrive shortly thereafter via White House car. She and I would enter the Oval Office to visit with the president, and after a bit, all three of us would walk over to the Mansion and go up the elevator to the West Hall and the family dining room. Johnson would be in festive spirits, telling one story after another, reminding Mary Margaret of some funny incident they had shared in a meeting in his office or at a gathering of notables at his ranch.

Sometime later, he would rise from the table and embrace Mary Margaret and me. We would depart the Mansion, and in the car driving home both of us would get a laugh out of the incident, which was so typical of Johnson. We both knew full well what this was all about. It was Johnson's way of saying to me, "Okay, Jack, I'm sorry I was so hard on you. Let me make it up to you, then let's forget about it."

One time my father, then in his late seventies, came to the White House to visit me. He was trembling with excitement. I took him into the Cabinet Room, where the president was involved in a public ceremony with several cabinet officers, surrounded by the press. When the president's eyes fell on my father, he grinned widely and said to the assembled officials and journalists, "I want you all to meet a great man from Houston, Texas. This is Joe Valenti, the father of my assistant Jack."

My father gulped, the color fled his face, and he stepped forward to be hugged by the president. His eyes grew moist. Never had anything so splendid happened to him. To be embraced by the president of the United States, in front of all these people! He never forgot it.

The president kidded with him, introduced him to all the cabinet officers, and later took him back into the Oval Office to give him some presidential souvenirs. My father was so overcome with joy, he could hardly speak. Later that day, the president said to me, "Your father is a good man, Jack. You are lucky to have him with you."

I understood. The president was telling me that he was glad he could give my father the gift of public recognition and affection that was possible only from the president. He knew what that meant to my dad, a simple, decent man to whom the presidency was a shining, holy institution and the president a man with near divine powers.

It was a characteristically generous gesture. I told the president, "Thank you, sir, for this morning; it meant so much to my father and to me."

Having spent a lifetime in and around the political arena, I have no grand notions about government leaders or anyone else who rises to fame. I have learned that the best of us is apt to be partly right and partly wrong. No one is bleached clean of the need for contrition, which means that all political commanders, businessmen, and famous celebrities are flawed. Those who declare themselves to be free of error are the ones to regard with the most skepticism. All public figures are subject to the vagaries of human emotion and even more prone than the rest of us to the dangers of infatuation with oneself. The most any of us can do is try to keep those impulses forcefully reined in.

It is said that Nero, emperor of all-powerful Rome, awoke one morning to declare to his adviser Seneca that he was truly a god, because he was without flaw. To which Seneca responded, "Sire, if we wish to be just judges of all things, let us first persuade ourselves of this: that there is not one of us without fault; no man is found who can acquit himself; and he who calls himself innocent does so with reference to a witness, and not to his conscience." This was not a diplomatic response to a certifiably mad despot, and the brilliant Seneca should have known better. Sometime later, Seneca was poisoned. Such are the rewards of candor.

What the people must pray for are leaders who will be right more often than they are wrong, leaders who believe that the humblest citizen of the nation is as important as the richest and most powerful among us. Perhaps we may be forgiven if we ask our leaders to be wiser than those who give them power and to be sufficiently armed with honor, character, vision, and good judgment that the tasks they obligate themselves to fulfill will not go unserved by all their skills and courage. Or perhaps we should follow the example of the leaders of the ancient church. In those early days, when the pope selected a priest to be a bishop, the priest was supposed to respond with "*Nolo episcopari*," meaning "I do not wish to be a bishop." It was the church's way of acknowledging that anyone who craved power was not fit to wield it.

Lyndon Johnson was never summed up as accurately as that moment at a huge dinner in New York City on January 13, 1969, seven days before he would vacate the White House for his successor, Richard Nixon. A beautiful book had been created for the event, with special essays by famous figures summing up LBJ's achievements in foreign affairs, civil rights, national defense, education, health, housing and urban development, the rights of elderly Americans, law and justice, transportation, excellence in government, business relations, labor relations, the environment, and consumer protection. It was a catalog of an administration ever restless, constantly pushing energy, passion, and commitment to their outer limits.

In one essay, Professor James MacGregor Burns of Williams College, a renowned historian, wrote: "Students of government, like myself, will remember Lyndon Johnson for a further and special reason. He was the first president to recognize fully that our basic social ills are so rooted in encrusted attitudes and stubborn social structures that no single solution or dramatic crusade will solve them, the first president to see clearly that only a total attack across the widest front, with every possible weapon, would bring a breakthrough, and the first president to propose basic institutional changes to make a total attack possible."

Toward the end of the evening, Ralph Ellison, celebrated author of *The Invisible Man*, approached the president and was embraced by him. Said Ellison to Johnson: "Mr. President, I just wanted to say to you that because of Vietnam you will just have to settle for being the greatest American president in our history for the undereducated young, the poor and the old, the sick and the black. But, Mr. President, that is a pretty fine epitaph."

The Vietnam imbroglio and the mounting protests against it hit Johnson hard. For all his herculean efforts to build the Great Society, his spirit had been brought low by the endless killing in Vietnam and the virulent opposition to that war that paid no heed to his triumphs in civil rights and all the other battles he had fought for those who had little and whose hopes were torn by despair. Perhaps he would have been consoled by the observation of Lord Bryce when he wrote: "Posterity fixes a man's place in history by asking not how many tongues buzzed about him in his lifetime, but how great a factor he was in the changes of the world, that is, how far different things would have been twenty or fifty years after his death if he had never lived." I believe LBJ knew that what he had created would not easily be dismantled, although he certainly knew others would try to do just that. Perhaps Lord Bryce's words would have had a hope-inspiring stirring within him. But no one save Lady Bird Johnson really knows.

For me it all began the first time I met Lyndon Johnson. It was in the early summer of 1956 in Houston, Texas, at the Shamrock Hotel. Warren Woodward, known as "Woody," was one of LBJ's trusted lieutenants. He had been an intimate member of LBJ's inner circle for years. I had met him casually, so I was surprised when he called me. He said, "Jack, the majority leader wants to meet you and a few other young folks in Houston. Would you be available next Tuesday around five p.m. for coffee at the Shamrock Hotel?"

Well, hell, why not? Like any Texan beyond the age of five, I knew who Senator Johnson was. He strode the state with seven-league boots, with far too much energy and presence to go unnoticed. Moreover, I liked what he was doing, and I affirmed that affection by voting for him every chance I could. Of course, Texas was probably the source of the political adage "Vote early—and often." I myself was beginning to be attracted to the old Texas maxim "When I die, I want to be buried in Texas so I can continue to be politically active."

"Yes, Woody, I'll be there," was my answer. I was looking forward to it.

When I turned up at the appointed hour at the opulent Shamrock Hotel, I found myself mingling with about a dozen young men and women, most of whom I knew somewhat. The Shamrock Hotel was the creation of Glenn McCarthy, a dashing, hard-drinking, hard-fighting maverick who had struck it rich in two oil fields that other, more experienced wildcatters had abandoned without success. Glenn promptly spent several million dollars to build what was, at that time, the most expensive, spectacular hotel in the nation. He launched it with a celebrity-studded extravaganza in the fall of 1949, and on this summer day in 1956, its glamour was still very much in evidence.

As we waited for the senator to arrive, Woody explained to me why this gathering had been called. Unlike most politicians, Johnson understood that the palace guard, the inner circle around senators and congressmen, inevitably grew old, tired, rich, and considerably less active. LBJ had the recent experience before him of the long-serving Texas senator Tom Connally (no relation to the soon-to-be governor of Texas John Connally). Tom Connally was chairman of the powerful Senate Foreign Relations Committee. He moved about the Capitol like a foreign potentate. Problem was, ole Tom didn't realize that the loyal corps of Texans back home who had brought him to power some thirty years ago were now dozing by the fire or tending to their ranches and their steadily producing oil wells.

Then along comes a young, ambitious governor of Texas named Price Daniel, who announces he's taking on ole Tom, icon of the Senate. When Senator Connally reaches out to his campaign guard, they pass along to him the dismal news that his political organization has shrunk and his county leadership had lost its zest. Better step aside, Tom, they said, you can't win. Connally, incredulous at first and heartbroken later, departed the field, a visibly devastated man shorn of power and influence. As was once said, "There is no more ineffective public man than one who is out of office."

Johnson vowed that would never happen to him. Even before the Tom Connally debacle, Johnson had begun identifying talented, energetic young people in every county in Texas and enlisting them into his legions. As his early supporters grew older and more weary, these fresh troops would take their place in the electoral field. This encounter at the Shamrock Hotel was the Houston piece of his state-wide search for young political warriors.

When LBJ entered that meeting room, you didn't have to ask, Is that the majority leader? Something electric emanated from him as he moved about the room, engaging each of us in turn with his full, sharp gaze. Then he talked briefly as he stood in the middle of the room, one hand thrust in his right-hand pocket, softly jingling coins.

I have no recollection of what he said, but it's hardly relevant. What I remember was how fast we wanted to sign up in the Johnson army.

On that day, four years into his leadership of Senate Democrats and two years as majority leader, Lyndon Johnson was at the summit of his Senate power. Against all odds, he was on the cusp of leading the passage of the first civil rights bill since Reconstruction, a bill that no sane observer ever thought had a chance of prevailing. It would be a stunning victory for the Senate leader, who dominated the Senate chambers with confidence, parliamentary skill, and an animal energy that was becoming legendary. He seldom slept when there was business to be done, which meant the senators didn't sleep, either.

And while he was awake, Lyndon Johnson had one priority—the Senate—to the exclusion of all mortal enticements. He knew every secret of the Senate and its members. He knew who was a drunk, who was screwing whom, and, most of the times, where it was happening. He knew what the senators coveted. He knew the sources of their funding. He understood and observed each senator's ambitions. He could pinpoint with precision their vulnerabilities as well as their wellsprings of strength and occasional fits of redemption.

In the long, raucous, and splendid history of the U.S. Senate, there has never been, even in senatorial legend and myth, a leader like Johnson. He had mastered the rules of that body. As Senate chieftain, he had produced two formulas that more than any others generated success. He never relaxed when there was work to be done, and he always looked beyond the next objective. He searched out alternatives with the same care other men devote to their families. He steered clear of trivia, which is the indigenous political virus. He never made trifles into serious business or allowed serious business to be treated as trifles. He played the Senate the way a grand master plays a world's championship chess match, making his move even as he contemplated four moves ahead, seeing what others saw dimly if at all, forecasting how this moment would affect all those that lay ahead.

To this effort, he applied a shrewd intellect more finely tuned than that of any other contemporary public man. John Gardner, LBJ's secretary of health, education, and welfare, himself a philosopher-statesman and Stanford professor, once declared that Lyndon Johnson was the most intelligent man he had ever met. (He made no such claims about Johnson's education credentials.)

LBJ was well aware that his graduation from Southwest Texas State Teachers College did not cut a wide swath in his current social circle. He always had a not-so-unspoken admiration for the supereducated, those who had been groomed since childhood for influence in public affairs. He liked to be surrounded by Rhodes scholars and graduates of Harvard, Yale, Princeton, and Stanford. But he also knew he was smarter, tougher, abler, and better suited for decision making than all those supremely educated advisers surrounding him. He was confident of his ability to see beneath the surface of things and of his willingness to do what had to be done, no matter how dismaying or heavily weighted the odds of failure might be.

When he became president, Johnson, like Kennedy, had no chief of staff. He brooded over the entire spread—and it was vast—of presidential responsibilities. If it was important to the nation, he wanted to know about it. This is not easy to do, which is why business schools emphasize delegating tasks and letting those to whom you delegate decide and act. But the presidency is not a business enterprise. It is about life and death, opportunity or lack thereof, raising a nation's hopes or dashing them, transforming expectations and translating ideals into reality. This is often why so many men and women from the business community flounder in the public sector. The business CEO can fire anyone who fouls up. He can make a quick decision and not have to run it by 535 colleagues to make sure he has a majority behind him.

LBJ understood this. He had a special knowledge of power, how to sense it in others and how to use it himself. He chose to keep his White House staff small and responsive to him. As he used to say, "If someone is going to make a big-ass blunder around here, I want it to be me and not some assistant of mine who thinks he's running the country."

He had another commandment. He would say, "It's not enough to do good, you have to look good." This meant that public scrutiny of your labors was part and parcel of the presidency. The presidency could not be stained by White House mismanagement, or a relaxed approach to the law, or venal acts of any kind. Therefore, every action you take must assume public knowledge. You cannot slide around the shoulders of the road; you have to keep it all on the pavement, within the lines, readily observable by traffic in both directions.

I collided with LBJ's code of White House conduct in a foolish kind of way. One day, I received a letter from Senator Tom Dodd of Connecticut. As I read the letter, it seemed fairly mundane and

harmless. Dodd was fulminating about how the navy was badly treating one of his constituents whose factory made parts for helicopters.
He wanted the White House to chastise the navy brass for cutting
this businessman out of a contract.

I promptly fired off a nice letter to the senator, saying that I was
sending his letter to the secretary of the navy, since what he was asking for was not handled by the White House. Within minutes of
signing the letter, it slipped my mind.

Three days later, the levees broke. The door to my office opened
and the imposing form of the thirty-sixth president filled the room.
Instantly, I saw the fury flaming in his eyes. In his hand was a flimsy
sheet of carbon paper with writing on it. He flung it on my glass-
topped desk and said in a low voice, "You're going to jail, and I will
not lift a hand to save you. Remember Matt Connelly? You're following right in his footsteps." (Matt Connelly was a press secretary for
President Truman. He had gotten involved in some unsavory conduct and been sent to prison.)

He saw the bewilderment on my face and picked up the flimsy
paper. "Did you write this?" I saw what it was, a copy of my letter to
Senator Dodd. I nodded. Then he reached into his inside jacket
pocket and pulled out another letter. "All right, now read this." It was
a letter from McGeorge Bundy to Senator Dodd. It read: "Dear Senator Dodd, I have no role in Pentagon contracts. Therefore I cannot
help you. Sincerely, McGeorge Bundy."

I had to admit, it was a crisply worded letter. Good work, Mac,
you bastard; clumsy judgment, Valenti, you dunce. In the Johnson
White House, you did not ever, ever, ever allow one whiff of potential scandal to exist. My letter was harmless, but to LBJ it was suscep-
tible to being misconstrued.

Then the president reached over and lifted the glass top on my
desk, slipped the copy of Mac's letter under it, and replaced the glass.
Still unhappy, he said, "I want you to read that letter every hour of
every day. And remember Matt Connelly." Whereupon he turned on
his heel and departed my office, heading down the hall to his own.

I kept the copy of Bundy's letter under my glass desktop for
about a week, where I felt its accusatory finger pointing balefully at
me. Then I made a command decision. I would remove the letter,

toss it in the trash, and take my chances that LBJ would not go poking around my office to see if my daily dose of moral medicine was still being administered. I am pleased to report I never was recalled to that particular woodshed. And I never went to jail, although if I had, I believe the president would have visited me.

The one puzzle I was never able to solve was how in the hell did LBJ find the copy of my letter? Was he padding around in the dark every night reading through thousands of documents to ferret out the mistakes of his dumb-ass staff? Frankly, I would not bet against it. But LBJ's strong distaste for anything that didn't "look good" was now fixed firmly in my mind and in the minds of every other Johnson aide. It made us prudent. So it was that LBJ's mission to prevent even the slightest hint of malfeasance in his administration was successfully achieved. His presidency was one of the few in the nation's history never to be burdened with even a whiff of illegal White House behavior by his staff or by the president himself. This was an achievement in which LBJ took great pride.

At the same time that he so effectively policed his staff, LBJ kept his sense of humor alive and thriving. One evening Lester Pearson, the prime minister of Canada, came to visit LBJ. The president hosted a small stag dinner at Blair House, a place for visiting presidents and prime ministers to stay right across the street from the White House. He carefully selected ten guests for the occasion. All had degrees from Ivy League universities, and some were Rhodes scholars, including the prime minister of Canada himself. I sat there, mentally clutching my Harvard MBA, between the White House national security adviser, McGeorge Bundy (graduate of Yale and former provost of Harvard), and Secretary of State Dean Rusk (Rhodes scholar), one chair away from Secretary of Defense Robert McNamara (Harvard MBA).

LBJ rose to his feet, glass in hand, smiling widely at his guests around the table. In a somber voice, he said, "I propose a toast to the best-educated group of men ever to sit down to dinner at Blair House. We have here tonight five graduates of Harvard, three from Yale, one from Princeton, three Rhodes scholars"—he paused theatrically to exhibit a wicked smile—"and one graduate of Southwest Texas State Teachers College."

Prime Minister Pearson almost fell out of his chair laughing. Johnson was mightily pleased with himself. He had made his point.

I remember chatting with a good friend, Dean Burch, former chairman of the Federal Communications Commission and campaign manager for Senator Barry Goldwater, the Republican candidate for president in 1964. Dean told me with some amusement a story about Goldwater, who came to Texas and spoke before one thousand passionately cheering oilmen at the Petroleum Club. So loud, so frenzied, and so vocally anti-LBJ was the reaction of these unofficial ministers of oil that on the ride back to the airport, Goldwater, still exultant from his reception, turned to Dean Burch and burst out with, "My God, Dean, we can carry Texas, we can do it. Have you ever seen anything like that before?" Burch nodded but said nothing. He had no desire to deflate his chief's emotional high, but his polling numbers were telling him that LBJ would carry Texas by almost 2 million votes (which, in fact, he did).

Although he may not have been popular with all the oil barons in Texas, LBJ always supported the oil depletion allowance, a tax incentive for oil production that was the oil industry's holy grail. Because of LBJ's congressional support for this measure, liberal-leaning Democrats fitted Johnson into the wrong political slot. They didn't do their homework. But in Texas, we knew better. You supported the oil industry in Texas because it employed so many people, just the way Vermont and Washington senators support syrup and apple growers and Wisconsin senators endorse the butter industry.

This pragmatic side of Johnson came forcefully into view in 1964, when the conservative Democratic bloc decided to bring down liberal senator Ralph Yarborough in the upcoming election by inserting into the Democratic primary a distinguished, popular (and conservative) Texas congressman, Joe Kilgore. Yarborough would be in deep trouble if this happened, and every political sage in the state knew it. Kilgore would give Yarborough fits and would be the favorite to win.

When President Johnson got word of this, he called me. "Come in right away, Jack, we have a problem." When I arrived, he leaned back in his Oval Office chair and said, "Jack, I want you to get hold of John Connally [then governor of Texas, elected in 1962]. You make it clear to him that if Joe Kilgore enters the primary against Yarborough, I'll do something I have never done in all my political career—I'll endorse Yarborough in the Democratic primary and campaign for him in every county in Texas."

"That's pretty strong stuff, Mr. President. He won't like it," was my response.

"I don't aim for him to like it. I just want him to know it. You tell John that I know that Yarborough has no affection for me. He hates my guts. He's impossible to get along with. He sees everybody as his enemy, and he believes he is the only virtuous man in America. I know all that. But there is one thing else I know, and it is that Yarborough votes with me, and Kilgore won't. Joe's a good, decent man and he's my friend, but he has no truck with my civil rights program. He's going to oppose me there and in everything else I want to do to help this country. Now, you make John understand that."

Within an hour, I had the governor on the line. "Goddammit!" exploded Connally. "The president lets Yarborough shit all over him and he keeps coming back for more. This is crazy. Yarborough is not my friend, he's not your friend, and he sure as hell isn't the president's friend. Can't he see that?"

"John, what you don't see is how Ralph votes. Sure, he can't stand LBJ, but he'll vote the way the president wants him to vote, and that's what counts."

John was now even more furious. "I have a mind to take him on. I believe Joe can wipe the floor with Yarborough. Ralph's so damn arrogant, he's lost a lot of supporters down here." He was silent for a moment. "I'll think about this, Jack. Tell the president I'll get back in a day or so."

"Thanks, John," I said. "You know the president loves you, and you know he's got some hard votes ahead of him. We can't lose anything that we have now, and that includes Yarborough."

John grumpily repeated that he would get back to me. And he did, two days later, to tell me that Joe Kilgore would not enter the primary. But Connally's tone was sour.

This was the moment I came to recognize what President Johnson had said to me some months earlier, that "John [Connally] is a brilliant politician and as charming as any man could be, but John has lost his social conscience. Too bad." Frankly, I wouldn't say that John had lost his social conscience, but it became clear to me that he was simply not tracking the same legislative trail as Johnson. They were steering by different compass headings. In particular, Connally just didn't feel comfortable with LBJ's passion for civil rights.

All of this truly saddened me. I adored John Connally. I remembered late in 1961, when John, then secretary of the navy, called me to say he had decided to resign his post and come back to Texas to run for governor. "I'd like you and your agency to handle my campaign in South Texas, from Houston on south. Will you do it?" Of course I would, but not without some doubts about my chances for success. A statewide poll showed Connally had about a 3 percent recognition with voters. We weren't exactly headed for an easy landslide victory, but I signed on. I recall that Connally came to Houston about a week later, and I took him to City Hall to mingle with the city fathers, where I had arranged for the press to be in full attendance. As we entered City Hall in the early afternoon, I hung back to observe. As John, looking like a film star, moved easily around the floor with a confident stride, what caught my eye was the sudden flurry of activity by the secretaries. They rose from their desks and flocked around the newly announced candidate, clinging to him with undisguised delight, some even holding out paper for him to autograph. The young men working at their nearby desks also came forward with more than typical interest. Hello, I thought, we have an asset here. Maybe he's not so crazy to run.

Connally was elected in the summer of 1962 after a rough primary runoff (in those days, a win in the Democratic primary meant it was all over, since the Republicans at that time posed little opposition). Shortly thereafter, his approval ratings headed skyward, and he was on his way to becoming one of the most popular Texas governors in recent history.

In my opinion, the man most like him in public life was John Kennedy. I was told Kennedy admired Connally, even though Connally publicly battered JFK during LBJ's abortive run for the nomination in 1960. Connally could be a tough sumbitch in the precincts, with a taste for the rough-and-tumble that the Kennedys certainly understood and indulged in themselves. JFK obviously held no animosity toward Connally, for he used one of his first appointments to name Connally secretary of the navy.

Both Connally and JFK were stunningly handsome, charming, impossible to ignore, and inordinately persuasive. When they rose to speak to groups, ruthless union, business, and political leaders would suddenly become like giggling schoolgirls in the presence of a rock star. It was amazing. It's true that LBJ was also nearly irresistible in small groups, but even with all his powers of persuasion, Johnson did lack some of the sheer magic commanded by Kennedy and Connally.

By an odd coincidence, I happened to be in Washington on July 5, 1960, for a visit with Congressman Albert Thomas. When I showed up, he waved at me and said, "Jackson, would you like to hear Lyndon announce for the presidency? I'm going over to the Senate auditorium. Want to go with me?"

Well, of course I did. As we made our way to the auditorium, I wondered why LBJ had waited so long to announce. It was just a few days before the Democratic convention. But my primary memory of that day was watching the Johnson entourage enter the auditorium from a side door. One staff member in particular stood out from the rest. She was blond, slender, and quite beautiful. She moved gracefully, with unself-conscious ease. Little did I know that I would meet her before long and that two years later we would be married.

Johnson's remarks held no surprises. He spoke carefully and calmly, essentially declaring that he was better equipped than any of the current Democratic candidates to assume national leadership. I thoroughly agreed, although I did have a growing affection for the senator from Massachusetts. John Kennedy appealed to me with his youth, wit, and graceful bearing. Had LBJ not entered the lists, I would have been an ardent supporter of JFK. But I was a Johnson man, and I intended to stay that way, no matter the twists and turns of fortune.

Some twenty-four hours later, I took a phone call from Jim Rowe, a veteran Washington hand, who as a very young, brainy lawyer some twenty-five years earlier had been a member of President Roosevelt's best and brightest of the forties. Would I be willing, asked Rowe, to go to Los Angeles and join the Johnson troops there? The mission was simple: Wrest away enough delegates tentatively committed to the other candidates and bring them into the Johnson camp. I signed on, not realizing at the time what a difficult assignment that would be, for I was unaware of the work being carried out so carefully and efficiently by the Kennedy battalions. I learned all too quickly.

After arriving at the convention, I set out on my assignment to convert Kennedy acolytes into partisans of Lyndon Johnson. My assignment was the New York delegation. I was jubilant. I would be doing the Lord's work. However, it soon became evident to me that the Lord was nowhere to be found. I buttonholed fourteen New York State delegates in a day and a half. Some of them were courteous. Some of them treated me like an alien carrying germs. And some were willing to chat with me. One delegate, whose forebears had emigrated from Sicily like mine, was kind to me—and candid.

"Jack," he said in a serious tone, "you've been sent on a suicide mission. We're Kennedy people. Hey, you're Catholic, you're Italian, so you ought to be, too. Not too many Italians and Catholics in Texas, am I right? There's no damn way any of the New York delegates are going to defect. I'm not saying Johnson is a bad candidate, I'm just telling you he won't win the nomination, and he sure as hell isn't going to get any New York votes. No way."

I was actually grateful to him for his candor. Maybe the reason I wasn't finding the Lord was that he was wearing a "Kennedy for President" button and had taken up residence in the New York delegation.

I relayed this dismal news to Rowe but did not chide him for insufficient intelligence gathering. I daresay he had to be hearing the same thing from other delegate scouts. It was not good. My gut told me that LBJ's run for the nomination was doomed. Jim Rowe said, "Jack, LBJ is going to meet with the Texas delegation, inviting leaders from other delegations as well. You need to be there."

Then one of those odd, even amusing, little foul-ups occurred. Somehow, an invitation sent by an empty-headed LBJ campaign worker wound up in the Massachusetts delegation. To everyone's surprise, who should show up for the Texas group's gathering but John F. Kennedy himself. The large room was packed, but I had had the good sense to plant myself on the floor right in front of the mike.

To his credit, Johnson made the best of an awkward turn. He

generously introduced JFK, who with assurance and a wide, mischievous smile grasped the microphone. He said, obviously enjoying the moment, "I think that Lyndon Johnson is the greatest leader the Senate Democrats have ever had. In fact, so splendid has been our leader's performance that the Democratic Party would be shrunk if Lyndon Johnson were not there, as the commander of all us Democrats. His best service to his party will be his continued leadership of our party in the Senate, and I most enthusiastically endorse that decision."

Even the most loyal of Johnson supporters had to laugh at JFK's ironic wit. It was masterful. My admiration for him soared. LBJ took it gracefully, for he knew better than to throw down any gauntlets. He and Kennedy shook hands, chatted privately for a bit, and then JFK and his entourage, including his brother Bobby, departed the room.

As befitted my role of spear carrier at that time, I was not mingling with LBJ, Sam Rayburn, John Connally, or any other big shots. Mary Margaret, my future wife, was there with Mrs. Johnson, in the majority leader's suite. She was privy to some fascinating pieces of history as LBJ greeted Sam Rayburn, senators, congressmen, and other luminaries including Philip Graham, publisher of the *Washington Post* and a Johnson supporter.

I sat with the other serfs and vassals in front of the TV set up in a large room for those working on the outer edges of the Johnson campaign. The TV announcer told us that Johnson had accepted an offer from JFK as his choice for the second spot. It had a stunning impact on the nation and most emphatically on the Texas delegation. I was caught by surprise—mind-boggled might be more accurate.

Some years later, I came to know the reasons why. It was plain to LBJ that with a Democratic president in the White House, the post of majority leader would lose much of its influence and possibilities of power. Assuming JFK won, the chief executive would call the shots and the majority leader could be only an ally, not a leader. Moreover, LBJ felt in his gut that he could be the decisive element in a triumphant campaign. The South was restless, fretting under its distaste for northern candidates, and most assuredly felt nothing but antagonism for a New Englander who was also a Catholic. LBJ knew that he could speak the language of southerners, understand their misgivings, and as a creek-dipping Protestant draw them to the Kennedy banner. If he declined the post and JFK lost, it would be, LBJ thought, due to his own pride.

So all of these factors worked on him. He finally accepted Kennedy's offer, to the outrage of his foes and the astonishment of his friends.

Within two weeks of the convention, my phone rang and the now-familiar voice of LBJ came on the line. "I want you and your agency to handle all the advertising, media selection, and TV production for the Kennedy-Johnson ticket in Texas. Kennedy is turning Texas over to me and the Speaker [Sam Rayburn]. Get in touch with Woody Woodward as quickly as possible," he said. "And then arrange to be in Austin for a meeting we will hold in about a week. You'll get clear instructions as to date, time, and place." There was a slight pause, then the voice grew stern. "I aim to carry Texas for this ticket. We are not going to lose Texas. A lot will depend on how well you do your job. Is that clear?" Yes, sir, it was clear, and as soon as I hung up, I plunged into my new assignment.

Within two weeks, candidate for vice president Lyndon Johnson was heading to Houston for some campaigning. I got a call from Woody Woodward, who asked me to set up a big luncheon at the Rice Hotel for Harris County Democrats and others from the area around Houston. There would be a crowd of some four hundred. I was given the names for a big head table, where I was also invited to sit. I had the head table place-carded and went over it carefully to make sure no noses and egos would be out of joint. Then I was off to the airport to meet LBJ and his entourage and ride in their small motorcade to the Rice Hotel.

There was a crowd of several hundred people at the airport to greet and applaud the candidate. As the chartered plane taxied to a halt, the door was flung open and Johnson and Lady Bird, all smiles, came down the ramp. They were followed by a sensational lady, whom I remembered from the Senate office building, when LBJ announced for the presidency. I asked Woody who she was. "That's Mary Margaret Wiley; she's one of the majority leader's top assistants." Woody looked at me quizzically. "She's mighty pretty, isn't she?" he said. Well, more than pretty, I thought, and then a grenade went off in my head. Without saying a word, I ran back to the hangar, got on the phone, and called one of my colleagues at the Rice Hotel. Luckily, he was near the reception desk and came on quickly.

"Get to the head table in the Crystal Ballroom right now. Find a place card for Mary Margaret Wiley. Pick it up and put it next to me and put the card next to me in the spot where you found Mary Margaret's card. Got it?" He got it.

When the majority leader and his staff arrived at the hotel, the Crystal Ballroom was already pretty much filled, and we hastened to seat everyone. I plunked myself next to this stunning woman and with a big smile said, "Hey, I'm the lucky guy today. I just won the raffle, and the prize was to sit next to you. How's that for good fortune?"

She looked a bit startled by this voluble fellow who was intruding on her, and I could tell I was making a less-than-stellar impression. Nonetheless, I sat down, uncorked every bit of charm I possessed, and poured it in a steady stream. Mary Margaret Wiley, I learned later, had ladies' men far more seasoned than I was hit on her time and again in Washington. My so-called charm was nothing new to her; she had heard it all before, and she was not buying any of my wit, gaiety, or endless attempts at being irresistible.

What she didn't know was that I was just gearing up. She was going to see a helluva lot more of me, though at the time the odds of my winning her over were so long, they wouldn't even be posted in Las Vegas. But first, before I would be able to launch my courtship, there was serious political work to be done. We had an election to win in Texas.

The key asset in the Kennedy-Johnson campaign in Texas was Lyndon Johnson, and everyone knew it. The battle was on, and LBJ was in total command, which is to say no one slept or dawdled. This was no campaign for the fainthearted. We traded in our watches for calendars. It was a twenty-four-hour-a-day assignment. My other clients simply had to accept the fact that I had to vanish from my agency scene to devote myself to this one crucial task: win Texas for the Kennedy-Johnson ticket.

Within days, every Johnson county leader in each of Texas's 254 counties had his marching orders. The Johnson forces were gearing up for the political fight of our lives. There was one obstacle, one overriding issue, and we all recognized it whether we liked it or not. It was JFK's Catholic faith. If you were an LBJ man, and you were also a thoroughgoing Protestant, you simply swallowed your prejudices and flung yourself into the fray as if you had conducted novenas all your life. As a Catholic myself, I was one of those in the front lines who resented the fact that religion posed such an obstacle, but it did, and we had to accept this and overcome it as best we knew how. In East Texas, in the big thicket, in the Bible Belt that stretched across the central plains and hill country, and in the northern tier of the state to the Panhandle, the animus toward Kennedy was particularly evident. This election was going to be close, we all knew that; this, of course, plunged LBJ only deeper and more energetically into the fray.

Lyndon Johnson had no ambivalence about Catholics or believers in any other creed. He was ecumenical long before that was fashionable. Both before and after being president, he could attend a Catholic church, a synagogue, or any one of a number of Protestant services with equal devotion. He believed in God, and though brought up in the faith of the disciples of Christ, he proudly watched his wife and daughters commit themselves to the Episcopal faith and saw no problem when his younger daughter, Luci, became a Catholic convert. He simply distanced himself from any kind of dogma, finding rigid doctrine as unappetizing in religion as he found it in politics. He recognized the Catholic issue as the principal thorn in the side of his campaign, and he deployed his troops in the field with this problem firmly in his sights.

In September 1960, my ad agency and I held the operational reins on a unique confrontation that both LBJ and John Kennedy knew had to take place sooner or later. It was the clash between the presidential candidate and the Texas Protestant leadership. Kennedy had pledged he would confront Protestant ministers on live television, a moment in which this religious issue kept so long beneath the surface would erupt into the open. No one would predict its outcome, and as I delved into the details of putting this show on the air, I began to have some anxieties, which I kept close.

We pulled the pin on this live grenade at 9:00 p.m., September 12,

1960, in the Crystal Ballroom of the Rice Hotel in Houston. Once the cameras began to turn, my job was done. The drama was now going to unfold in ways I could no longer hope to shape or control: It was Kennedy versus the Protestant ministers.

The ballroom was packed with Kennedy-Johnson supporters, local citizenry, a legion of print and broadcast journalists, and Houston ministers, many of whom unsmilingly declared their relish at the opportunity to give this young papist candidate his comeuppance. If I had dared, I might have gripped some rosary beads myself, but as one of my associates said to me, "Right now, Jack, we need longbows and cavalry more than we need prayer." I said nothing, but I thought we could use both.

I almost hugged John Kennedy when he finally appeared. The Kennedy people had told me the candidate would emerge from a door at the rear of the ballroom and walk to the microphone, but what he did was unexpected—and breathtakingly dramatic. With the large crowd waiting, the room growing tense, and the Protestant ministers ready for the kill, Kennedy suddenly appeared at the rear door.

Necks craned. Photographers' flashlights blinded the room, feet shuffled, murmurs grew louder. The ballroom came alive. And then I saw him. No one was with him. He was utterly alone. Not one aide or friend or security person was near him (though they were flung strategically around the ballroom). He paused, momentarily looking out at the crowd, and then strode, purposefully, with neither a nod nor a smile, through the aisle in front of the banked chairs where we had placed some fifty seats for those invited ministers who would question him. When he reached the small platform I had arranged, he sat down and mutely fixed his gaze on the cluster of ministers. It was a resplendent tour de force. Somehow that act of serenity, the march to the microphone alone with no one to guide, guard, or counsel him, set the whole meeting at tilt. I knew that some of those ministers had to feel admiration for his courageous entrance, as if he were saying to his doubters, "I am not afraid of you or this confrontation."

Kennedy spoke easily, warmly. He made it clear what he wanted to do for the country. Then he got to the core of the controversy, his religion.

"The views I have expressed are my views. But let me stress

again, I am not the Catholic candidate for president. I am the Democratic Party candidate for president. I do not speak for my church on public matters. And my church does not speak for me." He went on to say that "should I win this election, I will invoke every effort of mind and spirit to uphold the oath of the presidency."

It was a simple, eloquent unveiling of what he meant to do and how he meant to govern. The rest is history. The ministers were totally ineffective in their efforts to attack Kennedy's belief in separation of church and state. His opening statement declaring his personal convictions and their bearing—and lack of bearing—on his political life defanged his antagonists before they had a chance to spring on him. His statement was plain and clear. He would be a president first, and all else would be subservient to that duty, including his religion. In the question-and-answer period, the ministers' questions made little impression.

It seemed to me that Kennedy's calm, poise, and exhibition of conviction were proof against any more debates. Kennedy had clearly won, and news commentaries the next day verified this view. For the first time, our camp began to sense the possibility of victory. The telecast of that debate would be used a hundred times in other Texas cities and throughout the South, where it was imperative that we quash this religious issue before it hurt us at the polling booths.

LBJ was overjoyed and let me know as much. He knew better than most the necessity of a clear-cut win in the confrontation with Protestant leaders. We had done that, thanks to Kennedy's flawless performance in a dicey forum, where it could have easily gone the other way.

Meanwhile, Speaker Sam Rayburn and Lyndon Baines Johnson pursued voters in every one of Texas's 254 counties. I can still hear Johnson, his face contorted and his voice rasping as he called out, "No one ever asked who was Protestant or Catholic at the Alamo!" It was a pretty good summary of where we stood, and it sounded good to Texans, and frankly that's all we cared about.

On election day, the LBJ legions were at work all across the state. It was a massive effort, the most finely honed of any Johnson campaign. The final result was too close. The Kennedy-Johnson ticket, backed with all the efficiency of the Johnson organization, carried Texas by a mere 46,233 votes. It was a near thing, but it was a win. Texas was safely in the Democratic column. Lyndon Johnson had performed as he had pledged he would. He had carried Texas.

It was the same scenario throughout the country. It was close, but when it was all over, John F. Kennedy was president and Lyndon Johnson was vice president.

I think I knew LBJ as well as anyone outside his family. I admired him greatly. I followed him unswervingly as he became the most heroic figure in American history by pushing through the Congress the most far-reaching measures to advance civil rights and human justice, to provide federal aid for education, to finance medical care for the aged, to found Head Start, and to spearhead the War on Poverty.

I never wavered in my loyalty to Lyndon Johnson when he was alive, and I am still loyal to him through the long years since his death. But I never considered loyalty as a barrier to recognizing faults and flaws. No man or woman is without them. Had President Johnson been without those flaws, he would not have resembled the endlessly fascinating—and extraordinarily effective—figure that he truly was.

I will never see his like again. For a time, I was fortunate enough to stand by his side as he tried so hard and with such passion to make life better for a lot of Americans. It was a glory time. But it was also a painful time. Thankfully, because of phone recordings he made, our young Americans in college can listen to those tapes and hear this larger-than-life leader endlessly beguiling, cajoling, threatening, and charming those whose help he needed in lifting the lives, hopes, and well-being of millions of Americans. These young people look at one another and say, "He was a giant, and there aren't many around today."

Chapter 3

ALAMO STREET

My mother, Josephine, in 1920 in Houston at the time of her marriage to my father.

I was born at 1507 Alamo Street, in the First Ward of Houston, Texas. To be scrupulously accurate, I was born in St. Joseph's Hospital in downtown Houston, but from the moment I knew anything about Texas and its history, I insisted I was actually born on Alamo Street.

In retrospect, it was a shameless act of chauvinism, though at the time I had no idea what that word meant, nor did I care after it was defined for me. What is more "Texan" than to greet life on the street named for the holiest place in not only Texas history, but in all the deeds of recorded civilization? Of course it was chauvinistic. I also recall that before I was ten years old, I could recite (and believed!) the creed that inspired every Texas schoolboy: "Thermopylae has its messenger of death, the Alamo had none."

I should point out that in the Texas public schools at that time, the teaching of Texas history began in the third grade of elementary school. (I do pray that some latter-day political correctionist has not messed around with the Texas canon since I flourished in the third grade.) Texas schoolchildren were not introduced to the rest of American history until the fifth grade. The Houston Independent School District was never in doubt about which history should claim greater priority. And I never disputed their judgment.

Many years later, when I was at the summit of power in Hollywood, I was invited by my close friend Dick Cook, head of the Walt Disney film studio, to fly to San Antonio for the premiere of Disney's newest film, *The Alamo*. When the movie was over, I was standing in the lobby as all the guests streamed out, heading for the postfilm party, when two reporters came up to me. One of them, an attractive blonde who was with the San Antonio newspaper, said to me: "Mr. Valenti, did you like *The Alamo*?"

I leveled a firm gaze at her and said: "Young lady, I was born in Houston, Texas. I lived on Alamo Street. I went to Davy Crockett Elementary School and graduated from Sam Houston High School. And here you are asking me if I liked *The Alamo*?" She fled the scene quickly.

Early in the twentieth century, Houston's First Ward was populated by newly arrived immigrants and by first and second generations of new Americans who had taken root in Texas soil. Within its boundaries were Luna Park, just across from Alamo Street, and Houston Avenue, a major thoroughfare traversed by trolley cars transporting people to and from downtown Houston.

Alamo Street was the center of my universe. It was a long, unpaved street stretching for some three blocks without intersections, with drainage ditches on either side, inhabited mainly by Greek and Italian families. My parents were born here, the first issue of desperately poor peasants who had left a Sicily barren of hope to make a new home far from anything they had ever known. My grandparents had come to this strange, wondrous land, whose language they did not understand, whose culture they struggled to absorb, and whose mythology they sought eagerly to embrace. From the first day of their arrival, they tried mightily to be Americans. For them, to be American was as much a religion as their Catholic faith.

My father, Joe Valenti, was a small, good-looking man with a thick head of brown hair that stayed that way, even in his eighties, like Ronald Reagan's. He was a quiet man who loved being with his children, his wife, and her extended family. He was a clerk in the county courthouse, which in those days was the center of political activity in Harris County as well as in the city itself. There was a sweetness about him and a lack of ambition that contributed to his easygoing appeal. While I'm in full-disclosure mode here, I must confess that I differed from my father in this regard. A fierce ambition burned in me before I could even define the word. I knew I wanted to rise higher, much higher than my parents, although at my young age I could not fathom what that really meant. I knew I wanted to see more, know more, and feel more than what seemed to be my lot. Above all, I wanted to be educated, which to me meant gaining the tools that would let me leap to the highest point my ambition and abilities could take me.

My father was strict. When I got out of line or broke his rules, he didn't hesitate to take off his belt and give me a thorough beating until my butt and thighs were red. He didn't do it often, but it was enough so that I got a very strong notion of what was right and what was not. Later, he would give me a hug to let me know that he loved me despite the thrashing I got (and deserved, by his lights). Today's parenting experts would frown at the thrashings I received at the hands of my father, but I never felt abused. For better and for worse, when I got a whipping I deserved it, and I knew it.

My mother, Josephine, was a beautiful woman, particularly in her youth. She was the prototype of the Italian mother and lived for her two children, her husband, and her large extended family. I loved her dearly. She loved my sister and me with a fierce maternal devotion. My sister Lorraine was six years younger than I, a truly lovely girl, whose thick, dark curly hair framed an unforgettable face and a smile that matched the sun.

Lorraine is remarkable. She had a bad first marriage. She worked hard to raise her two sons, never whining about the unpretty hand fate had conferred on her. Then came a stroke of good fortune. She met and married a singularly loving, generous man whose company, which he had founded with his brother, became one of the most successful apartment builders in the country. Ted Dinerstein not only embraced her sons, Tom and Jack, as his own, but for the next thirty years and counting he lavished on Lorraine a steady stream of love and loyalty that most women only dream about. He proved the authenticity of the lyric, "Love is lovelier the second time around."

The kind of devotion my mother lavished on us would be described today as old-fashioned, for we knew our mother would have given her own life to save ours without hesitation. Okay, if love—pure, simple, and given without stint—is old-fashioned, I'll live with that. I'll also never forget it.

Our home on Alamo Street was a small frame house. We had a small living room and a smaller dining room, a kitchen, two bedrooms, and a screened-in back porch for a day bed, which is where I slept. (It had to be screened; Houston mosquitoes were the size of polo ponies, and meaner.) And one bathroom. When I was still very young I swore I would one day have enough of life's rewards never to live anywhere with just one bathroom, a sentiment echoed by Lorraine, once she was old enough to claim her share of bathroom time. My wife, Mary Margaret, and I agreed quickly on our wedding day that separate bathrooms was the key to a successful marriage. Whenever we traveled my definition of roughing it was a suite in the Ritz hotel in Paris with only one bathroom!

Just down the street, on the corner of Houston Avenue and Alamo, my father's parents, Jake and Mary Valenti, lived in an apartment above the grocery store they owned and operated. They had migrated to Houston from Palermo, Sicily, in 1890, just before the turn of the century, and were soon followed by my mother's parents the same year.

My mother's father was Bernardo De George (modified from DiGeorgio when he and his brother came through Ellis Island on their way to New Orleans, before settling in Houston). His first wife died in Houston after bearing him one son, Joe, and four daughters: Rosalie, my mother Josephine, Lena, and Mamie, who died before I was born. He sent off to Sicily for his second wife, who was to give birth to four more daughters: my aunts Lucille, Lillian, Julia, and Natalie.

My mother's father was a resolute man of severe brooding countenance who displayed a commanding presence whenever he entered a room. He was thoroughly Sicilian, and an immigrant "American citizen"—a designation that he considered sacred. Of medium height with a ramrod posture, he was an unbending old patriarch, with a thick, white mustache to match his abundant white hair, combed back in a pompadour. His word, once proclaimed in a mélange of Sicilian dialect and Texas Gulf Coast patois, became the irrevocable law of the household.

Bernardo and his brother were working on a plantation in New Orleans, when they heard about a thriving little town called Houston on the humid Gulf Coast, with a climate not unlike what they had left behind in Sicily. Some Sicilian friends from Bernardo's village had already congregated there and were putting out the word: "This is a good place; land is cheap; there are businesses to start; here there is opportunity." So my grandfather, his brother, and other Sicilians fresh from the barren Palermo countryside packed up their meager belongings and headed west toward a town named after the greatest man in Texas history, though they had not the foggiest idea who Sam Houston was. Little did they ever imagine that this little town would one day become the fourth largest city in the United States.

Like many poor Sicilian peasants, Bernardo and his older brother, Michael, wanted more than anything to find some land to own, a place where their children could become native-born citizens. It's hard to convey the depth of that yearning. Land was identity. Land was permanent. Land gave rootless peasants a chance to be somebody. A deed of ownership certified them as proprietors, who could no longer be ignored in society. It put their destiny in their own hands. And to these peasants, Houston was that place; it would be their home forever. Bernardo and Michael had come to stay—and prosper.

By the time I was born, my mother's father had become a fairly affluent businessman, despite his lack of education and irregular grasp of the English language. He was the proprietor of a spacious grocery store on the outskirts of what would become downtown Houston. He would go on to own more than sixty rental properties as well as the entire block on which his home sat. In later years, this area would become the heart of a wildly prospering, swiftly growing Houston, and many years after that, on the very site of my grandfather's home would rise the stately office building of the most successful enterprise in Texas, the Humble Oil Company, later to be called Exxon.

As fate would have it, my grandfather lost much of his property during the Great Depression. But he held on to the grocery store and his home above it and a number of lots and houses that generated monthly rents. The properties were sold in later years, too soon to reap the dramatic benefits of a rapidly advancing Houston real estate market. Had he held on, that downtown Houston property would have been worth many millions. As President Kennedy once said, "Life is unfair."

On the other hand, my grandfather's older brother, Michael, made it through the Depression with his holdings intact. He owned hotels, real estate, and rental properties, which made him a very rich man. My cousins lived in mansions on Montrose Boulevard and in River Oaks, then the enclaves of the very prosperous, all of which put them about as high up the fiscal and social ladder as one could climb in Houston. When I was young, I didn't really understand the difference between the way I lived and the way my cousins lived. It didn't take me too long to figure that out.

Alamo Street was a congenial place for a boy to grow up. Here the sons and daughters of Greek and Italian immigrants played together, went to school together, and generally got along pretty well. Indeed, since Greek was the language of my young friends' households, I spoke what might be described as "playground Greek" until the day we finally moved from Alamo Street. Native Texans lived there, too, like the Barnes family who lived right across the street. Three houses up was the Landers family, and across from them was the home of the prettiest girl on Alamo Street, Betty Green. And halfway up the street was Billy Koenig and his family, who were of German descent.

It was a funny thing about Alamo Street's inhabitants. None of the families had much to keep them from being dirt poor. But because there was no television to offer us visions of life beyond our neighborhood's borders, we simply didn't know that we lacked anything materially or where we fell on the social scale. Current-day pollsters would have been mystified to find no bitterness in our neighborhood about the harshness of life, or about how we Alamo Street folks were being shortchanged by the city's political overlords, or about any other inequities. We felt good about ourselves.

We children seldom wore shoes when we played together, so the soles of our feet began to take on the attributes of leather. We walked to Davy Crockett Elementary School about seven blocks away. A half mile from my house, we played baseball and football on Grote field, a flat slab of prairie dried by a pitiless Texas sun and harder than steel planking when you got knocked down in a scrimmage or tried to slide into second base.

My young Greek friends, with names like Chiacos, Kritson, Heidimanos, Voinis, and Pappas, always went to Greek school after public school to keep intact the culture of their families, though like all immigrants, the Greeks were determined their children would be American.

I'm always surprised when I read autobiographies of famous celebrities who prattle on about their dreary childhoods, filled with absent, uncaring parents, rejected affection, abusive treatment, and the other ills from which psychiatrists derive their livelihoods. My early life was populated by no such memories. My childhood passed most agreeably—which is not to say we didn't get into trouble once in a while. We were constantly outdoors, constantly figuring out ways to have fun, and sometimes our plans were not coincident with model behavior.

I don't remember who dreamed up our "great rotten egg" caper, but our merry band of kids all agreed it had possibilities. For weeks we hoarded eggs until they were about as rotten as eggs can get. We broke one open to test it, and it had the most god-awful smell. We almost choked as the odor filled the empty garage where we conducted our test. Yep, these eggs would do the job all right. That night, when we should have been home doing homework, eight of us snuck out to the corner of Alamo and Houston Avenue. We huddled down behind two large chinaberry trees to keep out of sight.

At that time of night, the streetcars didn't run as often as they did during the day, so all of us hustled out to the tracks armed with buckets of water and Octagon soap, the kind our mothers used to scrub clothes clean on their washboards. We wetted down the track for about fifty yards, and then we rubbed it with thick layers of Octagon soap. Someone yelled, "It's coming!" and we fled to our shelter of trees fronting Houston Avenue.

It was a typical Houston summer night, hot and humid, ensuring the streetcar's windows would be open. I was designated to stand at the streetcar stop and wave it down. Sure enough, the conductor spied me and applied his brakes, but the car only skidded down the soapy rails. With a whoop, my friends rose up and started hurling rotten eggs. Some of them scored direct hits, splattering the shirts of two passengers, and others broke on the floor of the car. We could see the screwed-up noses of passengers as they recoiled from the stench and the poor conductor struggling to stop the streetcar until he finally got it under control. By now, we were hightailing it out of sight, running as hard as we could back to our homes. We laughed until our stomachs hurt. But we all got home safely.

Then, two days later, the county commissioner, a short, fat fellow with a bow tie and cowboy boots, showed up in our neighborhood. It was an ominous sign. He strolled up and down Alamo Street, stopping here and there, ferreting out culprits. It turned out that one passenger had identified two of us, and from there it was easy to find the rest. That evening, the commissioner knocked on our door. My father knew him. The commissioner's office was in the county court-house, where my dad worked. He and my father engaged in conversation on the front porch and were soon joined by my mother. I couldn't hear what they were saying, but my knees shook with fear. I knew there would be hell to pay. And there was.

When my father came back into the house, he was in a foul mood. "All right, Jack, I know what you did, so don't try to talk your way out of this," he said in a menacing voice. If I could have thought of something that would have declared me "not guilty," I would have spoken up. But I was clean out of ideas. My father took off his belt and gave my backside a full-fledged whipping. I was yelping and crying and promising I wouldn't do it again, but the belt kept rising and falling. Finally, my mother entered and stopped my father.

She turned to me and said, "Jack, there were some ladies on that car who were trying to get home after working late. They did you no harm. Yet you caused them great pain. Suppose one of your aunts was on that streetcar. Suppose I was on that streetcar and your friends threw rotten eggs at me? How would you feel about that? And for what, so you and your friends could laugh at the misery of those decent, hardworking people? I should think you'd be terribly ashamed of yourself right now."

My mother's voice was soft but firm. I wanted to disappear off the earth. I said I was sorry, and I was. I crept off to bed, still weeping but less now from the belt whipping than from the pain of my mother's words and the sad expression on her face. I felt like two burlap sacks full of dog shit. It was not one of my proudest moments. I found out later that all my other friends had been subjected to variations on the same theme. Needless to say, I never got near a streetcar rail, Octagon soap, and rotten eggs at the same time again.

As a little boy, I spent every Sunday (with my father, mother, and Lorraine) at Grandpa De George's home above the grocery store, where his family lived. It was spacious, with at least five bed-rooms. There was a very large kitchen, a commodious back room, and a living room and dining room whose dimensions could embrace all of his considerable family for dinners and just plain get-togethers. An immense porch on the second floor surrounded the house on two sides, which we grandchildren used for our playground, peering through the railing to watch the passing human parade and play our games.

The De George house was always filled with grandchildren, sometimes as many as fifteen of them. We first cousins had a merry old time each Sunday. After early mass, the entire extended family of both my parents—including my mother's seven siblings, her brother Joe, the oldest, and six sisters, would gather at Grandpa De George's place. At Sunday dinner around 2:00 p.m., some thirty or so voices, adult and children, were raised in laughter, gossip, and lots of politi-cal talk. We were a noisy group. My uncles and aunts and their wives and husbands laughed and argued with one another, sometimes launching into fierce controversies that rocked the walls. There was petulance, stormy confrontation, and tearful reconciliation, but al-ways there was love. There was family. We knew who we were. We had a place to be, and we felt secure in it.

After dinner, my grandmother and the women of the family cleared the table, while the men gathered in the large back room to play poker or dominoes and to banter with one another. Uncle Joe's son, Bernard De George, known as Bunny, was one year older than me. We used to sit at the table watching the poker games. As we got older, we played as well. I got pretty good at it.

There was no television, and video games hadn't been invented yet, so Bunny and I made up our own games. We created a baseball league, using two decks of cards (the precursor of Fantasy Baseball). We conjured up names for our players, kept statistics, and Sunday after Sunday we would square off in our league games, sitting at a table on the wide porch, enjoying the late sunlight and occasional breeze. The rules were simple. An ace was a home run, kings were triples, queens were doubles, and jacks were singles. Twos and threes were strikeouts, fours were walks, and all other cards were outs. After a year or so, we had honed our game so that we had two decks of

cards with just the right number of face cards and aces to accommodate a nicely balanced game. In one year, we filled a beefy notebook
with the stats of each game, indexing the statistics, with playoffs for
the championship.

If I have one regret, it's that my own children don't have memories of large family Sunday dinners and the warm, enveloping embrace of numerous aunts and uncles and a dozen-plus cousins. We
may have missed a good many things when I was a child, but familial
love was not among them. In this way, our family was just like the
other families of Sicilian descent in Houston, most of whom emigrated from the same villages in the Palermo countryside. This extended family feeling inspired the Sicilian patriarchs to organize a
social club, the Philo Club, off Washington Avenue. It wasn't much
of a place, but it was large, and it had a kitchen and a small stage.

On scheduled evenings, grandfathers and grandmothers would
gather at the club, bringing their entire families, young and old, to sit
around, drink wine, eat, and talk and talk. Sometimes there would be
performances by the grandchildren, certainly not Tony Award caliber, but to this audience it was better than a Broadway sellout. It was
a close community, where everyone knew everyone else, where families intermarried until it was possible to say that any one person was
related in one way or another to just about everyone else.

Grandpa De George became the unofficial leader of this growing band of Sicilian immigrants. The political barons of Houston
wielded enormous power, but they paid court to these newly arrived
immigrants, who became U.S. citizens as soon as they were eligible
and voted religiously in each election. They had one other asset:
They voted as a bloc, which is red meat to politicians.

The district attorney of Harris County was John Crooker Sr.,
who was also my grandfather's personal lawyer. John Crooker founded
one of the most prestigious law firms in Houston, which later included Leon Jaworski, who would burst on the national scene in 1974
as a Watergate prosecutor. When Grandpa De George died, among
the honorary pallbearers were John Crooker Sr. and Captain James
A. Baker Sr., grandfather of President Bush's secretary of state, James
Baker. John Crooker's son, John Jr., himself a successful Houston
lawyer, told me that his father often said that Bernardo De George's

leadership role in the Sicilian community was a crucially important factor in Crooker's election as district attorney of Harris County.

When election time came around, my grandfather would call a meeting of Sicilian patriarchs at his home. There, my grandfather would select the candidates to be supported. The elders would depart the gathering and pass along the mandate to the members of their families and to friends who were not at the meeting. My grandfather had stern, intractable views about what his support was worth. He couldn't be bought with political "walking-around money," a few hundred dollars to pass around the neighborhood to make sure the voters went to the polls. Grandpa De George scorned these "gifts." He simply could not be bought. This shrewd old peasant had larger objectives in mind, which would be sullied by a bundle of cash. He stood aloof from the assumed venalities, knowing that the politicians had contempt for supporters whose hands were always out. His objective was not to fill his purse, but to make sure that his loyal assembly of friends would not be forgotten at City Hall or the county courthouse. He wanted assurances that when controversy visited his people, they would have loyal friends in high places who would listen patiently and courteously and act fairly. The Sicilians had good reason to be wary. They were an ethnic and religious minority in a mainly Anglo-Saxon, Protestant Bible Belt community. My grandfather commanded his political ramparts with an integrity that even the most biased of candidates and officeholders came to understand. When he talked, they listened, for the politicians knew beyond any doubt that Bernardo De George never reneged on a pledge and never deserted a friend, nor ever forgot an enemy.

As a small boy, I observed Grandpa De George closely and with considerable awe. He was a hard taskmaster. He did not tolerate advice from whippersnappers. He had unshakable confidence in his judgments, and once he took a position, nuclear bombs could not move him. When he spoke, he expected his family to listen. His values were rigid, never blurred by circumstance or anxiety. He placed great store in making it clear where he stood. No one ever misunderstood Bernardo, and when he was at a meeting, everyone knew who was in charge.

This unlettered man, his English thickly accented, was my first up-close look at what real leadership is all about. He spoke without artifice. He never allowed his passions full rein except when he confronted charlatans, liars, hypocrites, and latter-day progeny of Judas Iscariot. I have to confess, I tried to absorb all that he modeled. At this early age, I was fascinated to see how one leads others and earns their loyalty. I believe Lyndon Johnson would have found my grandfather to be a man "you could go to the well with."

My grandfather didn't realize how attentive his young grandson was to both his political philosophy and the commanding presence he brought to the daily business of dealing with politicians. I'm not sure that he taught me all he knew, but I never forgot what I learned from him about real leadership. I also learned something else that I treasured: my grandfather's sense of obligation, loyalty, and love for this new land that was now his beloved country.

In 1915, before the United States entered World War I, the *Houston Chronicle* ran the following item: "Harris County's Italian-American citizenship, estimated at 5,000, will send 50 volunteers to the sunny shores of the mother country. The attitude of the Italians in Houston over the war in Europe is a sense of indifference. Bernardo De George, a native of Italy, expresses it: 'We have never been friendly with Austria and our sympathies are with the Allies simply because Austria is fighting them. We know no other allegiance than the Stars and Stripes,' said Mr. De George."

That was my grandfather: brief and to the point, with no unnecessary flourishes. He knew no other allegiance except to the United States, which he loved more than life itself.

As I became more involved in politics on a local and national scale, I grew to appreciate, as my grandfather did, the value of people with common goals and common interests staying together in the voting booth. The power that comes to a group of persons able to assemble deliverable votes, without slipping across either legal or moral boundaries, is of considerable worth. As new generations spring upward from their immigrant roots, become college educated, and go into professions and business, they tend to widen their perspectives, and at the same time loosen the ties that bound them to a communal political position. This is why the Irish, Greeks, Italians, Poles, and the like can no longer assert their once vaunted political supremacy in their own neighborhoods. If their parents and grandparents were Democrats, many of them are now Republicans and independents. If once they gave seamless support to those whose names sounded like theirs and whose religious affiliations were the same, those loyalties are now only loosely held, their fathers' and grandparents' voting patterns casually observed. As a result, they can no longer present a united force that once gave them electoral heft.

There was only one way in which I would come to feel let down by Grandfather Bernardo. Up to the age of seven, I was fairly fluent in Italian. I could say my prayers in Italian and enter into conversations with the older generation that won me their admiration. Then one day, just past my seventh birthday, Grandpa De George delivered his ultimatum. "From now on," he said, "when the grandchildren are in the house, there will be no Italian spoken. My grandchildren will become Americans. English is the language of this country, and they will speak English like Americans speak English. They will speak it well. They will speak it so well, no one will doubt they are Americans."

That was it. No rebuttals, no debates. Whatever my parents or my uncles and aunts may have felt, it went unspoken. Once this edict went into effect, my ability to converse with the older generation of immigrants in their native tongue slowly faded. By the time I was in high school, I was taking courses in Spanish, not Italian, which wasn't even taught in the Houston Independent School District. My grasp of the musical Italian language was forever lost, causing me pangs of regret that I feel keenly to this day.

Later, in the White House, and most certainly in my long years in the Hollywood movie industry, whenever I encountered high-ranking Italian government officials or visited with cinema icons like Sophia Loren, Claudia Cardinale, Gina Lollobrigida, and Federico Fellini, I was hopelessly unlearned in their beautiful language, the tongue of my grandparents and all those relatives now either deceased or dispersed. I felt a sense of loss that sits like a canker in my soul. Yet whenever I flew into Italy, I always felt thoroughly at home. The minute I set foot on Italian soil, I was comforted. I knew I belonged. My roots were alive.

. . .

O ne truth became clear to me early in life, and that was the power of books. Out of my still undefined ambition, I became a tireless reader, hungering after books with all the zeal of a starving man stumbling onto a freshly laid banquet table. It was a consuming passion. I don't know why. While education was always a prime objective of my grandfathers and my parents, ours was not a bookish family. Not at all. My parents simply believed that education was the right compass setting for a future brighter than their lot, but we had no library in our home. Doubtless in my deep past there must have been a Sicilian ancestor who became enamored of Horace and Ovid, Tacitus and the Plinys younger and elder, and who read the Greeks as well. I wanted to believe that. How else could I explain my restless passion for books? After I finished devouring the school library, I plundered the downtown public library.

But I didn't travel by journeys of the mind alone. After all these years, I remember with splendid clarity my early teachers at Davy Crockett Elementary School: my first-grade teacher, Miss Corbett; my second-grade teacher, Miss Walker; and my fifth-grade teacher, Miss Hoskins. They confirmed the dictum of the wily old Jesuits who said: "Give us the child until the age of seven, and then others may have him." The Jesuits figured a child's character is formed early and once shaped becomes his moral and intellectual shield. From my first day in the first grade until I graduated from Sam Houston High School at the age of fifteen, these three teachers shaped my consciousness. All three read to their classes. Each day. They read the Brothers Grimm's fairy tales, Aesop's fables, and other children's books. I loved these reading periods, and I looked forward to them with an eagerness I was hard-pressed to understand. Then in the fifth grade, Miss Hoskins began to read *A Tale of Two Cities*, the Dickens masterpiece. Some might say that such a book was too much for young children to understand. Not the way Miss Hoskins did it. She read about ten minutes each day, and when she got to a sentence or an idea that seemed difficult, she would stop and explain what was going on.

I cannot say how educators today would judge Miss Corbett, Miss Walker, and Miss Hoskins, but I can report that some seven decades later, I can still hear their voices reading stories that unlocked my imagination and ignited my interest in a larger world that seemed endlessly fascinating. It seems to me that the Jesuits had it absolutely right, as did my three unforgettable teachers. What we learn when we are young is what sticks with us. Moreover, I believe that real values are something you learn at an early age, in school, in church, and at home.

And then there's the absolute magic that is released into the lives of children when they learn to read. My early teachers were so valuable to me because the way they viewed books made me excited about books, too. When they read to me, I wanted to read books by myself. I wanted to read lots of books. I became obsessed with reading. I began to build my own library, first with books I had my parents buy for me and then with money I saved myself.

As a small boy growing up, I read everything beginning with the Tom Swift series, the Frank Merriwell volumes, Edgar Rice Burroughs's alluring stories of Tarzan, and Harold Sherman's sports novels. Then, as I grew older, I discovered history, other nonfiction, and literary fiction, as I gobbled up works by Rafael Sabatini, Victor Hugo, Alexandre Dumas, and Claude Bowers. Later on came Lord Macaulay, Edward Gibbon, and Winston Churchill. I have read every word published by Macaulay (my favorite writer), including his unforgettable essays in the *Edinburgh Review*, his monumental *The History of England*, and his speeches in the House of Commons. I have pored over every book written by Mr. Churchill as well as his wartime speeches. I have read and reread—and listened to on tape—the immortal literary legacy of Gibbon, *The Decline and Fall of the Roman Empire*.

It is essentially these three writers from whom I developed my personal writing style. Alas, it has its defects. Since no one can match the symphonic writings of these masters, my own prose tends to overreach, but now it is too late. I have found no literary rehab center that can offer me a cure, so I do my best and can only hope you will forgive me my excesses.

But there were other writers who also became part of my family. William Shakespeare, of course. No literate human can claim to be even modestly educated without reading Shakespeare. To this day, when I fly about the world, I set a book of Shakespeare's plays in my lap and plug my earphones into a Walkman containing an audiotape of *Macbeth* or *Henry V* or *King Lear*. This way I can read the play in its written form and listen to the tape at the same time. To read *Hamlet* silently and simultaneously hear Paul Scofield's rich voice in the most wondrous renditions of the mother tongue in all of recorded literature is a sensual experience. I recommend it heartily to anyone enchanted by the riches of the robust English language.

I embraced the writings of Abraham Lincoln, who was without question a writer of such incandescence that no other American president has come within miles of his elegant literary craftsmanship. I count his second inaugural speech to be the most wrenchingly emotional piece of political persuasion the human brain could ever compose.

William Prescott created two epics that I have read with much pleasure, *The Conquest of Mexico* and *The Conquest of Peru*. I am an admirer of André Maurois, Balzac, and Maurice Druon, as well as of H. G. Wells, Francis Parkman, Anthony Trollope, John Steinbeck, Theodore Dreiser, John Updike, and the latter-day historians Arthur Schlesinger Jr., David McCullough, and Michael Beschloss. Oh yes, and Elmore Leonard, whose ear for real-life dialogue is so uncanny that he has no modern-day peer.

To be honest about it, there are some writers with whom I never connected, though God knows I tried. I never fathomed James Joyce. Yes, I know he is a literary icon, but I never could figure out why so many high school students were forced to read him. To give them a sense of what hell is all about, I guess. And then there are Henry James and James Fenimore Cooper. I find James to be a colossal bore. As for Cooper, I never could see what all the fuss is about. Maybe the Mohicans didn't survive because they were forced to write essays about Cooper's so-called regal prose. They chose to fade away rather than take on the task.

When I was about fourteen, I read a book that became the launching pad from which I leaped to other worlds of prose and poetry. The book was *The Story of Philosophy* by Will Durant. I was intrigued by the men he wrote about and by ideas that baffled me at first. But I read on. Will Durant is a master of clear, rhythmic, rich prose. He fed my interest. He fired my curiosity. Now I wanted to know about the philosophers he had illuminated for me. Plato, Aristotle, who were they? Francis Bacon, what a strange, compelling man; Voltaire, that impertinent gadfly, would become one of my most congenial literary companions; Nietzsche, whose name I could not pronounce for years and whose ideas also took me a long time to penetrate.

My love of language would serve me well, and in some ways that I never anticipated. When I was about ten years old, a minor miracle ignited something that is still alive in me at this very hour. My father was fascinated by the way I handled myself at the dinner table with my mother's enlarged family, so he decided to put me to the test. We were attending a political rally on behalf of the sheriff of Harris County when my dad said to me, "I've talked to the sheriff, and he thought it would be just fine if you got up and said something good about him." I was hesitant, as any ten-year-old would be, but I had a hankering to give it a try.

The sheriff's name was T. A. Binford, and he had been in office for over twenty years. In Houston and Harris County at that time, the county sheriff was an icon equivalent to a movie star, and he looked the role. Sheriff Binford was an imposing six feet four inches tall, with a pair of pearl-handled .45 six-shooters slung low from holsters on his waist and tied down in the manner of movie gunfighters of the Old West. He was always accompanied by a legion of lean, hard-faced deputies wearing Stetsons, equally well armed. You didn't want to mess with Sheriff Binford unless you were crazy or drunk or both.

So on this particular evening before the November elections (which for Sheriff Binford were as close to a sure thing as mortal man could make them), my father picked me up and lifted me onto the back end of a flatbed truck. I stood before a sound system that was primitive even by the standards of that day. I cannot for the life of me remember what I said, but I do remember the thrill that ran through me like a thrumming wire. Upraised faces were listening to me, actually listening. They even seemed to be admiring me. I looked them in the eye as I talked. Even at that absurdly young age, I knew something pleasingly addictive was happening to me. It wasn't a long speech, maybe two or three minutes, but I felt for the first time the magic that infects actors on a stage, the excitement, the sensual electricity of being aware that an audience is responding to what you are saying. It is a powerful surge in one's veins and brain. I never recovered from it.

From that moment on, I was fascinated by the art of connecting with an audience. I should have offered my gratitude to the sheriff, but I think he already understood. After my moment onstage, Sheriff Binford patted me on the head and bellowed in a deep voice, "Young man, you speak mighty good." Well, I accepted that at face value. Even at that age, I knew it was the better part of wisdom to go along with whatever the hell the sheriff said.

After that evening, I embarked on a lifelong study of the styles, manners, cadences, and rhythms of men and women whose public presentations I admired (and many I did not) and whose performances I burned into my memory. In short, I became a clinical observer of public speaking and public speakers. I even wrote a book about it, *Speak Up with Confidence: How to Prepare, Learn, and Deliver Effective Speeches.*

I have discussed the art of public speaking with Kirk Douglas many times. He confirmed that what an actor onstage feels before a live audience are the same emotions that a public official feels when he is addressing his constituents. He is performing, just as an actor performs. He strives to convince his audience that what he says has merit—much the same way the actor persuades an audience to believe in the character he is portraying. "Politicians and actors, we all come from the same DNA," said Kirk.

I always find it amusing when I hear someone deriding an actor plunging into politics. "What do actors know of politics and governance?" is the typical reaction. It is a myopic response. First of all, a good many actors are well-read, highly educated, and every bit as knowledgeable about public policy as public servants. But more important, the actor brings to the political rostrum an asset of inestimable value: the ability to speak lines convincingly, dramatically, and engagingly.

If one examines FDR, John Kennedy, and Bill Clinton, it's clear they shared an actor's gift for enlisting public approval and support. Ronald Reagan is the supreme exemplar of this phenomenon—

a movie actor who commanded the largest stage in the world with amazing grace and success. Reagan knew how to excite audiences, how to keep them in thrall to his voice. In movie parlance, he "hit his marks and said his lines." But the right of an actor to rise and speak his or her mind on political issues stems from the title we are all blessed with in this country, that of citizen of the United States.

After Davy Crockett Elementary School, I went on to Governor James S. Hogg Junior School and then to Sam Houston High School, which was the only high school located in downtown Houston. I chose Sam Houston High School because I had to earn money, which meant I had to work after school, and propinquity to jobs was essential.

I found that work through my godmother Lena Cannata, younger sister to my mother. Her husband, Fred Cannata, a sweet, quiet man, was general manager of the Horwitz Theaters, second-run movie houses owned by a maverick businessman, Will Horwitz. Uncle Fred allowed me to work after school as an usher in four Horwitz Theaters situated within five blocks of one another, on the perimeter of downtown. His boss, Will Horwitz, was not connected in any way to the major studios. As a result, the Horwitz Theaters played films only after their runs in the major cinemas on Main Street owned by the Hollywood studios that produced the films. Horwitz was one of a fiercely competitive group of independent theater owners who fought the majors for years and finally, in 1950, triumphed over them. The Supreme Court ordered the studios to divest themselves of their theater ownership, citing violation of the nation's antitrust laws. It mortally wounded the major studios. Eventually, that decision broke the back of the star-director-writer contract system that had kept the creative community functioning as indentured serfs, subject to suspension and being traded to other producers, the way MGM "loaned out" Clark Gable to play Rhett Butler in David O. Selznick's *Gone With the Wind*.

In my wildest imaginings, I could not have foreseen that almost thirty years later I would become leader of the Motion Picture Association of America (MPAA), an organization founded and funded by the same major film studios that were such implacable enemies of my first employer, Will Horwitz. It would be my mandate to design the industry's response to a challenge from its critics denouncing the slackening of creative discipline in the movie world. That discipline, once sternly enforced by the studios and the Motion Pictures Producers and Distributors Association (later renamed the Motion Picture Association of America), headed by Will Hays, had degenerated into a production code that was flawed and reeked of censorship. One of my first decisions would be to jettison that code and its oppressive fist—but all of that lay years in the future as I began my labors at the Horwitz Theaters.

My work consisted of being a part-time usher and also roaming the outer limits of downtown Houston to put up posters proclaiming the feature films exhibited by the Horwitz Theaters. After school, I would ride the streetcar into a neighborhood, enter a barbershop, or a dry-cleaning establishment, or a drugstore, and with my most winsome smile ask if I might put up a poster in their window. My native charm was never enough, so I turned to my secret weapon: free passes to the movies. That usually worked.

If I was putting up posters, my work ended by 6:00 p.m., when I took the streetcar back home and hit the books. If I was ushering, the day was longer, ending at 11:00 p.m. with the last screening. Now the wait for the streetcar would be longer, and when I finally got home, it meant only a few hours' sleep because my homework could not go undone. On those mornings after, I woke tired and was bleary-eyed as I began the long streetcar ride to school and a new day at the movie theater.

Inside me raged a desire to go to college when I graduated from high school, but I knew it would be impossible for my family to fund me; there was simply no money available. In those days, we knew nothing of scholarships. I only knew I had to earn money somehow, enough to get me into a full-time college program. Otherwise I had to find a job that would allow me to go to school at night. I dreamed of being a courtroom lawyer, performing in front of a jury, persuading them, engaging them, winning them over again and again.

One of my father's friends, Percy Foreman, was an assistant district attorney who decided to run for the top spot, challenging his boss in the Democratic primary. Percy was a hurly-burly kind of guy, thickset and formidable. Providentially for him, he lost his primary bid—and immediately set forth on a new career as a defense attorney. Within a few years, Percy became one of the most famous and successful defense attorneys in the nation. His mantra was that he'd never lost a client to the electric chair in Huntsville (the largest state prison in Texas). That may not sound like much of an endorsement, but we Texans knew that was a mighty fine accomplishment, since Huntsville led the nation in executions.

I recall chatting with Percy when I was about fourteen, telling him my ambition was to be a courtroom attorney just like him. "What I'd like to know, Mr. Foreman, is what law school I should go to. I want to go to the best law school in the country. Which one is that?"

He grinned. "Well, Jack," he said, "if you're going to practice law in Texas, then get yourself to the University of Texas Law School. They have a network of graduates all over this state, kinda like an exclusive club. They take care of their own. But if you want the best of the best, then go to Harvard Law." I didn't know Harvard Law from a horse barn, but if Percy said it was the best, that was good enough for me. Okay, Harvard Law, get ready, because here I come.

At age fifteen, when I graduated from high school, I was too young to get an office job, so my uncle Fred came to the rescue again. I was employed full-time at the Iris Theater in the role of usher, janitor, and part-time concession stand worker, popping the corn, bagging it, and selling it; I also worked with the projectionist after the last show, enclosing the film in its metal containers for shipping back to the branch offices of the film companies.

The Iris specialized in westerns. I saw enough western films to last several lifetimes, starring Hoot Gibson, Ken Maynard, Bob Steele, Hopalong Cassidy, and other studio-set prairie warriors. The good news was that I received $11 a week for my labors. The bad news was that it was a seven-day workweek, beginning each day with the first show around 11:00 a.m. and ending at 11:30 p.m. This meant I could not go to college at night, not now. So I bided my time and did what I could to gain what may be described as "life experience." The Iris workforce, as well as those of the Texan and the Uptown theaters a block away, consisted almost entirely of young women. These young girls served as usherettes, cashiers, ticket takers, and concession stand operators. They ranged in age from eighteen to near twenty-three. Some of them were quite lovely, and several in particular were most kind to me. One, whom I will call Christine, full figured, just turning twenty-one, with a perky smile, seemed to find this cheerful young fellow not entirely unattractive. After the last show ended, Christine and I would join another usherette and her boyfriend, whose most valuable asset was his car. Jalopy though it was, it was transportation.

We would ride out to Hermann Park, just off Main Street, in the late evening. Each couple found a quiet, private piece of grassy park and spread out blankets. It was during these secluded moments under clear, starry Texas skies that I learned what boy-girl interaction was all about. When Christine departed the Iris Theater to move to Galveston some months later, I was taken under the affectionate wing of Lois, who was twenty-two years old and almost as pretty as Christine, with the additional blessing of a truly sensational figure. She picked up my instruction in sensuality where Christine left off. I was sleeping less than ever, but I was learning there are compensations for sleeplessness. At fifteen, sleep was not the high priority that my lessons in sensuality were. But my hunger for books and education was as relentless as ever.

My book learning continued apace. I read incessantly, learning more and more about our nation and our planet. I was reading about great men and women and their ascent to power and influence and how mistakes they made sometimes demolished their dreams and ambitions. In my own mind, I grew increasingly impatient and apprehensive, which affected my sense of well-being. Sometimes even Lois's ministrations did not quell my anxieties. I felt excluded from a world that could open the way to learning more and reaching higher. Only a college education could satisfy my longings.

Then it happened. As it did so often for me in my later life, a new opportunity arose without any planning on my part. A friend at the Iris Theater opened up a new vista for me when I complained that my working hours were keeping me from going to school.

"Why don't you apply for a job at Humble Oil? They're a great company, and they often take on office boys. You might have a future there."

Humble Oil. It was arguably the best-run corporation in Texas, and probably in America, though I did not at the time fully appreciate what that meant. Humble Oil. Okay, why not? I called in sick the next day, to the displeasure of my manager. I wasn't happy about the outright lie, but what could I do? I went to the personnel office of Humble Oil on Main Street, not more than ten blocks or so from the Iris Theater. I filled out an employment form, smiled a lot, and exerted all the charm I could summon. The middle-aged lady behind the reception desk seemed to react favorably to me, but that could mean anything or nothing at all. "Come back next week, young man, and we'll see if we can find something for you."

I left the office floating on a billowy cloud of hope. The next week, after calling in with another terrible illness, I renewed my acquaintance with the nice lady in personnel. She beamed at me. "We have something. We have a hall boy slot open. Would you like that?" I had no idea what a hall boy was, nor did I truly care. Now I had a day job. I was free in the evening. I had a chance to go to college. How does one describe joy beyond words?

But she wasn't through. "The workday begins at eight a.m. You will report tomorrow morning to Mrs. Lurline Reinhardt on the third floor. She'll be your superior, and you will take your orders from her." Fine, I thought, just fine. I will serve Mrs. Reinhardt devoutly, lovingly, unstintingly. Then the lady offered the ultimate in unexpected gifts. "Your salary will be seventy-five dollars a month."

I almost collapsed on the floor. Sixteen years old, I was now making $75 a month! This was a bloody fortune—more money than I knew existed—and all that dough for working half the time I had been putting in at the theater, plus Saturdays and Sundays off. I managed a grateful grin, fled the office, and raced to the theater, where I called my uncle Fred. I told him I had to quit my job, because I was going to work for Humble Oil. Uncle Fred understood my excitement, but when I reported the news to the Iris manager, he said, "You can't quit. You got to give notice."

As I turned to leave, I said, "You've got my notice. I'm leaving now."

I found Lois to tell her I would no longer be working at the theater and probably would not be seeing her for a while. My evenings were to be occupied by excitement of a wholly different kind. Lois seemed to understand; she patted my cheek and kissed me. "Call me, will you?"

My new boss, Mrs. Reinhardt, was a tiny woman with fluffy blondish hair. She was nearing fifty, I judged. She was endlessly cheerful, sweet, generous, and to this just-turned sixteen-year-old, she acted as a second mother. My job was to sit beside Mrs. Reinhardt and answer the phone when she went to the restroom or to lunch. But mostly my chores were to take the business cards of visitors into the offices of the executives who populated the third floor, to escort visitors into those offices, and to deliver mail from the central mailroom. Once I got used to the routine, it was a halcyon existence. I was able to read my books between journeys to the executive offices. At first Mrs. Reinhardt filled every quiet moment with conversation, but after a while she smiled maternally as I read.

During summer recess from school, I made a friend on the hall desk who stimulated my mind as no friend had before. He was a graduate student at Rice University, no more than twenty-one years old, a handsome fellow with thick brown hair and inquiring warm eyes. He was brilliantly educated. He was well versed in the literary canon and gave me the ultimate grand tour of its endless fascinations as we sat side by side in that marbled Humble office corridor. My mind expanded exponentially as I accompanied him through a world populated by works from the world's finest authors. In quiet moments, he read from books he was studying in class: Shelley, Keats, Pound, and a fellow named James Joyce.

My hall mate's name was William Goyen, and he became celebrated as one of America's most gifted writers, acclaimed by critics and readers alike when his first book, *The House of Breath*, was published. We remained close friends until his untimely death. Many years later, I was able to thank his lovely wife, Doris Roberts, a talented movie and television actress who starred in the immensely popular show *Everybody Loves Raymond*, for the "PhD" in literature I received from Billy Goyen.

Almost immediately upon my employment with Humble, I was able to pursue the towering opportunity of my life—I could attend college. Earlier, I had determined there was only one rational choice for me. Actually it was the only choice, period. The University of Houston offered a great enticement: evening classes for working stiffs like me. Only four years before, in 1934, it had been accredited as a full-fledged university. Two years after that, Hugh Roy Cullen, a fabulously successful wildcatter, gave the university a gift of some $25 million, a wondrous sum in 1936. His gift would support new construction on campus, including the Ezekiel Cullen Building, named after its benefactor's father.

Mr. Cullen fairly loved having night-school students come to his office from time to time, so I got to know him quite well. He had attained only a fourth-grade education, but his uncanny instinct for finding oil was one of the best in Texas. Alas, he had primitive political notions, about as far to the right as one can get without falling off the planet, but to this day I am full of affection for this man. He cared deeply about young, money-short working guys like me, and he understood our hunger for a college education. If there had been no University of Houston, no Hugh Roy Cullen, I don't know what turn my life would have taken. So when my friends wonder how I can express such admiration for a man whose views about government and public policy were so contradictory to my own, my answer is simple: "He made it possible for me to get an education. I owe him gratitude."

The day I enrolled in the University of Houston was the most exalted day (strictly speaking, it was night) of my life. One month after I began my employment at Humble Oil, I started my university schooling. Classes would start at 6:30 and end at 9:30 each evening of the week. My first three courses were in English, history, and physics, which was as much as I could effectively handle during one semester; this meant it would take me some six years to graduate, unless I went to summer school, which I had already decided I would do.

My first night in English class, September 1938, I met Johnny

Goyen. (In an odd coincidence, he was a cousin of Billy Goyen, my instructor in advanced English at Humble.) He became my closest, most loyal, and most trusted friend for the next fifty-six years. At the time, Johnny was seventeen years old, a year older than I was. He was a tall, thin, nervous, handsome young man with a head of hair so thick, it looked like a wig. Most of all, he had a mischievous sense of humor that inevitably lifted the spirits of his friends. He was never boring. He would go on to become a city councilman in Houston, undefeated in twelve elections. He was popular enough to have become mayor, but he never had the fire in his belly to take on a big political campaign. He would have been a first-class mayor simply because he cared so much about others, understood how to form a consensus, and most of all, had the instincts that are the hallmark of a great leader.

The only time Johnny Goyen angered me was when he allowed himself to die. We knew he had heart problems. His doctor, the fabled surgeon Dr. Denton Cooley, pressed him for checkups and a possible heart bypass. But Johnny loathed hospitals, so he kept putting it off. The delay did him in. I have never forgiven Johnny for leaving this earth. Never again could we laugh together as we recounted the crazy things we did as teenagers, the small victories and moments of despair, stories of our college night school, wartime experiences, and the building of our lives and careers after the war.

Most of all, I miss the absolute loyalty we shared, knowing that the whole world could collapse around us and still we'd be standing in the ruins, unhesitatingly supportive of each other. When Johnny died at age seventy-one, it was as if that secret place where I deposited all my memories had been burglarized, emptied by some stealthy thief in the night, gone forever. The sad fact is that unless you can share memories, they begin to fade away.

Johnny and I shared a consuming passion: politics. There was the presidency of the student body, but that office represented students from both day and night classes. It wasn't likely a night student would ever be elected to that august post. Immediately, Johnny and I began stumping for the job, giving speeches at political gatherings that began at 10:00 p.m.! In our first election, Johnny was voted president of the freshman class and I was elected vice president. The next year, I was elected president of the sophomore class and Johnny was picked for vice president. We were building a dynasty. I campaigned on the slogan "For service a-plenty, vote for Jack Valenti." Pretty awful, wasn't it? When did we sleep? The short answer is, not much. When did we do homework? At 1:00 and 2:00 in the morning. As a result, we lived a monk's life. I yearned for Lois from time to time, but my course was set. I was going to graduate from the University of Houston, and then I was going to Harvard Law School; if that meant having to practice celibacy for a while, then I would do it, but damn sure not forever!

At Humble Oil, I rejoiced in my job. One of its attractions was that I could study during the workday when the floor traffic was slight. One day when Mrs. Reinhardt had gone to lunch, I was deep in my physics book, trying to fathom the formulas. Suddenly a shadow loomed over me. I looked up. Oh my God, I thought, it's Robert L. Blaffer, the chairman of the board! The color drained from my face. I was about to be fired for goofing off.

Mr. Blaffer looked at me sternly. He said in a deep voice: "What are you doing, young man?"

I swallowed hard. "I'm reading a physics book, Mr. Blaffer."

"Why would you be reading a physics book?" he said gruffly.

"I go to the University of Houston at night." My voice was strained. God, I loved this job. I needed this job, and it was now all over.

He broke into a smile. "Well now, that is just wonderful. We love to have our employees get all the education they can. You keep reading, and be sure to do your homework." Then he strode off down the hall. Dear Lord, I thought, thank you for letting me work here.

Humble Oil in those days was everything a corporation ought to be—shamelessly loyal to its employees, honest with them, and interested in making their lives better. Humble Oil was one of the first companies to have a savings plan where they matched every dollar you put in. I watched pipe fitters and secretaries retire after long years of service with hundreds of thousands of dollars in their retirement accounts, and this in the 1930s and 1940s. The leaders of Humble Oil would be appalled by the sordid behavior of latter-day Wall

Street and corporate executives who lie, cheat, steal, and break every moral compact in existence, betraying their employees and stockholders. Whenever I thought about Humble Oil in the long years that followed, I always mused to myself, Jack, you were one lucky bastard to have had your first real job at Humble Oil.

Then chance entered my life once again. My department shared our floor with the Humble advertising and sales promotion department, headed by an amazing man named Garner Allen Mabry, called "Pop" despite being a young man of twenty, because his wife had already given birth to a son. One day, Chester Lee, the administrator of the department, sought me out. He was a kind, good man who was immensely loyal to Pop Mabry.

"Jack, I know you have been badgering us to join the department. Well, I have an offer for you. Do you know how to type and take shorthand?"

I replied without hesitation, "Oh yes, Mr. Lee, I learned that in high school." This was a blatant lie. I could not type, and I surely didn't know shorthand. But I do believe the Good Lord forgave me. What else could I have said?

"Fine," said Chester. "This is May, and the job will be opening up in September. One of our secretaries is leaving then to move to Dallas. Okay with you?"

Is winning the lottery okay with me? "Yessir, Mr. Lee, I will be ready."

As soon as the University of Houston had adjourned for the summer, I had enrolled in the Letha Rhodes School of Business. After work each day, I would appear at Miss Rhodes's school ready to learn. I jettisoned everything else in my life, devoting myself slavishly to the process of learning how to type and to decipher the hieroglyphics of Gregg shorthand. It was difficult at first, particularly the shorthand. But then it got easier, and then it got to be a bit of fun. When September came, I was typing eighty words a minute and managing almost one hundred words a minute in shorthand. I was ready to rock and roll.

I have to confess, I wasn't the best secretary in the advertising and sales promotion department, but I was surely the most active and the most restless. One of my tasks was to maintain the subscription list of employees who received the *Humble Bee*, a monthly magazine published by the department. I disliked the tedious chore of keeping subscription lists (Chester Lee hadn't told me about this aspect of my new work, which I found so damn boring that it still bothers me). I know I fouled up the list from time to time, and surely there were people who didn't get their *Humble Bee* that month.

But I did take note of something. The head of the sales department, a large man named Frank Watts, and sometimes the chairman, Mr. Blaffer, or Harry Weiss, the president, had a signed editorial in the magazine commenting on various aspects of the oil business and its retail sales force. The editorials were ghostwritten by Pop's department, mainly by Walter Beach, editor of the magazine; conveyed to Mr. Watts, Mr. Blaffer, and Mr. Weiss for their approval; and published. I overheard Walter Beach complaining about an editorial to be signed by Mr. Blaffer that he found to be inadequate. When he was out to lunch, I sauntered over to his desk, picked up the editorial, and rewrote it, not too shabbily if I do say so. When Walter Beach came back, I said to him, "I hope you don't mind, Walter, but I did a bit of rewriting on this editorial. Want to take a look at it?"

He looked at me soberly at first and then grinned. "You did what? You rewrote the editorial? You think you're a writer?"

"Well, I sure want to be."

Whereupon Walter read the editorial as I stood there. When he finished, he smiled. "Jack, this won't win the Nobel Prize, but it is pretty damn good. You are now a member of the editorial staff."

I soared out of that office. Sixteen years old and on the Humble Oil editorial staff! What a life I was living.

In those days, travel was not by air, but by car, and the absence of air-conditioning made driving through much of Texas, particularly in the summertime, the equivalent of a steam bath mixed with dust that flew incessantly through the open windows. Pop Mabry, the director of the advertising and sales promotion department, was no remote manager. He wanted to see for himself the state of the service stations to which we provided our product and the morale of their operators. As it happened, Pop fell into the habit of asking me to accompany him on his numerous trips, many of which lasted a week at a time. I was not chosen for my executive vision or natural instinct for leadership. Pop needed someone to handle chores. He needed a staffer, a factotum, and I was it. But for me it was an unforgettable learning experience.

I sat next to him as he drove through East Texas, stopping at service stations along the way, chatting with the manager of the station and his team. We'd stop at a roadside diner in towns with funny names, say "howdy" to folks sitting at the tables, shake hands with farmers, cowboys, small-town businessmen, and just plain Texas folks who frequented these places, then sit down to a table with paper napkins and dive into chicken-fried steak laden with tasty gravy or a plate loaded with hot grits and eggs if it was morning. To hell with cholesterol.

I can honestly report that on these trips I never met anyone I didn't like. These small-town Texas people were up front, warm, friendly, and full of common wisdom. And I can tell you that you learn a whole lot about the heart of Texas when you drive through every one of the 254 counties in this huge nation-state, through all the different Texas cultural enclaves. West Texas is different from East Texas, and the southern part of the state with its large Mexican American population is truly different from the Panhandle. I never got tired of seeing new little towns and meeting new people full of easy banter and hospitality. God, I loved it—and this wasn't even the best part.

The big reward for going on these trips was being with Pop. Though he'd never graduated from college, he was an authentic intellectual with bountiful wit. He was a Shakespeare scholar who could hold his own with any Ivy League professor. He could passionately recite lines for hours without missing a beat. Often he would ask me to join in with him, repeating after him as he spoke. On some trips, he brought plays for me to read aloud as we drove. We'd go through dozens of famous soliloquies together. It was grand fun for me. I was dazzled by the elegant music of the language, and Pop was delighted that I enjoyed what he found indispensable. I doubt if any college course in Shakespeare could match the excitement of being with Pop and the Bard, roaring down a Texas highway, ignoring the fierce heat and the fiercer wind that blasted us as we drove.

Time flew by. I ascended the ranks of the department, with

prospects of rising higher. I cared so much about what I was doing. Advertising and its creative process made demands on the imagination that kept it wondrously alive. It all kept pouring energy and delight through me. However, on the horizon a dark blight approached that not one of us could have imagined. It would take me from Humble. It would shape my life in dramatic ways. It would teach me fundamentals of courage, discipline, and loyalty to comrades and country that are still deeply embedded in my soul. The nation would be going to war.

In the summer of 1940, Europe was engaged in a terrible struggle as the military forces of Nazi Germany slashed through any army that opposed them. We listened to the radio, riveted by the thoughtful commentary of H. V. Kaltenborn, Edward R. Murrow, and the flat intonations of Elmer Davis. I followed closely the Battle of Britain, as young English pilots battled hordes of German bombers assaulting that island kingdom. Even though I had never flown airplanes, I was endlessly drawn to the brave young men who flew them. But all these events seemed so far away. Hitler's depravity, and his unrestrained grab at land and power were obvious at the time. But it was oddly impersonal, a remote evil for me and for my friends.

The strange times reminded me of my childhood when I became infatuated with the only book my father owned. It was a thick rectangular volume, crammed with black-and-white photos of World War I. As a boy, I was pleased that my father had volunteered for duty when war broke out in 1917. He was shipped overseas as a private in the Forty-second "Rainbow" Division, commanded by the youngest general in the American Expeditionary Forces: Douglas MacArthur. To say that my father revered the general is the equivalent of saying an earthquake registering 9.5 on the Richter scale is large. If my father had to choose whom to follow blindly, the good Lord or General MacArthur, he would reenact Jack Benny's most famous skit: A mugger puts a gun to Benny's head and says, "Your money or your life." Benny stares at him, mute, not moving. The mugger snarls and waves the gun menacingly: "You hear me? Your money or your life." To which Benny replies, "I'm thinking, I'm thinking." That, dear friends, is my father.

I would pore over those World War I photographs hour after hour. I was struck by the obvious courage of the young men in their uniforms, some grinning wildly. The pictures, as I recall, did offer more than a modest glimpse of the inhumanity I was to experience firsthand. The photos were graphic and fascinating. I was drawn to them, and I wasn't sure why, except that I had never seen war before.

My dad would sit with me and we would talk about what I was seeing. He told me of the time General MacArthur's Rainbow Division was in combat in September 1918, in the last great battle of World War I—the Argonne Forest in France, where American losses were heavy. It was the first time in the war that a totally American fighting force was on its own, under the command of General John J. ("Black Jack") Pershing. It was not the kind of legendary battle where Americans were easily triumphant. Quite the contrary. My father recalled how the Germans, well dug in, fought with tenacity and effectiveness. He remembered the carnage, the stench of death, and the way his hero, General MacArthur, never stayed back of the combat lines. With great zest, my dad would describe how the general would lead his men in headlong attack on the enemy. The general, enthused my father, would lead the charge armed only with a riding crop, unfazed by enemy fire and disdainful of death, which inspired his men to great deeds on the battlefield. He never tired of telling me that MacArthur had received the Congressional Medal of Honor, the nation's highest tribute for valor in the field. I was transfixed. But the fact is that my father never personally witnessed the general on one of those death-defying charges. He just wanted to believe his hero did indeed challenge the enemy with that riding crop.

I was proud of my father and of what he had done when duty demanded it. I gloried in his service, feeling what a young boy feels when he realizes his father was a hero. I never forgot those moments with him and that book of war photographs.

Now, at age twenty, I had the first inklings that I was going to have to test my own courage to see if I would respond as my father had, to serve my country honorably and bravely. We were headed for war—a real one, when all I had known before were photographs.

In January 1942, a month after Pearl Harbor, when I was twenty years old, some two hundred of us at the University of Houston volunteered. We were told to stand by to be called up, which finally happened in 1943. We were now ready to be dispatched to various training camps to prepare us for combat. Pop Mabry summoned all my colleagues and friends at Humble Oil, and they gathered 'round me on my last day at work. Pop hugged me. "Jack, we will be looking forward to welcoming you home after you have served your country. This job will be waiting for you. May God bless you and bring you home safely. We know you'll do your duty bravely and your country will be proud of you."

It was an emotional moment. I felt loved by Pop and all the others. They were family, friends, loyal and trusting. The next day when I boarded a train for Sheppard Air Force Base in Wichita Falls, Texas, having said good-bye to my tearful mother and father and sister, I had an odd sense of anticipation. I was ready to be trained, ready to fight for my country. I think my old grandfather Bernardo De George would have been proud of his newly minted warrior grandson.

Chapter 4

WAR

At our squadron base in Solenzara, Corsica, in 1944, just before an early morning low-level bombing mission in Italy's Brenner Pass: bombardier/navigator Vic Rutz; pilot Hal Akers; me with my holstered .45 slung low like a western gunfighter; and "Hap" Arnold, a bombardier.

The University of Houston did not have fraternities, so my night-school friends and I formed our own, Tau Kappa Sigma, TKS. It didn't mean anything; we just liked the sound and rhythm of the three Greek letters. We were an unlikely fraternity anyway. We were all working-class guys, all of us at the same economic level, all of us bound together by circumstance and a hunger to learn, to succeed, to climb higher than where we were. Why else would anyone work eight hours a day and then spend three more hours going to college at night, every bloody night of the bloody week?

One day we were playing poker at the house of one of my friends. It was early in the afternoon on a Sunday. I had gone to early mass, and now I was relaxing with my buddies, kidding them, telling girl stories, and generally having a rousing good time. Furthest from our minds was any thought that our lives would be put in harm's way, our plans reshaped, and our dreams of a bountiful future after graduating from the university put on hold for a long time. A few in that room on that terrible Sunday would not come home again to any kind of a future.

We heard the news on the radio. The announcer's voice was slightly distorted by tension as he said, "Honolulu and Pearl Harbor have been bombed by Japanese warplanes." The card game was over, forgotten, as we gathered around the radio, looking at one another uncomprehendingly. We were not sure what all this meant. Bombed? Warplanes?

"Where the hell is Pearl Harbor?" someone asked. We soon found out. But we still had no idea where we would fit in.

Within two months, I had enlisted along with some one hundred

UH students, including Johnny Goyen and every single one of my friends around that poker table on Sunday. Johnny and I determined early on that we wanted to be aviators, though neither of us had ever even ridden in an airplane. Johnny chose the U.S. Army Air Corps. I chose the U.S. Naval Air Corps.

I presented myself at the naval recruiting office and signed all the papers necessary for induction into the V-7 navy program to be trained as a carrier-based combat pilot. A week later, I was taking my physical. The doctor poked around, thumped me, and listened. He seemed to find nothing that would bar me from being accepted. Except. Except my EKG and his stethoscope revealed I had a heart murmur, whatever the hell that was. The doctor shook his head. "I'm afraid you can't qualify, son. This washes you out."

I could scarcely believe what I heard. "Heart murmur? For God's sake, I am in great health." He responded with an understanding smile and turned to the next applicant. I was done. My naval flying career ended before it began.

Twenty-four hours later, I applied for the aviation cadet program of the U.S. Army Air Corps. Evidently the army's doctors regarded such things as heart murmurs more casually than the stiff-necked navy. I sailed through my physical—fit, fine, and formidable. Up yours, Navy.

Under the army air corps program, Johnny and I and the other UH enlistees were told to report back to the University of Houston and wait to be called up. Johnny and I were pissed. We wanted to go now, to get to the airfield and learn how to fly the damn plane. We needed to get into the war. Hell, our country was being attacked.

In January 1943, with the war a year old, we finally got the call. Our papers told us to report to Sheppard Field in Wichita Falls, Texas. We were ostensibly heading there for "basic training," but the real purpose was to humble and humiliate dumb-ass civilians who thought they were fit but weren't. Johnny and I and our contingent of UH buddies boarded a train stripped of every convenience and headed to Wichita Falls and our new assignment.

Johnny and I never slept on the overnight journey. We organized a crap game in the aisle of the train. By the time we arrived in

Wichita Falls, we had extracted a little more than $1,000 from our sullen comrades, which convinced us that our youth had not been completely misspent.

Sheppard Field was a collection of primitive wooden barracks, where for the first time I lived with a total lack of privacy of any kind. Our field instructors could not have been born of loving mothers; they must have emerged fishlike from some prehistoric swamp, equipped with bullhorns that resembled voices and a fanatical zeal to cripple every recruit within earshot. They also, I am convinced, manufactured the combat boots we were issued and in which we ran countless miles. This ostensible footwear must have had thorns in the soles and seemed designed to leave the hardiest of feet blistered and bloody.

Johnny and I groused about the mind-boggling stupidity of a program that forced aviators to drill and march anyway. We weren't going to walk anywhere. We were going to fly. If we had wanted to run around on concrete soil under a sun that could have fried alloyed steel, we would have joined the frigging infantry.

One thing I did learn was how to handle firearms, particularly the Colt .45-caliber automatic handgun. We learned how to disassemble the Colt and put it back together. The final test was doing this *blindfolded*! After a while, I could do it with ease. And after a time, I became a fairly good shot with that Colt. I carried my trusty weapon on every combat mission I flew. I never had to use it.

On page 107 you can see a photo of my good buddies Vic Rutz, Hal Akers, "Hap" Arnold, and me standing before our B-25 at Solenzara Air Base in Corsica minutes before we were ready to hit the skies for a morning mission. There I am, pulling on a glove, with my Colt .45 holstered on my right side, slung low like western gunfighters. Now what would I have done with that weapon? So I'm shot down in enemy territory. In a movie, I have my Colt in my right hand when a lone Nazi soldier emerges from the tree line. He is so frightened by my steadily aimed .45 that he surrenders immediately. Or perhaps a squad of heavily armed Germans appears, and I calmly take them all down with withering fire from my powerful Colt. Hello? Actually, I would no doubt fling my Colt to the ground, put my hands in the air, and noisily invoke the Geneva Convention. I know this much: It gives my image in photos visible panache and a nice touch of machismo.

Finally, with thanks to a humane God, we departed Sheppard Field for the next level of training on our way to becoming combat pilots. In West Texas State College in Amarillo, we would begin classes in navigation, meteorology, Morse code, aircraft identification, and all the other layers of learning that precede actual flying. I really enjoyed this schooling. Airplane identification was especially fascinating. After weeks of intensive study, a photograph of an airplane could flash on the screen for a bare half second and I would be able to identify it: Nazi ME109s, Jap Zeros, and our own Corsairs, P-51s, Thunderbolts, Lightnings, four-engine B-24s, B-17s, and twin-engine B-26s and B-25s (later to be my plane). I found I was pretty good at this war gaming. I grew to enjoy navigation and working with maps, something that had never been on my curriculum before. Morse code was another matter. It took me the entire term at West Texas State to translate the click-clicks into language I could understand, but I finally got the feel of wireless prose.

West Texas State was an oasis compared with Sheppard Field. It had one asset so remarkable that at first I could not believe my good luck. West Texas State's men had all gone off to war, so the college was now inhabited totally by young Texas coeds. They patriotically offered their considerable hospitality to make sure that men who were about to die would in their last moments on earth expire with nothing but congenial thoughts. During our three-month stay at West Texas State, we learned that war need not be hell! I did hate to leave, but it was finally time for primary flight training.

Johnny Goyen stayed in Texas for his flight training, while I was billeted to Ryan Field in Tucson, Arizona. At Ryan Field, I would sit in an airplane for the first time *ever* and learn to fly. Our craft was a Ryan PT-22, a small single-engine aircraft with tandem seating. The front cockpit was for the student, while in the cockpit just behind it sat the instructor. My instructor was a young fellow, a civilian type mixed in with the army air corps officers.

He grinned and said, "First time in a plane for you?"

I replied nervously, with a tinge of embarrassment, "Yeah."

"Well, don't worry, you're going to love it, and when we're

through, you will be one damn good pilot." I nodded and thought, Omigod.

I put on my goggles, adjusted my parachute, and climbed aboard. He clambered in after me, started the engine, and began to taxi, stopping at the edge of the runway. He ran up the engine, checked its vitals, and then pushed the throttle forward. We roared down the runway, and then, miracle of miracles, we were in the air! I had never told anyone in the Army Air Corps that I had a fear of heights, and not having ever flown, I didn't realize there is a difference between looking down from the top floor of a tall building and being in a plane and looking down.

I leaned over the side of the cockpit, gazing down on the landscape below as we wheeled and turned and gained altitude; to my astonishment, I felt nothing but exhilaration, growing by the minute. Sure enough, my fear of heights was nowhere to be found. The radio crackled in my ears. "Valenti, I'm going to do a stall and spin, do a few acrobatics, and then we'll fly straight and level, so you can take over."

Suddenly the nose of the plane rose, the engine sputtered, and we plummeted toward the ground, turning and whirling as if the plane were out of control. I damn near fainted! It was a disciplined stall, I later learned. As the plane spun downward, it stopped revolving and gradually leveled out. Then, unexpectedly, my instructor took the plane into a barrel roll, meaning that you're flying upside down for a few long, perilous seconds, and then you're upright again. Oh Lord.

"All right, Valenti, take the stick. Adjust the throttle on your left as you see fit. Maintain current altitude. Make some slow turns, nothing radical, then get back on level flight."

For the next half hour, I got to know the movement of the joystick. With my left foot, I pressed down on the rudder and slowly began to turn to the left. To my horror, the plane started losing altitude in the turn. "Valenti, give it a touch of the throttle, and pull up on the stick. You're letting the aircraft drift."

After an hour, I began to feel a little more comfortable, learning more about the aircraft and the movement of rudder and aileron. The instructor took over, and we landed in a sweet swish of wheels on concrete. Later that day, my instructor and several other instructors took a group of us in a briefing room to give us an education on how to fly this little Ryan aircraft. For the next several days, I went aloft, gaining more confidence in throttle and stick procedures as well as in getting the plane to do what I wanted.

One day, my instructor said to me, "Today, we're going to do some more acrobatics, and then I'll let you try a disciplined stall."

Sure enough, after a barrel roll or two, the headset crackled: "Valenti, put it into a stall. Go."

I pulled back on the stick and eased up on the throttle. The plane raised its nose, then began to shudder as the stall began. Abruptly, the nose dropped and we began to spiral downward from an altitude of about five thousand feet. The spiral grew tighter and faster. Then the radio: "All right, Valenti, get her out of this."

We were spiraling clockwise. I pushed down the left rudder, counterclockwise, and began gradually to push the stick forward, holding the throttle firm. To my utter delight (and probably to the surprise of my instructor), the little Ryan began to stop whirling. Now, I pulled back on the stick slowly, pushing the throttle forward. I was delighted when the aircraft began to level out and then climb. I had actually retrieved the plane from a deliberate stall! Awesome.

The tricky part was landing. My instructor was firm. "Valenti, any idiot can fly a plane in clear weather. But it takes a pretty good pilot to fly in bad weather and also to land. If you can't land, you're in trouble. So follow me closely. Concentrate on what I'm doing."

He flew over the airfield with his eyes fixed on the flapping flag in the middle of the field, indicating wind direction. He wheeled the little aircraft on its side as he did a 180 to guide the plane downwind from the runway. I heard his voice over the intercom: "Now, I'm going to slowly do a one-eighty again, lining up the runway." The Ryan performed a half circle until the craft focused on the runway.

"I am gradually losing altitude. I'm decreasing the speed. This little baby will land at about fifty. Now feel this with me as I very gently ease up on the throttle. . . . Now, get those twenty-twenty eyeballs on the runway. Turn on your depth perception. Watch this, I'm going to get close to the runway, then I will let her float a bit just a couple of feet above the runway, and then I will ease her down."

Sure enough, the plane began to float just as he'd said it would. I kept my eyes glued to the runway. Just when I thought we ought to be on the ground, we were; the tires told me we had made a gentle landing. Great, I loved it. Looked easy.

Two days later, after accumulating a grand total of nine hours of flying time, I met my instructor at the airfield at our designated time. As I began to climb aboard, my instructor clapped me on the shoulder. "Today's the day, Valenti. You are on your own."

I stood there in disbelief. I felt my heart pound heavily. I hadn't counted on this. My instructor saw my hesitation. "Look, you're doing just fine. Act as if I'm in the rear seat, but you'll be in command. You can do it, I promise." I thought, Well, that's easy for you to say.

I climbed in. I started the engine, breathed deeply, and then began taxiing to the runway. At its perimeter, I checked the engine. My heart was thudding against my ribs. It's hard to explain to those who have not gone through this rite of passage the flood of emotions that invades the nervous system. I pushed the throttle forward, and the Ryan leaped ahead, gathering speed as we moved down the runway. Finally, I eased back on the stick, and I was in the air.

I flew aimlessly for a bit, taking stock of my excitement. I breathed deeply, again, and again, thinking, Come on, Jack, settle down. You have to land this plane sooner or later. I tried a little barrel roll and to my astonishment pulled it off. I felt a little confidence pouring back into me. I put the plane into a stall and came out of it just as I had been taught. Another barrel roll. My confidence rising, I had a fleeting moment of calm. But soon enough, the time came. I headed back to the airfield, preparing to negotiate my first solo landing.

I rode the downwind leg, banked smoothly (so I thought), and lined up with the runway, decreasing my speed slightly, descending on what seemed to me to be a sensible course. I leaned back on the throttle just a tad and began to settle over the runway when to my dismay, I felt the plane dropping while I was still much too high off the concrete. When I realized I was going to crash my plane, I instinctively hit the throttle to the limit and the plane jumped forward, gained altitude. Sweat streaming down my forehead, I circled the field, fighting my anxiety. What a damn fool I was. My depth perception had wandered.

I circled the field, and as I flew downwind I could see a group assembled to bear witness to this nutcake who had come so close to totaling a fine little aircraft. I approached the runway, and this time I kept the throttle just right, descending at the proper speed. I flew over the edge of the runway, and easing the plane downward, I brought back the throttle, nuzzling the craft down until I could see the markings on the runway. I throttled back, held the stick firmly, and let the Ryan settle in, tires whistling, in what I judged to be a fairly good landing.

My instructor and my fellow cadets, about a dozen of whom had gathered to watch the first crash of their class at Ryan Field, all applauded. My instructor was grinning from ear to ear. "Okay, Valenti, you made it. The fact that you acted wisely and swiftly on that disaster of a first approach makes me certain you're going to be okay. You'll get your wings, my young friend."

It was a festive evening for me and my fellow fliers. That night as I tried to sleep, I replayed that near catastrophe over and over again. I learned that day that things will go wrong when you least expect it. That's when all your training, the discipline seared indelibly into your brain, will save your ass. You must act quickly, instinctively, and without hesitation. That's the essence of becoming an expert pilot.

I recall the sense of triumph when I graduated from Ryan Field, with my primary flight training at an end. I had survived. I had accumulated confidence in my ability to fly a plane. I knew I had a lot more to learn, but now I was eager to challenge the next station on the path to getting my wings. It would be Lancaster, in California's Antelope Valley. Basic flight training. Our aircraft, the BT-13, was twice as fast and a good deal larger than the Ryan PT-22. It was powered by a 450-horsepower, nine-cylinder Pratt & Whitney engine—powerful, sturdy, and noisy. It had a cruising speed of 170 mph at five thousand feet, but it could be pushed to 182 mph, and it had a maximum range of 725 miles.

At Lancaster we learned more about the art of flying, as well as navigation, flying by map, and compass course headings. We also learned, for the first time, the delicate dance of formation flying.

I got to know the dizzying excitement of low-level flying. I must confess, I was thrilled to the core when I put the BT-13 down on the deck fifty feet above the earth, throttle pushed forward, sailing along at speeds I had never felt before. It was exhilarating.

When we were finished with basic training, we were assigned to final flight training. I put in for fighter planes, with dreams of flying the Lockheed twin-engine P-38 Lightning. I was also fascinated with America's newest fighter, the P-51 Mustang, which was sleek, fast, and maneuverable. To my dismay, the orders came down that Europe needed B-25 pilots. The B-25, made by North American Aviation, was a storied two-engine aircraft, the valiant veteran (B-25H) of General Jimmy Doolittle's takeoff from an American carrier in the Pacific on his way to "twenty seconds over Tokyo."

I would not be flying fighter planes. I was greatly disappointed. But it was much better than flying the heavies, B-17s and B-24s. God, I hated those monsters, flying somewhere higher than Mars, burdened down with thick clothing and oxygen masks. Hell, the B-25, I had heard, didn't even carry oxygen. This turned out to be true. Fine with me.

My last flight training stop was Douglas, Arizona, where the craft of choice was a Cessna twin-engine plane, a flyable machine and great fun to drive, the prelude to actually piloting a B-25. The twin-engine Cessna had room for a student pilot and an instructor. We learned the intricacies of flying multiengine craft, so that we would be more companionable with the B-25. We flew across country, flying by map and compass headings. For the first time, I was introduced to the demanding discipline of instrument flying. The instructor would cover the windshield and the cockpit upper window with a green mat that he could see through with his glasses but was opaque to the student. This meant head-down concentration on the instrument panel, particularly the artificial horizon, as well as altimeter, airspeed, and needle and ball.

I'll never forget the first time I was cruising along on instruments when suddenly the instructor hit the feathering button to kill the left engine. The plane yawed violently, pitching like a horse gone wild. Immediately my training sessions kicked in. Swiftly I had to adjust flaps and keep a strong foot on the right rudder, or the plane would veer dangerously to port. I applied throttle to keep from losing too much altitude too fast and calmed down the yawing as best I could, guiding the Cessna to level flight, though we were losing altitude bit by bit. Once I got the plane under control, the instructor wanted me to get acquainted with how long the craft could stay airworthy as we slowly lost height in the air. We then got the port engine going again. I retrieved our lost altitude, and I got a rich lesson in one-engine flying.

The B-25 was a fearless, competent craft, but I always missed the glories of flying P-38s or P-51s. Later, when I was in flight combat, there was a four-squadron fighter group based just north of my base in Ancona, Italy, populated entirely by black pilots. These black fliers, later to be famed as the Tuskegee Airmen, now the 332nd Fighter Group, flew P-51 Mustangs. These pilots were the best of the best. They escorted the heavies, the B-24s flying out of Foggia and Bari in the south of Italy, protecting them from the malevolence of Nazi ME109s. In all the sorties they flew as protective cover, they never lost a single bomber to Nazi aircraft. I remember once jeeping up to their field to chat with them and inspect their planes. They were a warm-hearted bunch of combat professionals. They knew I was envious of them and how hotly I wanted to climb aboard that P-51 and sail away.

The day I got my wings at Douglas Field, pinning on my gold second lieutenant's rank and adjusting my creaseless officer's cap, I realized that I had come a long way from that callow young student at the University of Houston. I was beginning to learn how to be a combat pilot, although combat was still a couple of months away.

Next stop was Mather Field in Sacramento and then on to Greenville, South Carolina, for real combat training. My most notable memory of Mather Field, where we actually got into the cockpit of a B-25 and began learning to trust it, was a cross-country nonstop flight to Minneapolis, returning after an overnight. My co-pilot had a sister enrolled at the University of Minnesota. He had called her in advance, and she invited us to join her and some friends at their sorority party. She was thrilled that young pilots would be available, as most of the young men at her school had gone to war.

We were greeted most hospitably. There were about a dozen other guys there, also in uniform, all having a jubilant time. My friend's sister had me meet one of her best friends, a golden-haired beauty with the bluest eyes I ever saw. It so happened that she had broken up with her boyfriend before he enlisted, which was just fine with me. All of us had a famously fun time. My buddy and I got to bed around 3:00 a.m. It was one helluva party for all of us, dancing, singing, doing a little drinking, and engaging in long conversations. I spent what few hours I had left trying to figure out how to spend another night in Minnesota. I chatted with my co-pilot, who agreed with my idea.

I put in a phone call to Mather Field. "We have a bit of engine trouble, nothing serious, but we will have to overnight again. We'll be in the air at first light tomorrow." I was worried about how the duty officer would take that blather, for which I would be surely convicted of perjury. But he never really protested, except to say, "Funny thing, your aircraft had been checked thoroughly before you took off."

"Really?" I said. "Well, we will be back at the base when we arrive tomorrow."

The training continued at Greenville Air Force Base in Greenville, South Carolina. Here our rugged training was simulated war in the air. We used Myrtle Beach as our firing platform for on-the-deck strafing and for checking out bomb runs and emergency procedures. Our endless training, day after day, began to take full effect. By the time we were summoned overseas, we were, in truth, almost professionals. The operative word is "almost." The only way to become a professional pilot in wartime is to be in actual combat.

We boarded a troop ship for Naples, Italy, and after a five-day voyage we were finally in the real war. It was September 1944, two months after the D-Day landings, when we landed in Naples and were assigned to squadrons in the 57th Bomb Wing of the 12th Air Force. My group was the 321st and my squadron the 448th. Along with my fellow pilots and a group of bombardiers, we were transported to our base in Solenzara, Corsica.

A bleaker, more forbidding place I had never seen. It was a barren slice of land cheek by jowl with the Tyrrhenian Sea, an unruly body of water separating Corsica from mainland Italy. No wonder Napoleon got the hell out of there as soon as he could, although he came from a much better neighborhood—the northern part of the island. I remember how cold it was—penetrating cold that was to get worse as winter began.

We clambered out of our transport planes in the late morning and were greeted by a captain, a surly fellow whose name I do not recall. We got aboard jeeps, and the captain directed us to our new "home." He pointed to an empty space with seven or eight tents nearby.

"Here's where you live," he said.

"Excuse me, Captain, but just where is 'where we live'? There's nothing here," I said, though why I decided to be the spokesman for my comrades, I cannot fathom. They were smart enough to stay silent.

Captain What's-his-frigging-name glared at me. Then he smiled a crooked grin, the kind Al Capone must have displayed before he whacked the dumb-ass who triggered his temper.

"Well now, Lieutenant, by 'home' I mean you'll build it right here. You'll be issued sleeping bags and cots, but if you want a roof over your heads tonight, you had best get off your lazy asses and start building. I know what you're thinking—where are the enlisted men who ought to be doing the building. You're in the best goddamn group in the whole Twelfth Air Force. And those enlisted men have more important chores to do than put up your tent while you sit back on your fat butts. Those enlisted men will save your stupid lives by keeping your planes ready and willing to do what they have to do. So, you build. Now."

Okay, nobody ever explained it that way to me before.

To my surprise and delight, several officers who weren't flying that day came out of their tents to lend a hand. Within seven hours, we had put down makeshift planking for a floor and raised a tent to give some relief from the winds that came up. Four cots were delivered to us, plus four bulky but life-warming sleeping bags. "Hap" Arnold, bombardier; Hal Akers, pilot; Vic Rutz, bombardier/ navigator; and I, the four musketeers of the 448th Squadron, assembled our sleeping arrangements as best we could. Our first priority, according to our fellow fliers, was to make a stove out of aircraft fuel containers and use high-octane petrol for heating. As I look back on this, I cannot imagine how, in all our time in Corsica, that tent never blew up.

I got to know and love the B-25, first the H-model and then the more powerful J-model, with boosters on the wheel (the pilot's steering mechanism). It was powered by two Wright Cyclone engines, air-cooled, fourteen-cylinder engines with Holley carburetors that could each deliver 1,850 horsepower. All engine controls were mounted on a control pedestal between the pilot and co-pilot. Its fast cruise speed at 2,000 rpm was 210 mph, though we went over our targets at 200 mph. We carried no oxygen equipment, so we never flew higher than fifteen or sixteen thousand feet. The only reason to go that high or higher would be terrible weather conditions at lower levels. We were trained at those altitudes to keep looking at our thumbnails. If they started to turn blue, we were suffering oxygen deprivation and had best get lower, and fast. Our takeoff speed was 120–130 mph, drawing forty-four inches of mercury. On the approach, the landing speed was 125–135 mph.

The key instrument gauges I had before me on the instrument panel became my constant companions on whom I depended for my very life (without them I would have been one dead pilot): airspeed indicator, artificial horizon, pilot's directional gyro, glide path indicator, gun sight rheostat, nosewheel position indicator lights, fuel gauges, needle and ball, altimeter, bomb bay doors, and flap position indicators. The prize of them all was the radio compass—without this baby, there'd be no crossing the Atlantic (which later I was required to do). The base instrument panel was crowded with all sorts of other gauges, but these were the ones we flew by. Today, this equipment would look primitive. Modern military aircraft today can pinpoint their position within a few meters. We were lucky to pinpoint the right zip code.

The stated combat range of the B-25 was 1,350 miles, but I never bought that. The only way to push the B-25 to that range required perfect weather, no headwinds, no heavy cargo, and an altitude where leaning the fuel was feasible.

When I flew as flight leader my crew numbered five, for then my plane carried a bombardier/navigator. Otherwise we had four in our crew and toggled our bombs off the lead plane. It worked this way: We flew steady over the target, with the pilot of each plane in the nine-craft flight watching the flight leader. When the flight leader opened the bomb bay doors, the rest of the flight opened the bomb bay doors. The second I saw bombs exiting the lead plane, I hit the bomb toggle and dropped my bombs, although on some missions we carried a bombardier and his Norden bombsight on board at least two of the wing planes, especially if we were going into heavily defended areas where the possibility of losing the lead plane made it necessary to have backup bombardier support.

We flew low, sometimes on the deck delivering fragmentation bombs supporting the Fifth Army's advance, but more often we flew at seven–eight thousand feet or more for better precision in placing our bombs on the target.

The B-25 was a brute for punishment. It possessed two rudders, starboard and port. If one engine was shot up and lost—and that happened frequently—and if the remaining working engine retained its in-line rudder, the B-25 would fly on one engine better than any craft I know. It wasn't invincible, however, and on one engine it continued to lose altitude, but at a slower rate than other planes.

We were armed with a flexible turning turret that fired two .50-caliber machine guns just aft of the pilot on the J-model—farther back on the H-model—as well as a tail turret and waist gunner. Two blister .50-caliber guns on each side of the fuselage firing forward gave us vital firepower for strafing.

The B-25s flew a cocoonlike formation, tightly woven together in nine-plane flights with wingmen putting their outer wing edges a bare few feet behind and under the wings of the flight leader. In this seamless webbing, the firepower we could bring to bear on ME109s was awesomely concentrated. The Nazi fighter planes were wary of our .50-caliber defenses in our tight, well-nigh impenetrable formation. They relished hitting the heavies, the B-17s and the B-24s, which flew a looser formation. So they pretty much left us alone.

Though well armed and defensible, the B-25 was still vulnerable to German 88 mm antiaircraft guns. Pilots of bombers in the European theater will tell you, almost to a man, that the .88s were one of the fiercest weapons of the war. The Germans who handled them were craftsmen who knew their weapon and handled it with deadly skill.

Since we were based in Corsica, we had to navigate over the Tyrrhenian Sea to get to our targets on the mainland. Later on we were billeted in Ancona, Italy, on the Adriatic Sea, across from Yugoslavia. The Nazis had deployed several crack divisions in Yugoslavia, but they never conquered the insurgents in a land festooned with surly mountains and thick forests, all of which made for a most inhospitable terrain. Though I admired the bravery of the Yugoslav partisans in refusing to cave in to the Nazis, I never wanted to crashland in those forbidden forests. If you did, you wouldn't get found until the next century.

One of the 321st Group's prime objectives was the interdiction of Nazi troop movement in a narrow gash cut in the Italian Alps, a channel way called the Brenner Pass, dividing the Rhaetian and Nordic Alps. Since the time of imperial Rome, the Brenner Pass has been a 275-mile crucial passageway from Innsbruck, Austria, to Verona, Italy. We got to know it quite well indeed. On our maps were names of small towns and a few not so small, none of which I had ever heard of before and every one of which I wished I had never visited from the air. Verona, so sweetly catalogued by Shakespeare, sits in the south of the pass, which wiggles north to and through San Margherita, Rovereto (a bitch of a place with unsavory antiaircraft guns everywhere), Trento, Lavis, San Michele (I damn near got killed at this place named for a saint), Ora, Balzano, Brennero, and finally Innsbruck, the farthest point the B-25 could fly from its Corsican base and get home before fuel was exhausted.

The landscape of the Brenner Pass was surrounded by some of nature's loveliest mountains to be found anywhere. As we flew up the pass, the glistening spires of these immense piles of earth, stone, and snow caught the sun, flashing across our pathway, shining, glowing, and offering their beauty freely to all who came close, as we most surely did. But we didn't spend too much time basking in the handsome beguiling landscape. Our prime mission was to rip apart that indispensable Nazi logistical lifeline into Italy. Our objective was to blow up bridges, ferries, railroads, trestles, roads, and any and all wheeled transport in and about the pass so that the Nazis, if they moved at all, moved slowly, fretfully, and with painful relentless costs in casualties.

Even today the name Brenner Pass ignites a constriction in my throat. Once when my children were in college and high school, one of them suggested that we take a family vacation at Lake Como. It is arguably one of the most enchanting places on earth, but it never happened. But the fact is I have never been there. Well, not exactly. It is an odd twist of fate that I know it best from an airman's map. It was inscribed in my mind with the permanence of brain matter.

Sometimes with one engine shot away, it was not possible to get back to base and you had to find somewhere to put down, unless you had a peculiar desire to be captured in enemy territory. The 321st Group brass instructed us on alternatives to returning to base if we were hit, particularly coming out of the Brenner Pass, a truly scary adventure in the sense that it was like flying in a tunnel with only one way out. If we got hit badly, with a fatal blow to an engine, and the pilot-commander determined he couldn't make it back to the base, one alternative was somehow to get clear of those shimmering, jagged spires rising higher than our altitude and head for Lake Como. But getting to Lake Como wasn't enough. You had to find and land (or crash-land) on the Swiss side of the lake. No prisoner of war camps in Switzerland.

I spent hours poring over maps of Lake Como. I began to know that terrain better than its inhabitants. I honestly believed I could guide my plane blindfolded, if it still had flying strength, to the Swiss side. I knew exactly what I had to do. The tricky part was doing it. Thank the Lord, I never had to try.

One emergency procedure we learned—over and again—was ditching in the sea. Because we had to get back to our base overflying the Tyrrhenian Sea, understanding how to ditch was serious business. If the sea was rough, it was best to try to approach parallel to any uniform swell pattern and touch down along the crest of a swell or just after the crest passed. If the sea was irregular and the wind strong, it would be necessary to try to set down into the wind and on the falling side of a wave. On two separate occasions, I really thought I was going to have to follow those instructions. Somehow, I coaxed my plane home, and just in time. I must confess that the prospect of ditching filled me with nightmares. There was something about settling down in a sullen sea, knowing the plane was going to stay afloat for a few minutes at best, that gave me hives. Still does.

Our squadron commander, Major Gus Farwell, much respected and admired by his pilots, bombardier-navigators, airmen, and ground crew, was a tough guy who was proud of the 448th Squadron's record of never turning back on a mission and having one of the highest accuracy bombing records in the European theater. He used to admonish the pilots, "Remember, on the bomb run get your ass glued to your seat, keep the formation tight, don't even think about aborting, don't think about anything except what you were ordered to do. You toggle on the leader and get your ass the hell out of there. Keep cool, and let your co-pilot watch the flak and throw up." Nice turn of phrase our squadron commander had.

He also had a point. On each and every one of the fifty-one combat missions I flew, the progression of emotions never varied. First, excitement filled our veins as we were briefed by group intelligence in the early morning before the mission; then anticipation mounted as we taxied toward the runway. We took off, seconds apart, to reach altitude with our load of four one-thousand-pound bombs (and sometimes six). With a load of six one-thousand-pound bombs, getting into the air got dicey. The drill was to stomp the brakes, then push the throttle to the firewall. A few seconds later, release the brakes. The B-25 would leap forward like a scalded tiger. Then you had to keep the nosewheel down as long as you could to gain the airspeed you needed to get this bulky animal in the air. I always muttered a silent prayer of gratitude when we left the metal runway a few feet before it ended, heading toward our in-air formation assembly, flying in our cuddly protective pattern to our target.

We moved evasively when we neared antiaircraft fire, so that it would be more difficult for the German .88s to mark us. But on the bomb run, it was all head-down concentration, because the plane had to be flown steady, steady, steady, so the lead planes could sight on the target. Then came the fear, sweaty, throat-grabbing, belly-twisting fear. It never varied.

We knew that when the flak was puffy and black, it was not supposed to be lethal, but it damn sure could be. Your plane rocked and pitched from the rolling sound waves of exploding shrapnel from the .88s. That shrapnel, too, often found our plane. When your plane was hit by shrapnel, you could feel the crunch and crack, and you could only pray it hadn't hit anything vital. On a number of missions my plane got hit, leaving gaping holes in the wings and fuselage. But when the puffs of flak turned orange, you knew the gunners had your altitude. They had you bracketed, and you were turning your craft on its side, hearing your engines scream as you pushed the throttles to the wall and got off the premises fast before that next barrage blew you out of the skies.

As a pilot, you never forget your first mission—at least I never did. I was flying as co-pilot, with Lieutenant Swanson, a veteran, in the left seat. We rocked in at eight thousand feet, heading toward the target, Ora, Italy, in the Brenner Pass. We were not quite there when the flak began. Big black puff balls filled the sky. Then I felt the thump and the tearing sound as shrapnel found our plane. I thought, Those bastards are trying to kill me. It was not a good moment. It was the first time in my life that anyone deliberately shot at me—wanted me dead. Jesus.

Lieutenant Swanson seemed oblivious to the chaos in the sky. He was doing what he was trained to do, flying his plane with no regard for anything else, even killer .88s. For those first few minutes I was, as we say in Texas, as useless as tits on a boar. Then Swanson's voice on the intercom broke into my frozen thoughts. "We're on the bomb run. Straight and level."

No matter what was thrown at us now, we had to maintain a steady course to give the bombardier in the lead plane time to focus his Norden bombsight. On a run, ten seconds is a damn eternity. All you can do is hunker down and hope the .88 gunners were all drunk the night before. Then comes the most delicious moment of all, the upward jerk of the plane as the bombs are loosed. In that instant, Swanson turned the craft into a ninety-degree tilt, and the airspeed indicator went crazy. We got out of there as swiftly as the B-25 could slide and run, which was not fast enough for me. In the coming weeks, when I was in the left seat as command pilot, I would be the one who kicked the B-25 on its side to end a run over the target.

As we streaked home toward our base in Solenzara, I began to understand with a clarity I had not known before that there was a distinct possibility I could be killed. This was a disquieting thought, to say the least. I also fully appreciated, for the first time, that I would be staking my life on the reflexes I had developed through endless repetitions in training. I knew I would do whatever I had to do because I was prepared for whatever came my way. I had a crew to think about, and it was my job to get them and me home unharmed. I do believe that these sentiments were what every young flier, soldier, sailor, or marine feels the first time in battle. It's unlike anything else you have ever known, but it is also something you cannot avoid.

Back in our crudely built piece of a barn that we called an officers' club, the pilots and bombardier/navigators would knock back what seemed to be gallons of cognac, Scotch, or whatever. The best thing about being a combat pilot is that you had booze when you got back to base. It did tend to ease one's anxieties. We would trade horror stories, draw a few laughs, and then saunter as best we could to our tents and our sleeping bags, falling off into sodden dreams, feeling the fuzzy warmth of liquor inside us, which got us to sleep without too many nightmares.

In 1993, I was interviewed by Brian Lamb on C-SPAN. Lamb is a unique TV personality in that his lack of ego equips him to be the superior host that he is, extracting from those with whom he talks a full catalog of their experiences. He was querying me about my career in the White House and in Hollywood. It was going smoothly. Then, without warning, he caught me by surprise. Looking me squarely in the eye, he asked me: "What did you learn from the war?"

I've been on TV a good many times before and since, but that was my first experience with that question. Without thinking I answered, "I learned to do my job when I was scared out of my mind. It was actually primal fear, belly-spilling, throat-grabbing fear." Afterward I reflected on my unscripted response. It was succinct and to the point, and for me, at least, it was true.

After the war, I often wondered how it was that very young men who did not want to die never turned back in the face of deadly fire. My squadron never aborted a mission because of a curtain of .88 mm antiaircraft fire or swarms of ME109 fighter planes. Never. We knew we were going to get hit, we knew there would be casualties, but we never turned tail and ran. Why? How does this happen? The only conclusion I could draw comes from my own experience. Whatever men, and now women, do in war for which generals and admirals confer medals can be explained very simply: They do it because it's what they have been trained to do. It's not about medals or certificates of valor. It is all about duty. And when they go beyond that line, beyond the call of duty, it is because they will not betray their buddies, their comrades-in-arms. They will not let them down, because each of us knows that our buddies will not let us down.

Once when I lost one engine to enemy fire, I had to slowly straggle back to my Corsican base, my altitude dropping. I looked to my left and then to my right. There I saw two B-25s from my squadron, one on either side of me. They had dropped out of the full formation as it sped back to our base to watch over us if we had to crash-land or ditch. They were also there to let us know we were not abandoned. I cannot express even now the overpowering gratitude that I felt. That is part of the bond that develops among men who share the experience of facing an enemy who wants to kill them.

I also learned what years later I commended to my colleagues in business, in the White House, and in the movie world as "professionalism," the ability and inclination to do every piece of the job exactly right, never to cut corners or treat the task at hand casually, always to live up to the obligation you have for those who count on you, and to do all this even when it scares the hell out of you. The professional does his job right every time, without regard for anything else.

That's what I learned in the war, without really knowing I had learned it. It was beyond question one of the richest and most valuable lessons to absorb and understand. Still, it must be said that World War II, which has been called "the last good war," was not good at all. It was brutal, callous, and cruel, filled with depravities, as are all armed conflicts. War is a savage, barbaric struggle in which the aim is not merely to survive, but to win at any cost. It is an activity to engage in only when all else fails and the cause is just.

World War II came to an end, but I wasn't safely home yet. The army air corps had no intention of leaving valuable B-25s sitting on

Italian runways while we joyously headed home. No, not at all. We had to fly our planes back to the States. Well, what's wrong with that? Plenty.

On the day I was to begin the flight back to America, I gathered up my crew, including my valiant buddy Victor Rutz, bombardier/navigator from Spokane, Washington. We had flown many combat missions together. Vic was funny and easy to be with, and he knew what he was doing at all times, and at all times he did it superbly well. My co-pilot was a young fellow who had flown only a few missions in the right seat, and though he was eager, he was still a rookie. We had to load up three enlisted men to transport back with us. Then we were off. First, we flew to Marrakech in Morocco. We spent the night at the air base, refueled, downed some food, and slept. The next morning, we checked our plane to make sure it was operational, went over our new maps, and were off to Roberts Field in Monrovia, the capital city of Liberia. Again the same routine: Spend the night, sleep a little, and pore over the maps.

The next day, our compass course heading was Ascension Island, a tiny piece of land—I mean seriously tiny—in the very middle of the Atlantic Ocean, a little speck on the map with one runway. It was 1,018 miles away. With the B-25 moving forward at 200 mph, you figure the time in the air is going to be about five hours, maybe longer, all things working in your favor, though we would be battling headwinds. Once I was aloft, my first move was to tune my radio compass to Ascension Island's powerful radio beacon. If I kept my eye on my radio compass, it would guide me in, unless the needle began to wander, which would mean there were problems with the radio signal. Not good. If it failed completely, well, let's not think about that. With clear skies and full tanks, we wouldn't have any trouble.

But the weather, as predicted, turned sour when we were some forty minutes out of Roberts Field. The clouds were angry. Slanting, relentless rain limited my visibility. I had to come down out of those dark clouds bursting with rain to some three hundred feet off the ocean level in order to see what there was to see. The problem with this was fuel capacity. The lower you flew, the more fuel you consumed. The higher you flew through a thinning atmosphere, the better able you were to conserve the petrol. Vic, even with all his skills, could not do dead reckoning in this kind of weather. If we went higher with no horizon to sight, you could forget about dead reckoning.

At some point, worried about the expenditure of our fuel, I went up, though I did consume petrol to get to a higher altitude. We found more congenial weather there, but our view of the ocean was totally obscured by thick clouds. Now the radio compass was our guide. Radio compass, dear loyal colleague, please do not let me down.

Vic reminded me that according to his rough calculations, we ought to be nearing Ascension Island. I frowned. Couldn't see a damn thing, though the radio compass was steadily pointing to the west. Then, in a flash, the compass needle went crazy, flopping 180 degrees, now pointing east. I hit the mike to alert Vic, who was in the Plexiglas nose cone.

"Jack," he said, "I think we overshot the island."

He was right. "All right," I said, "we're going to the deck and find out where the hell we are." I put the nose down and settled out about 400 feet above a swirling ocean. The radio compass heading stayed steady on east, and we were definitely riding west. I wheeled around as swiftly and carefully as I could, given how close the plane was to the sea. I headed east, following the radio compass, now back on course. Suddenly we saw it, a patch of land thrown up by the Atlantic. Hello, hello, you lovely little lost bitch of an island. I contacted the tower and got landing instructions. I settled on an approach. I eased back the throttle, got level with the runway, and put it down. What I didn't know was that the frigging runway ran uphill—that is, the part where I planned to lay it in soft and sweet was much lower than the end of the runway. My plane bumped into the runway with a thud, then another one, as we struggled uphill. I cursed the maps, our briefers at Roberts Field, and the incompetents who manned the Ascension Island tower: None of them had made any reference to this aberration. Bastards. I brought it to a stop and climbed out. Vic grinned at me, saying, "I was in the nose cone. It wasn't pleasant, but we made it okay." Sweat had formed on my forehead, and my hands were trembling. It was a lousy landing. But we got down safely.

Ascension has a bizarre history. This was the place called St. Helena, the site of Napoleon's final exile in 1815. I can imagine the frustration of this ruler of most of Europe on being consigned to this dismal patch of earth. There are more sea turtles and sooty ferns on the island than humans. But to be honest, at this moment I was mightily pleased that Ascension Island existed. No way we were going to get to Brazil and then on to the States without this refueling stop. All hail to Ascension/St. Helena. Sorry about that, Napoleon, but you should have kicked English butt at Waterloo.

The next morning would be tough. Our destination now was Natal, Brazil, some 1,447 miles to the west, with no Ascension Island to orient us or to land on, nothing except the sweep of the sea. I have to admit that I had some anxieties. Absurd as it may sound, I would rather ride a bombing run at five thousand feet with Nazis targeting me than face angry weather and roiling seas for long stretches of time with no place to land. I slept uneasily in my bunk, listening to the winds pummeling Ascension Island.

Dawn came quickly. Vic and I huddled over the weather reports and our maps. The weather, it seemed, had turned ugly. So what else was new? I checked out my aircraft. For the millionth time, I marveled at the sturdiness of the B-25 and continued to pray that those Wright Cyclone engines didn't conk out on me. Actually, I had never lost a Wright Cyclone engine except to antiaircraft fire, so I had every reason to trust their airworthiness. But I still could not shake my concerns. Maybe, I thought, it's better to be alert, with nerves at battle stations, than to affect a confidence I most assuredly didn't have this morning.

We took off with the sun in our faces and then turned to head west with the sun at our back. No more than an hour over the ocean, the weather turned really grim. If the sun ever shone steadily over the Atlantic, it was surely not on my flight watch. The winds were roaring into us now, slowing us down. The rains had begun, and the cloud ceiling began to drop palpably. My rookie co-pilot's demeanor revealed he was not having a merry old time. The rain pelted our windshield. I was at about four thousand feet and decided to run higher to find more suitable climes. I leveled out at ten thousand feet and began to lean the fuel, stretching the petrol as long as I could.

After a while the rains began to weaken, but cumulus clouds

clustered around the plane. Dirty gray fluffiness was all we could see. I went on instruments, flying by needle and ball, altimeter and artificial horizon. Now I was concentrating, every nerve edge taut, calling on my reserves of energy. For over two solid hours, I flew the aircraft on instruments, with an intensity I had never before experienced. The weather was nasty, the clouds thick, heavy, sour, threatening. I wanted to turn over the wheel to my co-pilot, but I figured if we were going into the drink, it had better be me at the wheel, although who cared about blame when you hit the water. Some helluva difference it would make.

Sweat began to collect on my forehead as my eyes strained to read the instrument panel. I took off my gloves and tried to wipe my face with one hand as I gripped the wheel with the other. We were being bumped hard now, jarred ceaselessly by the slanting winds that drove the clouds. It just never stopped. I wondered how long the B-25 would be able to withstand this pounding.

Vic appeared over my shoulder, hanging on with both hands to a guardrail. He didn't say anything. Vic was a gutsy guy, seldom betraying any anxiety, which was mighty helpful to me then. He had checked the compass heading but couldn't do any decent dead reckoning, not with this yawing and sliding. We were probably off course, but Brazil had a very large coastline; we sure as hell weren't going to miss it. I had a nagging worry about fuel, but I figured what the hell, let's go down to the deck to find some relief from this fierce weather. I nosed the B-25 down, and sure enough, we soon broke free of the cumulus, and at some six hundred feet off the ocean I leveled out. We were more comfortable, but it was fuel expensive, and the rain was hard.

The sky overhead softened gradually, and once more I headed back to about eight thousand feet. It was better now. Our radio compass had fastened on to Natal's high-power antenna. Vic suggested I adjust the compass heading, and suddenly there it was, the airfield, right in front of us.

I landed at the airfield with maybe fifteen minutes of fuel aboard. From Natal, we flew a little more than 1,000 miles to Belém in northern Brazil near the equator, and from there we jumped to Atkinson Field in Guyana, some 890 miles from Belém. Next on the itinerary was Borinquen Field, Puerto Rico. There we experienced the undiluted joy of waking up after a night's fitful sleep knowing that our next stop, 1,345 miles north, was home. We were headed to America via Hunter Field in Savannah, Georgia.

As we neared Hunter Field, I tuned in a Savannah radio station. Coming in sweetly was the honeyed voice of Doris Day crooning "Sentimental Journey." It sounded so good to me that I almost said aloud, "Thanks, Doris, for welcoming us home. Mighty nice to be here."

I remember vividly putting the B-25's wheels down gracefully on Hunter Field's runway and taxiing to a stop at the nearest slot open on the revetment. We climbed out, Vic and I and our passengers, big smiles on our faces. I looked up at the aircraft, my faithful, steady companion, a machine that had absorbed tremendous punishment but kept flying, even if it struggled on occasion to respond to my commands. Somehow, it never failed to get me home. And it had done so now, for the last time.

As I stood there, I felt a warm surge of affection for this machine. I knew I had become a damn good pilot—no, more than that, I had become a professional pilot. I knew every feature of my craft. I knew what it could do, and I knew what it could not. I knew I could fly in good weather and bad. I could fly with great skill in dangerous environments. When it was killing time in the skies, I had confidence I could guide my plane, ready for any emergency.

So I patted the side of this great mechanical beast and looked up at the pilot's window. Under my breath, I said, "Thank you, Lord. Thank you and this brave airplane for letting me return home safely. I don't intend to press my luck."

I never piloted a plane again.

As the years passed, as my children were born and grew to adulthood, I never talked about the war. My children often asked me about what I did and how I felt, but I had no answers for them. My daughters, Courtenay and Alexandra, are both part of the movie industry; Courtenay is in film production, and Alexandra is a scriptwriter and music video director. Both of them, and my son John, kept insisting I should sit before a videocamera and recount my war experiences. Their argument was, "If not for us, at least for your grandchildren."

I never did it. But here in this book, I have recounted for the first time how one young American came to know war both as it bears eloquent testimony to the human spirit and as it exemplifies unspeakable inhumanity.

In 1975, I attended a new film festival in Deauville, a quaint little picture-postcard town in the Normandy countryside of France. As the festival came to a close, I decided to take my wife, Mary Margaret, to visit Omaha Beach and the American Cemetery. I had never been, and they were only thirty kilometers from Deauville.

Nothing could have prepared me for the sight of row upon row upon row of marble tombstones, as far as the eye could see, each one marked with a cross or a Star of David. There lay 9,387 American fighting men, more than half of whom were between the ages of eighteen and twenty-three. As I looked out on that silent expanse, I was suddenly overcome with emotion. I ran ahead of Mary Margaret, tears streaming down my face. I could not look upon those graves without asking myself, Why did I survive when they didn't?

Some years later, when my son John was about fourteen, I brought him to Deauville to see Omaha Beach and the American Cemetery. I wanted him to see first-hand the gift he, and all of his generation, had received from young men he would never know. We walked to the bluff above Omaha Beach and looked down on rolling waves folding gently over the shore. John was astonished at how close the bluff was to the sand where, I told him, our young men were pouring out of landing craft while the Nazis, on this very bluff, assailed them with machine gun and mortar fire.

"John," I said, "just remember that in spite of close range killing going on all around them, our young men never turned back. They kept coming and coming, even as their buddies were falling around them."

Then I took him to the American Cemetery, a hundred yards or so distant. It was American soil now, deeded to the U.S. by a grateful France. The American flag waved in the sea breeze as we walked among the grave markers in silence. I asked my son to read the words etched on markers, so he could fix in his memory the brief statistics of a young warrior's life—name, rank, outfit, and the day he died. We walked for a long while among those graves.

As we retraced our steps, I turned to John and said, "I wanted you to see this, to be near these young men who were just a few years older than you in some cases, because they gave you the grandest gift that human beings can give to others—the gift of freedom. It's a gift bought and paid for in blood and bravery."

As we stood next to each other, I put my arm around him and said, "Never forget what you saw here today. These soldiers, these boys, died before their lives could be lived. We all owe them a debt we will never be able to repay."

That was a long time ago, but John never forgot. After he saw Steven Spielberg's *Saving Private Ryan*, the finest epic of war ever filmed, he called me and said my words reverberated as he was watching that brilliant opening scene. "You said those young boys never turned back, even as so many were cut down in the water. And you were right. They never turned back. Never."

He remembered.

Chapter 5

THE PEACE YEARS BEGIN

Our sainted bosses give Weldon and me a good luck send off as we begin our brand-new enterprise, Weekley & Valenti Advertising, on January 2, 1953. *Left to right:* Abe Penny, Weldon Weekley, my partner, "Pop" Mabry, our sainted boss, and my smiling self.

The war years are over,
The peace years begin.

W hen the war ended, I took off my uniform for the first time in almost three years. I raced back to Humble to be lovingly greeted by my friends there. Pop had a little celebration for me. I was now home. I was back on my job. The country was ready to start driving again.

But meanwhile, I had to go back to the University of Houston. I had one more semester before that coveted degree was mine, which meant I had to ponder my future. I was prospering in Humble's advertising group. I had been promoted several times. Pop and Humble's outside advertising agency, headed by a brilliant, imaginative man named Joe Wilkinson, had informed me I had a creative gift that would carry me far in the advertising world.

In the winter of 1945, just before we turned over a new year, I knew I had to make a decision. In some five months I would get my diploma from UH, an educational journey I had begun some seven-plus years earlier. I knew I wanted to go on to graduate school, but where and to what end? Did I apply to Harvard Law School and fulfill my boyhood ambition to become a lawyer, my goal since I was ten years old? Or did I choose to stay in the world of advertising and marketing, which had claimed my interest and earned me some measure of success? I was deeply torn. The courtroom mightily attracted me. Yet the pull of words and ideas also tugged me toward advertising. Quo vadis?

I don't know what finally tilted the scales. I do remember thinking, If I don't go to Harvard Law School, what's the next best choice?

Someone had told me that Harvard Business School was the best of the best. Why *not* go to Harvard Business School? I did some research, which described Harvard Business School as the West Point of American business. That had a noble sound to it. Another attraction was the presence of a giant of a teacher, Neil Borden, professor of advertising and mentor to most of the advertising titans in New York. So it was that I wrote Harvard Business School for the application forms and filled them out with great diligence and no small amount of anxiety.

I reported to Pop Mabry that I had applied to Harvard's Graduate School of Business Administration. "That's a good choice, Jack," he said. "How are you fixed for funds?"

As usual, Pop was right on the mark. That was a problem. I had been in the service for almost three years, and the sorry fact was that I was pretty much broke. Pop knew that, and he responded in a way that was entirely consistent with the sensitive, loving, generous man he had always proved himself to be. "I don't want you to worry about finances, Jack. Just study hard. Meanwhile, when you have time off at Harvard, I'll put you back on the payroll for or whatever time off you have. That way you can have a few dollars in your pocket."

Fortunately, it turned out that my money needs were not nearly as severe as they might have been, thanks to an act of Congress unlike any other. As I look back on it today, I consider the G.I. Bill of Rights to be one of the greatest pieces of legislation ever enacted, right next to the Voting Rights Act of 1965. It granted war veterans full payment of expenses (tuition, books, lodgings, and so on) at any university or college whose admission department granted entry. That the American economy after the war soared to historic heights was due, in part, to the G.I. Bill of Rights. It educated an entire generation of Americans. The energy and ambition it released in millions of young, now educated veterans was the most profitable investment Congress had ever made.

But there remained one considerable hurdle for me: I had to be admitted to Harvard. Soon after filing my application papers, I received a message that could only have come from an institution that was very sure of itself and its constituents. Essentially, it read as follows: "Mr. Valenti, you are scheduled for an interview at Morgan

Hall at 2:00 p.m. . . . ." on such-and-such a date. It was as if they were casually asking me to hop a streetcar to go somewhere in downtown Houston, not travel half a continent away to Boston. There was no indication that Harvard would reimburse me for the transportation and lodgings. (They did not.)

Once again, into the breach came Pop Mabry. When I told him about Harvard's peremptory request, he smiled. "Tell you what. I have to be in New York for a Jersey Standard public relations meeting [the Standard Oil Company of New Jersey was one of the principal owners of Humble Oil] around that same time. Why don't you accompany me as my assistant? We'll go to New York, and then I'll put you on a plane to Boston, at Humble's expense, of course. You come back to New York, and the two of us will return to Houston." I could have hugged and kissed that man.

I arrived at Harvard Business School promptly at the appointed date and time and found myself sitting across a desk from the assistant dean of admissions, a slender young man of no more than thirty. He gazed at me through wire-rimmed glasses with searching scrutiny.

"Thank you, Mr. Valenti, for coming here to see me. Am I pronouncing your name correctly?"

I nodded. "Yes, sir, you are."

"Good, then let's proceed. I regret very much that I have no knowledge of the University of Houston. I have checked with the college and the other graduate schools, and no one from the University of Houston has ever applied to Harvard. Rather odd, don't you think?"

I said, "Well, there has to be a first time." He looked at me uncertainly. I kept going while he was considering his response. "Also, the University of Houston is a very new university only eleven years old. One day I would like to be able to say that I attended the youngest university in the country and that I also graduated from the oldest—and the best." I smiled winningly, pleased with my turn of phrase.

The assistant dean frowned. My sense of humor was clearly alien to his. "Yes, I see," was his offering. Then he began to quiz me. He was obviously interested in my military career and the combat missions I flew. He said, "Unhappily, I have weak lungs and couldn't pass the physical. I regret that, don't you see?"

We chatted for another half hour, discussing my academic record and, as they say, "my hopes and dreams." To my surprise, he seemed avidly interested in my activities as president of the student body while still a night student. Going to college at night was simply beyond his ken. It was something that the lower classes did, which made it all the more incomprehensible to him. To my mind, the gulf between us seemed impossibly wide.

I got on the plane back to New York to meet up with Pop Mabry, unsure what my chances of admittance were. As we flew home from New York, Pop said to me: "You did the best you could. You served your country honorably in war. You were at the top of your class at UH. I sort of feel this fellow will consider you a nice prize for Harvard."

Two and a half weeks later, an envelope arrived with "Harvard Graduate School of Business Administration" printed on the outside. Inside were the words I'd been longing to hear: "You are admitted to join the Class of 1948." Hot damn. I was in! How could I have so misjudged the young man who interviewed me? Clearly he was a wise and discerning young man—not to mention a great judge of talent.

On a breezy September day in 1946, I arrived in Boston and found my way by taxi to Harvard Business School. I still couldn't believe my good luck as I carried my bags to Gallatin Hall, where I would reside my first year. (All the living halls at HBS are named after former secretaries of the Treasury.) I was twenty-five years old. Three years had been taken from me, though I never once regretted my wartime experience. Nonetheless, I knew I had lost three years, and I aimed to make up for that lost time by working my butt off.

At 8:30 a.m., I entered my first class, in Baker Hall. The thing that struck me most was the sunlight. I was going to class in the daytime—and full-time, no less! There were four hundred men in the Class of '48, each section containing one hundred students (alas, no women). To my surprise, I found that my section was populated exclusively with war veterans, all as eager as I was to make up for lost time. Probably because of my intense involvement in UH campus politics, I was selected to serve on the student council to represent my section. I do know that none of my classmates were stricken with the political bug the way I was.

It was on that crisp autumn opening day alongside the Charles River that I first got to know my new friends and classmates, with whom I would forge an unbreakable bond of affection and respect. We were new students, all eyeing one another warily as we met for the first time. It was a truly formidable group of intellects, the most tirelessly energetic, fiercely competitive, ceaselessly ambitious men I had ever known. Most were graduates of the nation's elite universities. After their military service, most of which involved combat in faraway places, my colleagues were eager to reclaim their lost years.

The pace never slackened in the classrooms or in the study groups working late in the evening, dissecting a new case about the travails of a corporation and designing a plan to remedy whatever was plaguing the company. The energy of the conversations reminded me of the B-25: It all seemed to happen at full-to-the-firewall velocity. We had no time to waste. Well, perhaps we did find a few hours of leisure for visiting Wellesley College, where we did our best to take Severance Hall, Tower Hall, and the other stately dormitories near Lake Waban by storm.

I confess I came to Harvard with an insouciant assumption that I would be first in the class. As it turned out, I had to ride at full gallop just to stay the course. The air crackled with split-second retorts, on-the-spot extemporaneous rebuttals in class, and sheer genius when we labored in the evening in our study groups. As I recounted years later, I learned as much from my classmates as I did from the rigors of the classroom.

At that time, the president of Harvard was the celebrated James Bryant Conant, whose prestige gave Harvard an aura unique among institutions of learning. The dean of the Graduate School of Business was Donald K. David, who could have been CEO of any Fortune 500 enterprise in the nation. His calm, warm demeanor made him very appealing as well. The faculty was also without peer. It was like a championship athletic team, with every player having a good shot at being admitted to the Hall of Fame and an all-star bench to relieve the starting team. It was the glory of Harvard Business School that its preeminence was neither artificial nor hollow. It was real, and made so by an incandescent group of teachers whose voices I can still hear and whose restraining and supportive hand I can still feel.

It is fair to say that other than the war and later my White House years, no other experience made such a profoundly deep impression on me. It furnished me with everything I needed to navigate and survive my long years in Hollywood. To confront a war and Harvard Business School before I turned twenty-six gave me a sense of assurance about my abilities and possibilities—as well as an awareness of my flaws. Harvard Business School was my mace and shield in my long career. Not often do young men have such a singular opportunity to stretch the mind and broaden its reach.

From my band of student brothers in the classes of '48–'49 at Harvard came some of America's matchless business champions: Tom Murphy, a big Irishman with a sense of humor as large as his frame, a founder of Capital Cities Broadcasting and later the owner of ABC; John Whitehead, a wizard chieftain of Goldman Sachs, later deputy secretary of state; the wondrous Al Casey, CEO of the *Los Angeles Times*, then CEO of American Airlines and the Resolution Trust Corporation, then postmaster general of the United States; Don Davis, the athletic, no-nonsense CEO of the Stanley Works; Lester Crown, the quiet but amazingly effective CEO of the Material Services Company and principal stockholder in General Dynamics; Richard Bryan, the sturdy, incisive head of White Motors; Jim Burke, visionary CEO of Johnson & Johnson; Jack Garrity, a rousing intellect and a managing partner of McKinsey & Company; Al Winnick, who became one of America's great leaders in apparel; and Jack Dowd, a top executive with Hershey Chocolate. And there were more in that special class. These men were all, in my judgment, unusually fit for leadership. What they all had in abundance was an integrity, a sense of honor and fair play, which, to the nation's loss, is in short supply these days in too many business arenas. They were a glittering assembly that in the long annals of Harvard Business School stood forth as a "class of stars," whose impress on the face and form of American business was unique, deep, and memorable.

Harvard founded a new way of teaching business: the case method. Each problem we tackled in class, discussed in our group study sessions, and confronted in frequent tests was set forth in a narrative that required us to choose which pathway to take in order to best serve the company in question. To newcomers like me, the case method was frustrating. Unlike Euclidean geometry with its eternally pure equations, the case method offered no one answer, no golden passkey to the solution. What was required was thinking through the problem; examining the numbers; assessing the company's place in the competitive arena, its products, its leadership, and its employees; and then using disciplined inquiry to fashion the decision the smart CEO would make. Our professors were merciless in attacking a student's formula for decision making. And if you chose to sink into your seat and stay mute, the professor would seek you out just when you were least prepared. I always feared that accusatory finger pointing at me, followed by, "What is your opinion, Mr. Valenti?" Especially when I was riven with doubt.

Harvard's administrators understood that we had lost time serving in the war, so they offered my class the option of going full steam ahead, taking no summers off, and finishing our studies three months earlier than the normal two-year requirement. Most of the class jumped at the chance. I sure as hell did.

Although the intense environment made us very close, my classmates and I never talked about the war. Not once. We knew without asking that we all did what was required of us, and that we had all suffered the same doubts and fears. We all understood that war had no heroes. You just did what you had to do, and what was so heroic about that? That didn't leave much to talk about.

What we did talk about—more than just a little—was what we were going to do when we graduated. We were taught that we were the select few who would guide, manage, and change for the better all that business in America stood for and achieved. Alas, too many of us, including me, began to inhale this stuff to the point where a few years after graduation, if we all weren't running the company we worked for, we'd think we must be failures. It took me quite a while to figure out that Harvard Business School was dealing in some hyperbole here. But a little hyperbole never hurt anybody.

I thought about the future seriously and often, and in my thesis on that topic, I wrote that I would go back to Humble Oil and renew my career there, and when I judged the time to be right, I would depart Humble to start my own advertising agency. I had no doubt about that plan.

Years later, I began to see more clearly what I saw only dimly at graduation time: Nothing is ever achieved without the help of other people. Opportunity knocks for some and not for others. Luck and timing play crucial roles. My own life is an example of extraordinary opportunities presenting themselves. I have lived a fascinating life that could never have happened without the unexpected entry of chance and fate and people who gave me an opportunity.

When we graduated from Harvard Business School, all of us scattered to pursue our dreams. Four of us from Texas piled into a Chevrolet and drove nonstop to the Lone Star State. When the journey ended in Houston, I embraced my parents and my sister, and the next morning I reported to Pop Mabry, ready to start work.

At that time, Humble Oil, a giant in exploration, refining, and production, was trailing its competitors at the retail service station level. Success at the pump had eluded Humble—and it was the only place it had. Humble had grown used to one triumph after another, and this failure frustrated it. Frank Watts was installed as the new supreme manager of all retail sales. He had his orders: Make Humble Oil a leader in the retail sales arena. So he was determined to make Humble service stations number one in Texas, not the laggard fifth they were now.

Pop Mabry called his team together. The managing partners of Wilkinson, Schiwetz & Tips, our advertising agency, were summoned to the meetings. Also there were Abe Penny, top assistant to Pop, Jack Shannon, who headed up the public relations section, Walter Beach, Weldon Weekley, and I. We labored for days (and some nights) over our advertising, marketing, and sales promotion strategy.

I cannot remember who came up with the sparkling idea, the key to lifting Humble from the also-rans to the top tier, but the logic went like this. Texans drive their cars longer, faster, and more often than drivers in any other state. They drive not only city streets, but highways as well. Even for Texans it's difficult to distinguish one gasoline from another, although millions of advertising dollars are spent to do just that. Then, in one of our strategy meetings, someone said: "What else would attract drivers and their families to a service station other than gasoline? When they're on the road, what is it that sooner or later every automobile is going to try to find? What is it? It's a clean restroom."

At first we all grinned. Kind of funny. Yet the more we circled this idea, the more attractive it became. I said, "Terrific idea. Let's get it going." Suppose, Pop suggested, we advertise and promote Humble service stations as having the cleanest, most sanitary restrooms in all of Texas? To most drivers, gasoline was gasoline. But suppose that "cleanest restrooms" become our central theme? Would that engage Texas drivers? We all pondered that. I murmured, "Well, what we are doing now sure isn't engaging too many folks."

So it was that "the cleanest restrooms in all of Texas" became our essential selling point. We had a key marketing asset. Humble had for years sponsored the Southwest Conference football games on the radio, and Texans were certifiably barking mad about football. With Kern Tips providing his superb play-by-play voice on the air, we had the listeners. Even our opposition conceded that point. In a state where college football was a religious experience, Pop thought we should ask our ad agency to fill those game commercials with the "clean restroom" theme.

Weldon introduced the thought that we needed more than advertising. We had to make sure that when customers drove into a Humble service station, they truly got what we had promised. "We have to infuse service station managers and their personnel with a spirit of pride through this new campaign," he said. "Why not begin to stage sales meetings in every nook and cranny of Texas, making these not typical dull gatherings, but meetings full of fun, interesting things to hold their attention?" Weldon went on to say, "Jack and I will write scripts for these meetings, we will act in them, we will make every hour of those meetings so interesting that the service station guys will *want* to attend."

I jumped in at that point, pleased that Weldon had brought me into the action circle. "Yes, we can preach our clean restroom theme by making sales meetings fun as well as educational. No campaign is going to succeed if the people who man our service stations aren't enthusiastic. We must draw them in, enthuse them, make them feel like they are on a crusade."

Pop grinned. "That makes sense. Let's go do it." Weldon and I created four separate meeting scripts over the next month, working around the clock, testing on each other the ideas we wanted to put in the scripts. We wrote little plays starring the service station manager and his employees. Weldon and I would play all the parts, the guys at the station, the drivers who came in looking for clean restrooms, as well as scenes where a driver comes in with his family and finds a filthy, unappealing restroom instead of a Humble restroom. Corny? Absolutely. Kind of silly? Indeed. But dullness, the blight of most sales meetings, had been replaced by fun. And if the spoken lines were not Academy Award caliber, it was still unlike any sales meeting the service station people had ever attended. For the first time, they could laugh at the goings-on and join in the applause when the driver complimented the service station manager on his attention to a family's needs.

Over the next months, Weldon and I and the rest of the Mabry legions traded our beds at home for victory laps on the road. We would go out for a week, holding sales meetings in East Texas, in Lufkin, Tyler, Marshall, and Longview, then go back home and out again to South Texas, to Corpus Christi, San Antonio, to Browns-ville, along the Rio Grande, which Texans called "the River Road," then on to West Texas, into the Davis Mountain area to El Paso, then to San Angelo sheep country. After a rest, we canvassed the hill country, Dallas and Fort Worth, the Panhandle, the Red River, Abi-lene, Amarillo, and Lubbock. Then east to Beaumont, Port Arthur, and Orange on the Sabine River and then on to Galveston, Houston, and their environs. It was hard work but great fun. We were seeing up close what Texas was all about. Frankly, I loved every moment of it, especially our performances.

My experiences driving with Pop Mabry early in my Humble ca-reer, stopping at little diners and cafés all over Texas, chatting with the locals, listening to the inhabitants of a state who loved the land and the place they lived, were bearing fruit all over again. Once again I was seeing this huge, hospitable, friendly state up close. The time I was spending in the farthest reaches of Texas made me feel at home with men and women I truly admired. And once again I felt a surge of pride in Texas—and Texans. My chauvinism was in full flight.

From the fifth-place cellar, Humble now rose to number one in gasoline sales volume. Frank Watts, the company sales manager, was glowing with praise from Humble's top brass. Pop Mabry, saluted by Frank Watts, was joyously embracing his staff. We even got write-ups in the national advertising magazines. You can be certain that our competitors were fuming and either firing their ad agencies or demanding that something be done to counter this "clean restroom" bunkum that was reverberating through the state.

I was also spreading my creative wings. For the next nine years, I turned out a weekly Saturday column for the *Houston Post*, which added up to some 478 columns and maybe half a million words. I have to confess and do declare that my style needed some tutorials, but no one can doubt that sustained writing, putting your butt before a typewriter in a disciplined fashion, much as I did at Harvard Business School every week, makes for better writing. And I was taught a valuable lesson while being both pilloried and praised in the "Letters to the Editor" section. Those whippings I took from readers of the *Post* led me to understand that anytime you go public, you will not be universally loved—an indispensable lesson for me later in the White House and Hollywood.

When I pointed out to Arthur Lara, who hired me, that the paper was under no obligation to print some of those letters to the editor, he remonstrated quite wisely, "Well, Jack, at least they are reading you." Which is how I became devoted to a quatrain written by British author Hilaire Belloc: "When I am dead, I hope it may be said, his sins were scarlet, but his books were read." Yes, I like that.

Throughout the early part of 1952, Weldon, his wife, Rosalie, and I were discreetly talking about starting our own advertising agency. I was pushing for it hard. It had been almost four years since I'd graduated from Harvard. Granted, I was single (and thoroughly enjoying my social life), so the risks for me of disengaging from the warm corporate embrace of Humble Oil were minimal compared with what the Weekleys, with their two sons, would be putting on the line. But to my amazement, this quiet, thoughtful man and his brainy wife began to view the prospect with the same excitement I felt. He and Rosalie were ready to make the move. (Today, Weldon says with some amusement that when they decided to take the leap off the cliff, they both decided that was the perfect time to have a third child. Young David Weekley, that third child, became one of the largest and most successful home builders in the nation, so I like to think I had a beneficent effect on the Weekley family fortune.)

I drove out to Weldon's home in West University Place early one evening with the last rays of the summer sun fading slowly. The three of us, Weldon, Rosalie, and I, sat on their front lawn and concentrated on the big question: Whom do we approach to be our first client? Without that first client to cover the monthly nut of our new company, the risks would be too great. We talked for about an hour. When night fell, we went inside the Weekleys' modest home. Weldon said, "Let's start with our marketable skills. Who would want them? Another retail gasoline marketer, right?"

I said, "You're right. I have an idea. The one outfit that is struggling much as Humble did some years ago is Conoco, the Continental Oil Company. Someone told me last week that Conoco was looking for a new agency. I know a fellow named Charlie Perlitz who's the number two guy at Conoco."

Some two years earlier, Pop Mabry had "detailed" me to work on a community charity drive, headed by Charles Perlitz. I "eager-beavered" the job, working twice the hours that were called for, so I thought Mr. Perlitz would remember me. I said, "Why don't we prepare a campaign presentation and run it by Perlitz? If he likes it, I believe he'll send us on to the top sales and marketing people."

Weldon nodded appreciatively. "I say let's get to work on our presentation."

For the next month, we labored every night, constructing and polishing the presentation we would offer to Conoco. The core of our pitch was "We were the creative force behind lifting Humble retail sales to first place. We can do the same for you." For a company like Conoco, vexed at its limping retail sales, it just might hit a nerve.

Mr. Perlitz fortunately did remember me. He not only agreed to meet with us, he showed an undisguised interest in our pitch, and when it was over, he picked up the phone and called Harry Kennedy, vice president of marketing. Two days later, we were in Mr. Kennedy's office.

Kennedy was a rotund, cheery executive who was gracious

enough to lavish considerable time and attention on us. After we had presented him with our case, he said, "You're saying to me that you can do some magic for Conoco's sales like you did with Humble?"

"Yessir," Weldon and I responded in chorus.

"What we're saying, Mr. Kennedy," I injected, "is that we are knowledgeable about the Texas retail gasoline marketplace. We believe that we can do two things: enthuse your sales force and your service station managers, and infuse your advertising with melodies it has never sung before."

Kennedy nodded approvingly. "All right, I like that. I'll ask Mel Hatwick, who's our head of advertising, to meet with you. Mel is responsible for all public communications. He has the authority to retain you, if he believes it makes sense, which, by the way, I do. Call Mel's office tomorrow, and he'll find time to meet with you."

We danced out of his office. We were about to undergo the final test. If we passed Mel Hatwick's scrutiny, we would be home.

Three days later, we sat across the desk from Hatwick. He had obviously been briefed by his boss. He was friendly and seemingly interested in hearing us out. He said, "You're coming in at an opportune moment. Conoco is looking for new creative help. Harry Kennedy was impressed with your presentation. Let's see how I feel about it."

We spent some forty minutes emphasizing our Humble experience and offering some ideas for Conoco. When we were done, Mel did not attempt to keep his views under wraps. "I'm attracted to what you have to say, and I like the way you say it. I am particularly attracted to the ideas you have for building enthusiasm with our service station operators. I want you on our team."

Could that be it, a home run in the first inning? We stood up and shook his hand. He smiled heartily and said, "I suggest you come back tomorrow so you can meet with our lawyers and draw up a contract that meets our needs and I hope yours as well."

As Weldon and I drove off, I said, "What do you suppose he means by 'meets his needs'? He never talked about fees. What do you think?"

Weldon was thoughtful for a bit. "We are not in the driver's seat here. Conoco will be our only client, at least for a while. That means we don't have a lot of leverage, and I think Mel knows it."

At our next appointment with Mel, we met two conservatively dressed gentlemen, both somber and packing large briefcases. Mel spoke up. "Jack and Weldon, I have a contract here for your scrutiny. I have to tell you that there is no running room here. The contract is what we believe is fair for both parties. Why don't you take a few minutes to go over it in my outer office."

Essentially, the contract was fairly simple. We would be paid a retainer of $40,000 per year for two years. We would be exclusive to Conoco during the first year. If in the second year we wanted to add another client or two, this would have to be approved by Conoco.

At the time, I was making $7,500 annually at Humble, and Weldon was making a thousand more. So $40,000 sounded pretty good to us, until we did the math. Out of that retainer fee had to come the cost of our office, our equipment, and a salary for Mildred Davidson, a paragon of efficiency in our Humble office who wanted to become part of our new agency—and our own compensation plan.

Quickly, we recognized we would have to be constantly watching our costs if we were going to survive. But we both knew we had no negotiating room. Take it or leave it. I said, "All right, Weldon, we'll just have to slog through this first year and then take on new clients. I do believe if we handle it right and show Mel our financials, he'll okay the new clients."

Weldon nodded. "Okay, let's go back in and sign the contract."

We immediately went to see Pop Mabry, our mentor, our sainted boss, our loving friend. How would he take the loss of what he called his "bright young men"? Pop was standing behind his desk when we came in, his eyes crinkling.

He grinned. "Now why do I think this is just not part of the day's business? You've got something on your mind, right?"

We described what we had been up to the last month, ending with our Mel Hatwick meeting. "Pop," Weldon said, "we love you and owe you so much. But Jack and I think the time is right to start our own agency. You have given us the great experience that allows us to climb the next mountain."

I was emotional. "Pop, we do love you. Without you, we would have had no chance to do what we want to do now. For me personally, I can never forget what you did for me, taking this very young, green hall boy into your office and taking him under your wing. I can never repay you for what you gave me after the war and when I was at Harvard. Without you, I just could not have made it."

Pop came from around the desk and embraced Weldon. "You did this on your own, Weldon. You never let me down, ever." Then he grabbed me and held me close. "Little Friend, you came to me when you were just a boy, and here you are, a war hero and a fine, wonderful man. I'm proud of you."

He leaned against his desk. "I want you both to succeed, and you will. God knows we will miss you here, we will miss you both a lot. You are my family, but sooner or later families disperse because new opportunities come along. Just know I am always here if ever you need me."

Weldon and I both had glistening eyes when we left Pop's office. Later in my life, I came to understand with greater clarity the absolute sweetness and loyalty and love this man lavished on us. How rare was our good fortune. We were immensely lucky to have such a boss. In the ensuing years, I seldom turned down a request from a young college graduate, man or woman, to see me about a job, even when I had no job available. More specifically, I wanted to reach out to all those young men and women who would work with me in the years ahead. I wanted to treat them as Pop Mabry had treated me.

It had been fourteen years since I had begun my first day on the job at Humble. I never forgot those years. And I have never forgotten Pop Mabry. He was one of three men who changed my life. The second would be the president of the United States. And the third would be a Hollywood mogul, first among moguls.

I'm sure my Harvard Business School professors would have been aghast at the early days of Weekley & Valenti. Weldon had a friend who owned a little one-story building—actually it was about two cracked panels past being a shack—at 2706 Richmond Avenue, and he offered to rent us a four-room "suite." We moved in on January 2, 1953. Weekley & Valenti was ready to rock and roll.

Our rent was $75 a month, which we both thought was excessive, but we had no choice. Weldon took one room for his office, I took another one, and Mildred settled into the third. The fourth we used for files and storage. How small were they? To use the old cliché, I had to go outside to change my mind. Weldon and I vowed we would never invite any client or prospective client to visit us in our offices; we would go to theirs. We kept that vow. One good thing about these offices was that they motivated us to work our asses off so we could get the hell out of 2706 Richmond Avenue. A year and a half later, our landlord built a nice brick building next door, and we moved into new quarters. Now, clients would be welcome.

Weldon and I poured all our energies into Conoco's business. We worked morning to night and weekends as well. Poor Rosalie saw precious little of her husband in those early days. Within a month, we had put together the format and scripts for sales meetings, duplicating our triumphs at Humble Oil. Weekley & Valenti prospered. Weldon and I agreed on a division of labor. We both stayed deeply involved in the creative process; Weldon managed the administrative duties, and I became the rainmaker for new business, making presentations to prospective clients. We sought and received Conoco's permission to bring on our next client, the American Petroleum Institute. Then we lassoed San Jacinto Savings & Loan (founded by my old friend Joe Allbritton, who later came to Washington to run the Washington afternoon newspaper the *Star* as well as to buy Riggs National Bank; and I became a director of every enterprise Joe presided over). We gained other new clients: the Continental Bank, Tenneco Life, and the oil field service companies owned by my friend Ray Shaffer from Fort Worth.

We had a creative plan almost from the first day of our agency. And we stuck to it. It emerged from two advertising geniuses whose methods and philosophy Weldon and I judged to be worthy of imitation. One was David Ogilvy. At the age of thirty-seven, he founded Ogilvy & Mather, which became one of the finest agencies in the world. Ogilvy's touchstone was his concept of what advertising was all about: "I do not regard advertising as a medium for entertainment or art, but as a medium of information." That is truth to the tenth power squared. He added to that, "If it doesn't sell, it isn't creative."

Years later, when I worked for President Johnson in the White

House, I put David Ogilvy's name on the list for a state dinner. I met him there and told him of my long-held admiration of him. He smiled, seeming pleased.

The second fount of wisdom for W&V was an advertising titan named Ted Bates, who founded the agency that bore his name. His insight was called the "unique selling proposition," or USP. It was simple. When you write copy for an ad, it ought to stress the unique value of the product, how it does what it is advertised to do better than anyone else's product, and why you should buy it. It is all very well to be cute, funny, and entertaining, but tell the customer what the product does and how well it does it. A lot of advertising these days has forgotten to emphasize Ted Bates's USP.

Then we brought on what would be a most important client for me (even more so than for Weldon, for reasons that will soon become clear). It was Dresser Industries, a very large oil field equipment enterprise moving into esoteric sensor devices, the kind that were much sought after by the civil defense unit of the federal government. It was this client that gave me freedom to pursue Mary Margaret Wiley, whom I had never lost sight of in my mind, now one of Vice President Johnson's most trusted aides.

I presented a plan to Dresser that involved going to Washington to meet with civil defense officials. The objective of my plan was to persuade the civil defense authorities to test Dresser's new sensor device. I did not see any reason to tell them that my close association with Houston's congressman Albert Thomas was going to be a key factor. He was the all-powerful chairman of the House Appropriations Subcommittee on Independent Offices. This meant that Thomas was the supreme arbiter of how much money each federal government regulatory agency got to run its business—the Federal Communications Commission, the Federal Trade Commission, the Civil Aeronautics Bureau, and all other federal regulatory groups, including the one that was my ultimate prize: the U.S. Office of Civil Defense Mobilization (OCDM). Albert Thomas controlled all the purse strings, which made him a very important person in Washington regulatory circles.

I announced to Dresser that I would have to make a number of trips to Washington to try to close the deal. I told them I aimed to make our case to Leo Hoegh, former governor of Iowa and now head of the OCDM. I saw no reason to mention my other, even more valuable objective: the winning of Miss Wiley.

Dresser bought my strategy. Immediately I called Mary Margaret. "I'm heading to Washington day after tomorrow. May I take you to dinner?"

To my delight—and surprise—she said, "Yes, I would like that."

Several Houston friends of mine, Welcome Wilson and Johnny Goyen, were also in Washington at the time. I scheduled a drink with them at the Mayflower Hotel and asked Mary Margaret to meet me there so we could dine at the hotel's fine restaurant. I was chatting with Johnny and Welcome at the bar when Johnny motioned to me. I turned and there she was, standing in the entrance to the bar. She was ravishingly beautiful, with a tiny, shy smile that seemed to say she was glad to see me. At least that was what I wanted to believe.

I flew across the bar to meet her. I wanted to take her in my arms, but I resisted. I knew Mary Margaret would not appreciate any romantic antics in full view of a curious public.

I bade good-bye to my two friends. Mary Margaret and I sat down to dinner, where I plied her with all the charm I could summon. There was an authentic shyness to her. When she spoke she usually had something to say. She was a quiet surveyor of her surroundings, with an appealing lack of pretense and a special gift for listening. I must have blathered on for some time, but she never exhibited any dismay or impatience.

Somehow, this was the beginning. For the next year, I commuted as often as possible to Washington, each time drawing her closer to me, though in barely perceptible degrees.

Meanwhile, I kept to business, Dresser's business. My first priority was to meet with Albert Thomas in his office.

"Albert," I said as I explained to him Dresser's new technology, "I need your help in getting me in to see Governor Hoegh."

"Well, Jackson," said Thomas, "I think I might be able to help you." Whereupon he picked up the phone and told his secretary to get Governor Hoegh. Within a few minutes, the governor came on the wire.

"Governor, Albert Thomas here. . . . I was calling," Thomas said

in response to whatever Hoegh had said, "on behalf of my close podner in Houston, Jack Valenti, who has a lot to do with my being up
here in Congress."

Hoegh must have grasped the lay of the land. Thomas was laying
down the close connection, conveying that Jack Valenti was a valuable asset to the chairman of the Appropriations Subcommittee on
Independent Offices, keeper of the keys to the government's funding
vault. In short, he was certifying me.

"Do you think you might have some time to meet with him? I
sure would be grateful if you did."

You can bet the ranch, the bowling alley, and the drugstore that
Hoegh damn sure wanted Albert to be grateful, and if Hoegh had to
meet with Valenti, this redneck cracker from Texas, he would. Of
course he would be glad to see Jack Valenti.

I made my thanks to Albert, got on the phone with the Office of
Civil Defense Mobilization, and made an appointment to see the
governor in the early afternoon of the next day. I then called Dresser
to tell them to send their top technical guy that night to decipher the
Dresser device for the defense agency the following day.

When I got to Hoegh's office at the appointed hour with my
Dresser expert in tow, the governor was waiting for me with about
seven members of his staff. The Dresser technical director exposed
the assembly to the magic of the new device. They asked a bundle of
questions. After an hour, Hoegh asked me and my colleague to wait
in his reception room for a bit.

An hour and a half later, we were called in by Hoegh. Once inside his office, he wasted no time. "We like your proposal. We would
like to enter into a contract to test your sensor methodology. If the
test meets our expectations, we will draw up a longer-term contract
arrangement with Dresser."

We all shook hands. I uttered a silent prayer of gratitude to the
magician named Albert Thomas, and we departed. Once we were
outside hailing a cab, the Dresser executive was bewildered but
deliriously happy.

"My God, how did you do that?" he said, his voice stammering.
"In all my years, we have never, ever, gotten so quick a response to a
presentation. How the hell did that happen?"

I saw no need to trouble the happy man with complicated explanations. No need to invoke Albert's name. Let Dresser move forward with the confidence of knowing that with Weekley & Valenti as their guide, no peak was too high to scale, no objective too difficult to achieve. I thought it best to leave it that way. My Dresser friend would be back in Texas tomorrow, and word of the miracle of Valenti walking on water would spread. No way we are going to lose the Dresser account, was the message I passed along to Weldon, who laughed and congratulated me.

The big part of the deal, though never mentioned, was that Dresser Industries had paved the way for my courtship of Mary Margaret Wiley. It was the most successful venture of my life.

What was different about Mary Margaret? First there was her natural elegance. Then she possessed a reticence that I found irresistible, a quiet centeredness that was completely unfeigned. She was unimpressed by glamour and resistant to the charms of hordes of men who were attracted to her, both for being a gorgeous woman and for being an important member of LBJ's political team. She was always more amused than contemptuous of her suitors and their displays of rapture.

Even though she seemed wary of my sometimes overenergetic attention to her and held back from revealing what she was thinking and feeling, I had this odd sense that she was not resisting me so much as feeling her way toward, as the cliché goes, "getting to know me."

The more I got to know Mary Margaret, the better I came to understand the deep loyalty she conferred on those close to her. Once her friendship was offered, it was not easily withdrawn or casually tended. I cannot pinpoint the precise moment she began to move close to me, and I cannot recall that moment in time when I realized, to my surprise, that I was ready, even eager, to give up my bachelor's life. It was all quite mysterious, but at the same time perfectly clear.

As Mary Margaret and I grew close and marriage neared, Lyndon Johnson drew me increasingly into his inner circle. I wrote some speeches for him, as well as some political memos. (Of course, this was all pro bono. The vice president was very big on pro bono work.) We talked a lot about political issues, how Texas was trending, and what I thought about the Democratic Party's future strength not only in Texas, but in the nation. I sensed I was being tested. But he seemed to find my views worthy, and sometimes he even smiled and said, "I agree with you." That is like scoring 1,600 on your SATs.

LBJ liked to be surrounded by people with what he judged to be blue-chip credentials, and mine seemed to fit the bill. As a young man, I had wanted an education so badly that after working at my job all day, I went to college every night. That kind of resolve had a high value to Johnson. Moreover, I was a Harvard graduate. And I had gone to war. I had fought in battles. He counted that a huge asset. The fact that I had survived was an added benefit.

In early 1962, Mary Margaret finally surrendered to my tireless attentions. We were married on June 1 at St. Anne's Church in Houston. It was a small wedding. Mary Margaret's father was in the hospital. At her request, Vice President Johnson gave her away at the altar and then returned to his pew alongside Mrs. Johnson. My closest friend, Johnny Goyen, was best man. Afterward, Weldon and Rosalie Weekley had a reception for us at their home, honored by the presence of the vice president and his wife as well as Mary Margaret's mother and my parents and sister.

Just after this, Vice President and Mrs. Johnson invited us to travel with them to the inauguration of President Juan Bosch of the Dominican Republic. We were also their guests when LBJ flew to Rome to represent the United States at the funeral of Pope John XXIII. We had more long talks about politics. I was feeling more comfortable in the presence of the vice president. I hoped he felt the same about me.

But everything else aside, the plain fact is that Mary Margaret was the key to my growing intimacy with LBJ. He trusted her completely. He respected her judgment about people and political issues. In crisis she was absolutely calm, and her first and last thoughts centered on how she could best serve Lyndon Johnson. It was never about her personally. He knew she would never betray him. Ever. To those who have never lived in the fiery cauldron of politics, it may be difficult to understand that such unquestioned loyalty and wisdom capable of transcending all else have a measureless value to high-stationed public men and women.

I have in the privacy of my own thoughts often wondered what inspired LBJ, in the first minutes after he was thrust into the presidency, to instruct the Secret Service, "Get Jack Valenti aboard Air Force One." Since LBJ had no doubts about Mary Margaret's skill in divining the essence of people, I have to assume that I had been endorsed by Mary Margaret. To LBJ, that was the gold standard.

Weekley & Valenti continued to grow. By now, whenever we sought a client that was also being pursued by a major New York agency with branches in Texas, we knew the drill. The New York agency would send its varsity to woo the client, putting on a dog-and-pony show. The New York agency would have far more people and resources than we did. We had to offer something the other agency didn't have (in our estimation). And that was the creativity and energy of a single agency as steward of the account on the ground in the local community, every day, every week.

So our pitch to the prospective client went something like this: "The chairman of the other agency and his experts will return to New York and you will never see them again. Why don't you ask that agency to introduce you to the person or persons who will worry about your account here in Houston twenty-four hours a day, who will be working to serve you seven days a week. Weldon and I will be the persons at Weekley and Valenti who will be on the job for you from here on out. So why not let us go head-to-head with the other agency's counterpart to Weldon and me. You can judge for yourself who can best serve your company."

It usually worked.

Weldon and I had a rule we never broke. We never "bet on the come." That is, we never hired new employees until we had the account on board to pay their salaries. Thanks to our accounting counsel, Bob White, and Weldon's strict fiscal rules, we never spent a dime unnecessarily. We made it clear to clients that their business was our business, something to be treated with respect, frugality, and tireless creative energy and vision. That was why from day one of the agency's existence, we were in the black. I think it is fair to say that Weekley & Valenti was the most profitable agency in the region.

Moreover, we were both in touch with each and every client at least once a week, on the phone or in their office or at lunch or at dinner, often with their wives or husbands. I kept a little notebook with times and dates for a phone call to each client. This discipline was never breached. It's a simple fact that there is no substitute for caring about the client, and in a personal way.

I enlarged Weekley & Valenti's business by becoming active in political consulting. Since my earliest days following my grandfather around to visit his political constituents, I had been fascinated by the county courthouse and City Hall crowd. I loved the tumult of political rallies and the grit and grind of street politics. Memories of my first public speech at age ten stirred up nameless streams of excitement, the kind that light up hidden spaces inside you and make you want to go back for more.

But most fascinating, at least to me, was the intersection of politics and instinct—those unrequested signals from the brain that say, Don't go the way others tell you to go; go this way, without knowing precisely why. Animals are born with instinct. It's what allows them to survive. As far as humans go, we can develop our instincts to some degree through experience, but I believe first-rate instincts are something you're born with—or without.

Political professionals understand this. The problem arises when a candidate, looking for specific answers from his campaign aide, feels uneasy when he gets a response like "My instinct tells me that no matter what the polls are saying, we ought to go public with this new initiative." It is the most imprecise of all the art forms (except trying to make a first-rate movie). There are no precise answers, only blurry perceptions that are not really seen but "felt."

Moreover, campaigns are seldom won or lost by reason of a single "smoking gun" issue unless the issue is a gut wrencher, war or depression. Rather, they are like raucous boxing matches, the candidates dancing in and around one another, each striving to outwit, outmaneuver, and outthink the other. Political instinct is knowing when to strike and when to hold back and seek higher ground, when to let loose the dogs of war and when not to. Each campaign must be alert to sudden shifts in strategy and tactics. A campaign is 24/7, and it is not for the indolent, nor is it for torpid minds and timid spirits.

I did have some tested strategic weapons that I kept always at the ready. First, the campaign theme must be simple, easily understood, and repeated constantly over and over again. Second, never let the opposition divert you from your aims and strategy. Third, when the game gets dirty, don't respond in kind except to instantly knock down accusations that are plainly wrong and potentially lethal. Fourth, it is essential that your candidate be "liked" by the voters. When you have candidates like John Connally and Albert Thomas, that's no chore. But the rest of the field may require some coaching time to plant "likability" where previously the ground may have been barren.

There is an old military term called *friction*, defined as that which happens that was not in your original battle plan. As friction grows, you make adjustments quickly, decisively, and without qualm. Politics is steeped in unpredictability, which means friction is a daily virus. Maybe that's why I liked it so much.

We handled the successful election of Houston's mayor Lewis Cutrer and several campaigns for Congressman Albert Thomas, were in charge of advertising and radio in Texas for the 1960 Kennedy-Johnson presidential campaign, and we co-managed the triumph of John Connally as governor of Texas in 1962. I am immodestly proud of the fact that Weekley & Valenti never lost a political race where we were put in total charge of the creative political advertising. This was why Weldon was pleased when I told him I was going to be involved in the Kennedy-Johnson visit to Texas in November 1963, its centerpiece being the huge dinner honoring Congressman Albert Thomas on November 21, 1963, in the Sam Houston Coliseum, where the president and vice president would be the principal speakers.

Neither Weldon nor I imagined that the spectacular Albert Thomas dinner would be the last day and night I would be an active partner in Weekley & Valenti. Our long, loving, exciting, fruitful, never-once-a-quarrel partnership would be over, although our friendship would endure. Building a new business from scratch turned out to be the grandest fun. We won client after client and never lost a client that had come aboard. It was fiercely hard work, but the way Weldon and I operated in tandem, the work wasn't work at all, it was a challenge, it was exhilarating, it was consuming. God, I loved every minute of it.

Within hours of the end of the Houston dinner, the eleven years Weldon and I had spent together would be over. Weldon would move from success to success until years later when he retired. But it would be different, very different, for both of us. For me it would be a radical revision of my life.

Before the next day had ended, I would be embarked on my new life in the White House.

The Longest Day was about to begin.

PART II

THE
WHITE
HOUSE

Chapter 6

THE GREAT SOCIETY

On one of LBJ's vigorous walks around the circle on the south grounds of the White House, with Vice President Hubert Humphrey.

The first full day of the presidency of Lyndon Johnson came on early. The morning of November 23, 1963, was cold, and after less than three hours' sleep, I woke strangely full of energy. My new life as special assistant to the president of the United States had begun. Everything was all so new. While I could navigate every part of Texas with full confidence, now I was right in the middle of the biggest league of them all, the epicenter of governing power. I can't say I was nervous, but I sure as hell knew I was setting out on the steepest learning curve of my life. I knew I would have important duties to perform, and I was determined not to fall on my ass doing them. I quickly shaved, showered, and presented myself downstairs at the breakfast table of the Johnson home.

Mrs. Johnson was at the table, as was the president, who was on the phone. Federal judge Homer Thornberry (a former congressman who had succeeded LBJ in the Tenth District of Texas before being appointed to the Fifth Circuit Court of Appeals) had just walked in. LBJ nodded to Homer, Cliff Carter, Bill Moyers, and me. The president was speaking to Robert McNamara.

"Bob," he said, "I'm on my way in. Meet me at the office in an hour. I'm in my vice presidential quarters in the EOB [Executive Office Building]."

He put down the phone and said to Moyers, Thornberry, Carter, and me, "You all sleep well last night?"

"Darling," said Mrs. Johnson, "I don't think anyone in America slept well last night. How could they? But most of all," she continued, nodding to us, "how do you feel? You surely didn't get a lot of sleep."

"There's work to be done," said the president. "We've got to get ready for the funeral. There'll be a lot of presidents and prime ministers heading our way." To his wife he said, "Have you talked to Mrs. Kennedy?"

"My dear, it is a bit early, don't you think? I'll talk to her. If ever a human being needs comforting, it's that sad woman. I cannot comprehend how she will hold together after what she has gone through. It's beyond human endurance."

Within twenty minutes, the president, Thornberry, Moyers, Carter, and I were in the presidential limo (soon to become a heavily armored vehicle), heading for the White House. Once in the car, the president got on the phone to Walter Jenkins. If Johnson had had a chief of staff, it would have been Walter, although Jenkins considered himself just another assistant. In the days and months ahead, I came to know Walter very well. I was struck by his kindness, his efficiency, and his total self-effacement. He was utterly devoted to LBJ, with whom he had worked for over twenty years. He was Johnson's closest confidant and the only one who knew everything about LBJ and his family.

It was to be a long, long day. First LBJ stopped by the Oval Office to tell JFK's secretary, Mrs. Lincoln, of his sorrow and to obtain several sheets of presidential White House stationery. He wanted to write a personal note to both Caroline and John Jr. He did not use the Oval Office for any meetings, and he held off moving into the president's office for three more days. He met with Bobby Kennedy to express his deep regret and condolences once again. McGeorge Bundy provided him with a briefing in the Situation Room. CIA director John McCone gave him a private intelligence briefing in his vice presidential quarters, where he would work for the next three days.

For the next several hours, he met and talked on the phone with J. Edgar Hoover, director of the FBI, Mac Bundy, and Bob McNamara, among others. At 11:15, he accompanied Mrs. Johnson to the East Room of the White House to view the coffin of President Kennedy, along with congressional leaders from both parties. Later, after attending a public service for President Kennedy, he met with President Eisenhower. He chatted with Speaker of the House John McCormack about a soon-to-be-announced speech to a joint session of the Congress, followed by more meetings and phone conversations with labor leaders, business leaders, governors, and journalists.

It was a morning of nonstop activity, Johnson seemingly un-daunted by lack of sleep; the day poured into evening. Sometime after 11:00 p.m., the new president wrapped up a seventeen-hour day, his first in office. Once more I rode back with him to his Spring Valley home, which was now my home.

Several days later, the president said to me, "Let's walk a bit before we head to the White House." We emerged from his residence with Secret Service agents fanning out on either side of the president. We began a brisk walk down the street, the president apparently enjoying the crisp, cool morning. I was at his side, wearing an old trench coat, my face grim. The next morning, the *Washington Post* carried a photograph of LBJ in full stride, with a smaller, unsmiling, trench-coated fellow by his side. The caption read, "The President takes an early morning stroll accompanied by an unidentified Secret Service agent." LBJ got a rich laugh out of that.

The Secret Service detail had ballooned to a dozen or more agents. They were everywhere. The Secret Service had lost one president, and they damn sure weren't going to lose another. Suddenly I recalled what LBJ had said to me about a year earlier, in describing a conversation with President Kennedy. JFK was telling LBJ that he had attended a meeting with the head of the Secret Service, who was describing the methodology of presidential protection. President Kennedy told Johnson, "If an assassin is willing to give his own life, no president is safe."

Johnson understood the role of his guardians. He knew these agents would do everything required to carry out that responsibility, including taking a bullet, to save the president's life. Now that no longer seemed like such a remote possibility.

Eleven days after the Dallas nightmare, the Johnsons moved into the White House. They had not disturbed Mrs. Kennedy in all that time. When the former first lady departed, the Johnsons moved in. So did I. I took up residence on the third floor of the Presidential Mansion. The living quarters of the first family were on the second floor. My lodgings were a smallish sitting room, a small bedroom, and a bathroom. As I recall, at that time there were three other little suites on the third floor. Whenever I tell college students how I became a boarder in the White House, I suggest to them if ever they are on

Jeopardy!, the TV quiz show, and they confront the question "Who are the only two assistants to a president who actually lived in the White House?" they can give a ready answer: "Who were Jack Valenti (with LBJ) and Harry Hopkins (with FDR)." (I also make it clear to them that if it is a double Jeopardy question, I want 10 percent of their winnings.)

I came to know that there is a downside to living in such close quarters with a president—especially this president, who slept just four to five hours a night. Whenever the other assistants went home around 8:00 p.m. or so, I stayed. I *was* home. Then, around 10:00 p.m. or so, LBJ would call me to the Oval Office. He'd say, "Let's go upstairs, have a bite, and talk."

We would sit in the family dining room on the second floor of the Mansion, munch on some food, and drink some coffee. He would ask me what I'd been up to that day, how I'd fared with the assignments he had given me, and how the speeches I was tending to were progressing. But most of all, he wanted information—whatever I had heard from members of Congress or had picked up in the press lobby.

He would listen, nod, and ask a few questions. Then he would take off on some problems he had run into during the day. We would go over some of his "night reading," a thick pile of memos from the staff, most of which required presidential decisions, and memos from his cabinet, some of which requested counsel from the president. By the time the conversation came to an end, it was nearly midnight. He would say, "Good night," and I would stumble upstairs to my beloved but mostly underused bed.

Invariably, the phone would ring the next morning between 5:15 and 5:30 a.m. The president's voice would come booming through the handset: "Come on down, Jack, we have work to do. I'll have breakfast ready for you." Dazed, I would fall out of bed, shave (how I avoided cutting my throat in my stupor, I'll never know), shower, and get to the side of the leader of the free world. He would be sitting up in bed (not in the master bedroom), with telephone consoles to his left and papers piled high on a hospital-type hinged table tray. Some food would be sitting in front of him, and to the side was a tray with eggs and fruit on it. My tray. My food.

One morning, the president made his usual 5:15 a.m. call and asked his usual question: "Well, Jack, what are you doing?" That morning, I spoke without thinking (not wise when you're in dialogue with LBJ).

"Mr. President," I said, "I've been lying here hoping that you would call."

My attempt at early morning humor didn't go far. His response was a brittle, "Well, get down here fast."

The Johnson White House staff settled in quickly. LBJ had moved his own people in without fanfare, trying hard not to disturb the still-intact Kennedy staff and cabinet. He had publicly and privately affirmed that as the new president, he would carefully tend the Kennedy legacy. LBJ had vowed to implement JFK's policies, both foreign and domestic, and do his damnedest to pass Kennedy legislation now bottled up in Congress. For the press and others trying to get a handle on Johnson's conduct in those early days of his presidency, understanding his pledge to continue Kennedy's policies was critical. To this end, LBJ went to considerable lengths to hold fast to every Kennedy White House aide and every Kennedy cabinet officer. The Kennedy people who eventually departed all did so on their own schedule, with no pushing from Johnson.

I took up residence at a desk opposite Kenny O'Donnell, Kennedy's chief political aide, in the large office next to the Oval Office. I made a concentrated effort to establish a warm relationship with this laconic, seasoned old Boston pol. I wanted to extract as much knowledge from him as I could. It was not easy. O'Donnell was guarded and always skeptical. But over the days that followed, he came to believe in the authenticity of my admiration for John Kennedy, and he softened visibly.

The essential aspect of my tutelage under O'Donnell was to understand and remember who the key players were in Congress and in the various departments of government. But more important, I needed to know who could be trusted and who could not, whom to court and how, and who needed to be handled some other way. I made it my business to listen more than I talked. I wanted to absorb all I could about Washington's political terrain so that eventually I could move around without O'Donnell's guiding hand. Once O'Donnell felt I was trustworthy, he opened up and I was able to learn quickly. He was not a social animal, but I swiftly understood why JFK wanted him around. If kneecaps had to be busted, Kenny was the guy who could wield the ax handle.

Myself aside, I believe the Johnson staff was the finest ever assembled by a chief executive. This assessment is based not only on their performance in the Johnson White House, but also on their subsequent careers at the highest levels of government, media, education, and business.

Bill Moyers was a native Texan and an ordained Baptist minister who had begun working in LBJ's office in his teens. At age twenty-eight he was appointed deputy director of the Peace Corps, which was organized and run by Sargent Shriver, brother-in-law to JFK. A year later, Bill had become a key member of President Johnson's inner council, and he would go on to serve Johnson as assistant for domestic policy and press secretary. After he left government, Bill became publisher of the Long Island newspaper *Newsday*. From there he stepped into perhaps his best-known role as public broadcasting's most famous television commentator, a shrewd observer of America's frailties, follies, and triumphs.

Also part of LBJ's Senate and vice presidential team was George Reedy, a shambling figure with thick white wildly vagrant hair. A crafty veteran of Washington wars, he would become press secretary when Pierre Salinger was selected to fill a vacant seat in the U.S. Senate from California. Reedy departed the press post owing to illness and later became dean of the School of Journalism at Marquette University and author of several books.

Horace Busby was a graceful prose stylist, a perceptive political observer, and a longtime LBJ counselor. His tenure reached back into LBJ's celebrated 1948 election as U.S. senator. He would go on to publish one of the most widely read political newsletters in the nation's capital.

When Bill Moyers replaced George Reedy as press secretary, he and I called up Joe Califano from Bob McNamara's Pentagon staff to replace Moyers as domestic policy assistant. Califano, a brainy Harvard Law graduate whose round-the-clock work habits became legendary, would become secretary of health, education, and welfare in the Carter administration as well as managing partner of one of

Washington's best-known law firms. The author of five widely respected books, he is now chairman (and founder) of the National Center on Addiction and Substance Abuse, a nonprofit drug abuse research center in New York.

In 1965, Harry McPherson joined the staff. Harry, a brilliant lawyer, was assistant secretary for education at the State Department but had previously worked for LBJ in the Senate and had written a seminal book about that experience. Harry joined us as special counsel. Harry's poetic way with language made him one of the best writers in LBJ's White House.

In 1965, LBJ called in Marvin Watson, a longtime Johnson political ally, whose tenure in the LBJ battalions dated back to the 1941 and 1948 senatorial elections in Texas. Marvin would be in charge of political coordination with the Democratic National Committee and of other inside political issues.

At the same time, the president brought in Douglass Cater to become his assistant. Cater had caught Johnson's eye as a popular, respected writer for the *Reporter* magazine. Cater's White House duties would include serving as chief designer of the Public Broadcasting Service and the National Endowments for the Arts and Humanities. I'll never forget the day LBJ brought Doug to the White House to sort of interview him. "Let's go for a swim, Doug. Okay with you?" said the president. Well, of course it was, so Doug, Bill Moyers, and I followed the president to the swimming pool. Doug's eyes almost popped out when LBJ, Bill, and I threw off our clothes and jumped into the pool, nekkid, as we say in Texas. After a moment's hesitation, Cater stripped and plunged in, too.

As we splashed around, the president began chatting with Doug about his ideas for making the Johnson administration more effective. I daresay many of us have been interviewed in odd places, but as Doug said later, "Nothing compares with my waterlogged birthday-suit interview with the president."

I hired Richard Goodwin to join the speechwriting brigade. I was impressed with his elegant writing style. He had worked in the Kennedy White House, then the State Department. When I met him he was a speechwriter for Sargent Shriver at the Peace Corps. It was Goodwin who came up with "the Great Society," taken from the title of a book written in the earlier part of the century by Graham Wallas. I extracted the phrase from one of the first speeches Goodwin wrote, thinking we should save it for more significant use. It became the canopy for Johnson's rapidly growing social and economic programs for America.

Johnson called on another of his former senatorial aides, Lloyd Hand, to join the staff. Lloyd was a charmer, an extremely bright lawyer with an intuitive feel for handling prickly situations and crafty politicos. LBJ made him chief of protocol and part of his White House staff as well. Lloyd eventually left the White House to run for lieutenant governor of California, in a race that he lost by a whisper. I always believed that if he had won and had gone on to be governor, he would have been a contender for the presidency. And that, dear friends, would have been the highest summit any former LBJ aide would have climbed.

Lloyd's wife, Ann, also became a star in Washington. Several years ago, she surprised her friends by becoming a jewelry designer, swiftly achieving extraordinary success. Powerful women in Washington know that wearing Ann's jewelry designs is a mark of taste and distinction.

In early 1964, I became a fan of Liz Carpenter, Mrs. Johnson's chief of staff. Liz was smarter, funnier, and wiser than almost anyone I met in the extraordinary Johnson White House. She was feisty and possessed of a wit that knew neither rest nor bounds. She was an invaluable member of LBJ's White House cadre.

McGeorge Bundy, national security adviser to President Kennedy, stayed on as Johnson's key foreign policy aide. So did Larry O'Brien, head of the Congressional Liaison Office. These two men, with their vast experience under fire, proved to be crucially important to LBJ. He trusted them and relied on them.

Moyers and I brought three of the very first class of White House Fellows inside the West Wing in 1965. The Fellows was a group created by LBJ with the help of John Gardner, a philosopher, teacher, and author who later became LBJ's secretary of health, education, and welfare. Each year, some fifteen men and women, best of the breed under thirty-five, would come spend a year in Washington at the highest reaches of federal government. Moyers and I plucked the pick of the litter: Tom Johnson, who in later years became publisher of the *Los Angeles Times* and president and CEO of CNN; John DeLuca, who later became the deputy mayor of San Francisco and president of the Wine Institute of America; and Charles Maguire, a crackerjack writer who later became a successful consultant.

My own duties included managing the president's schedule: As appointments secretary, I decided whom he saw, whom he didn't see, and where he should go to speak or make an appearance. Kenny O'Donnell had held this post for Kennedy, and as he put it to me, "Any time you decide who gets to see the president, where he goes, and when, that's real power." I was also in charge of presidential speechwriting and served as a member of LBJ's inner task force on Vietnam. During my White House tenure, I attended every meeting the president convened on that tragic conflict.

The speechwriting design apparatus for President Johnson was the same as in the Kennedy White House. In the Kennedy White House, the line staff assistants composed JFK's speeches under the direction of Ted Sorensen, who was special counsel and also primary speechwriter. It worked the same way with the Johnson speechwriting brigade. The special assistants to the president, those who were on the daily firing line of White House policy, did the writing. This meant that in the Johnson White House, the speeches were written by Moyers, Busby, McPherson, Califano, Reedy, Goodwin, Cater, Bundy, and me. Like the Kennedy staff, we had no specially designated "hit team" of nameless, faceless speechwriters caged in the Executive Office Building across the way from the West Wing.

It was my responsibility to assign each speech to a special assistant and to work with the writer and the president on the editing to make sure it was what LBJ wanted, in both style and substance. Beginning with the Nixon White House, speechwriters have been housed in baronial offices in the Executive Office Building across West Executive Avenue, half a world away from the West Wing. Believe me when I say that each of those talented writers would have given a kidney to be housed in a broom closet in the West Wing, simply because that was where the Sun King dwelled.

Many years later, William Safire, *New York Times* columnist, and I and others formed the Judson Welliver Society, composed of former speechwriters to presidents and named after the first White House speechwriter (in the administration of Warren G. Harding). We meet irregularly at dinners where we invite writers in the current administration to join us. Our agenda is to tell war stories. It's a bit self-indulgent, but it's good for laughs and to revive those memories of past literary glory.

Neither Kennedy nor Johnson had a chief of staff, which any political pundit will tell you is quite surprising. A chief of staff has been standard equipment in every White House beginning with President Eisenhower, brought back by President Nixon, and employed by every president since. So how on earth did the West Wing function without one? Simply put: very, very well. Each assistant had an area with which he or she was tasked, whether it was domestic policy, foreign policy, legal matters, press relations, appointments, cabinet relations, secretarial functions, speechwriting, political issues, cultural affairs, or congressional matters. Each top assistant had the authority to insert into the president's "night reading" any memorandum on any subject. Each assistant could see the president any time LBJ had a free moment, and immediately if the matter was urgent. From time to time, the president would invite top aides to sit in on cabinet meetings—gatherings with the secretaries of state, the Treasury, or defense and the attorney general—or he might call his assistants together in the Oval Office to discuss key issues and trade information.

If the attorney general had a problem, he would call the special counsel. The Departments of State and Defense would call the national security adviser, members of Congress called the congressional assistant, and so on. But some key members would call any one of the special assistants with whom he or she had a relationship. The LBJ White House was wide open to communications with those the president deemed to be crucial to his aims, mainly members of Congress on both sides of the aisle. No member was left behind.

One of the assets of such an arrangement was that no one person on the White House staff was the nexus of all wisdom and information. When there is a chief of staff, he or she inevitably becomes the exclusive funnel through which all information flows to the president. I believe one reason JFK and LBJ were able to recruit the ablest and most talented to serve in the White House was that it was a house of equals, all of whom had ample access to the president and all of whom were involved in decision-making meetings.

I've mentioned that the quality LBJ valued above all others in his White House staff was loyalty. As he put it, "If you are the smartest fellow in the room, but you aren't bound by loyalty to the president, you are not useful." Loyalty according to Johnson meant "You won't ever betray the president." Sometimes loyalty to the president exceeded normal limits, which takes us to the story of how the "great wall" almost got built.

Marvin Watson is a first-class public servant, a deeply religious man whose connection with Johnson dated back to early LBJ days in Texas. He was there for LBJ's first run for the Senate in 1941, which he lost to Governor W. Lee ("Pappy") O'Daniel in an election marred by O'Daniel's manipulation of the way votes were reported. Marvin was so loyal to Johnson that anything the president ordered him to do he did without hesitation, never once questioning the instruction.

All this is background to a phone call I received from Joe Califano a year after I had departed the White House for Hollywood. "Jack," said Califano in a voice charged with frustration, "we have a problem. It seems the president and Marvin were strolling outside the entrance to the West Wing, and the president was made aware that his off-the-record guests coming in through the West Basement could be seen by reporters lurking outside. He went a bit off the handle. He ordered Marvin to build a wall shielding the West Basement entry from the front of the White House."

"Not a good idea," I said, though I wasn't pointing out anything Joe had not already figured out for himself.

"That's why I'm calling," he said. "The staff thinks it's crazy and will cause all kinds of bad press for no good reason. We've decided you have to get involved. We've all struck out."

I agreed I would try to intervene. That day, I called the president and asked if I could see him. He told me to come in the afternoon of the next day. I called Joe back and reported I would see LBJ. "Well, you'd better hurry. I think Marvin has already got the mortar mixing and is now stacking the bricks."

The next day, I greeted the president in the Oval Office. He was in pretty good spirits. "Mr. President," I said, "I just heard about the wall you're building. I congratulate you. This is something we should have done a long time ago."

The president grunted his approval. I went on, "Those pesky reporters shouldn't have a clear line of vision to your off-the-record guests, and this will definitely put a stop to that. The nosy bastards."

LBJ smiled.

"Of course," I said, "we'll all have to hunker down while the press has a field day with this. I can imagine Herb Block's cartoon now [Herb Block at the *Washington Post* was one of the nation's premier political cartoonists], and TV comedians will be all over this with their ridiculous jokes. But it will be great not to have any more snooping reporters jotting down the names of folks coming in the West Basement. To hell with the barrage of bad jokes about you and the wall. You'll have the satisfaction of knowing you are right, even if a lot of folks do find it very funny."

I could see Johnson's eyes narrow. He said nothing, but the heavy eyelids were a sign that he was moving into full combat mode. He looked at me intently, still mute. Then he got up and said, "I've got a meeting now. Thanks for coming by."

The next day, Califano called, his voice jubilant this time. "I don't know what the devil you did, Jack, but the wall won't go up. All of us owe you dinner."

When you're part of the president's staff in the White House, there is one lesson you absolutely have to learn. You may have said or written almost anything in your private life and no one noticed, but say something like it now as a presidential assistant and you could find yourself in a pile of tar and turds. Or to put it another way, one learns quickly in the big league of national politics that even a completely innocent comment can bring down heaps of outrage and ridicule if the timing is off or if it's a slow news day and you've just put some ripe red meat on the spit.

On June 8, 1965, I flew to Boston to make a keynote address to the American Advertising Federation, one of the premier advertising associations in the country. It was one of the rare times I left the

White House for something other than presidential business. Since I was now at the right hand of the new president, the AAF thought I would be a good draw.

It was a packed house. I had done my homework, and I knew the speech cold. I admit I thought it found a responsive audience. Mostly the speech was about my new duties in the White House—the kind of thing that was almost always well received. I returned to Washington the same day, and when I got back to the White House, the press office had left me several messages informing me that there was a run on copies of my Boston speech. George Reedy, the press secretary, and his aides were in a state of bewilderment.

"What the hell did you say that is so damn interesting to the press?" Reedy wanted to know.

"Read it," I told him. "There's nothing there that is classified information."

Reedy shook his head. He knew better. And sure enough, the press had seized on one of my lines—"I sleep better at night because Lyndon Johnson is my president"—with unbridled hilarity. The ridicule fell in torrents. Herb Block's cartoon in the *Post* depicted a Simon Legree–type plantation owner whipping a Valenti look-alike slave who's crying out, "I sleep better at night because Lyndon Johnson is President."

I did suggest to a couple of friends in the press to reread the last paragraph of the speech. I review it here for those who read this book to judge for themselves:

Once during the deadly days of the Nazi terror, when France had been overrun and the heel of the Nazi boot was on the neck of the French, Winston Churchill spoke to the French people: "Français! C'est moi, Churchill." He told them not to lose heart, that in due time the free world would stir itself and relieve the French of their long night.

"So," he said, "sleep well, my Frenchmen, sleep well to gather strength for the morning, for the morning shall come."

I sleep each night a little better, a little more confidently because Lyndon Johnson is my President. For I know he lives and thinks and works to make sure that for all Americans, and indeed, the growing body of the free world, the morning shall always come.

What the hell could I do except hunker down and take it? But that line stuck to me like a recurring rash. Years later, I flew to Austin to make a speech at the Headliners Club and afterward drove to the LBJ ranch to spend the night with the retired president. I told him, "I can't escape that line. In Austin today, the master of ceremonies introduced me by saying, 'This is Jack Valenti, who once said that he sleeps better at night because Lyndon Johnson is president.'"

Johnson eyed me with some mirth. "I don't know why you get so upset, Jack. Do you know how few presidential assistants ever say anything memorable?"

Actually, that made a lot of sense to me.

LBJ's Courting of Senator Harry Byrd to Free the Kennedy Tax Cut

From the first day of his presidency, Lyndon Johnson had firmly latched on to four key priorities: civil rights in all its forms; health insurance for the elderly (Medicare); federal aid to education; and the Kennedy tax cut. For each of these priorities, LBJ had a timeline. Because he was convinced by Walter Heller, chairman of the White House Council of Economic Advisers, that a tax cut was indispensable to increased prosperity, and because Johnson knew his Great Society required a growing economy, he put that at the head of the list. So in early 1964, LBJ had his gun sights trained on the tax cut stuck in the Senate Finance Committee, whose master and chairman was Senator Harry Flood Byrd from Virginia. All of President Kennedy's remarkable powers of persuasion had made no impact on the courtly, cunning Virginia senator, who kept a firm hold on his committee. The tax cut was in solitary confinement, unable to get to the Senate floor.

The Byrds of Virginia were as close to a First Family as it is possible to be in Virginia. The senator's brother was Admiral Richard Byrd, the celebrated explorer of the Arctic. Senator Byrd tended his power in the Senate as he cultivated his apple orchards, which lay blissfully productive on the beautiful acres of the Byrd estates. Both his power and his apples were ripe, fat, and shiny. One of the very first visits paid by the new president was a helicopter trip to the Winchester mansion of the senator.

Harry Byrd was neither an easy target nor an accommodating one. Budging Byrd from his immovable position, according to the congressional liaison people who had managed Kennedy's Capitol Hill affairs, was a chore to be ranked with Hercules' cleansing of the Augean stables. But Hercules had one advantage: He was divinely inspired. Alas, only ordinary mortals were available to deal with Senator Byrd.

President Johnson knew Byrd intimately from his Senate majority leader days. He and Byrd had a mutual respect for each other. They had worked together in the Senate whenever the issue or its outcome moved them. Both Johnson and Byrd treated each other with a congeniality fed by the realities of power and influence, for each man had ample stores of both.

LBJ determined he must approach this most regal of Senate proconsuls with great care. He invited the Virginian to lunch with him on December 5, 1963. This was to be no ordinary luncheon. Its setting was the small office just off the Oval Office of the president. It was the first time Johnson had hosted a lunch there. He took great pains to make certain everything was perfect, selecting the menu himself. The president invited me to sit with him through the lunch as a working assistant and friendly observer. Senator Byrd was characteristically gracious to me.

The two of them ate at their leisure, refreshing the meal with quiet reminiscences of Senate days. As the president poked aimlessly at his dessert, he said easily, "Harry, that tax cut is mighty important to me."

Byrd, impassive, his cheeks pink and cherubic, replied, "Now, Mr. President, you know that we cannot have a tax cut without serious cuts in the budget, substantial cuts."

"Yes," said the president calmly, "but my latest studies tell me I would be fortunate, really fortunate, if I could get it down below $105 or $107 billion." (Today, that would be chump change.)

"Too big, Mr. President, too big," said Byrd, shaking his head.

The president continued to toy with his dessert, swirling a remnant of ice cream with his spoon. "Hmm. Well, Harry, just suppose—

and I say just suppose, because I don't think it can realistically be done—just suppose I could get the budget down somewhere under $100 billion, what would you say then?"

The senator leaned forward, his ancestral genes on full display as he reached for a glass of water with assured grace. He sipped before replying.

"Mr. President, I would say that if you got the budget under $100 billion, we might be able to do some talking."

The president's face moved closer to Byrd, craning across the small table until they were almost nose to nose. "Harry, I am going to try my damnedest to somehow get the budget under a hundred, and if I do, will the tax cut come out of your committee?"

Byrd moved back ever so slightly to escape Johnson's advance. He tugged at his earlobe. "Yes, I would say if you can bring in a budget less than $100 billion, I think it is quite possible the committee members would consider bringing the bill to the floor, though I can't speak for them personally."

The president knew that if Byrd was amenable, the committee would damn sure consider the tax cut, and if Byrd nodded, the committee would send the bill to the floor. Johnson also knew that once Byrd pledged his word, it was unbreakable. The president got up quickly, stuck out his hand, and said, "Harry, we've got a deal. It's been good spending time together. I don't see enough of you."

With one arm under the elbow of the senior senator from Virginia, the president escorted Byrd to the door. Then he got on the phone to Kermit Gordon, director of the Bureau of the Budget. "Get in here, Kermit, and bring a meat cleaver. We have some butchery to perform on the budget."

When, a week later at a press conference, Johnson announced a budget of some $98 billion, it was a stunner to the press and the public. No one expected such a low number. True to his word, Senator Byrd cut the shackles on the Kennedy tax bill. The committee voted it onto the floor, and it passed easily. Johnson, with great enjoyment, signed the bill six hours after it was cleared by the Congress. Johnson did have flaws, but sitting around after a bill he had fought for was ready to be signed into law was not one of them.

LBJ's Titanic Struggle for Civil Rights
and Human Justice

The next test of LBJ's leadership was what came to be known as the
Civil Rights Act of 1964. It had to run the gauntlet, as Johnson so
well knew, of the all-powerful southern senators who ruled the standing committees. Lying in the shadows was the filibuster, which could
tie the Senate into parliamentary knots, bring debate to a halt, and
kill the bill. Johnson knew he had to hit this head-on. He needed
more than a simple majority. He had to assemble enough votes to
stave off a filibuster. Cloture (which overrides any attempt to filibuster) requires a two-thirds vote, and with all one hundred senators
voting, that meant locking up sixty-seven votes, which in turn required the support of Senator Everett Dirksen, minority leader of
the Senate. The capstone of the Johnson presidency, insofar as LBJ
was concerned, would be achieving his far-reaching agenda for civil
rights and human justice. Now he was being put to the test.

One night, as he was preparing to fire the opening salvo in the
most important political battle for human justice in the history of
the Republic, LBJ called me into the Oval Office. He had been on
the phone most of the day, testing the waters for his civil rights bill
with key members of Congress. Casually, I mentioned some reading
I'd been doing about a historic political meeting that had taken place
in St. Mary's Church, Putney, England, in 1647. There, the officers
of Oliver Cromwell's New Model army had gathered. General Henry
Ireton, the lord protector's son-in-law, had called the meeting, which
turned into an unexpected debate.

General Ireton made it clear in an impassioned speech that he
wanted to confer voting rights only on those who owned property. As
he finished speaking, a tall, rangy man stood up. He was Colonel
Thomas Rainsborough, a man of humble origins who, through highly
effective leadership under fire, had been personally promoted for
valor on the battlefield to the highest ranks in the army by Cromwell
himself.

Facing Ireton, he said in a calm voice, "The poorest he in England has as much rights as the richest he in England." As he went on
to enlarge on that theme, the convened officers murmured their ap-

proval of Rainsborough's courage. Although Rainsborough's simple words did not carry that day, his belief shaped England's values of freedom and liberty and later found its fullest flowering in the American dream.

After I finished my story of the Putney meeting, LBJ nodded approvingly. He asked me to repeat the last part of the story, which I did. He had never heard of either Colonel Rainsborough or General Ireton, but if anyone ever understood the political philosophy of Colonel Rainsborough, it was Lyndon Johnson. Johnson's own humble beginnings in Texas, and his rapport with the poor and the undervalued, were never more than a millimeter beneath the surface of his passions. It was a side of LBJ that many, particularly liberal Democrats from the East and the Northeast, would never fully understand.

Readers of this book today may find it difficult to imagine just how thick the minefields were that stood between Johnson and his desire to right civil wrongs for blacks in the nation. The barriers were cultural, psychological, and, above all, political. Southerners ruled the Senate committees and, by extension, the Senate itself. Their expert knowledge of parliamentary rules that guided Senate procedure made them proof against any maverick colleagues who chose to contest their will. No president before LBJ had dared to confront the human injustices that divided the country by region, religion, and race. LBJ had no illusions. It would be a bitter, bare-knuckled struggle, but he had to win. Failure was not an option—at least not the way he saw it.

Johnson's special assistants as well as his congressional liaison staffers were mounted up and ordered to ride into the corridors of the House and Senate. As a southerner myself I was one of his aides dispatched to take on members from states and districts below the Mason-Dixon Line. When I visited the members on my list, my approach to win support for the civil rights bill went something like this: "Sir, you know this bill is right, and you know it is needed. It really is just basic Christian doctrine being set into law." I would continue invoking Christian duty and the spirit of our Founding Fathers, until I ran out of steam. Then I brought out the velvet glove. "I think you know the president will win the election this November. He will be in office for at least four more years, maybe eight. With that in mind, he wants you to know he will always remember your vote for him on this bill."

The moment was usually followed by silence on the part of the member as he considered that potentially rich reward. And this time I let the member catch a glimpse of the steel behind the glove. "And the president also wants you to know he will never forget your vote against him on this bill."

Hardball? Bare-knuckle barroom tactics? Yes and yes. But it was the best way I could think of to convey just how determined the president was to see this bill pass. Some members didn't take kindly to my approach. Their backs stiffened or their hackles went up. I expected that. But I knew that when I left their offices, they would not be treating my message with casual regard. They knew that to lose this highest priority of his agenda would not be forgiven. They knew LBJ could be, as we say in Texas, "one tough sumbitch." With a president in the White House who was the odds-on favorite to win in November, our appeals would not be ignored. On the other hand, Johnson's southern opponents would not take kindly to our full-court press. They would be angry.

At this point, the key entreaty belonged to LBJ, as he personally reached out quietly to the Republican leader of the Senate, Everett Dirksen of Illinois. Both sides had girded for war over the civil rights bill, with the specter of a filibuster brooding over every debate. When the time finally came for a vote, in a moment that later would be described as "momentous," Senator Dirksen rose to speak from his minority leader's desk. He ended his remarks by saying, "This calls for cloture and the enactment of a civil rights bill."

It was over. The Republican minority leader had thrown his weight behind the president. The southern senators were dismayed, but their ranks were broken, and the Civil Rights Act was signed into law on July 2, 1964, a few hours after it had been passed by the House. With the aid of Senator Everett Dirksen, the president had achieved the second of his top priorities, the Civil Rights Act of 1964, within months of his first.

Next on the agenda was the Voting Rights Act, an indispensable cornerstone in building a fortress of protection for civil dignity. This time, the pressures bore in on Johnson from the black civil rights leaders, from the liberal wing of his own party, and from his close advisers. But LBJ refused to be stampeded into a vote on the floor he was not certain he could win. Wily Texas poker player that he was, he waited for the right cards. Timing was everything. Like a panther on a hillside, LBJ was patient. He would know when the time was ready to spring.

On March 7, 1965, a day that would become known as "Bloody Sunday," six hundred civil rights advocates moved out of Selma, Alabama, onto U.S. Route 80 to cross the Edmund Pettus Bridge. Their destination was Montgomery. They were met by a large contingent of Alabama State troopers with nightsticks, dogs, and tear gas at the ready. The marchers, led by Hosea Williams and John Lewis (Lewis would later become a congressman from Atlanta), were barred from moving from the center of the bridge by a converging battalion of officers. When they tried to continue their march, the troopers moved in with nightsticks flailing. One trooper hit Lewis across the head, and as he slumped to the ground, the trooper fell on him, slamming his heavy club into Lewis's chest, face, and head. Lewis was near death when the beating stopped. Blood streamed in rivulets all over the bridge as the civil rights marchers were viciously beaten. That night, the national TV networks broke into their regular programs to show the assault on the marchers. Viewers, including President Johnson, were revulsed. It was ugly.

Two days later, James Reeb, a Unitarian minister from Boston, was attacked by three white men while he was eating dinner in a black restaurant in Selma. The black community erupted in anger, and a lot of white people felt the stirrings of shame. I sat with the president, taking stock of this racial turmoil gripping the country.

"Any news?" he said.

"Not really, Mr. President, but if Reeb dies, all hell will break loose."

LBJ was somber. "Let's go over what I'm going to say to the members this evening." Johnson was preparing to unveil his voting rights bill to a group of congressmen at the White House, in advance of a televised speech to a joint session of the Congress he was planning for the following Monday. The moment had come. Johnson knew he had to seize this racial turbulence and put it in service of the nation. The time for his long-planned Voting Rights Act had finally arrived.

In the middle of the president's congressional briefing, I got word that James Reeb had died. It was a terrible moment. The president, with Vice President Humphrey in tow, quickly took the private elevator to his living quarters on the second floor of the Mansion. They got on the phone to call Mrs. Reeb.

Meanwhile, the fates were busily working to help the president. George Wallace, governor of Alabama and an unrepentant segregationist, gave Johnson a surprise gift. Late in the afternoon of Friday, October 12, a UPI story reported that Governor Wallace had sent a telegram to the president requesting an immediate meeting to talk about the Selma incident, which the UPI story quoted the governor as saying "posed a great internal problem." LBJ knew that providence could turn tragedy into triumph—and that this could be one of those times.

LBJ acted quickly. Without even seeing the telegram itself, he fired back a response: "Yes, Mr. Governor, I would be happy to meet with you. How about tomorrow?"

Johnson believed wholeheartedly that southerners ought to talk to southerners. They spoke the same language, having come from similar cultures and traditions. So some weeks before, LBJ had pressed his old friend Buford Ellington, governor of Tennessee, into service. Ellington's task was to persuade Wallace to meet with the president to see if together they could clean up the mess this human conflict was causing. Now, Wallace, who had been doing a little dance with Ellington, was giving LBJ what he sorely wanted, to go mano a mano with the Alabama governor. The governor's strategy was to try to turn public attention away from police brutality to protesters who were blatantly breaking the law, those whom Wallace called "agitators."

It was noon on Saturday, March 13, just six days after the beatings on the bridge in Selma. Into the Oval Office came Governor Wallace. In the room with the president were Nick Katzenbach, Dick Goodwin, and I. We stood nearby observing how Johnson's large frame dwarfed the smallish Wallace. They were certainly a political odd couple. I watched Wallace closely. He had a prizefighter's face, with flat features that might have been smashed a number of times in the ring when he fought as a bantamweight boxer. His head was round, with thin lips that looked as though they didn't smile much. He carried himself carefully, not looking up into LBJ's face.

It was a scene worthy of Steven Spielberg. The diminutive Wallace settled into the beige couch, with Johnson sitting in his customary rocking chair. Johnson pushed the rocker closer to Wallace, who leaned back in the cushy sofa as far as he could, probably wondering why the hell he had sought a meeting with this president who was either going to physically assault him or swallow him whole. LBJ motioned for Wallace to speak his piece, since he had asked for the audience, and the governor launched into a rant about Communists and "outside agitators." When the governor was done, LBJ said, "Now, George, I know what you ought to do, and that is open up Alabama's schools to kids of all races. You can do that. You've got the power to do it."

Wallace, looking as helpless as a gaffed trout, insisted he didn't have the authority to do that, "because the power belongs to the local school boards, not the governor."

Johnson was not buying it. "George, don't shit me, you can do whatever you choose to do." He paused, then said, "You spent all your life working to help the poor. Why are you doing this? Why are you off on this Negro thing?"

Then Johnson's voice softened as he said, "Think about 1988, George. You and I will be dead and gone. What do you want to leave behind? Do you want a marble monument that reads, 'George Wallace, He Built,' or do you want a piece of pine board that reads, 'George Wallace, He Hated'?" Wallace was now clearly spent, breathing heavily. Here he was, allowing himself to be crushed under the weight of this mad brute from Texas, doubtless wondering why the hell he had ever left the safety of his home state.

LBJ took Governor Wallace by the arm to escort him to the Rose Garden and the waiting press. When the governor shook my hand on the way out, it seemed to me that he had shrunk before my eyes. LBJ told the assembled reporters that the next march from Selma to Montgomery would be peaceful, and it was. Wallace wasn't converted into a civil rights advocate, but Johnson had taken something out of him that affected the tone of public discourse, for the better, even in Wallace's home state. But only after the failed assassination of Wallace some years later, which confined him to a wheelchair for the rest of his life, did he seem to change course as Johnson had urged him to.

Monday, March 15, came early. LBJ once more went over the written remarks that he would present to the nation and a Joint Session of the Congress at 9 p.m. that evening. Now it was time for him to lay out the reasons why he would not agree to anything less than full voting privileges for all Americans. I walked with the president through the Diplomatic Reception Room alongside Marvin Watson and Larry O'Brien. At 8:46, fourteen minutes before his scheduled address, the president, O'Brien, Watson, and I stepped into the presidential limo, which pulled away from the South Entrance of the White House heading to the Capitol.

LBJ gazed silently out the window, seemingly engrossed in the night. Marvin, Larry, and I didn't try to furnish any chitchat. For some reason, a passage from Shakespeare's *Julius Caesar* kept running through my mind: "There is a tide in the affairs of men / Which taken at the flood, leads on to fortune; / Omitted, all the voyage of their life / Is bound in shallows and in miseries." This night was Johnson's flood tide. Tonight he would take the nation to a place where no president save Lincoln had ever ventured.

Right on schedule, "Fishbait" Miller, the long-serving doorkeeper of the House, bellowed the traditional introduction: "Mr. Speaker, the president of the United States." Johnson strode with firm steps down the aisle. Hands reached out to touch him or to catch a fleeting handshake. The chamber was packed with nearly all 535 members of both bodies. Ambassadors, justices of the high court, cabinet members, military brass, and guests in the galleries filled every seat.

The staff—Moyers, Busby, Goodwin, Watson, Califano, McPherson, O'Brien, and I—were standing on the side of the House chamber with a full view of the president as he mounted the rostrum to be introduced by the Speaker of the House, John McCormack from Massachusetts, intoning the ritual words that Speakers have used for over half a century on every such occasion: "It is my distinct honor and high privilege to present to you the president of the United States."

The president's speech had been swiftly put together but exhaustively vetted by a number of us, most usefully and finally by LBJ himself. The first draft was composed by Dick Goodwin. Moyers, Busby, and I had been involved in the editing. But LBJ was the key author; he'd made it clear to us what he wanted to say.

The House chamber's occupants listened to Johnson's words, some warily, some with hope, some with hostility. As Johnson moved through his indictment of a society that would allow terrible disparities in the dispensing of justice, he made it plain that the time had come to balance the scales. Then he came to what he rightly judged to be the crux of his argument: "Their cause [the Negro cause] must be our cause. Because it is not just Negroes, but really it is all of us who must overcome the crippling legacy of bigotry and injustice." He leaned forward, peering over the rostrum into the eyes of the assembly in front of him, as the audience sat preternaturally quiet, not quite sure what to do or feel. Then in pure Johnsonian fervor, the personal touch that Johnson had inserted in the speech: "And we shall overcome."

It is hard to describe the frenzy that followed. The entire assembly was on its feet, applauding, some members shrieking, crying out, and hugging one another. I cannot speak for the rest of the staff standing next to me, but I daresay their veins, like mine, were bursting with blood that rushed from head and heart. God, it was magnificent.

But Johnson was not through. In a passage he had rewritten, he spoke both tenderly and firmly. "I never thought then, in 1928 [while he was teaching school to destitute Mexican American children in Cotulla, Texas], that I would be standing here tonight. It never occurred to me in my fondest dreams I might have the chance to help the sons and daughters of those students and to help people like them all over the United States." He hesitated, again fixing his gaze on faces upturned to him. Then he said confidently, "But now I do have that chance, and I'll let you in on a little secret." A slight pause. "I mean to use it."

Once more, an audience whose emotional exhaustion had almost reached its limits, nonetheless sprang to its feet, applauding, whooping. Afterward, every senator and congressman I spoke with told me that this was a night they would always remember. One member from what we southerners call "Yankee country" said to me, "I never really cared much for those arrogant Texans, no personal offense to you, Jack. But I've got to admit, I underwent a divine conversion when I heard Lyndon Johnson. He made me proud to be an American."

The Voting Rights Act was passed on April 4, 1965, its opponents bowing to overwhelming public support. Johnson's approval rating soared to 70 percent. History records that in the tiny span of four months, President Johnson, in the first session of the Eighty-ninth Congress, had pulled off one of the most astonishing achievements of the modern presidency.

On April 11, 1965, the Congress approved the Elementary and Secondary Education Act, the first time in the life of the Republic that the federal government was authorized to offer aid to education at the elementary and secondary school levels. It was an ingeniously composed piece of legislation. The bill did not offer grants to individual school systems, which would have barred Catholic schools from being part of the final measure because of constitutional restrictions. Instead it provided grants to individual students, thereby finessing constitutional barriers. Now, for the first time, students could go to college with loans, scholarships, and grants provided by the federal government. After a walloping victory, Johnson signed this legislation into law at the little schoolhouse he had attended as a boy in Stonewall, Texas.

On July 28, 1965, Johnson flew to Independence, Missouri, and with former president Truman by his side signed the bill that created Medicare, medical aid to the elderly. It marked the fulfillment of a pledge by Johnson to pass Harry Truman's medical insurance bill that had never cleared Congress during Truman's tenure. LBJ was never happier than when he put his signature to that bill with a grateful ex-president at his elbow.

What Johnson had done was hit the presidential and congressional "trifecta." It is a record-breaking, stunning triple victory that may never be duplicated.

More than any other national leader, Johnson always heard the ticking of the electoral clock. He never fell victim to the illusion that one success would lead to a never-ending victory roll. He knew that from one moment to the next, the tides could turn. The public could develop amnesia, and the accomplishments of an administration could be barely remembered, if at all. He kept urging his staff and his cabinet, "Let's get as much done as we can while we can, because sooner or later it's all going to end." But even LBJ, whose sixth sense was exquisitely honed, did not realize that it would be Vietnam that would derail the nation's sense of purpose and would wound Johnson himself so terribly that he would voluntarily leave office before his Great Society was fully realized.

An unforgettable night in October 1964, with LBJ running against Barry Goldwater and campaigning for Bobby Kennedy in his race for the U.S. Senate at an intersection in Manhattan, with thousands of New Yorkers going wild with enthusiasm. There we are: the unidentified leader of this Italian neighborhood, the president, me, and Bobby Kennedy, our arms raised in a triumphant forecast of the election. I kind of liked the applause.

LYNDON JOHNSON AND BOBBY KENNEDY

There are few subjects guaranteed to pique public interest and stir public debate more than the uneasy relationship between Lyndon Johnson and Robert Kennedy. Between these two resolute and complex men there would develop a mutual antagonism that was baffling to both friends and observers. I couldn't help but feel saddened by that turn of events, for had these two men set aside their differences, they could have constructed a political combination unbeatable by any known political force.

My first meeting with Bobby Kennedy was an unlikely encounter, to say the least. It was in the very early part of 1964, a few weeks after LBJ assumed the presidency and before Bobby had resigned as attorney general, though there was speculation in the press that he was preparing to make some move. He came to the White House to attend a cabinet meeting. I had just stepped into the corridor outside the president's office heading toward that same meeting. Bobby Kennedy and Mike Feldman, a former JFK aide, were striding briskly by. We were all on our way to the Cabinet Room for the meeting with the president.

Bobby stopped in front of me. I looked at him and smiled, but before I could say anything, he spoke to me brusquely. "I don't appreciate the leaks coming from the White House and from you. I suggest you cut it out." His face was deadpan, his gray eyes like granite. To say I was stunned is one of the great understatements of the decade. My surprise was amplified by the fact that I had just learned what a leak was, so green was I to the Washington jungle. I stammered something, I can't remember exactly what. Bobby turned and strode off, with Feldman in tow.

I recovered from my shock as best I could and followed Bobby to the Cabinet Room. Feldman had already doubled back to his office, and I took my seat behind the president's chair. Bobby sat in the attorney general's chair, two seats from the president and not more than three feet from me. He never looked at me, nor I at him, though I did sneak a glance at him for a brief second or two.

I brooded about this all the next day. It was clear to me that Bobby had singled me out as the source of stories published in the press about him and his relationship to the president and about the probability of Bobby being the vice presidential nominee. But stories about LBJ and Bobby were floating all over Washington, and for the life of me I could not pinpoint any one specific story Bobby might be referring to.

When I reported Kennedy's accusation about me to the president, he nodded and said, "This is not about you, Jack. This is about me. Don't let this bother you." But it did.

I could not imagine why Bobby thought I was his enemy. First, whatever else I might have been doing, I was not leaking anything to the press. Second, to this point it had never occurred to me that anyone would have to choose between Kennedy and Johnson—not that this would have been a difficult choice for me. I had no difficulty being totally loyal to President Johnson and at the same time honoring the younger brother around whose shoulders the entire Kennedy legend was now wrapped. But if there was any truth to the rumors in Washington, perhaps the time was coming when Bobby's ambitions and those of the president could no longer run parallel—especially if Bobby was beginning to cast a covetous eye on the presidency itself.

For the moment, anyway, the issue seemed to be the vice presidency. Tension about whom Johnson would choose as his running mate was seeping into every cranny of the White House, and everyone who worked there knew it. The machinations of Kennedy partisans, the tiptoeing around the subject that was the staff ballet in the West Wing, the unsettling political climate it was creating: All these were building to a head. I myself favored Hubert Humphrey for the post, as did most of the Johnson White House aides. I was convinced he was the choice the president was going to make. Yet not all the political signs pointed to that conclusion.

On June 4, 1964, the president and Bobby Kennedy met in the Oval Office. The subject was the Olympic games, in which Bobby took a strong interest. They talked together for one hour and twenty minutes behind closed doors, while reporters in the West Lobby worked themselves up into various stages of hysteria. What were the president and Bobby talking about? Olympic games? As our British cousins might say, "Not bloody likely." Give it to us straight; it's the vice presidency, isn't it? And so it went.

Kenny O'Donnell, chatting with me while our two principals closeted themselves, said that the New York papers were going to carry a story in tomorrow's editions that Bobby was preparing to resign from the cabinet and run for the Senate in New York. O'Donnell didn't elaborate on this, and I didn't press the point. Then Dave Powers, an intimate aide to JFK, came in, his usually cheerful Irish face in torment. A large group of photographers and reporters had clustered around the attorney general's limousine outside the West Basement, and Powers had just ordered it moved to the South Grounds, which was off-limits to the press.

Finally, Bobby emerged from the Oval Office. He nodded perfunctorily to me. His mood seemed pleasant enough—certainly not the demeanor of a man whose political hopes had just been dashed. O'Donnell and Powers accompanied him through the rear of the West Wing to where his car was waiting. During the rest of the day, although I was in and out of the president's office, LBJ offered no account of the meeting. I said nothing.

The next morning, as we ate an early breakfast in the president's bedroom, he mentioned Bobby's visit for the first time. "I was very impressed with Bobby yesterday," he said. "He was right up to snuff on his facts, knew them cold, and made a very fine presentation. Damn able."

"Did you discuss anything else?" I asked.

"Yes, we did," said the president. "I asked him about the civil rights program and told him I was going to move it forward if I did nothing else. All in all, it was a good meeting."

The next day, O'Donnell again raised the subject of RFK. He said he believed that if Bobby and the president were to spend more time together privately, their relationship would grow closer. Bobby, he said, was increasingly impressed with the president's steadfast resolve in the face of opposition, particularly on civil rights. O'Donnell was scornful of several of RFK's junior aides, and he came down especially hard on Paul Corbin, an assistant of some kind who seemed to have been stirring up support for Bobby for vice president.

I offered no comment one way or the other. What passed through my mind was a question about O'Donnell's intentions in making his contempt for Corbin so obvious. Was this a false scent across the trail? Could Corbin really have been acting on his own, without approval from the attorney general? It struck me as a bit unusual for Ken to be so outspoken about people who might be considered part of his own band of brothers.

For the president, the day's schedule wore on. He met with the national coal policy people, with John L. Lewis and his mine union executives, and with the coal mine owners in a forty-five-minute session. Then he called in O. A. Knight and his oil, atomic, and chemical union executives to meet the coal group as the Lewis group left. LBJ enjoyed mingling union leaders and business executives in the same room. It was part of his long-held belief that getting people of disparate views in a room together was bound to produce something better than a stalemate. It was all very fraternal, this odd mix, and LBJ found it all splendidly attractive.

It was nearing 7:00 p.m. on June 5, 1964, after these union conferences had finally concluded, when the president told me to accompany him to the Situation Room in the basement of the White House. At that time, the Situation Room, centerpiece of strategy planning for the White House, was located in the basement of the West Wing, amid a warren of small offices and cubicles that constituted the province of the national security adviser. It was austere and antiseptic, a room beyond the pale of any decorator's touch, designed for function alone. A rectangular metal table sat in the center of the room, flanked by a number of straight-backed, metal-bottomed chairs calculated to keep meetings short. On one wall was a large world map, where at this particular moment pins and colored markers displayed the disposition of U.S. naval forces. Along another wall was a battery of phones, including a direct wire to No. 10 Downing Street as well as direct, instant pickups to the War Room in the Pentagon. And of course, there was a direct line to the president.

Just outside the Situation Room lay the center of White House communications, machines and teletypes constantly clacking and whirring with incoming messages. Here, teletypes on twenty-four-hour duty ceaselessly transmitted cables to our embassies all over the world, and cables coming into the State Department and the Pentagon were sped through to the Situation Room for transmission to the national security assistant's staff and to the president. The famous "hot line" was a teletype machine residing in the Pentagon. When activated, it spewed its incoming messages to its counterpart in the Situation Room communications center. Within only a few seconds of being received in the Pentagon, any Russian-language message would be click-clacking in the basement of the White House. Several minutes later, an unofficial translation would clatter through.

There were two entrances to the Situation Room. One was through the main communications center, and the other could be approached only directly from within the office area of the national security adviser. On this evening, Secretaries Rusk and McNamara, together with McGeorge Bundy, awaited us. We examined top-secret documents and intelligence reports on the situation in Laos and South Vietnam. The president, as usual, had little patience for all the military jargon and military assessments. "We need more diplomatic ingenuity, not more statistics," he said.

Bundy was pessimistic that diplomacy could succeed in getting any other nations to give us a hand. The president said we simply had to try harder. He looked with great care at the reports in front of him. "Why can't we bring in more civilian governors and administrative advisers to help improve the civil problems?" he asked. "Why not get USAID, Agriculture, and Peace Corps people in there to help their farming?" He turned to McNamara. "There's nothing that will give a farmer greater hope for the future than to see larger yields from his planting."

The president stood up and, as he was wont to do, roved the floor, jingling his keys and coins with one hand in his pocket, gesturing fiercely with the other. "Dammit, we need to show more compassion for the Vietnamese people. When their own armies move across the countryside and destroy crops and livestock, the poor farmers get no recompense. When I talked with the South Vietnamese foreign minister, this was one of the problems he mentioned. Can we help more on the civil and agriculture side of things? Can we push the South Vietnamese government to get their compassion out in the open where the people can feel it and see it? We've got to see that the South Vietnamese government wins the battle that gives its people hope in the future and trust in their government."

He sat next to Rusk and with a smile said, "You know, when I was a schoolboy in Johnson City, we had a teacher that none of the kids really liked. He was kind of a bully and not a very good teacher, either. A bunch of us talked about giving the teacher a good lesson by punching him around a bit. Sure enough, one day about seven of us boys ran into the teacher as he was crossing a small footbridge. Somebody said, 'Let's get him,' and I took the lead, trotting toward the teacher. When I got right up on him, I realized he was a pretty big fellow, and he was ready to take us on. So I turned around to get help from my friends, and I saw, to my horror, that they had turned tail and run. I was with the teacher alone. I got out of there fast. What I am saying is, if I have to turn back here, I want to make sure I am not in too deep to do so. That would be a case," said the president, "where no one would be a winner."

As we left the Situation Room, the president grabbed Bundy by the arm and asked him to talk to Bobby Kennedy about Vietnam, particularly about how Kennedy viewed Ambassador Henry Cabot Lodge's work in Saigon.

The next day, June 6, after a National Security Council meeting on Laos in which a decision was made to overfly Laos with regular reconnaissance, we boarded helicopters for New York. The president was scheduled to unveil a bust of David Dubinsky, president of the International Ladies' Garment Workers' Union, at the health center of the ILGWU in Manhattan. President Johnson's appearance in the garment district was a wild scene. Thousands of New Yorkers surged to greet him when he arrived. Dubinsky, spry, elfin, shrewd, was jubilant. The president embraced him, laughing uproariously, with Dubinsky glorying in every minute.

After the unveiling, we attended a small luncheon that included Mayor Robert Wagner. It was fortuitous that Wagner was there, for I had business to transact with him. The luncheon was being held in a small, busy room full of conversation, so I had no chance to approach Wagner privately. But after lunch, I saw my opportunity when we were both on our way to the men's room. Standing at the urinal next to mine, the mayor had no choice but to listen to me.

"Bob," I said, "you just can't get into a blood feud with Adam."

He and Adam Clayton Powell, Harlem's congressman and the powerful chairman of the House Education and Labor Committee, were rattling sabers over who was going to be in charge of the poverty enterprise in Harlem. The mayor's man was Dr. Kenneth Clark, a prestigious black educator. Powell had put his banner in the hands of one of his key lieutenants. The New York City newspapers loved the smell of blood, and a messy situation was getting messier with each passing day. The president had asked me to ride shotgun for Adam Clayton Powell.

"Bob, the president has got a bundle of education bills before Adam's committee that he wants passed, and quickly, including some for the War on Poverty. This is very important to the president. He would be grateful if you let up on Adam and let him concentrate on the president's legislation. The president is aware of your needs, and he will take care of them."

Standing in front of a urinal may not be the ideal venue for high-level political persuasion, but I wasn't going to pass up any opportunity. I was also aware that I needed to complete my missionary work before Wagner zipped up and disappeared into the throng upstairs.

He was mute for a few seconds. "All right, Jack," he said. "I'll call a cease-fire, but only for the time being. I want to be helpful to the president."

"That's just fine, Bob. And the president will be helpful to you."

I reported all this to the president without going into detail about the site of Wagner's conversion. He nodded approvingly. I made a mental note that negotiating in a men's room seemed to have its advantages.

Back out on the streets of New York, the president, with Dubinsky by his side, walked past thousands of cheering, cheerful people.

LBJ, in visibly good spirits, remarked to Dubinsky, "I'm going to do much better in New York than a lot of people think." Dubinsky nodded in agreement. There was certainly no question in the old labor leader's mind about which way his union members were going to vote.

On Sunday, June 7, Michael Forrestal, a key aide in the national security adviser's group, called the president at 3:00 a.m. to inform him that one of our planes had been shot down over the Plain of Jars in Vietnam. At 10:00 a.m. the same day, Forrestal phoned to ask me to call the president for permission to set up a National Security Council meeting. The president agreed, and the meeting was held at 12:30 p.m. The decision was made to continue aerial reconnaissance, but the president pressed for more specific recommendations and plans. "Where are we going?" he asked with some vehemence.

All those around the table were in agreement about a plan of action, with the exception of General Curtis LeMay. LeMay wanted to get tougher, much tougher, and right now. LeMay, tough, cigar-chomping, and always ready for a "nuke in the park," was the commanding general of the Strategic Air Command. As we left the meeting, the president told me he worried about LeMay. "I get anxious and look for the fire exits when LeMay wants to get tough. Frankly, he scares the hell out of me," the president said. He wasn't joking.

Johnson was steady and composed in these meetings. His questions were searching. His dismay at what he considered lack of forward planning was held in check so that his questions were posed softly, quietly. Forrestal told me privately that he thought "the president is putting his finger on the deficiency in our total planning now." I became increasingly aware, as I participated in more of these national security and cabinet meetings, of how few times Bobby Kennedy spoke up. He was silent, withdrawn, keeping his own counsel. This was in stark contrast, Forrestal told me, with his behavior in meetings over which President Kennedy had presided. Then Bobby had been outspoken, quick, and ready to advance his opinion.

It was on June 13, 1964, that Bobby expressed his desire to go to

Saigon as our ambassador. The president had called me into his office on that day. We talked of some pressing issues that demanded his attention, then he turned to me abruptly and said, "Have a talk with Bundy. The two of you come back to me with suggestions about who should go to Saigon to replace Lodge."

Ambassador Lodge had recently written the president suggesting that he (Lodge) thought it was time for him to depart Saigon. The president was uncertain about the former Republican vice presidential candidate. LBJ knew Lodge's public image had value, but the president told me he felt Lodge was leading with slack reins. Lodge was having problems with his staff, stemming mainly from his insistence on making every decision himself. Under the circumstances, the president was willing to go along with Lodge's desire to be relieved of his post.

Later that day, I called Mac Bundy and we chatted. Bundy told me what I already knew, that Bobby Kennedy had written the president to say that if LBJ thought it was a good idea, the attorney general would be willing to go to Vietnam as our ambassador. With obvious pleasure, Bundy informed me that the attorney general felt his relationship with the president was improving.

The president had asked Dean Rusk, Bob McNamara, Mac Bundy, and Bobby Kennedy to give him a list of the three people they thought best qualified to go to Saigon. Interestingly, all four men put their own names at the top of the list. Bundy suggested this was to show the president that each of his top advisers was willing to make whatever sacrifice the president asked.

During breakfast the next morning, I told the president about my visit with Bundy. The president, propped up in bed with a tray in his lap, chewed calmly on a piece of bacon. He sipped his hot tea as he listened to my report.

"Are you going to name Bobby Kennedy to the post of ambassador?" I asked him.

He was thoughtful for a second, and then he said, "No, I am not. I would be accusing myself for the rest of my life if something happened to him out there. He could do the job. He could do it damn well, but I can't trust the security there. Someone or some group might want to do him in. I couldn't live with that."

He paused and then asked, "Who would be your choice between Maxwell Taylor, George Ball, or Roswell Gilpatric?"

I was prepared for the question. Without hesitation I answered, "My choice would be Roswell Gilpatric."

The president surveyed me quizzically. "Why?" he asked.

"First," I said, "I think Ball is better suited to your own needs here, where he can be in constant touch with you. Talking to you by cable ten thousand miles away is not the same. I count Ball too important a voice at your council table to have him in Saigon." (Little did I know that a year later, George Ball would prove to be the most prescient man in the room when the pivotal decisions on the war were being taken.)

"Second, I think Gilpatric is one of the ablest men I know. He would be a first-rate administrator, a no-nonsense captain, and he would turn in accurate reports. I think he would be tough enough when he had to be. You could trust his judgment.

"Third, I am bound to say that from the standpoint of who the public would have more faith in, Max Taylor is your man. But I would send Gilpatric, because I think he would do the job you want done."

The president nodded, and we talked at length. Finally, I gathered all the papers we had gone over and prepared to go to my office to await the president's arrival in the West Wing. He clambered out of bed and put on his robe. He seemed engrossed in his own thoughts. As I left the room, he looked up and said, "Have lunch with Clark Clifford [one of LBJ's closest confidants] and me today. We will be discussing what you and I just talked about."

At noon, I met the president and Clark Clifford in the family dining room on the second floor of the Mansion. As we sat down, we began talking. The president questioned Clifford about his choice for ambassador, but before Clifford could answer, the president (as he often did) launched into his own views, as if he wanted to test them out. To my surprise, he floated the names of Taylor, Ball, and Gilpatric, reviewing their various merits in language not unlike my own earlier that day. He concluded with emphasis on Max Taylor and the national confidence he inspired. Clifford agreed. I understood why. Johnson wanted instant public approval for his new envoy, and Taylor, the soldier's soldier, would be publicly praised. The president mentioned that Bobby Kennedy had volunteered his services, but Clifford gave no response to that.

So General Maxwell Taylor, confidant to President Kennedy, close friend and trusted counselor of Bobby Kennedy, a ramrod-straight soldier with extraordinary tenacity and a scholar's mind, became the president's chosen instrument in Vietnam. In a way, Max Taylor was coming full circle, since in 1961 he and Walt Rostow had written for President Kennedy a blueprint for action in South Vietnam that involved American troops in numbers larger than anyone was considering at the time.

The time for deciding about Bobby Kennedy as a vice presidential candidate had arrived. On July 29, 1964, at 1:00 p.m., the president met with Bobby in the Oval Office, where on so many occasions the attorney general had conferred with his older brother, a time when Bobby Kennedy was the second most powerful man in the country and no one doubted the reach of his power. On this day, Bobby came without any special status other than what his new leader might choose to bestow on him.

They met and talked alone, these two unique yet similar men. They talked for almost two hours. After the meeting, Bobby went to Mac Bundy's office, where the two conferred in private.

The president reported to me that he had told Bobby he would not take him as vice president. The election fight, the president said, was going to be waged in the border states and the southern states, as well as the Midwest, places where Bobby would be an unacceptable vice presidential candidate. The president was direct, giving the news to Bobby "with the bark off," as he put it. It was a blunt political appraisal, but an accurate one. Bobby may have taken issue with the view that he was "unacceptable," but the basic thrust of the logic would have made sense to him, I suspect. Publicly, the president announced that he was not choosing anyone in the cabinet, without naming Kennedy specifically.

According to Mac Bundy, Kennedy was fine with this. Bobby was calm when he emerged from the president's office (as was the president when I visited him minutes after Bobby had departed). I have always felt that on the level that matters most, these two men respected and admired each other. Unfortunately, I know that men close to both of them helped poison the rapport that otherwise might have taken root—to the detriment of the nation. President Johnson had a deep affection and admiration for President Kennedy. That respect was plenty big enough to carry LBJ past the minor humiliations he had suffered at the hands of RFK's staff members and possibly, inadvertently, from Bobby as well. (I use the word *inadvertently* because I don't want to believe Bobby deliberately engaged in LBJ bashing.)

Proof that the president bore Bobby no ill will came in October, when LBJ told me that Bobby Kennedy had just called. "He needs my help in New York. Ken Keating has been a good senator. He'll be tough to beat, in spite of the Kennedy mystique. So we're heading out to New York on October 14. I'm going to visit Mrs. Kennedy and then we have the speech at the Al Smith dinner." The Al Smith event was a big traditional Democratic Party dinner at which the faithful gathered in varying degrees of jubilance. Then the next day the schedule called for us to start upstate and end up in Manhattan, all on the same day. I had to get our advance people on board.

Working with the Democratic National Committee and Kennedy's campaign staff, we labored 'round the clock to organize the trip. On October 14, the president was suffering from a sore throat. He was hoarse and feeling a little grumpy, but we had a long day ahead. At 8:45 a.m., the president boarded Air Force One. Marvin Watson and I accompanied him. At 9:50, we arrived at Teterboro Airport in New Jersey. It was a warm, sunny day, and some four thousand people were there to greet him. Governor Richard Hughes and Senator Harrison Williams welcomed the president and rode with him in the motorcade. Our first stop was the Bergen Mall in Paramus, New Jersey, where LBJ was cheered enthusiastically by a huge crowd. The president made some remarks, keeping them brief to save his voice.

Then it was back to the airport en route to Wilkes-Barre. Pennsylvania governor David Lawrence came aboard for a brief visit. LBJ reclined in his chair and took a fifteen-minute nap. Then, a little after noon, we landed at the Wilkes-Barre/Scranton Airport. There were twenty thousand wildly cheering people in attendance, plus a high school band striking up "Hello, Lyndon" and a crowd of uniformed "Ladies for Lyndon." The president made brief remarks to energetic applause. Hey, this is the American political ritual.

Then we were in the air once more, this time on our way to New York City. At the airport to welcome LBJ were Ethel and Bobby Kennedy and Mayor Wagner. The motorcade took us through East Harlem, where crowds thronged the sidewalks. Finally, around 2:30 we arrived at the presidential suite at the Waldorf Towers, where Bobby Kennedy joined the president for a brief chat. Jacqueline Kennedy, having been informed of the president's throat problems, arranged for Dr. Jim Gould, a throat specialist who treated President Kennedy, to come to the suite to examine LBJ's throat and administer some medicine. Then, a little before 4:00 p.m., an unexpected phone call came in, with two of LBJ's key advisers on the line—Clark Clifford and Abe Fortas.

"Mr. President," said Clark, "some bad news. It appears that [LBJ aide] Walter Jenkins was arrested on October 7 in the men's room of the YMCA. It was the night of the *Newsweek* party, and a number of members of Congress and the White House staff were there. It was a police bust. They were monitoring that restroom, and Walter was apprehended"—his voice faltered—"for engaging in misconduct with a man. Walter was hospitalized this morning for nervous exhaustion. Abe and I have been trying to keep this story under wraps, but we can't hold it much longer."

The president's face was grim, etched by lines of weariness. "You and Abe stay on top of this."

Thirty minutes later, another call. George Reedy, press secretary, was on the line. "Jack, is the president there?"

"Yes, he is, in the next room."

George's tone was urgent. "I have to talk to him."

I strode to the large bedroom, told the president that Reedy was on the phone, and got on the extension.

"Mr. President, there's a big story going to break tomorrow or the day after. I understand you talked to Clark and Abe."

The president was quiet for a moment. "Who knows about this?"

George said, "By tomorrow, everybody. It'll be a big story, sir. The newspapers will be all over it."

The president was preternaturally calm, though I knew his gut and heart were ripped apart. "I'll have to put out a statement. Say that I have accepted Walter's resignation." Neither man discussed the effect the timing of this story might have, given that the election was coming up in less than a month. They didn't have to.

LBJ called Mrs. Johnson to inform her. She was devastated. When he told her that no one would be making any comments to the press except him, Mrs. Johnson demurred. "No, Lyndon, we can't let Walter hang out there all alone. I intend to put out my own statement standing by him."

Nothing the president could say swayed her. I wanted to hug this extraordinary woman, who loved Walter no more than the president did but would not allow the president's instinct to protect the White House, or anything else, to stay her voice in support of her friend.

Happily, fate intervened. George Reedy's forecast of a big newspaper story the next day was only partially accurate. In a confluence of highly improbable events, at exactly the same time Jenkins's misadventures were making their way onto the printed page, Moscow produced a crisis on a global scale. Nikita Khrushchev was toppled in a Kremlin coup. The morning papers would be carrying the second-coming-of-Christ-size headlines about the Soviet dictator's collapse and the power shift in the Soviet Union. The Jenkins story would run on the first page, but in smaller type, and amid all the tumult in the Communist empire, the Jenkins story wouldn't gain any traction.

How LBJ got through that evening I will never know. It was enough to break the will and spirit of any mere mortal, yet through no sign or expression did he betray the fact that angry serpents were crawling all over him. The first thing the next morning, he was on the phone to Nicholas Katzenbach, the acting attorney general. I was on the phone as well.

He said to Katzenbach in clear, firm tones, "I want you to make a full investigation of the Jenkins matter. Let the chips fall where they may. As my chief legal officer, I want you to know that the orders I give you are to be carried out with absolute impartiality. Is that clear?" I thought that was pretty damn clear. Then LBJ told me we would be keeping our appointments that day. "I've got to do it. I can't let Bobby lose that election if I can help it." So by a little before 9:00 a.m., we were on our way to LaGuardia. Bobby Kennedy's campaign in the state of New York was under way.

We arrived at LaGuardia and clambered aboard a chartered DC-6, headed for Rochester. The president motioned for all of us to leave him and Bobby alone, which we did. On the trip, LBJ called Clark Clifford and Abe Fortas. The subject was Walter Jenkins, who was clearly weighing heavily on Johnson's mind. He loved Walter, and the trouble he was in hit Johnson hard.

At the Rochester airport, the president and Bobby and Ethel came down the ramp to be greeted by a large crowd, some of them waving banners reading, "Welcome Mr. President" and "LBJ for the USA." On the platform at the airport were various members of the Kennedy clan, Mayor Bob Wagner of New York City, and Governor Averell Harriman. The platform bulged with local leaders as well as political nabobs from the surrounding counties. Before a crowd of some three thousand people, Bobby introduced the president. LBJ waxed enthusiastic about the election of Bobby Kennedy and how much it meant to the future of New York. The crowd cheered endlessly. Taking Bobby by the shoulder, LBJ moved with him into the crowd, grabbing hands and smiling.

Once again we were back in the DC-6 and on to Buffalo, where the wild, welcoming crowd at the airport reprised our hospitable greeting in Rochester. LBJ and Bobby climbed into a limo on their way to City Hall, where a crowd estimated at fifty thousand had gathered. LBJ and Bobby spoke. Although what they said was lost in the din, who cared? The crowd's reaction was nonstop cheering.

Finally, we pulled Johnson and Bobby off the platform to join a motorcade back to the airport. LBJ, his political senses at high alert, stopped the motorcade at one point so he could alight, dragging Bobby with him, to greet a group of nuns clustered on the curb. They giggled as LBJ and Bobby shook hands with all of them, their faces illuminated by wide smiles. LBJ looked delighted, too.

At JFK Airport, the motorcade formed around 5:30 p.m. and

moved through Brooklyn, where at LBJ's instructions it stopped twelve times so that LBJ and Bobby could greet surprised and joyous onlookers. It was Johnson's firm belief, though the Secret Service disagreed, that surprise was a president's best defense against a would-be assassin. If the assassin didn't know LBJ was going to stop the caravan, he wouldn't be ready to shoot, would he?

It had been one long day. Presidents and presidential candidates, even senators, don't ever really get tired. How could they, when all they hear is, "God love you, Mr. President," and, "We pray for you, Bobby"? It must be like having an endless stream of stimulants administered intravenously into every vein. They just don't want it to end. But for presidential assistants, days like this eventually give way to total fatigue. More than a bit spent, I wandered back to an empty Secret Service car in the rear of the motorcade to catch some sleep, little knowing that I'd soon get a taste of what was keeping the president and Bobby Kennedy so alert.

I was jogged awake by a Secret Service agent. "Mr. Valenti, the president wants you up front in his car, and right now."

I leaped out and did a Jesse Owens record-breaking dash to the front of the motorcade, which was held up at an intersection where it looked like a hundred thousand people were going completely crazy. LBJ and Bobby had shifted to an open car and were standing on the backseat. To LBJ's right, as I climbed aboard, was a balding man with rimless glasses, holding a mike. The president grabbed my hand and pulled me on the seat between Bobby and him. Then he turned to the balding man, saying, "Okay, Tony, you're on."

The man, who I later found out was the Democratic leader of this very partisan, mostly Italian American crowd, yelled into the portable mike, pointing toward me. "And we have here one of our own, the closest man to the president, our friend and compatriot Jack Valenti." To my amazement—and I might add to my heightened sense of well-being—the crowd's loud response filled the dark night air. Hey, I'm loved! At that moment, LBJ grabbed my right arm and Bobby got hold of my left, and now we were all three on the backseat of that open car in the night, our arms upraised in triumph.

The motorcade was in motion once more. We moved slowly

through the boulevard choked with people on both sides. I was still standing there between LBJ and Bobby, arms waving, a huge smile on my suddenly much beloved face. Ah, these wonderful New Yorkers.

After ten minutes or so of unalloyed public adoration, the motorcade stopped. The leader of the Italian American district disembarked, and another fellow leaped on. He was small and wiry, with wispy hair. It turned out he was the leader of the famous Jewish district we were heading into. The president leaned down, his lips close to my ear. I thought, Oh yes, he must want to seek my counsel.

The president's voice was low but firm. "Okay, Jack, you can get out now."

As I stepped down from the open car, I felt a sudden, terrible sense of loss. My short time in the sun (or the moon, in this case) was over. Now all I had left were memories of a time when at an intersection somewhere in Manhattan, I was admired, loved, and honored by thousands of my fellow citizens. For a moment I found myself thinking, Hey, I'm going back to Texas and run for the Senate myself. Then I sobered up. Hell, this stuff sure was addictive.

Johnson won the presidential election. He won it big. He triumphed by the largest percentage of votes cast in the history of twentieth-century presidential elections. On election night, when the outcome was clear, a seemingly inconsequential event occurred that, had it been handled differently, might have been the catalyst of reconciliation between these two Democratic political giants. During the campaign, President Johnson had gone far beyond providing "enough help" to the then-aspiring senatorial candidate in New York. When the ballots were counted, the president had carried the state by over a million votes and Bobby Kennedy had won by some six hundred thousand. Political pros and the press recognized that the coattails of the president had been long enough and strong enough to carry Bobby Kennedy to victory over Senator Keating.

Yet somebody near Bobby must have cautioned him against giving any credit to the president.

On election night, Mary Margaret and I sat with President Johnson and his family and friends at the Driskill Hotel in Austin to watch the returns. The camera picked up the newly triumphant Robert Kennedy in his New York City headquarters, with his wife, children, staff, and friends, all beaming joyously at a noisy, wound-up crowd of supporters. As Bobby started speaking, he began to thank all those who had made his victory possible. He cited his wife and Governor Averell Harriman, and he lauded each member of his staff by name, calling out a list of names of prominent Americans who had also aided him. As Bobby looked up from his notes, I found myself silently urging him to speak: *C'mon, Bobby, let's hear it.* But the outpouring of gratitude was over. The name I wanted so much to hear never came.

President Johnson made no outward sign that the omission had registered. His expression throughout the speech by the senator-elect never changed. But I certainly felt the absence of Bobby's appreciation for the hard stumping the president had done on his behalf. To be honest, I felt ill. What an opportunity lost.

President Johnson and the Motorcade in Mexico City That Gave Me Heartburn

In 1966, I had to confront a terrifying decision that involved the safety of the president.

President Gustavo Díaz Ordaz of Mexico had issued an invitation to LBJ to meet with him in Mexico City for the dedication of a statue of Abraham Lincoln. Johnson quickly accepted. Apart from his affection for Mexico and an eagerness to be part of honoring Lincoln, there was another reason for the president's swift assent to the Mexican trip. A few months earlier, LBJ had sent several thousand marines to the Dominican Republic to quell a civil war that threatened Americans. LBJ figured that a visit to Mexico would soften criticism of that expedition.

The president called me to his office. "I am sending you and Bill Moyers to advance my trip to Mexico City. Bill will take care of the press issues. You take care of the rest."

The next day, Bill and I were aboard an air force jet to Mexico City, where we set up our headquarters in the American embassy. Within hours of landing, Bill and I were about our tasks. I toured the presidential guest bedroom in Los Pinos, the palace of the Mexican president. I took particular care to inspect the guest bathroom.

LBJ had a thing about bathrooms, and specifically showerheads. (I am not saying that civilization as we know it would collapse if the president encountered a showerhead that was not up to his Olympian standards; I *am* saying I would rather bear witness to the end of civilization than confront LBJ in a substandard bathroom.) I left Los Pinos pleased with what I saw, especially after I had ordered the installation—with the permission of the Mexican security officials—of a new huge showerhead to the president's exacting requirements. As you, dear reader, have observed, special assistants to LBJ had numerous very important duties.

I rode the entire length of the proposed motorcade route from the airport to Los Pinos. I went over all the minute details of a presidential trip with the Mexican security officials, and everything seemed to be in place. Two days before the arrival of the president, I met again with the U.S. ambassador, Tony Freeman, and top Mexican officials. Tony was a superb diplomat. Fluent in Spanish, affectionate toward Mexican culture, he was as good an ambassador as you could hope to find. In an offhand remark, I said, "Oh yes—the president's armored limo is due to arrive via cargo plane tomorrow."

The ambassador's eyebrows shot up. "Why does he need his armored limo here?" Well, I wanted to say, for starters we'd like to ensure the safety of the president. Do we not remember Dallas? But instead I said, "Tony, he rides in that armored limo in all public motorcades. Moreover, the Secret Service would go ballistic if he didn't ride in that car."

But with some anxiety, Tony said, "Jack, you had best talk to the foreign minister. We have a problem."

I still didn't understand. "Problem, what problem? He has to ride in that limo from the airport to the presidential palace." Tony made it clear now. He gave me a tutorial in the culture of Mexico, especially with respect to how the Mexican president conducts himself in public. The Mexican president never rides in an enclosed vehicle. The people must see him.

Tony said, "Let me put it this way. You have three alternatives. One, the president and Mrs. Johnson ride in his limo, and the Mexican president rides in his open limo. Two, the two presidents ride in the open limo. Three, you cancel the visit." None of these sounded good to me.

Tony was sympathetic to my plight. "Look, Jack, perhaps I should talk to Antonio Carillo-Flores [the foreign minister], who is a former ambassador to the U.S. and an intimate friend of President Johnson. We'll see if this problem can be resolved according to your needs."

Within an hour, Tony was back to me. "No chance," he said. "The foreign minister just talked to President Díaz Ordaz. He will ride in his open limo."

I left the meeting to consider my choices. But I really had no choices. This was not about showerheads, or meeting sites, or whom to spend time with. This was about the president's personal safety. I immediately conferred with Bill Moyers. Bill and I both had a momentary laugh about this dilemma and then we both realized this was serious business. Bill said, "Jack, I don't see any other course except calling the president. And I'm glad that you're calling him and not me." Bill did have a devilish sense of humor. I got on the phone and asked the White House operator to connect me with the president, who was at his ranch in Texas, preparing to fly to Mexico.

"Mr. President, we have a problem—" I began, but before I could complete the sentence, the president's voice roared through the wire.

"For God's sake, Jack, that's why you're in Mexico City, to fix problems and not to bother me."

"But, Mr. President, you don't quite understand." And before he could override me, I poured out the problem to him. Now his voice moved into a lower register and got quiet, which meant he was getting pissed. "I really don't care what kind of car I ride in. Hell, I'll ride a burro if that's the only way to get to the city. Whatever you and Moyers and Ambassador Freeman decide, that's okay with me. Now let me get back to work." Click. End of conversation.

Well, that wasn't okay with me. I tried next the only thing I could think of: I called J. Edgar Hoover.

When the FBI director came on the line, I dumped the whole load in his lap. Oddly enough, Hoover was serene. "If I were you,

Jack, I wouldn't worry at all. Put yourself and the president in the hands of the Mexican secret police. They will take care of everything. Actually, I do believe the president would be safer driving down the boulevards of Mexico City than he would be in New York City." Hoover did promise to send down a cadre of FBI agents. They would be in Mexico City within hours. "Don't worry," was his parting suggestion.

But I did worry. I met again with the director of the Mexican equivalent of our Secret Service. He was a courteous, gracious, and thoroughly menacing man. Moyers and I then met with Tony Freeman again. I told Tony of my conversation with both the president and Hoover. I said with as much confidence as I could muster: "Okay, Tony, here's the decision. Tell the foreign minister that President Johnson will ride with the Mexican president in an open car."

Tony was obviously pleased. A diplomatic incident had been averted.

Air Force One landed in Mexico around 5:00 p.m. LBJ and President Díaz Ordaz greeted each other warmly. Then both got aboard the open limo. LBJ was in fine form, embracing the Mexican president, and obviously looking forward to the huge outpouring of Mexican affection he was sure to receive. Some three hours later, in the waning moments of daylight, the motorcade moved through 3 million or more cheering Mexicans before arriving at its final destination, the presidential palace of Los Pinos. It was to be the largest, friendliest crowd the president would see in his entire presidency.

Moyers and I were greatly relieved. But I was curious. How had everything gone so smoothly? I arranged a private meeting with the head of the Mexican secret police. My private question to him was, "How the hell did you do it?" It turned out that the Mexicans had prepared an extraordinarily detailed set of plans, which were carried out to perfection. They were plans I daresay we couldn't implement in the United States. First, prior to the president's arrival, hundreds of known dissidents and potential troublemakers were rounded up and put under lock and key until the president flew back home. Every single building on the motorcade route had been inspected; the police knew the names of every occupant of every room. Windows were closed unless a security officer with a weapon was in the window.

Snipers were on rooftops all along the route. Seventeen medical stations were located in strategic positions, with an English-speaking doctor and nurse at every station. It was a total immersion plan with several thousand police, security forces, soldiers, and supporting personnel at the ready. It was also a classic example of security plans deployed with nary a mistake or omission or unexpected friction.

Ambassador Freeman's estimate and Hoover's forecast were both right on.

The President Circles the Earth to Meet the Pope

Few adventures ever came close to matching the unlikely odyssey of President Johnson in 1967. At that time, I was already one and a half years into my job as president of the Motion Picture Association of America. On December 17, I watched the morning news; the lead story was about the untimely drowning death of Harold Holt, prime minister of Australia. I sorrowed because I considered Holt a superior political leader. He was greatly admired by LBJ. I knew the president would be in a blue funk today. But the hours moved swiftly, and the thought of Holt drifted slowly from my mind.

Later in the morning, I received a call from President Johnson in my MPAA Washington office. "You busy?" he asked.

My answer was quick and to the point: "For you, Mr. President, I'm never too busy."

"Good, then come on over to see me right now."

I put on my jacket, walked past the Hay-Adams Hotel, crossed H Street, and moved swiftly through Lafayette Park, then across Pennsylvania Avenue. The guards at the Northwest Gate recognized me and waved me in. In those days, security at the White House was more relaxed than it is today.

The president greeted me in the Oval Office and told his secretary to hold all calls, that he was not to be disturbed. Then he sat in his rocking chair as I settled into the couch to his right. "What I am about to tell you is for your ears only, Jack. No one else must know of this besides you and my pilot, understand?" His voice was low, stern.

Now I was curious. What the hell could be so top-secret that

Colonel Cross and I would be its sole custodians? He leaned into me. "I will be attending the funeral of Prime Minister Holt, but I am not coming straight back to Washington. I'm going on to Vietnam and then to Rome. I want to meet with the pope, and I don't want one damn living human being to know those plans."

Yep, that was top-secret all right. I nodded my understanding and said nothing. I was transfixed.

"Now, I know you have a contact at the Vatican, right?"

I nodded. "Yes, sir, I know Monsignor Paul Marcinkus. He is a top aide to the holy father." Marcinkus was indeed one of the holy father's closest advisers. He was born in Cicero, Illinois, built like an NFL linebacker, bold, assertive, and gifted with a persuasive charm that worked equally well in Italian and in his native English. He was essentially the pope's expert on America and Americans.

"All right, you get in touch with him. Let him know what I want to do, and find out if the pope will agree to meet with me." Then he paused and said: "I want to talk to the pope about American prisoners of war in Vietnam. Maybe he can help with a prisoner exchange of some kind. I don't sleep well at night knowing brave men are in those Vietnamese prisons. We've got to find a way to get them out."

"What time frame are you thinking about, Mr. President?"

"The funeral won't be for a few days. I figure we'll get to Rome around Christmas Eve. And one thing more: Don't make that call to the Vatican from the White House or your home. Find a pay phone that's private. Understood?" Yes, sir.

I departed the White House, trying not to break into a run as I returned to my office to find my Filofax. I located the phone number of Monsignor Marcinkus, changed some bills into quarters, and drove to a Gulf service station on MacArthur Boulevard, a few blocks from my home. I got the international operator, told her my number, and fed the phone a handful of quarters.

Marcinkus got to the phone promptly.

"Well, Jack," he said, "to what do I owe the honor of this call?"

I didn't waste time with small talk. "The fact is that my friend wants to meet with your friend. Is that possible?"

You don't spend a lifetime at the Vatican without being acutely sensitive to intrigue, secrecy, and hints of conspiracy. He got it fast. "What time did your friend have in mind?"

"Around Christmas Eve, I think, but I'll be in touch with you in plenty of time to set it more precisely."

"Where can I ring you back?"

"I'll call you. You can expect a call from me at exactly this time tomorrow. Is that suitable?"

"I'll be standing by my phone. Call me." His voice was calm.

I had no sooner returned to my office when my secretary said the president was on the line. "Yes, sir, Mr. President."

To my surprise, he didn't order me to the Oval Office. He spoke quickly on the phone. He said: "Tell your contact that he should not be in touch with our embassy or anyone there. Tell him that my representative, Jim Rowe, will be there in two days to go over the logistics and he alone will handle everything. When will you speak to your contact?"

"I already have, Mr. President. I'm calling him tomorrow at this same time to follow up."

I could almost see him smiling. "Good work, Jack, good work. Come see me the minute you hear from him. And I want you on the trip with me. Can you do that?"

I reckoned I could find the time.

The next day, I hovered over that pay phone at the Gulf service station. If someone had come up to use it, I think I would have either assaulted him or tried to ransom the phone. No one came close. At exactly the appointed moment, I started dropping in my quarters. On the second ring, Marcinkus picked up. "That you, Jack?" I heard his voice clearly.

"Yes, I'm here. Do you have any news?"

"Yes, and it is good. My friend agrees to the meeting, and he understands the approximate time. You'll let me know more specifically, won't you?"

"Yes, I will. Meanwhile don't talk to anyone there who works for my friend. No one, and I mean no one."

He understood. "Furthermore," I said, "you will be hearing from a man named Jim Rowe, who will call you to lay out the logistics of the meeting. He will be your only contact other than me."

Again, he said he understood, and he would welcome hearing from Mr. Rowe.

It was to be a circumnavigation of the globe by air and land that had no precedent in the chronicles of American presidential travel. We were to be in the air 19.5 hours while covering 28,210 miles. LBJ was to meet with fourteen leaders of foreign countries.

We took off from Andrews Air Force Base, stopped at Travis Air Force Base in California, then on to Honolulu and finally Canberra, the capital of Australia, where the president attended the funeral of Harold Holt. I should note that this was the only time we slept in a hotel in a real bed for the entire trip. We next flew to Melbourne and on to Korat Air Base in Thailand, where the President met with American soldiers and aviators. It was the same scenario at our next stop, Cam Ranh Bay in South Vietnam. Soon we were airborne again, this time heading for Karachi, Pakistan, where a meeting had been arranged between LBJ and Pakistani President Ayub Kahn.

At approximately 7:00 p.m. on December 22 we landed at Ciampino Airport on the outskirts of Rome. The airport was cordoned off by security guards. The president, Walt Rostow, Frederick Reinhardt (the U.S. ambassador to Italy), and I quickly boarded a chopper and flew to Castelporziano, the hunting lodge retreat of the president of Italy. No press was allowed. LBJ was greeted by President Saragat, his daughter, and her two children, and we all proceeded to a large drawing room on the second floor, where we were introduced to Prime Minister Aldo Moro, Foreign Minister Fanfani, Ambassador Corrias, Ambassador Malfatti, and Admiral Spigaj. As the two presidents met alone with interpreters in an adjoining room, the rest of us from LBJ's party, including Marvin Watson, chatted with the Italian president's guests.

Soon LBJ, Ambassador Reinhardt, and I were back aboard the chopper for an appointment at the Vatican. Once we were airborne I found out that we were going to land in one of the Vatican's inner gardens, a small circumference at best, in the dark, with a pilot who had never made a dry run. It was going to be a bit hairy. I decided not to share my concerns with the president. Soon we were above the Vatican. The pilot began to circle to get his bearings. We circled once, twice, three times until the president pressed his mouth to my ear and said, "What the hell is going on?"

"The pilot has to set down in a small location, sir, and he's getting himself set to float in. No problem."

Like hell, I thought. Dear God, what a travesty of justice and divine belief it would be if the president's helicopter crashed in the Vatican gardens just yards from the holy father. Well, at least we would have the pope giving us last rites.

Finally the pilot began to float above what appeared to be a tiny opening in the foliage below. As we began to drop, the opening got larger, and ever so slowly, swaying a bit from side to side, we finally touched ground with a confident clatter after what seemed an eternity.

There to greet us was my old cloak-and-dagger friend Monsignor Marcinkus, as well as Archbishop Benelli, the Vatican's assistant secretary of state, and Count Galeassi, the Vatican administrator.

Marcinkus squeezed my arm as we made our way to the Vatican limousine. "You took the hard way, didn't you?"

I grinned. "Yes, but if we had crashed I could have said at the Pearly Gates that the pope himself gave me extreme unction."

"No such luck," Marcinkus replied. "I would have done it myself."

When we arrived at what is known as Cortile San Damaso, the president beckoned me to his side. "I want you in this meeting with me," he said. "Perhaps we'll have Rostow come in later."

He and I took the elevator to the second floor, where we were escorted to the papal antechambers and on to the pope's library, which was spacious and richly splendid with very high ceilings. The holy father was waiting for us there. He was of medium height with fine features and a warm smile. He was clad in white and he lifted his arm in a half-benediction as he greeted the president. LBJ shook his hand vigorously. I realized as I stood there that this room had been privy to the most private pleadings and plans of counselors and popes for centuries. The pope turned to me and I knelt to kiss his ring. Even as my lips touched the ring, his hands, firm and insistent, were urging me up.

He smiled and said very softly in English, "I am glad you are here. It is good to see you again." I silently commended Marcinkus for good staff work.

The meeting was very friendly, and the president pressed the holy father for help getting American prisoners of war in Vietnam released. Later, as we were preparing to depart, Marcinkus put his hand on my shoulder and whispered, "Please tell your boss that my boss thought it was a fine meeting." I did repeat those words to LBJ, who seemed to find them quite suitable—in fact, very suitable.

We flew from Rome to the Azores and, finally, back to Washington, where we landed at Andrews Air Force Base on December 24, Christmas Eve.

Chapter 8

CROSSING THE RUBICON

With Secretary of Defense Robert McNamara, after a nail-biting meeting on Vietnam in the Cabinet Room of the West Wing.

E very act of public policy has a back story. Every decision has an ancestor. The history of American involvement in Vietnam goes back many years, through many presidents. As always, the first decision is key. From it flows the next decision, and the one after that, until a body of precedent and policy is locked together so tightly that to try to isolate its parts is well-nigh impossible. Each decision along a certain path contributes to a momentum that is increasingly resistant to change. Disengagement becomes complex and difficult, and the chief executive and his advisers face alternatives that are limited by the decisions that came before them.

One of the aspects of my life I enjoy most is speaking to high school and college students. I like to challenge these students, none of whom were born when Vietnam raged, with a question that is impossible to answer definitively. I tell them that on that nightmarish day of November 22, 1963, when Lyndon Baines Johnson raised his right hand on Air Force One to swear an oath that formalized his new status as the thirty-sixth president of the United States, the United States had some sixteen thousand fighting men in Vietnam. They were described as "advisers," but they were heavily armed and in the field of battle. The question I pose to my young audiences is this: "If the United States had not had any soldiers in Vietnam in 1963, would the new president have sent them in?"

At some point in the discussion that follows, invariably one student will raise a hand and say to me, "Well, what do you think?" My answer never varies.

"I believe LBJ would not have sent in troops for the simple reason that his first objective was to build the Great Society. He knew this would be expensive and demand his focused energies. A war in a jungle half a world away would intrude seriously, and perhaps fatally, on his goal of lifting up the quality of life in this nation." And I always conclude by saying, "Who really knows the answer to a purely hypothetical question? I can only give you my personal view."

When Lyndon Johnson was sworn in on Air Force One, he instantly understood that he could not, and must not, disconnect from the policies of John Kennedy. It would be both dismaying to the American people and inappropriate to do so before he had time to assess exactly what his options were. He made it clear publicly that he would honor the murdered president by holding fast to his policies, domestic and foreign. He believed that this was the best way to serve the American people and his own presidency.

Indeed, five days after his accession to the presidency, he stood before a joint session of the Congress and said firmly, "President Kennedy said let us begin. I say let us continue."

In the summer of 1965, LBJ came face-to-face with a Kennedy commitment that would not go away. What should he do about Vietnam? The war was going badly. Should he commit more American troops to the conflict? As luck would have it, Lyndon Johnson was the only one of four presidents to be challenged with this most difficult dilemma: Get out, or get in with more, much more. All three previous presidents had gotten by without reaching this fork in the road. Truman, Eisenhower, and Kennedy had examined the situation, and each had bought into the "domino theory," the notion that if one nation in Southeast Asia fell to communism, the rest would follow, one by one.

In the hot summer of 1965, the curtain went up on what was now the central crisis of the Johnson administration. The Pentagon high command had examined the war, and in their judgment the South Vietnamese armed forces were not capable of stemming the tide of reinforcements from the North. The war was now going so badly so swiftly that the Joint Chiefs concluded it would be lost very soon, unless the United States was prepared to commit large numbers of ground troops, *now*. The specter of the domino theory hung over these sessions like Banquo's ghost. Yes, there was an alternative: American forces could be evacuated immediately. But were we prepared to give up on a course that three previous presidents had deemed vital to America's interests? The unaskable question had been asked. Now it had to be answered.

At 10:40 a.m. on July 21, 1965, in the Cabinet Room of the White House, an important meeting took place, just hours after the return from Vietnam of Secretary Robert McNamara and General Earle Gilmore Wheeler, chairman of the Joint Chiefs of Staff. The green draperies were drawn in the Cabinet Room in the West Wing of the White House, a spartan, sparsely furnished rectangle. Usually those draperies were kept open during meetings, providing a view of the Rose Garden and beyond it the graceful white façade of the Mansion. Today, the Rose Garden was aglow with a profusion of colors, the gardeners having only recently planted new blooming flowers. The lawn had been cut the day before, so the thick carpet of grass was neatly clipped and its edges trimmed, a soothing sight. But this was no time for such pleasures.

Around an immense octagonal table sat fifteen men. The president had not yet joined the gathering; his high-backed, black leather chair was empty. In front of the vacant chair was a yellow foolscap pad and three sharpened pencils, and to the side of the pad was a carafe of water with two glasses. These fifteen men were the president's closest advisers. He had put his trust in their judgment over the previous months, and whenever there was a crisis in Vietnam, these were the men he summoned for counsel. Some of them were members of the National Security Council. Some were not. Three of the men were assistants to the president. The fifteen in attendance were Robert McNamara, secretary of defense; Dean Rusk, secretary of state; Cyrus Vance, deputy secretary of defense; McGeorge Bundy, special assistant to the president for national security affairs; General Earle Gilmore Wheeler, chairman of the Joint Chiefs of Staff; George Ball, undersecretary of state; William Bundy, assistant secretary of state and brother of McGeorge Bundy; Leonard Unger, assistant to Bundy; Richard Helms, deputy director of the CIA; Admiral "Red" Raborn, director of the CIA; Henry Cabot Lodge Jr., ambassador to Vietnam; Carl Rowan, head of the U.S. Information Agency; John McNaughton, assistant secretary of defense; Bill

Moyers; and me (Moyers and I sat behind and to the right of the president).

Each of these men had read the top-secret recommendations of the defense secretary, and the subject of the meeting, as everyone knew, was to advise the president on a course of action. Get in, or get out.

At precisely 11:30 a.m., the door to the Cabinet Room opened and the president entered. Everyone stood up and murmured greetings. Johnson was wearing a gray suit with a blue-flecked tie and a pale blue shirt. He looked grave, even a little worn, but his stride was forceful. He nodded to those around the table before sitting down. There was a moment's pause as the president looked swiftly around the room, fixing each man's eyes with his own. His face was a mask.

He nodded to McNamara and, speaking very softly, addressed him. "Would you please begin, Bob?"

McNamara was a favorite of the president: LBJ thought very highly of President Kennedy's choice of the Ford president and former Harvard Business School professor for secretary of defense. His embrace of McNamara had much to do with the extraordinary precision of McNamara's mind. LBJ had always appreciated intelligence, which in McNamara's case was coupled with the remarkable ability to retain—and produce when needed—staggering amounts of detailed information. The president reveled in aides "doing their homework," and McNamara was always knowledgeable, always informed.

I confess I always felt wonderment when I heard McNamara race through a presentation with facts and figures calculated to the tiniest detail. I remember one time when the president asked McNamara for a summary of our deployment in Vietnam, the secretary of defense had every single number at his command, without looking at his notes. Without missing a beat, he said, "We have 187 aircraft, 14,673 troops, including 345 special forces . . . ," and went on and on in that vein.

LBJ found this exactitude dazzling. Once, when the president and I had a moment alone following one of these impressive displays, I was struck by a thought. I turned to the president and asked him, "How do we know the numbers Bob gives us are real?"

The president looked at me quizzically. "What do you mean?"

"I mean, how do we know with certainty that the facts about our deployments are what he said they were? We have no way of checking on what he said."

The president said, "Are you intimating that Bob is cooking the numbers?"

"No, sir, but I am saying we aren't doing an audit on any of the Pentagon arithmetic." The president was silent, as if he were weighing what I had just said. But I don't recall any time before or after when the accuracy of McNamara's numbers was questioned by anyone around the table, including LBJ.

On this day, McNamara began with a summary of his top-secret memorandum. He spoke without pause or hesitation. The last part of his summary concluded with a statement that to support 200,000 troops in Vietnam, the United States should have at least that many in the reserve units. He recommended calling up 235,000 reserves a year from now, eventually replacing them with regulars. By mid-1966, said McNamara, we would have approximately 600,000 additional men available.

When he had finished, the president, who had listened impassively, said nothing. He leaned back in his chair, a yellow pencil in his hand. He pointed the pencil at McNamara and spoke, his husky voice almost inaudible. "What I would like to know is what has happened in recent months that requires this kind of decision on my part. And what are the alternatives? I want this discussed in full detail, and I want to hear from everyone around this table."

I leaned forward in my chair, seated just behind and to the right of the president. His hand holding the pencil was steady. He seemed perfectly calm and composed, and I recognized his mood. He had summoned his disciplines. He was preparing to circle the problem, approaching it from all sides, determined to use the intense rigor he brought to bear on any difficult problem to decide how deep into uncharted territory he was prepared to go.

He continued: "Have we wrung every single soldier out of every country that we can? Who else can help us here? Are we the sole defenders of democracy in the world? What are the compelling reasons for this call-up? What results can we expect? And again I ask you, what are the alternatives? I don't want to make snap judgments. I want us to consider all our options. We know we can tell the South Vietnamese we are going home. Is that the option we should take? What would follow from that?"

I watched Rusk. He lit a cigarette carefully. He said nothing, holding the president in his fixed gaze. Seated to Rusk's right was George Ball, in profile to me, seemingly ready to speak yet keeping his own counsel for the moment.

General Wheeler piped up. "The big problem, sir, is good combat intelligence in Vietnam, but the Vietcong are creatures of habit. By continuing to probe, we think we can make headway."

George Ball stirred in his chair. He raised his hand tentatively, and the president nodded to him. "Isn't it possible that the VC will do what they did against the French—stay away from confrontation and not accommodate us with a head-on fight?" Ball asked.

The president turned to Wheeler, and the general responded, "Yes, that is possible, but if we constantly harass them, they will have to fight somewhere."

McNamara interposed at this point. "If the VC don't fight in large units, it will give the ARVN [Army of the Republic of Vietnam] a chance to resecure hostile areas. We don't know what VC tactics will be when the VC are confronted with one hundred and seventy-five thousand Americans."

Admiral "Red" Raborn, newly appointed chief of the CIA, was heard for the first time. "We agree. By 1965's end, we expect North Vietnam to increase its forces. It will attempt to gain a substantial victory before our buildup is complete."

The president frowned. "Is anyone here of the opinion we should not do what this memorandum says? If so, I want to hear from them now."

Ball answered, "Mr. President, I have grave misgivings about our ability to win under these conditions." He paused. "But let me be clear. If the decision is to go ahead, I will support it."

The president turned his great bulk sideways in his chair to face Ball. "But, George, is there another course in the national interest, some course that is better than the one McNamara proposes? We know it is dangerous, but the big question is, can it be avoided?"

Ball took up the challenge with some eagerness. "There is no course that will allow us to avoid losses. But if we get bogged down, our cost might be substantially greater. The pressures to create a larger war would be irresistible."

The president persisted. "Tell me, then, what other road can I take?"

"We can take our losses and let their government fall apart, Mr. President, knowing full well there will be a probable takeover by the Communists. This is an unpleasant alternative, I know."

The president nodded. "I can take unpleasant decisions. But I want to know the best case you can make for your thoughts."

"We have discussed it," said Ball. "I have had my day in court," referring to his lengthy memos to the president importuning LBJ to support his contrary views.

"I don't think we have made any full commitment yet, George," the president said. He paused to let his words sink in, then went on. "I want another meeting, more meetings, before we take any definitive action. We must look at all other courses of action carefully. Right now I feel it would be more dangerous to lose the war than it would be to risk a greater number of troops down the road. But I want this fully aired."

Rusk now drew the president's attention. "What we have done from 1954 to 1961 has not been good enough," he said. "We should have probably committed ourselves more fully in 1961."

Carl Rowan, the first black man to head the U.S. Information Agency, spoke up. "What bothers me most is the weakness of the [Nguyen Cao] Ky government. Unless we put the screws to the South Vietnamese government, one hundred and seventy-five thousand men will do us no good."

Lodge intervened. This slim, elegantly clad Brahmin, so confident of his identity, was a curious figure at the table. LBJ liked him, though I never really felt that he would hand Lodge the scepter of authority. Nevertheless, LBJ felt comfortable with this aristocrat sitting at his council table.

"I don't think we ought to take this government seriously,"

Lodge said. "There is simply no one there who can do anything. We have to do what we think we ought to do regardless of what the Saigon government does. As we move ahead to a new phase, we have the right and the duty to do certain things with or without the government's approval."

The president listened, saying nothing. He leaned back again in his chair, as if considering Lodge's comments. Then he turned to Ball. "George, what do you think?"

Ball's answer was firm, his voice clear. "I would not recommend that you follow McNamara's course."

"Can you offer a viable alternative? I want to hear you out, truly hear you out, then I can determine if we can follow your suggestions, which I am prepared to do if I am convinced."

"Yes, Mr. President," Ball replied. "I think I can present to you the least bad of two unpleasant courses. What I would present is a course that is costly but can be limited to short-term costs."

The president seemed satisfied. "All right, let's meet again at two-thirty this afternoon to discuss George's proposals."

I suddenly felt claustrophobic, so I got up and pulled back the drapes. The heavy rumble of a jet plane overhead filtered through the window. The White House policeman standing at the west end of the walkway leading from the Mansion to the West Wing watched his colleague patrolling slowly from the Southwest Gate to the guardhouse that sat on the edge of the circular asphalt drive. A cement walkway curled from the guardhouse to the president's office. The Rose Garden was bursting with color.

The president stood up, and the others at the table immediately got to their feet, pushing back their chairs. When the president left the room, they all departed via the side door leading into the West Wing corridor, carefully removing their papers before leaving. Within minutes, a White House policeman and a Secret Service agent entered the room, carefully tore off the first pages of the memo pads on the massive desk, and deposited them in burn bags.

At 2:30 p.m., the same fifteen men gathered again in the Cabinet Room, and within minutes the president entered, took his chair, and the meeting began again.

"All right, George," said the president, nodding to Ball.

Ball crisply arranged some papers in front of him. From my seat, I could barely see what was on them: neatly typed paragraphs with what appeared to be Ball's handwriting scrawled on the edges. Ball cleared his throat and began.

"We cannot win, Mr. President. This war will be long and protracted. The most we can hope for is a messy conclusion. There remains a great danger of intrusion by the Chinese. But the biggest problem is the problem of the long war.

"As casualties increase, the pressure to strike at the jugular of North Vietnam will become very great. I am concerned about world opinion. If we could win in a year's time, and win decisively, world opinion would be all right. However, if the war is long and protracted, as I believe it will be, then we will suffer a loss of prestige as the world's greatest military power proves itself incapable of defeating guerrillas."

He went on: "Every great leader in history was not afraid to make a tactical withdrawal if conditions were unfavorable. The enemy cannot even be seen in Vietnam. He is indigenous to the country. I truly have serious doubts that an army of Westerners can successfully fight a determined foe in an Asian jungle."

The president listened with obvious interest. Ball's last statement triggered a response. He said: "This is important. Can Westerners, in the absence of accurate intelligence, successfully fight Asians in jungle rice paddies? I want McNamara and General Wheeler to seriously ponder this question." With that, the president again nodded to Ball, and the undersecretary continued his exposition.

"I think we all have underestimated the seriousness of this situation. It's like giving cobalt treatment to a terminal cancer case. I think a long, protracted war will expose our weakness, not our strength. The least harmful way to cut losses in South Vietnam is to let the government decide it doesn't want us to stay there. Therefore we should put proposals to them that they can't accept, although I have no illusions that after we are asked to leave South Vietnam, that country will soon fall under Hanoi's control."

The president said to Ball, "But, George, wouldn't all our allies in Asia say that Uncle Sam was a paper tiger, wouldn't we lose credibility by breaking the word of three presidents, if we did as you propose? It would seem to be an irreparable blow. But I gather you don't think so."

"No, sir," responded Ball. "The worst blow would be if the mightiest power on earth was unable to defeat a handful of guerrillas." Substitute "insurgents" for "guerillas," and forty years later Ball's nightmare scenario would visit the Pentagon's war plans in Iraq, and eat greedily at their vitals.

"Then," said the president, "you are not basically troubled by what the world would say about our pulling out?"

"If we were actively helping a country with a stable viable government," Ball replied, "it would be a vastly different story. Certainly the Western Europeans see us as having gotten ourselves into an imprudent situation."

The president allowed himself a smile. "But I believe that these Vietnamese are trying to fight. They're like Republicans who try to stay in power but don't stay there long." The president grinned, shrugged, and said, amid the laughter that floated over the table, "Excuse me, Cabot." Lodge managed a smile.

Ball continued, "[Nguyen Van] Thieu spoke the other day and said the Communists would win the election."

"I don't believe that," said the president. "Does anyone believe that?" McNamara, Lodge, Bill Bundy, and Leonard Unger all expressed contrary views.

The president hunched against the edge of the table. "There are two things troubling me. First, I'm not sure that Westerners can ever win a war in Asia. Second, I don't see how you can fight a war with the support of a government that changes every month. Now, go ahead, George. Anything else?"

Ball continued, "What our Western European allies are concerned about is their own security—that is, troops in Berlin have real meaning for them; troops in Vietnam have none."

Mac Bundy thrust himself forward in his chair. "The difficulty I have with accepting George's argument is that it would be a radical switch in policy without visible evidence that it should be done. George's whole argument gives no weight to losses suffered by the other side. A great many elements in his arguments are correct, though. We need to make it clear to everyone that this will not be quick and that no single action will bring swift victory."

"Yes," said Ball. "My problem is that we'll get bogged down and won't win."

Dean Rusk now joined the conversation. The secretary of state was one of the most enigmatic men I encountered in Washington. He always spoke in a dispassionate manner. He rarely made long speeches in meetings, preferring to sit quietly until prodded by the president into revealing an opinion. He reserved his thoughts for private talks with the president. It could have been written about Rusk what was once written about Queen Elizabeth I's faithful counselor William Cecil: "Yet what Cecil thought, few could discover. Heart and soul a servant of the state, this was a man wholly discreet; one of those who have no windows in their breasts."

I found Rusk a congenial man, always courteous, yet I have often thought that I knew Dean Rusk as little the last time I saw him as I had the first time I met him. Once, he called me to come to his office on the seventh floor of the State Department to discuss the possibility of the United States reinstituting its ambassador to the Vatican. He wanted my judgment, as a Catholic, on the issue. We sat, the two of us in the enormous office of the secretary, he behind a smallish desk out of proportion in the vast room and I in a chair facing him. He ordered a Scotch from his mess, and I had one with him. We sipped our drinks, ate a sandwich, and talked. Rusk was obviously well-informed about the past history of our relations with the Vatican. In one of the rare moments when I saw him relax, he was amiable and humorous and yet retained that sense of detachment that consistently set him apart from his fellows.

In this Cabinet Room meeting, the secretary of state said: "If the Communist world finds out we will not pursue our commitment to the end, I don't know where they will stay their hand. I have to say, I am more optimistic than some of my colleagues. I don't believe the VC have made large advances among the Vietnamese people. It is difficult to worry about massive casualties when we say we can't find the enemy. I feel strongly that one man dead is a massive casualty, but in the sense that we are talking, I don't see large casualties unless the Chinese come in."

Here Lodge interposed. "I feel there is a greater threat to start World War Three if we don't go in. Can't we see the similarity to our own passivity at Munich? I simply can't be as pessimistic as Ball. We have great seaports in Vietnam. We don't need to fight on roads. We have the sea. We have the air. Let's consider meeting the VC on our own terms. We don't have to spend all our time in the jungles."

There was spirited talk around the table, more or less going over the same ground. The president stirred fitfully. "I think we have said enough today. Let's adjourn for now. I am calling a meeting for to-morrow at noon, to hear in person from the Joint Chiefs. I want them to tell me personally what they think, and I want to tell them what I think."

The next day, July 22, 1965, at noon sharp, the meeting got under way. Present were the president; McNamara; Vance; General Wheeler; General Harold K. Johnson, chief of staff of the U.S. Army; General John P. McConnell, chief of staff of the U.S. Air Force; Admiral D. L. McDonald, chief of naval operations; General Wallace M. Greene Jr., commandant of the U.S. Marine Corps; Secretary of the Air Force Harold Brown; Secretary of the Navy Paul Nitze; Secretary of the Army Stanley Resor; McGeorge Bundy; Clark Clifford; and me.

The president began. "I asked Secretary McNamara to invite you here to discuss these problems and the ways to meet them. I want you to hear from the chiefs the alternatives open to you and then recommendations on those alternatives from a military point of view.

"As I see them, the options open to us are these: One, leave the country, with as little loss as possible; two, maintain present force and lose slowly; three, add one hundred thousand men, recognizing that may not be enough and adding more next year. The disadvantages of number three are the risk of escalation, high casualties, and the prospect of a long war without victory. I would like you to start out by stating our present position as you see it and where we go from here."

Admiral McDonald, chief of naval operations, spoke up. "Sending in the marines has improved the situation. I agree with McNamara that we are committed to the extent that we can't move out. If we continue the way we are going now, it will be a slow, sure victory for the other side. By putting more men in, it will turn the tide and let us know what further we need to do. I wish we had done this long ago."

The president, his face somber, asked, "But you don't know if one hundred thousand men will be enough. If you don't know where we are going and what will happen, shouldn't we pause and find this out?"

Some minutes before this meeting began, the president and I had been alone in his office. LBJ felt bound by President Kennedy's actions and pledges, and the prospect of unhinging the linchpin of the Kennedy commitment was disturbing to him. Yet there was that doubt that kept skittering through his thoughts.

Admiral McDonald responded to the president, "Sooner or later we will force them to the conference table."

"But," persisted the president, "if we put in one hundred thousand men, won't they put in an equal number, and then where will we be?"

"No," said Admiral McDonald. "If we step up our bombing—"

The president interrupted with some acerbity, "Is this a chance we want to take?"

"Yes, sir, when I view the alternatives. Get out now or pour in more men."

"Is that all?" the president asked.

"Well," said McDonald, "I think our allies will lose faith in us."

The president managed a tight smile. "We have few allies really helping us now."

McDonald continued, "Take Thailand, for example. If we walk out of Vietnam, the whole world will question our word. We don't have much choice."

The president turned to the secretary of the navy, a tough-minded intellectual. "Paul, what's your view?"

Paul Nitze answered, "In that area not occupied by U.S. forces, things are getting worse, from what I observed on my trip out there. We have two alternatives, Mr. President. Support the Vietnamese throughout their country, or stick to the secure positions we do have.

We need to make it clear to the populace that we are on their side and then gradually turn the tide of losses by aiding the ARVN at certain points."

"What are our chances of success?" asked the president.

"If we try to turn the tide by putting in more men, it would be about sixty-forty," said Nitze.

"If we gave Westmoreland all he asked for, what are our chances?"

"We could certainly expand the area we could maintain. In the Philippines and Greece, it was shown that guerrillas can lose," Nitze said.

"Would you send in more forces than Westmoreland requests?" asked the president.

"Yes, sir."

"How many? Two hundred thousand instead of one hundred thousand?"

"We would need another one hundred thousand in January," said Nitze.

"Can you do that?" the president queried.

"Yes, sir," said Nitze.

McNamara spoke up. "The current plan is to introduce one hundred thousand men with the possibility of a second hundred thousand by the first of the year."

The president frowned. "What reaction is this going to produce?" he asked.

General Wheeler replied, "Since we are not proposing an invasion of the North, the Soviets will step up matériel and propaganda, and the same with the Chinese. The North Vietnamese might introduce more regular troops."

The president wasn't satisfied. "Why wouldn't North Vietnam definitely pour in more men? Also, why wouldn't they call on volunteers from China and Russia?"

Wheeler answered the president. "First, they may decide they can't afford to. At most they would put in two more divisions. Beyond that, they start to strip their country and invite an attack on our part.

"Second, on asking for volunteers—the one thing North Vietnam fears is the Chinese. For them to invite Chinese volunteers is to invite China to take over North Vietnam."

"Don't you anticipate retaliation by the Soviets in the Berlin area?" the president asked.

"You may have some flare-up, but the lines are so tightly drawn in Berlin that it raises the risk of escalation too quickly. Lemnitzer [Supreme Allied Commander of NATO] thinks there will be no flare-up in Berlin. In Korea, if the Soviets undertook operations, it would be dangerous."

The president nodded and addressed McDonald. "Admiral, would you summarize what you think we ought to do?"

McDonald flashed a brief smile. "Yes, sir. First, supply the forces Westmoreland has asked for. Second, prepare to furnish more men, one hundred thousand, in 1966. Third, commence bringing in air and naval forces, and step up air attacks on North Vietnam. Fourth, bring in needed reserves and draft calls."

"Do you have any idea what this will cost?" queried the president.

McNamara, with his usual precision, said, "Yes, sir. Twelve billion dollars in 1966."

"Do you have any idea what effect this will have on our economy?" asked the president.

McNamara answered quickly. "It would not require wage and price controls in my judgment. The price index ought not to go up more than one point or two."

General McConnell spoke. "If you put in these requested forces and increase air and sea effort, we can at least turn the tide to where we are not losing anymore. We need to be sure we get the best we can out of the South Vietnamese. We need to bomb all military targets available to us in North Vietnam. As to whether we can come to a satisfactory solution with these forces, I don't know. With these forces properly employed, and cutting off the VC supplies, we can surely do better than we are doing now."

The president scribbled something on the pad of paper in front of him. "Do we have results of our bombing, and has it, in your judgment, been as fruitful and productive as we anticipated?" he asked.

"No, sir," McConnell replied. "They have been productive in South Vietnam, but not as productive in the North because we are not striking the targets that hurt them."

The president faced McConnell, fixed him in his gaze, and

spoke very slowly. "Would you go beyond Westmoreland's recommendations?"

"No, sir."

The president was silent a moment. Then he asked, "If we follow Westmoreland's requests, doesn't it really mean that we're in a new war? Isn't this going off the diving board?"

"If we carry forward all these recommendations, it would be a change in our policy. We have relied on the South to carry the brunt. Now we would be responsible for satisfactory military outcome," McNamara said.

"Would we be in agreement," said the president, "that we would rather be out of there and make our stand somewhere else?"

"The least desirable alternative is getting out," General Johnson replied. "The second least is doing what we are doing. The best alternative is to get in and get the job done."

The president's voice hardened. "But I don't know how we are going to get the job done. We don't have the allies we had in Korea. Can we cut off supplies to the North?"

"No, sir," replied McNamara, "we can't prevent chartered ships entering Haiphong."

"Have we done anything to stop them?"

"No," said McNamara, "we haven't put the pressure on them, as we did in Cuba. But even if we did, it wouldn't stop the shipping."

The president spoke very slowly. "Are we starting something that in two or three years we simply can't finish?" He was zeroing in on the key question, and the men around the table knew it.

"It is costly to us to strangle slowly. But the chances of losing are less if we move in," said Brown.

General Greene, stiff-backed, every inch a marine, spoke. "The situation is as tough as when it started, but not as bad as it could be. Here are the stakes as I see them. One, the national security stake; it is a matter of time before we would have to go in someplace else. Two, there is the pledge we have made. Three, there is our prestige before the world.

"If you accept these stakes, there are two courses of action. One, get out. Two, stay in and win. Now, how to win in the North and in the South? I would like to introduce enough marines to get the job done: two marine divisions and one air wing. We have twenty-eight thousand marines out there now. We need an additional seventy-two thousand."

McNamara said, "Mr. President, General Greene suggests these men over and above the Westmoreland request."

"Then you are saying you will need eighty thousand more marines to carry this out?" the president asked.

"Yes," Greene replied, "I am convinced we are making progress with the South Vietnamese. In the North, we haven't been hitting the right targets. We should hit petroleum storage, which is essential to their transportation. Also, we must destroy their airfields, their MiGs, and their IL-28s.

"Then we should attack the industrial complex in the North and blockade Cambodia, to stop supplies from coming through there. How long would it take? Five years, plus five hundred thousand troops. I think the American people would back you."

"How would you tell the American people what the stakes are?" the president asked Greene.

"The place where they will stick by you is the national security stake."

The president leaned forward and said, "If we come in with hundreds of thousands of men and billions of dollars, won't this cause China and Russia to come in? No one has given me a satisfactory answer to that."

"No, sir," General Johnson said, "I don't think they will."

The president smiled wanly. "MacArthur didn't think they would come in, either."

"Yes, sir, but this is not Korea," said General Johnson.

The president continued, "But China has plenty of divisions to move in, don't they?"

"Yes, they do," replied General Johnson.

The president leaned forward. "Then what would we do?"

There was a long silence. The room was absolutely still. General Johnson finally said, "If so, we have another ball game."

The president leaned back in his chair. "What is your reaction to Ho Chi Minh's statement that he is ready to fight for twenty years?"

"I believe it," General Johnson replied.

"What would you describe as Ho's problems?" asked the president.

"His biggest problem is doubt about what our next move will be."

The president asked whether or not we were being careful about civilian casualties. He had laid down strict instructions that civilian targets and civilian areas were not to be touched. "Are we killing civilians in these Vietcong areas?" he asked.

General Wheeler answered, "Certain civilians accompanying the Vietcong are being killed. It can't be helped."

Stanley Resor, secretary of the army, now spoke up. "Of the three courses, the one we should follow is the McNamara plan. We simply can't go back on our commitment. Our allies are watching carefully."

"Do all of you think the Congress and the people will go along with six hundred thousand men and billions of dollars being spent ten thousand miles away?" the president asked.

Resor said evenly, "The Gallup poll shows people are basically behind our commitment."

"But," said the president, "if you make a commitment to jump off a building and then you find out how high it is, you may want to withdraw that commitment."

There was no answer from those in the room. He sighed. "I judge, though, that the big problem is one of national security. Is that right?"

There was murmured assent from those at the meeting. "Well, then," said the president, "what about our intelligence? How do the VC know what we are doing before we do it? What about the B-52 raids? Weren't the Vietcong gone before we got there?"

McNamara answered, "They get information from infiltrating the South Vietnamese forces."

"Are we getting good intelligence out of the North?" the president asked.

"Only reconnaissance and technical soundings," said McNamara. "We have none from combat intelligence."

The president leaned back in his chair, looking at each man in the room. Before the meeting, he had instructed Bundy to prepare a paper on how we got to where we were and to cite the tough questions that needed to be asked. "What Bundy will now tell you is based not on his opinion or mine, but on what we hear from some congressmen and senators," the president said.

Bundy read from a paper in front of him, ending with a list of questions. How long is this going to take, and how much is it going to cost? Can we take casualties over five years? Aren't we talking about a military solution when the solution is really political? Why can't we do a better job of interdicting North Vietnamese supply lines? Why are our bombings so fruitless? Why can't we blockade the coast? Why can't we improve our intelligence? Why can't we find the VC?

With the president admonishing those present to ponder the questions posed by Bundy, the meeting adjourned. Later meetings were held morning, afternoon, and night over the next five days, as the president strained to extract every differing view he could find in the government and bring it to the table to be examined. Finally, as the president described them at one of the meetings, the options boiled down this way. "One, we can bring the enemy to his knees by using our SAC [Strategic Air Command] and other air force. I don't think our citizens would want us to do this. I sure wouldn't.

"Two, another group thinks we ought to pack up and go home. I don't think too many of our people want us to do this. Ike, John Kennedy, and I have given our commitments.

"Three, we would stay there as we are, suffer consequences, and continue to lose territory and take casualties. You wouldn't want your boy out there crying for help and not getting it.

"Four, go to Congress and ask for great sums of money, call up the reserves, and increase the draft. Go on a war footing, declare a state of emergency. There is a good deal of feeling that ought to be done. We have considered this. If we make a land war in Asia, then the North would go to its friends China and Russia and ask them for help. They would be forced to increase aid. For that reason, I don't want to be dramatic and cause tension.

"Five, give our commanders the men they say they need, out of forces in this country. Get such money as we need and must have. Use our transfer authority to get money we need until January.

"Six, say to the South that they must get their military to get to work and make what gains we can. Meanwhile we will explore ways to find peace, explore them every day."

It became clear as the days wore on that options four and five were the ones looming as alternatives. There was much unease. Crystal balls were clouding up all over the government, and "through a glass darkly" was the mood of the moment.

I have inspected my own thoughts a thousand times, and I come to the conclusion that the president's choices had indeed narrowed down to these. He came to this conclusion reluctantly, resisting all the way. He had no illusions about the war. He had no great faith in the predictions of the military, but he had no sound countervailing arguments. And he was aware that there was only one man at the table who counseled getting out now and cutting our losses.

What I found so telling later was of the men around that table, almost all of whom were the prime advisers to President Kennedy, all were opposed to George Ball's recommendation. Not one spoke up to second Ball and urge his course on the president.

The president had one final meeting on Vietnam. It was with the congressional leadership, the top leadership from the House and Senate. It convened on Tuesday, July 27, 1965, at 6:35 p.m. in the Cabinet Room. The president outlined what he had chosen to do. There was spirited questioning on the part of the leadership, but no one opposed the move except Mike Mansfield, the Senate majority leader, who was silent through most of the discussion.

As the meeting neared its end, Mansfield, puffing on his pipe, took the floor. "I could not be true to myself if I didn't speak," he said. "This position has a certain inevitability. Whatever pledge we had was to assist South Vietnam in its own defense. Since then there has been no government of legitimacy. We owe this government nothing, no redemption of any pledge of any kind. We are going deeper into war. Even total victory would be vastly costly. The best hope we have for salvation is a quick stalemate and negotiations. We cannot expect our people to support a war for three to five years. Remember, escalation begets escalation."

Mike Mansfield represented that breed of public man who always speaks his mind when his country is in danger and he believes that his voice will add substance to the debate. He never dealt in personal recrimination. No man in the Senate doubted Mansfield's rock-like integrity. But other than Senator Richard Russell of Georgia, no one opposed the final decision.

The president nodded to Senator Mansfield, his old colleague and friend.

Mansfield's discontent was remarkably prophetic. What might have happened if the president had listened to Mike Mansfield and given his views more weight? We will never know, for with Mansfield's comments to the president, the meeting had come to its end. The die was cast, the decision taken.

At 12:30 p.m. on Wednesday, July 28, 1965, the president held a televised news conference in the East Room of the White House. He informed the nation of what he planned to do. "We intend to convince the Communists that we cannot be defeated by force of arms or by superior power. They are not easily convinced. In recent months they have greatly increased their fighting forces, their attacks, and the number of incidents. I have asked the commanding general, General Westmoreland, what more he needs to meet this mounting aggression. He has told me. We will meet his needs.

"I have today ordered to Vietnam the Air Mobile Division and certain other forces, which will raise our fighting strength from seventy-five thousand to one hundred and twenty-five thousand men almost immediately. Additional forces will be needed later, and they will be sent as requested. This will make it necessary to increase our active fighting forces by raising the monthly draft call from seventeen thousand over a period of time to thirty-five thousand per month, and stepping up our campaign for voluntary enlistments.

"After this past week of deliberations, I have concluded that it is not essential to order reserve units into service now. If that necessity should later be indicated, I will give the matter most careful consideration. And I will give the country adequate notice before taking such action, but only after full preparations.

"We have also discussed with the government of South Vietnam lately the steps that they will take to substantially increase their own effort—both on the battlefield and toward reform and progress in the villages. Ambassador Lodge is now formulating a new program to be tested upon his return to that area.

"I have directed Secretary Rusk and Secretary McNamara to be available immediately to the Congress to review with the appropriate congressional committees our plan in these areas. I have asked them to be available to answer the questions of any member of Congress."

We had crossed the Rubicon.

Chapter 9

BACK TO THE HILL COUNTRY

In my office right next door to the Oval Office, with Vice President Hubert Humphrey.

From the first decision to give aid to Indochina in April 1950 to the crossing of the Rubicon in the summer of 1965, the hoops of commitment bound the United States tighter and tighter. Every president, as the record so clearly shows, accepted as a fact of life that Southeast Asia was essential to the security of the free world. Once you let Southeast Asia fall to Communist domination, went the prevailing opinion, the unraveling of that part of the world would begin, with all the attendant threats to our national security.

This view was staunchly held by every American administration since 1950. Of course, there was risk in going in further in Vietnam, but what of the larger and even more crippling risk of losing American credibility in Asia? How could we justify all that was said and done, not by one president, but by four presidents, counting Johnson, if we suddenly shifted gears and left the South Vietnamese alone to fend for themselves? What would have happened if thousands of Vietnamese were massacred by a vengeful Ho Chi Minh?

All these concerns seem so simple to refute at this writing. "Retrospective wisdom," opined Edmund Burke, "does make us all so intelligent." But every public man knows he cannot take refuge in what might have been. He has to stand or fall on what happens at the time it happens, or as LBJ used to say, "What order do I give at nine a.m. tomorrow morning?"

No one around Johnson felt comfortable about Vietnam. LBJ hated it. He fumed because he couldn't negotiate a way out of it. Johnson's strategy never varied, and he made that strategy clear to his advisers. But I was never sure it was clear to the American people. What he strove to achieve was a negotiated settlement.

Once after a meeting on Vietnam, I followed the president back to his office. I sat down across from him. He put his hands behind his head, leaned back, and murmured, "If I could just get to the table with Ho Chi Minh, we could find a way out of this damnable war."

LBJ's favorite biblical injunction was from Isaiah: "Come, let us reason together." He truly believed if he could get into a room with Ho Chi Minh, they could find a mutually agreed-on settlement to end the war. But meanwhile, the war raged on, and LBJ suffered under its terrible burden.

I was privy to some of Johnson's bleaker moments. Each morning when Bill Moyers and I went to LBJ's bedroom, by 7:00 a.m., he was already on the phone to McNamara and the Pentagon. His first question was always, "What were our casualties?" His face turned grim each time as the Pentagon recited to him the list of killed and wounded twelve thousand miles away. One morning as the bleak, wintry news was conveyed to him, I spoke as he put down the phone.

"I don't know how any human can handle that kind of a report, Mr. President, I really don't."

He looked up, a dreary expression on his face. "I'll tell you exactly what it's like. It's like drinking carbolic acid every morning."

There was one particular incident that furnished those of us around him with a more complete view of how LBJ coped with the carnage in Vietnam. This particular morning as he was on the phone, I heard him say, "When did it happen? Can they rescue him?" He listened for a bit and then broke in, "Bob, I want your people to go all out to rescue him, get him out of there before he's captured or killed. Understood?"

When he cradled the phone, he said to me, "A young naval aviator from one of our carriers has been shot down in the sea near Haiphong. McNamara's going to get him out, and now."

An hour later, he was in the Oval Office chatting with several of his aides. Twice he was on the phone to McNamara: "Bob, what's the news on that flier?" McNamara was obviously saying they were trying to locate him and lift him to safety, but so far no luck. The president fretted visibly. Some two hours later, I was back in his office when the phone rang. It was McNamara.

The president leaped to the phone. "Bob, that's the best news you have brought me in a long time. Is he all right, is he hurt?" He listened for a bare few seconds, put down the phone, and whooped.

"They found him, he's safe, he's okay, in good shape, and wants to get back to duty. That's the best news in a long time."

One lone combat pilot. His plight and his possible death or imprisonment had obsessed the president. I suppose that pilot had become to Johnson the exemplar of all the other young men in this war, in harm's way, putting their lives on the line for their country. I had never seen Johnson as happy as he was when McNamara called him. "They found him, he's safe, he's okay."

In all the meetings on Vietnam in the White House, I never spoke up. Nor did any of the other Johnson aides. We all reserved our comments and ideas to pass on to him privately. Because I knew he read carefully all the memos assembled in his "night" reading, I put most of my thoughts on paper. It allowed him to consider carefully whatever I was thinking and even to reread the memo if he was so inclined.

On March 31, 1968, I was at my job at the MPAA when my secretary came in. "Mr. Valenti, the White House is on the phone. The president wants to talk to you."

I picked up the phone. "This is Jack Valenti."

The White House operator's voice was crisp. "Mr. Valenti, please hold on, the president is calling."

Johnson got on the phone. Without any small talk he said, "Are you going to watch my speech tonight?"

"Of course," I said. "I'm staying home tonight so I can watch it."

"That's good. When I am through, wait about a half hour and then give me a call. We can talk."

This was a bit odd, I thought, but as the day wore on I forgot the feeling. That night, I watched the president's speech, and when he announced his decision not to run for reelection, I was thoroughly shaken. I dialed the White House and was told the president would call me back. In about twenty minutes, he did.

"Well," he said, "what did you think?"

"Mr. President, I think it was a huge mistake. I just can't believe it. I am sick at heart."

There was a slight chuckle in the phone. "When you get a chance, come see me. We'll have a nice talk." He hung up.

Within two days, I was in the Oval Office talking to the president. He settled back in his chair and said, "The reason I made this decision was very simple. I wanted the North Vietnamese to know I had no more political ambitions—that whatever I did from here on would only enhance the prospects of peace. I figured this was the best way to get them to the negotiating table. I had just run out of options. Now I think I can beat Nixon, but it would be close, so close that it would be hard to govern, to get the rest of my agenda passed. I think a fresh face, like Hubert, can now come in, start new, and bring the country together. I believe that."

Six months later, in August 1968, Hubert Humphrey prepared to take the giant rostrum in the Conrad Hilton Hotel in Chicago to accept the nomination of the Democratic Party for president. Upstairs in his seventeenth-floor suite, a group of men were sitting around a table, working to create a first-class acceptance speech for our hero. Bill Connell; Gus Tyler, an influential labor union intellectual; John Stewart; Max Kampelman; and I had crafted a speech that Humphrey didn't like, and rightly so. Speechwriting by committee bears few blossoms. Hubert came into the room to visit with us and convey some of the changes he had made.

The night was warm even for August. We had the windows open, overlooking Grant Park across the street. As we worked, we heard the clamorous noise of thousands of protesters. My eyes suddenly became irritated. Tears began to stream. I wiped my eyes with my handkerchief, but the irritation increased. I saw Bill Connell wiping his eyes, and suddenly all of us were wiping away. Someone walked over to the window, and I heard a voice saying, "My God, come here." We all dashed to the windows, and what we saw stunned us. There was a riot in progress in the park. Tear gas swept through the crowd and was wafting in still, dense waves to our floor. I could see scuffling in the crowd. Policemen in growing numbers were battling the protesters, pushing them back with nightsticks flailing as television cameras recorded the ugly fracas for viewing on TV sets all over the country.

My first thought was for the safety of the protesters and police, but following quickly on its heels was the political assessment "What rotten timing for Hubert." My dismal forecast became dismal fact. The messy battle in Grant Park between mostly young American college students and the Chicago police produced the political equivalent of fingernails scraping a blackboard. It so unbalanced the Humphrey election strategy that when he began his campaign in Detroit on Labor Day, Richard Nixon had a double-digit lead.

I did something I have never done since: I took leave from my job and traveled with Humphrey on his chartered campaign plane for over a month. Each day, I could see the rise in Humphrey's fortunes in the growing size of the crowds that turned out for their candidate.

On the last Sunday in October, Humphrey came to Houston, where he was to be introduced by President Johnson for one last campaign rally in Texas. I had flown to Houston earlier to be with the president. To my sorrow, a rift, small at first but growing, marred the relationship between LBJ and Hubert. Humphrey had given a speech in Salt Lake City, which in part seemed to distance him from Johnson's Vietnam policy. LBJ was not pleased. In several phone calls, I pleaded with the president to repair things. He was fuming about the Salt Lake City speech but didn't blame Humphrey so much as those near him, who in LBJ's view were pouring poison in Hubert's ear.

On this day, the Astrodome was jam-packed, some fifty thousand faithful gathered to show their support of the Democratic candidate for president. At 4:40 p.m., Lyndon Johnson mounted the stage to give Hubert Humphrey the heartiest possible political embrace. He made it clear in his impassioned speech that Humphrey's election would reunite a divided country under fresh, enthusiastic, inspiring new leadership. LBJ poured it on, his rhetoric rising like the rumble of thunder. When his speech was done, he turned to Humphrey, enveloped him in a Texas bear hug, held on to him, and then waved to the crowd, which was going berserk with joy. It's difficult to imagine that Hubert wasn't deeply moved by this heartfelt endorsement by the president.

Alas, Eugene McCarthy was sulking in his tent. Humphrey had

urged him to issue an endorsement of Humphrey's candidacy after the Chicago convention. McCarthy, who had lost the Democratic nomination to Humphrey, demurred, saying his young legions would not take kindly to such an endorsement. Well, why not, Gene? Do your young legions prefer Richard Nixon? Throughout September and October, McCarthy circled the arena with a languor and diffidence that was hard to fathom—or to swallow. Finally, he gave what Hubert judged to be an endorsement drained of particulars and commitment. It didn't mean spit.

To the everlasting detriment of the country, Richard Nixon won the 1968 presidential election. I wanted to weep. The final results were so close. If we had had another week of campaigning, I believe Hubert would have triumphed. With 73,211,875 votes cast, Nixon's margin of victory was 25,552 votes. I ached. I often wondered how many sleepless nights Humphrey must have suffered, thinking about what could have been. And I wondered what might have been if Gene McCarthy had gotten off his ass and pledged his support to Hubert early on in the campaign with real enthusiasm. But I was torturing myself. Nixon had won.

Tragically, neither of the hopes that motivated President Johnson's decision not to seek reelection materialized: Humphrey's election campaign had failed by a whisper, and a swift, successful resolution of the Vietnam peace talks was moving further and further away.

Some days after Nixon defeated Humphrey, Mrs. Johnson called our home. Would we be free to have lunch with the Johnsons later on that day in the family living quarters on the second floor of the Mansion? Of course, I told her. There were five of us there that Sunday, November 18: LBJ, Mrs. Johnson, Mary Margaret, our little daughter, Courtenay, and me. We watched television, *Issues & Answers*, with Walt Rostow, national security adviser, as the guest. Courtenay was well behaved and happy to see her good friend "the prez." Then we went into the family dining room for lunch.

The president began to talk about the difficult challenges he had faced in the past six weeks before the election. He was upset with McGeorge Bundy. Beginning in early October, he said, it looked as if there would be a favorable break in the Paris peace talks. Hanoi began to display a willingness to go forward. Then Walt Rostow reported to the president that McGeorge Bundy was preparing to make a speech about Vietnam that might have a negative effect on the president's peace initiatives. LBJ said he instructed Rostow to call Bundy immediately and ask him to postpone the speech because Hanoi and the United States were in a delicate negotiating moment and an agreement might be imminent. Rostow did call Bundy with the president's urgent request, but Bundy, who had left the White House a year earlier to become president of the Ford Foundation, went ahead with the speech.

Almost immediately, our intelligence-gathering agencies reported that Hanoi had interpreted the speech as follows: Bundy was one of LBJ's closest advisers. His brother Bill Bundy was LBJ's chief operating officer in the Vietnam strategy. Therefore, Hanoi concluded, the speech reflected the views of the president. Hanoi instructed its representatives in Paris to withdraw from the negotiations and fly back to North Vietnam, setting progress back to a state of limbo.

It would be thirteen days before the United States could even get Hanoi back at the table. The president said Bundy's speech and some of Vice President Humphrey's comments indicating that the president would call a bombing halt without any preconditions were the principal causes of the hiatus. Then the president spoke bitterly of another problem, this one coming from Nixon. When it appeared that the gut issues with Hanoi might be resolved, and Ellsworth Bunker, our ambassador to South Vietnam, had reached an agreement with President Thieu of South Vietnam, the glittering prize of peace seemed realistic. The president and President Thieu had even agreed on a joint statement. But it was cruelly evident that Nixon's aides—and Nixon himself—were secretly doing all they could to avoid a bombing halt before the election. Intelligence was forwarded to the president about back-channel deception. Allegedly, Anna Chennault, widow of General Chennault, leader of the famous Flying Tigers in China, had gotten through to Thieu to urge him not to accept any terms. The incentive offered to Thieu was that the South would get a better deal with Nixon in charge and that the speeches by Bundy and Humphrey indicated a sellout of Saigon. The president was apoplectic at Nixon's unacceptable deceit. He was ready to go public to announce this betrayal. It was Dean Rusk, backed by Clark Clifford, who cautioned him against doing this. Rusk said if LBJ went public it could rupture the country even if Nixon lost. But it would be catastrophic if Nixon won. LBJ was not mollified, but grudgingly stayed quiet.

The president said he had been keeping both Humphrey and Nixon informed of progress with the peace talks and that Nixon had pledged to the president that he would support him in his aims. I counted this to be classic Nixon duplicity.

Then LBJ leaned back in his chair and began to discuss more philosophical matters, saying, "I am at odds with Scotty Reston [the celebrated *New York Times* columnist] and Walter Lippman [a very influential syndicated columnist]. They believe that the great thrust in the future will come from China and its Communist system. I don't believe that at all. If it turns out that stabilized governments in Asia are unable to carve out their own destiny, then I'm wrong. But I see nothing in the future to dictate that a Communist system is the direction other Asian nations will take. History will have to be the judge of all this, but I am convinced I'm right and that communism is wrong."

Although frustrated by recent events, the president seemed unperturbed at the prospect of leaving the White House in two months. He seemed comfortable with his decision not to seek another term. When he unreeled himself from the dining table, he picked up Courtenay and gave her a big kiss. She laughed happily.

Once the Rubicon was crossed, our choices in Vietnam narrowed sharply, until ultimately we had just one: to push for negotiation. Papers published long after our withdrawal from Vietnam in the early seventies provided some answers to the questions we had wrestled with. Ho Chi Minh made it clear that no matter how many additional troops we sent in, the North would match the number. He and his successors were prepared to fight five years, or ten years, or for a generation, with no regard for casualties. This was the kind of tenacity we faced, unknowingly.

Lessons We Learned or Should Have Learned from Vietnam

So many years later, Vietnam still lies in the public landscape like a poisoned beast sprawled awkwardly across the reluctant memories of Americans.

It began for noble reasons. We wanted to deter aggression against a small country supposedly fighting a Communist invasion. At the time three presidents—Eisenhower, Kennedy, and Johnson—had believed with stout assurance in a "fixed truth": the domino theory. It asserted that if South Vietnam fell to the Communist insurgents, all of Indochina would be marching under red banners. We later learned that the domino theory was not a fixed truth, but was instead a defunct mythology.

It was reinforced by President Kennedy when on September 9, 1963, two and a half months before his death, he was interviewed on NBC by David Brinkley. The following exchange occurred:

> *Brinkley:* Mr. President, have you any reason to doubt this so-called "Domino theory" that if South Vietnam falls, the rest of Southeast Asia will go under?
>
> *President Kennedy:* No, I believe it. I believe it. I think that the struggle is close enough. China is so large, looms so high just beyond the frontiers, that if South Vietnam went, it would not only give them an improved geographic position for a guerilla assault on Malaysia, but would also give the impression that the wave of the future in Southeast Asia was China and the Communists. So I believe it.

As an observer and participant in all the White House meetings about that unwholesome Vietnam struggle from 1963 to 1966, I can only describe it as a "dark vast" (using Samuel Beckett's memorable phrase in another context).

So what did we learn or should we have learned from Vietnam?

First, no administration can long sustain any war that loses public support. Once the people begin to question a military adventure, once the belief in its worth and long-term value begins to shrink, it is like a heavy body let loose down a hill. It is beyond the control of the one who let it loose. No war can be won without public support. I believe that de Tocqueville, more than 200 years ago, had the most insightful wisdom when he wrote, "The people grow tired of a confusion whose end is not in sight." When the people withdraw their support of a military venture there is no choice but to get out.

Second, no conquering armed force in a foreign country can ever contest successfully against an insurgency where sect, religious, clan, and family loyalties always trump "democratic" governments, and where the insurgencies live among the people like fish in the sea. The only way a native insurgency can be defeated is when the citizen population of the conquered country itself turns on the insurgents. Until the local populace is ready to say "enough," the insurgency will go on—and on. Foreign countries always loathe occupiers no matter the occupiers' benign motives.

Third, while it is very fine to hate the enemy, we first must "know" him. We ought never to consider a military venture into alien lands without knowing with as much precision as possible what kind of people we are about to challenge—who they are and what is their religion, their ancestral traditions, their ethnic background, culture, mores and customs, their resolve?

All of the above was operative in the LBJ Vietnam years. I carefully chose my timing to urge upon President Johnson that he meet with some Indochina historians to listen to them tell him about the cultural, religious, and historical roots that roiled within the tenacious warriors in the north. Wouldn't it be useful for him and his advisers to understand with more clarity just who these northerners were, what they believed, and who they worshipped?

LBJ agreed with me. "Check it out with Bundy."

I met with Mac Bundy in his national security adviser's office in the West Wing. I said, "Mac, why don't we invite Bernard Fall and other serious historians of Indochina to the White House? Let the president hear them and ask questions, like, who are these people, what do they believe in, what provokes them, why are they the way they are? Wouldn't this vital knowledge be in the president's best interests as he tries to figure out what the hell to do or not to do?"

Bundy, whose crisp, orderly mind and talent for biting, brief memos had won the favor of the president, leaned back in his chair and said, "Jack, we have our own historians and experts on that part of the world at the Agency [the CIA] and State. They know as much or more than any outside historian. But let me think about it." Nothing came of it. Moreover, I never met any of "our historians." I am certain the president didn't either.

Fourth, no one questions the bravery and devotion to duty and country that is the hallmark of America's generals, admirals, and Pentagon civilian commanders. But we have to remember that none of them is all-wise, none of them free of the errors that infect every military campaign ever waged in the history of warfare. The great Prussian military strategist Carl von Clausewitz noted a long time ago that battles never turn out the way strategists plan them. The critical factor is something he called "friction." Friction, observed von Clausewitz, "is that which happens in battle that the battle plan never anticipated and which multiplies as the battle progresses. . . . Friction," said von Clausewitz, "is what distinguishes war from war games."

In hindsight, what becomes so startlingly clear from the Vietnam experience is that so many of the military's recommendations made to President Johnson turned out to be wrong.

I make no claim that our commanders in Vietnam and their superiors in the Defense Department were deliberately applying some delusional juice to their numbers. Not at all. But the fact is that too many of the forecasts from the Pentagon were proven in hindsight to be wrong.

LBJ struggled mightily and painfully to get to the negotiating table with the North Vietnamese. He sought the views of the best advisers available to him, mostly from the ranks of Kennedy's administration. After the agony of five days of constant meetings in July 1965, he counted only two who were opposed to staying in Vietnam: George Ball and Mike Mansfield, who passionately urged him to cut his losses and get out. But the other twelve to fourteen key counselors were antagonistic to the views of Ball and Mansfield. I confess I hated the war, but I had no ready alternative. What Ball forecast was his own speculation. None around the table could say for certainty his view was the correct one.

It's easy today, forty-two years later, to see clearly what was seen dimly then, if at all. But decisions must be made at the time they must be made. Waiting is not an option. I sorrowed for President Johnson. To have waged the most successful war against poverty, injustice, discrimination on behalf of the poor, the old, the sick and the black, to have done more than any president save Lincoln, and then to be devoured by a wretched war not of his choosing, is even at this writing too sad to comprehend. Every reach to greatness has its shadows. So it was with this larger-than-life leader.

When on January 21, 1969, LBJ came back home to his ranch in the hill country of Texas, he truly retired. He made few speeches. The only board membership he accepted was that proffered by the Mayo Clinic in Rochester, Minnesota. He spent time at the LBJ Library, but mostly he led a reclusive life on his ranch, which was tiny by Texas standards. He devoted considerable energy to writing his memoir, *The Vantage Point*, published in 1971. He summoned to the ranch a number of former aides, including me, to help in the research, the structure, and the writing. We spent considerable time at the ranch, working in collegial fashion to cobble together the story of his presidency. It is not surprising that no great piece of writing was ever composed by a committee. Even a lesser composition grows more unruly when a battalion of writers convenes to write it. Unfortunately, these long sessions at LBJ's ranch brought to mind William Buckley's richly venomous comment "I would rather have the first fifty names in the Boston phone book govern this country than the entire Harvard faculty." My own view, after the publication of Johnson's memoir, was that I'd rather have one trained chimp with a typewriter writing LBJ's book than a committee of fifty of the best and brightest. *The Vantage Point*, was, sad to say, a pretty dull volume. It was not a bestseller.

In 1972, I found myself raging over the most reprehensible case of amnesia that ever infected a political party. I was sitting before my

TV set watching the Democratic presidential convention. It was not a pretty moment, to my way of thinking, and I daresay it was also an affront to the majority of the American public.

Except for a speech by Senator Ted Kennedy, former president Lyndon Johnson had become a nonperson, expunged from the Democratic Party with all the scouring skills Marxist propagandists used to revise Communist history. Aside from Kennedy, no one mentioned Johnson's name. To add insult to this injury, the convention hall was festooned with photographs of Franklin Roosevelt, John Kennedy, Harry Truman, Adlai Stevenson, Speakers of the House, and other lesser lights, some of whom would be quite obscure to most Americans. I do not recall seeing even a Kodak Brownie snapshot of LBJ.

It was all so Orwellian; the managers of the convention knew exactly what they were doing. They wanted no part of the only president since Lincoln to encode human rights and human dignity in national law. It was written of Lord Burleigh, chief adviser to Elizabeth I, that "he never deserted his friends until it was no longer convenient for him to stand with them." There was an awful lot of inconvenience on display in the 1972 Democratic convention.

I wrote an op-ed piece for the *Washington Post* airing my views about this sorry state of affairs. LBJ called me from his ranch the day after its publication. "Jack, thank you for that article in the *Post*," he said, "but, please, don't come forward anymore to defend me. It can hurt you, and I don't want that. You have a duty to the movie industry, and I don't want your loyalty to me to cause you problems."

I said, "Mr. President, that's one order from you I cannot and will not obey."

Deep in his gut, Lyndon Johnson always knew that his life on this earth would be short. In relaxed moments, he would declare that all the Johnson men in his family, including his father, died young. He insisted he would be no different. Sometimes I think one compelling reason he stepped down from the presidency was that he feared the prospect of dying in the White House or suffering an incapacitating stroke like Woodrow Wilson. He looked upon that as a catastrophe that was simply unacceptable. It would not be good for the country.

So it was that after he left office, LBJ let his hair grow long and took on an appearance older than his years. He resumed his habit of incessant cigarette smoking, which he had given up after his near-fatal heart attack in 1955. He resumed his less-than-healthy eating habits, his weight ballooning as he abandoned the discipline he had taken on when he was president. It was as if he didn't give a damn about his appearance or his health and welcomed death, for he knew it would be appearing on his doorstep soon.

On Sunday morning, 6:30 a.m., on January 21, 1973, my home phone rang. President Johnson was on the line. I was getting dressed for an early-morning indoor tennis game. His voice was spirited, but a tinge of weariness seeped in. "I told Bird that you were my only friend in Washington who would be up at this hour on a Sunday morning."

"How are you feeling, Mr. President?" I asked.

"Well, I feel pretty good right now. But in the afternoon I get these angina pains, hurts like hell. I try to lie down to feel better." He went on to say that he and Mrs. Johnson had decided to spend a few days in Acapulco.

I said, "The sun will be good for you. You always enjoy it down there."

He agreed. "Yeah, I think it will. Acapulco is at sea level, so the altitude won't bother me. We want you and Mary Margaret to join us."

I told him we would be glad to accept his invitation. He encouraged me by saying that Mollie Parnis, famed dress designer from New York and a close, dear friend of the Johnsons, would also be a guest.

"Now, I don't want you trying to take Mollie off by yourself. She's coming down to be with Bird and me. You understand that?" There was laughter in his voice. We talked on for some minutes more.

When he hung up, I felt that his bantering mood was promising. Maybe the sun in Mexico would make him feel better. We had vacationed with the Johnsons several times in Acapulco, staying with them at the spacious, fully staffed home of Mexico's former president Miguel Alemán, situated on a lovely lagoon just off Acapulco Bay and very private. Alemán was a longtime friend of LBJ's.

Several hours after my conversation with the president, I caught a plane for San Francisco on my way to Palo Alto. Douglass Cater, my brilliant colleague in the LBJ White House and now a professor at Stanford, had invited me to be a guest speaker to his class. Doug, his vibrant wife, Libby, and I sat on the patio of the Cater home in Palo Alto. In about a half hour, we would drive over to Stanford and meet the students I was to address. We were having a merry time, re-living our never-to-be-duplicated days when we both served LBJ, swapping stories.

The phone rang; it was for me. My secretary was on the line. "Mr. Valenti, I think you ought to know President Johnson just died at his ranch." Some thirty-four hours after my conversation with him, death sought out the thirty-sixth president in his ranch bedroom in Stonewall, Texas. He died alone, gasping for breath, seconds after he had buzzed the Secret Service for aid. He was sixty-four years old.

My shaking hands when I cradled the phone told the Caters the whole story. We sat there, the three of us, holding back tears and not doing a good job of it, remembering, aching, reaching back to those glory days now gone forever. Of course, I canceled my talk, and that night I was on a plane heading back to Washington.

Mary Margaret and I shared our burden of grief with each other. We had to tell Courtenay, now nine years old, that her dear friend "the prez" had died. She was distraught. David Brinkley, then Amer-ica's premier TV journalist, called me. Would I, he asked, be willing to sit beside him in NBC's special telecast booth and help him com-ment on the return of LBJ's body to Washington to lie in state in the Capitol rotunda?

I said I couldn't. I had to be with Mary Margaret and the John-son family with the coffin. David was insistent. "Jack, you can do a lot more good for the president talking about him to twenty-five million people than you can standing there in the rotunda." David was right.

In NBC's studio in Washington, as I spoke to that enormous un-seen audience, I watched the monitors showing countless officials from around the world, as well as thousands of just ordinary folks whose future had been brightened by this president, pass slowly by the flag-draped coffin. Somehow I could not believe that any man-made box could contain the massive restlessness of LBJ. I fully expected him to come storming out of that coffin, exhorting his aides to get off their butts because there was work to be done.

The next day, Mary Margaret and I were aboard Air Force One with Mrs. Johnson, thanks to the kindness of President Nixon. Once we were airborne, I walked slowly to the rear of the plane. There it was, the coffin covered by an American flag, the coffin of the thirty-sixth president. It hit me with the impact of a balled fist that nine years earlier I had gazed on the flag-draped coffin of the thirty-fifth president, lying in the same rectangular space now occupied by his successor. It was eerie. I had flown in this same plane from Dallas to Washington, with the body of John Fitzgerald Kennedy. Now I was flying on it again, this time from Washington to Austin, and this time the body draped in the flag was that of Lyndon Baines Johnson.

All of a sudden, I was back at the Shamrock Hotel on that day seventeen years earlier when I'd first met LBJ. It was so clear to me. He loomed over me, energy unbounded, eyes riveted on me as if he were looking so deep inside me that everything was revealed. I stood there for a time beside the coffin. It was all so very sad, so very strange. Mary Margaret came and stood beside me. She had served this president far longer than I, working long days and nights over many years, always sustained by the feeling she was doing something for the country that was good and needed by serving this man who would lift the hopes of millions of Americans he would never meet.

Three others on this plane shared my thoughts. They, too, had been on the flight from Dallas to Washington. Mrs. Johnson sat in dry-eyed grief, having shed so many tears already. She had known this moment would be coming but had hoped it would be years from now. Her hands were folded in her lap. The great partnership of her life had ended. She was alone.

Liz Carpenter, too, had been on that earlier flight. Liz, who could never resist a comic line, was now slumped in her seat, wrapped silently in long-ago memories.

Nearby, Marie Fehmer, the president's secretary, who had been so unflappable, so firmly in control on that Dallas flight, sat unseeing, sorrowing as the plane moved steadily toward the birthplace of the president.

We had all been by his side when he needed us, fought beside him, serving him in all those battles he commanded, battles to rid this country of what he called the "damn shame" of rights denied and hopes abandoned, stood there with him as he accepted the grateful embrace of the poor and the underserved, those discriminated against for their race, or age, or poor health. Now we were riding with him to the very end, to be by his side when they put him to rest in the earth of his beloved hill country, an earth he knew so well and loved so much.

In October 2004, a month after I had stepped down as chairman and CEO of the Motion Picture Association of America, a ceremony was held in my honor. Three senators hosted a small reception for me with about thirty close friends in attendance. They were John Warner, courtly Republican senior senator from Virginia, former secretary of the navy, now the powerful chairman of the Senate Armed Services Committee; Fritz Hollings, Democrat from South Carolina, a feared debater and towering force in the Senate; and Daniel Inouye, long-tenured Democratic senator from Hawaii and a genuine hero, the only member of Congress to be awarded the Congressional Medal of Honor for valor above and beyond the call of duty on the battlefield.

These three bulls of the Senate were at the peak of their power and influence. After a half-hour reception in the LBJ Room in the Capitol, all of us stepped into the gallery overlooking the Senate chamber. The three senators stood in the well of the Senate as Warner, in his rich, clear baritone, recounted the history of the Senate and spoke warmly of my service in wartime and in the White House. Then Hollings, his patented South Carolina drawl larded with wit, spoke generously about me. Then came Inouye, who knew Mary Margaret before I did and was the senator I had known the longest, heaping praise on Mary Margaret and me.

Then came the surprise. Senator Warner asked me to step to the floor of the chamber. When I did, all three senators escorted me to the chair and desk of the Senate democratic leader. Hollings said, "This is the chair and desk occupied by Lyndon Johnson during his tenure as the majority leader. It was from this desk that he ruled over the Senate with force and command never seen or heard in this American parliament before or since."

Senator Inouye beckoned me to sit where LBJ sat for his six years as the youngest Senate commander in its history. I sat down, my hands moving slowly and quietly atop his old desk. From the gallery, my friends applauded. As for me, I cannot really describe my emotions. Perhaps it was foolish of me to be so charged with long-ago memories. Then, eerily, I could feel the powerful presence of Lyndon Johnson. Silly? I guess so. But the feeling was palpable, just as real as anything I've ever felt.

Then the spell was broken. I rose from that chair to embrace my three old Senate comrades with heartfelt affection and gratitude. Later on, my friends in the gallery, some of whom had been part of government in Washington for many years, told me they did not believe such a scene had ever taken place before on the floor of the Senate. It was unique. And only three such prestigious captains of the Senate could have brought it about.

And I do solemnly swear that Lyndon Johnson was there that night, in that historic Senate chamber that he knew and ruled for so long.

When I sat at his old desk, I could feel his hand on my shoulder.

PART III

HOLLYWOOD

Chapter 10

LEW WASSERMAN:
THE HOLLYWOOD CURTAIN OPENS

Lew and Edie Wasserman and I at the LBJ Ranch in November 1964.

Around 2:30 in late February 1966, two remarkable men arrived at my White House office.

Lew Wasserman was no ordinary movie mogul. As I put it once, "If Hollywood is Mount Olympus, Lew Wasserman is Zeus." Taciturn and publicity shy to a degree that bordered on the pathological, Wasserman would be a movie titan for over sixty years. He was now the chief executive officer of MCA Universal Studios, one of the major film and TV production and distribution enterprises in the American movie industry. At age twenty, Lew Wasserman had been handling publicity for a local nightclub in Cleveland when he was asked to join MCA, which at that time booked popular dance bands in Chicago and New York. Thirteen years later, Wasserman was president of a talent agency that had become a dominant force in Hollywood.

As the new head of MCA talent agency, Lew immediately charged into the studio fiefdoms. Soon, some 60 percent of all the major TV and movie stars in Hollywood, including Clark Gable, Jimmy Stewart, and Bette Davis, were handled by MCA. These stars, writers, and directors, including Alfred Hitchcock, were guarded and guided by MCA's black-suited agents. They may have operated like ghostly figures outside the public eye, but these MCA legions roamed Hollywood from its outer peripheries to its innermost circles, penetrating every studio. They wooed and won just about any star they coveted.

It's difficult for Hollywood outsiders to fully grasp the leviathan power wielded by Wasserman in his heyday as chief of the MCA agency. At one point Jack Warner, the Warner brother who ran that venerable studio with an impish smile and an iron fist, became furious with Bette Davis, a Warner box office star. He suspended her over some perceived slight—that is, he took her off the Warner pay-roll, leaving her in career limbo. Immediately she called Wasserman, her agent. Lew ordered his agents to call their clients now working on Warner's studio lot and "suggest" to them that they should fall ill, absent themselves from work the next day, and assemble at a nearby restaurant for a meeting with Wasserman—whereupon some 70 per-cent of all the actors on the Warner lot were stricken with vague but debilitating ailments.

The next day, when Jack Warner learned of the epidemic that had struck his studio, leaving every sound stage silent, he fumed and raged. It did not take him long to learn what had happened and why. He put in a phone call to Wasserman, who was mysteriously unavail-able. Finally, after two days Warner got Wasserman on the phone. "Lew, I've missed you. I've been trying to call you."

Wasserman was equally gracious. "It's good to hear from you, Jack. What can I do for you?"

"Well, I was thinking of what I could do for you, like suspending every actor who refuses to show up for work," Jack said equably.

"Fine," said Lew, every bit as calm. "You'll be in court. It will be nice to see you there, Jack."

Silence on the other end of the line. Then Jack said, "Or, I could welcome Bette back to the studio."

"That would be kind of you," said Lew. "I know she would be pleased."

The next day, Bette Davis received a lordly hug from Jack Warner, all the sound stages were back in play, and Warner and Lew had lunch together. Such was the majesty with which Lew Wasser-man presided over a town populated by kings and lords who put much store in their own power. Lew's power was just that much greater. For all their fame, actors, directors, writers, and producers were daily assaulted with anxieties and insecurities. In Lew's protec-tive embrace, they felt cocooned from real or imagined distractions, freeing them to undertake their creative work.

It was Lew who changed forever the fiscal foundations of Holly-wood, when he made a deal for Jimmy Stewart that gave the actor a percentage of the revenues of *Winchester '73*, a western that few at the studio thought would have mass appeal. Actually, Lew had constructed a double dip, linking the western with another movie that the studio had higher hopes for—*Harvey*, in which Stewart played alongside a large invisible rabbit. When Lew offered Stewart's services for both films at a low salary, but with a percentage of revenues on *Winchester '73*, the studio thought it had hit a home run; they were getting Jimmy for chump change on the western and at an equally low cost for their favorite, *Harvey*.

They were wrong. Both movies were hits, but it was *Winchester '73* that was a real honey at the box office. Stewart prospered. Wasserman triumphed. Every star in town felt envious of Jimmy Stewart and his magician agent. Once more, Lew had outwitted the moguls and in one contract had redefined the parameters of compensation in a way that would become more or less the norm for big stars going forward.

Some four years before the meeting in my office, Lew Wasserman had departed the agency business by buying Universal Studios. He turned over the agency's clients to his colleagues, who organized their own agencies. MCA as a talent agency was no more, but Wasserman now had a view of Hollywood from the mountaintops. It was a piece of delectable irony that Lew's revolutionary profit arrangement for famous stars now hung heavy around the necks of Universal executives, but Lew never fretted. He just went about figuring out new ways to balance the scales.

On the day we met, Lew Wasserman was fifty-three years old, lean and tall, with penetrating, observant eyes shrouded by large black-rimmed glasses, his hawkish face perennially tanned, his frame superbly tailored and fit. Wasserman was a commanding and often fearsome presence. It is certainly true that Lyndon Johnson had the largest impact on my life. Had he not brought me to Washington and installed me in the seat of national power, my life as this book describes it would have been the stuff of fantasy. But it was Lew Wasserman who was the central force behind bringing me to Hollywood, and I never forgot that, or him.

Like Lew, Arthur Krim, the chairman of United Artists, along with his partner, Bob Benjamin, had radically reshaped the movie industry. UA, famously founded by Mary Pickford, Charlie Chaplin, and others years before, had been bought by Krim and Benjamin in the early fifties. Then they did something that was, by Hollywood standards, revolutionary. They eschewed real estate, or studios with sound stages, or any of the accoutrements of the typical sprawling movie giants. Their business/creative model took a totally new shape and form: a film studio without studios, free from all the overhead such physical premises imposed.

Directors, writers, and producers would come to UA with a movie idea, a treatment, a scenario, a script, or a book to be adapted. Krim and Benjamin would agree to do the movie, subject to approval of the script and budget. Once they had read the script, approved the budget, and green-lighted the project, they literally said, "Go make the movie and come back to us with a finished print." No wonder the best creative brains in movieland could not wait to work with United Artists. No script development teams or spiraling ladders of approvals to climb: It was a director's dream, as well as a haven for producers. UA's New York office on Broadway was an ordinary place, devoid of opulence. Tattered carpets covered a floor on which sat ancient furniture that proclaimed to visitors, "This is a low-cost operation; we put our money in the movie and the marketing."

To say UA was successful is to grossly understate the case. In the years before Krim and Benjamin sold UA to an insurance company named Transamerica (one of the few bad moves the two of them ever made), United Artists won more Best Picture Academy Awards than any other movie company. If the movie industry had a Hall of Fame, UA under the leadership of Krim and Benjamin would surely have occupied a premier place in it.

Few people ever knew that in the last two years of the LBJ presidency, no single person was more influential with President Johnson, no one had won LBJ's trust and admiration more, than Arthur Krim. LBJ found Krim to be soft-spoken, without self-importance, given to speaking in compact sentences garmented in logic and common sense. Krim's selfless personality endeared him to Johnson. Krim sought no plaudits, avoided the press, and aimed only to be of value to the president. Period. Only a few of us in the White House knew of Krim's intimacy with the president or how often the Krims spent the night on the second floor of the Mansion.

. . .

After a few pleasantries, Wasserman and Krim got down to business.

Wasserman said, "Jack, we've come to talk to you about the top leadership post in our industry. That post is open, and Arthur and I want to offer it to you. We can assure you the board of directors will elect you unanimously."

I was astonished. I had heard about the Motion Picture Association of America, certainly, but hadn't ever given it much thought. When I did some homework on the MPAA, I learned that according to gossip, Ted Sorensen, Pierre Salinger, Adlai Stevenson, and even Richard Nixon had at one time or another been considered for the job of running the organization. But because the position demanded unanimous approval from its board, no one had been given the crown. I learned that the MPAA derived from an institution created by the immigrant founders of Hollywood—Samuel Goldwyn, Louis B. Mayer, Joseph Schenck, Jesse Lasky, and others—in 1922.

The MPAA was born as the result of various Hollywood scandals, most notably a sex orgy ending in the death of a young starlet that involved Fatty Arbuckle, a major film comedy star at the time. The national press went crazy, with banner headlines of arrogance gone wild, sexual aberrations, and other gory tales. This all lay heavily on Hollywood's founding moguls, who had become passionate patriots in their new land. Excessively sensitive to public opinion owing to their eagerness to be part of the American mainstream, the old pioneers took decisive action. They quickly organized the Motion Pictures Producers and Distribution Association (forerunner to the Motion Picture Association of today), whose objective was to bring—in their words—sanity, decency, and morality to the screen. It wasn't merely window dressing: Hollywood's first moguls meant to do just that.

To build the association and give it a moral leadership, they reached into President Harding's cabinet and tapped Will Hays, postmaster general at a time when that cabinet post had heft and influence. They agreed to give Hays, who was considered a pillar of purity in an otherwise sleaze-ridden administration, large powers in return for which he would serve as the public face and conscience of the movie industry.

It was Will Hays who, in the thirties, created the Hays Code. For more than thirty years, this code was the iron-fisted moral arbiter of screen stories, dialogue, manners, and customs. It literally ruled the content of film (not exactly a model of the First Amendment). The source bed of its power was the fact that the major studios owned all the first-run theaters in the land. If any outside producer could not get a seal of approval for his film from the Hays office, his film would be relegated to the purgatory of second-run movie theaters. Few producers were keen to take on such a dismaying power.

Years later, in the fifties, a power stronger than the Hays office showed up in the form of the Department of Justice. In a historic Supreme Court antitrust case, the government compelled the studios to sell their theaters, and the stranglehold of the Hays office on film content began to ease up a bit. In 1945, Hays was replaced by Eric Johnston, a tall, handsome, ingratiating man who was an intimate of General Eisenhower, among others. Johnston, I was informed, was a bit removed from the workaday duties of his Hollywood job, being content to serve on the board of United Airlines, to perform foreign chores for President Eisenhower, and to spend little time in Hollywood (or in Washington, for that matter). New York was more to his taste. From his desk in the MPAA office in Manhattan, he ran the association's worldwide operation with loose reins. But he was well connected politically, and the moguls seemed to find him suitable. Indeed, his lengthy tenure seemed assured, until he died unexpectedly in late 1964.

So it was that I found myself listening to Wasserman and Krim as they outlined the scope of this key post in the movie industry. I heard them out, and then I said, "I really do thank you for offering me what seems like a dream job. But frankly, I can't leave the president now. He wouldn't take kindly to it, so I have to say no to you, although I am deeply grateful."

They both nodded as if this were the answer they expected. They stood up. As they were leaving my office, Wasserman turned to me and said, "Jack, we understand your reluctance. But we'll be back, so keep thinking about this."

Sure enough, in two weeks Lew called me. "Have you thought about our offer?" I told him I had, but my answer was the same. I just couldn't leave the White House. Later that same week, Arthur Krim called. I surmised they were double-teaming me. I was a bit amused and surprised that these two giants of the industry were still pursuing me. Then, a month after his first visit, Lew called me again. He was going to be in town, and could he come by to visit? Of course, I said. And two days later, he was once more in my office.

He said, "Jack, Arthur and I are not going to keep intruding on you. But I have one question that I want you to answer, not today, but in a couple of days, after you've had a chance to think hard about your answer."

He definitely had my interest. "Question?" I said. "What's your question?"

He said, "Before I put it to you, do we not agree that this job is a temporary one—that you won't be here one second longer than LBJ is president?"

"Of course," I answered. "When the president leaves, I leave."

"Okay, so your job is temporary. Agreed?" he said.

I said, "No question about that."

He said, "All right, here's the question: What do you want to do with the rest of your life?" He rose from his chair. "I'm not pushing you, but this job will not stay open indefinitely. It has to be filled, and soon. So get back to me as soon as you have the answer to my question."

Frankly, I had not thought about the rest of my life. But after Lew departed my office, I found his question hit alarmingly close to home. I knew I didn't want to go back to my advertising agency. I also knew I didn't want to go back to Texas and go into land development or oil production, which a number of my close friends in Houston had suggested. I just didn't think it would be fun, although there was lots of money to be made in either of those arenas. I was, I admitted to myself, enticed by a new job that would be exciting and, yes, fun every day. The White House with Lyndon Johnson was burnout duty, but it was sublimely stirring, with a new challenge every day. Even though I was bone tired, I was eager to wake each morning and be about my tasks. Only a job like that would do, so perhaps I needed to take a closer look at this MPAA position.

I discussed the offer with Mary Margaret, who instantly recognized that I was intrigued. My earlier work at Humble Oil and my post–Harvard Business School advertising agency years were in the creative arena, and she knew the creative process was always stirring within me. As Mary Margaret and I talked, I began to come to a conclusion. Movies, TV, yes, that's what I would like to do with the rest of my life. I told Mary Margaret I had made my choice. She smiled. She had known before I did what I would decide.

I was now keen to take the job. Mary Margaret, however, was a better judge of a particular obstacle I faced. "The president is going to be unhappy about this," she said. "He's not going to like your decision. You know he doesn't react well to anyone who chooses to leave him, and particularly someone he relies on as much as he does you." How right she was.

I called Lew Wasserman and let him know of my interest. Somehow, he didn't seem surprised. I surmised Lew, the master negotiator, had already factored in my response to his question. "What I have to do now, Lew," I said, "is to let the president know of my decision. I've got to have his blessing."

There was a moment of silence. Then Lew asked, "What's your judgment? Is he going to let you go or not?"

I had more confidence in drawing to an inside straight than in fathoming the complexities of LBJ's thought process. "I think he'll agree to it when I tell him how close I'll be, just across the street."

Lew chuckled. "To LBJ, across the street might as well be a hundred miles."

Once again, Lew's prophecies were on the mark. Later that afternoon, I hit the red button on my phone console, which connected me directly to the president.

"What's going on, Jack?" came LBJ's familiar accent.

"Do you have a free moment for a private chat, Mr. President?"

Now the voice was lower. LBJ did not like surprises. "What's the issue?"

"I'll come right in and go over it with you, okay, sir?"

"Yeah, come in now."

I was in the Oval Office in a few seconds. He looked up from his desk, his gaze heavy on me. Before he could say anything, I sat down quickly a few feet from him and very briefly recounted my conversation with Lew and Arthur. I ended my summary with, "And I would like to take this job, but I would be instantly available to you at any time, with my office across the street from here."

I must report that even at a distance of many years, the memory of his response still rattles my teeth. The truth is that the wrath of Achilles was mild compared with Lyndon Johnson giving full vent to his grievances. To say he was highly pissed off is a huge understatement. Mary Margaret had divined it all. The resignation of someone in his inner circle was, to Johnson, a personal affront to be responded to with the force of a category 5 hurricane. I choose not to accurately recount what he said because even at this distance I still shudder and because my conscience is so easily tormented. I will say that the nicest thing he called me was "Benedict Arnold."

Finally, as the last of his obloquy drained away, the phone rang. He picked it up. "Dick, this is Lyndon Johnson." It was either Richard Russell or Richard Helms, CIA director. "Yes, come over right now. Bring whoever you want to brief me, but I don't want an army accompanying you. Just one other person, understood?" It was Helms, and he obviously understood.

The president put down the phone. I stood up and said, "Can we talk further about this, sir?" He glared at me, unmistakably furious, but didn't answer. I nodded and got the hell out of the Oval Office. Now I had a bad-ass problem. I knew I would not leave the White House without the president's blessings, but that surely wasn't going to be forthcoming any time soon. And I knew the MPAA job was not going to languish unfilled for long. What I needed was reinforcements.

First I talked to Mary Margaret. Then I rallied my spirits and called Lew. "Lew," I said, "I need help. Can you and Ed Weisl [MCA Universal's legal counsel and LBJ's close friend] chat with the president? Make it clear that I will be as accessible to him in my new job as I am right now in the West Wing."

Lew listened quietly. "I'm going to be in Washington next Tuesday. I'll bring Ed with me. Maybe we can get an appointment with him."

Tuesday came, and Lew and LBJ confidant Ed Weisl had their

appointment with the president. I waited impatiently at my desk, some fifteen feet from the internal entrance to the Oval Office. The extent of my problem was immediately brought home to me when Lew and Ed entered my office.

"Well," I said, "what's the verdict?"

Ed Weisl smiled. "If you count being thrown out of the Oval Office by the president good news, then it is a happy day." They told me that the president was still furious at their effrontery in trying to spirit away one of his chief aides. LBJ had much affection for Weisl and equal respect for Wasserman, but it was becoming clear that either I left without the president's blessing or I gave up the notion of being the new head of the MPAA. It was one of those Hobson's choices—either the firing squad or the electric chair. Not good news at all.

For the next four days, I mournfully reviewed my options. I had one last idea. If I could have a private meeting with the president, with Mary Margaret by my side, I might be able to convince him the MPAA job had benefits for him as well as for me. Mary Margaret had worked for him for almost ten years. She would rather have her fingernails pulled out with a Stillson wrench than betray him. Johnson knew that. Her loyalty was beyond question, and loyalty was the indispensable connection to LBJ. Moreover, LBJ had total confidence in her political savvy and her judgment.

There was a meeting on Vietnam that afternoon in the Cabinet Room. I sat in my usual place behind and to the right of the president. When the meeting ended, before he had a chance to leave the room, I said to him, "Is it possible Mary Margaret and I might have dinner with you this week while Mrs. Johnson is out of town?"

To my delight, he said without rancor, "Yes, let's do that. Tonight."

At 8:00 p.m. that evening, the president, Mary Margaret, and I were in the family dining room on the second floor of the Mansion, just the three of us. He was in a rather jovial mood, telling a story about a phone conversation he had had with Senator Everett Dirksen, Senate Republican leader, with whom Johnson had an affectionate relationship. He did a perfect imitation of Dirksen's deep-throated baritone, the inflections right on target. It was very funny.

When the president dug into his tapioca pudding, I turned to the business at hand. It seemed the right moment. When LBJ was into his beloved tapioca, his resistance was at its lowest. I said, "The truth is, Mr. President, I can be of great value to you as head of the MPAA. I will insert into my contract that I will be available to you for three months if need be. I'll also be available to you on a daily basis. My office would be just across the street. You will have an additional assistant with no expense to the government, in a sense a pro bono assistant." I knew that LBJ was mightily attracted to anything pro bono.

Mary Margaret moved in at that moment. "Mr. President, Jack believes this job will not be available for much longer. He wants it, but not if you believe that his taking it will cause you problems. We both love you, and we want to do what you believe is right." She spoke softly and warmly, secure in the knowledge that LBJ understood the value of her long service to him. It was indeed the right insertion at exactly the right moment.

The president leaned back in his chair. "Jack will be marketable no matter when he leaves the White House, now or a few years from now. I think he ought to stay in public life. He's good at that, and he can continue to do good things for his country. But I understand what you're saying."

I pushed no more, nor did Mary Margaret. I sensed the softening in his tone and in his body language. So we drifted into political chitchat, the president off again into one of his stories. It was a pleasant, and to my mind rewarding, evening—which was why I was caught totally off guard several days later. Around 6:00 p.m., the president called me. I bounced briskly into the Oval Office. LBJ stood up and came around his desk. He put his arm around me.

"I've got some great news for you. Today I talked to Prime Minister [Aldo] Moro in Rome, and tomorrow I want to announce I am appointing you the U.S. ambassador to Italy. Both the prime minister and the Italian ambassador are happy about my choice."

He was grinning now, a wide, satisfied expression. He turned back to his desk to fetch a color photograph off the top, then thrust the photo into my hands. "That's the residence of the American ambassador in Rome, maybe the best embassy residence anywhere in Europe," he said triumphantly. True. Villa Taverna was the most elegant of ambassadorial homes, famous for its architecture and am-

With my one-year-older first cousin, Bernard De George, outside the home of our maternal grandfather, Bernardo De George, in Houston.

Here I am in my younger days in Houston.

The pilots and bombardiers of the 448th Squadron in our so-called "officers club" in Solenzara, Corsica, 1944.

Left: Me in basic flight training in Lancaster, California, 1943. *Right:* With my B-25 in Ancona, Italy, in 1945.

Left: Vice President and Mrs. Johnson with Mary Margaret and me on our wedding day, June 1, 1962.

Below: Walking with Courtenay, and Mary Margaret holding John, on 31st Street in Georgetown, 1966.

Courtenay giving a kiss to "the Prez" in the Rose Garden of the White House.

With Bobby Kennedy, 1965.

Henry Kissinger and me, 1967.

Opposite

Above (left to right): Louis Nizer, celebrated New York lawyer and author; Olivia de Havilland; Mrs. Nizer; and me at the 1969 screening of an enhanced color version of *Gone with the Wind* at Radio City Music Hall in New York City, thirty years after the film's world premiere in 1939.

Below: Dinner with Gina Lollobrigida, at her villa in Rome, 1966.

On the set of *The Bobo*, with Peter Sellers and his wife, Britt Ekland, 1967.

Here I am in the early 1970s with Paul Newman, Barbra Streisand, and Sidney Poitier at the announcement of their new movie company, First Artists, in New York City.

With Sidney Poitier, 1971.

With President Ford, 1975.

Johnny Carson, Joanna Carson, Hugh O'Brian, and me in Beverly Hills, 1978.

Sharing stories with Kirk Douglas and Burt Lancaster.

With Clint Eastwood and Courtenay Valenti.

Shirley MacLaine, me, and Gregory Peck at the Cannes Film Festival.

Here I am at the rostrum announcing a new TV rating system in the East Room of the White House; Vice President Gore is on the left and President Clinton is on the right.

Roman Polanski and me, dining in Honfleur in the Normandy
country of France in 2002 during the Deauville Film Festival.

Relaxing with Michael Douglas at the Augusta National Golf Course.

Mary Margaret Valenti, my wife of 44 years
and counting.

Conferring with Governor Arnold Schwarzenegger in Washington, D.C.

With Italian prime
minister Silvio
Berlusconi in the
PM's office in
2004. He had just
conferred on me
the highest civilian
award given to a
non-Italian citizen,
the Knight of the
Grand Cross.

A playful,
affectionate
touch of the cheek
with Berlusconi
at the reception
following the
award ceremony.
Mary Margaret
is in the center.

In Beverly Hills
with King Abdullah
of Jordan.

biance. "Moreover," he went on, "Dean Rusk tells me he has a contingency fund that he will make available to you so you can entertain on the right scale without digging into your own resources. Pretty nice, eh?"

What I knew was that if you approached a crowded event in Washington and called out, "Mr. Ambassador," half the people in the room would turn around to face you. Washington was filled with ex-ambassadors, few of whom ever went back to their hometown digs.

I took a slow, deep breath. I had to be careful, very careful. I nodded and said, "Mr. President, I am so grateful to you, as well as being a bit awestruck. What an honor. But, sir, I am forty-three years old, and I'll be an ambassador not one second longer than you are president, which means my ambassadorial tenure will be over in six years. So when I'm forty-eight or so, my public life will be done. On the other hand, the MPAA job has the potential of starting a career that will last a lot longer." (Needless to say, I didn't have an inkling of how very long that would turn out to be.)

At that moment, I think I broke through. The president was obviously disappointed. But if there had been anger before, it was there no longer. He patted me on the shoulder and tossed the photo back on his desk. "All right, now this is what you ought to do. Call Paul Porter [Porter was a former chairman of the Federal Communications Commission and a founding partner of Arnold & Porter, one of the finest law firms in the town] and ask him to negotiate your contract. Paul will get you everything you ought to have. These Hollywood guys are smart, and they know how to slice a contract to their benefit. Paul will see that you are protected."

It was an exquisitely executed turnaround, typically Johnsonian. When he came to a conclusion, he moved swiftly to implement it.

On the morning of April 25, I dispatched my formal letter of resignation right to the president's desk.

> DEAR MR. PRESIDENT,
> The economic commitments to my growing family cause me to regretfully submit my resignation as Special Assistant to the President, effective May 15.
> I cannot competently tell you what it has meant to

serve, and hopefully to be of some small value to the
President of the United States. Although I will no longer
be a member of your staff, my loyalty to you and my
commitment to your cause will be undiminished.

It was a hard letter to compose. I kept it brief, stripped of various
sentiments I yearned to express, but I believed the letter conveyed
my feelings, however constrained by formality. I did attach a small,
very personal note to accompany the letter.

To my amazement, that very evening I received a response from
the president.

> DEAR JACK:
> This has been a very long day.
> Your letter of resignation and the personal note just
> came in, and I wanted to acknowledge both before
> knocking off for the day.
> You know how much I will miss your companionship,
> your good cheer, your brilliant mind, and your store-
> house of information. You have been someone very
> special to me for a long time—first because of Mary
> Margaret, and then Courtenay, but really all the time—
> it was you, yourself.
> I guess I just didn't want to admit that a man should
> need another man quite so much. This move will be
> good for you and your family, and they must come first.
> They deserve anything you or I could do for them
> because all of them have already gone a long way with us.
> You have served your country with devotion and dis-
> tinction, and you can always be as proud, or prouder of
> that, as you are of your fifty-one missions. You served
> me, though, even more—and I thank you, and love you,
> and am very proud of you.

It was signed, "Lyndon B. Johnson."

I confess when I read the letter, I wept. They were tears of joy
and tears of gratitude that I had been able to spend so much time
serving my country and serving a president whose passion to make
this country greater eclipsed all other considerations. Even now, after
so many long years have passed, that letter still touches a profound

well of affection and loyalty that lies deep inside me. I owe so much to that man. It is a debt I can never repay. The world I was about to enter would be filled with drama, and glamour, and tremendous satisfaction, but my years in the White House were the summertime of my life.

So it was that I showed up on an April afternoon in 1966 in the press lobby of the White House to announce my resignation. Dozens of reporters and photographers were gathered. It was for me a moment rife with contradictory emotions: I felt real regret that I was disconnecting from the most substantive job I would ever have, and at the same time I was filled with eagerness to begin a new life in a dazzling, uncharted world. I had come to Washington as a Texas advertising executive and political consultant, untested in the brute sport of presidential politics. I was leaving blessed with the aura of presidential favor, no longer completely unknown, and certainly no longer untested.

I had trouble controlling my emotions that final day. It was especially difficult when I was offering my gratitude to the president for allowing me to perform on the largest stage in the world. I remembered how when I was very young I used to think about "my destiny," knowing only that there was something out there—something shining with challenges gathered in unarranged shadows, and that one day I would have my shot at that future. And now it was all around me. Youthful dreams do come true. It was a long leap from Alamo Street to the White House and now to Hollywood. I confess it was kind of magical—unplanned, unexpected, and completely beyond the bounds of everyday life.

But humility was clearly in order, too. Each day in the White House, LBJ, who understood the dangers of hubris, made sure his top assistants grasped the necessity of not inhaling all the praise heaped on them simply because they worked near the president. That's why he insisted every day on pouring spoonfuls of humility through our clenched teeth. We didn't think we needed it. But he knew we did. The truth is that any one of thousands or more young men and women in the country could have done the work that I and the other assistants to the president were chosen to do. The operative word is "chosen." Just as JFK had his own band of "chosen few," so did LBJ. So would every president in the years ahead, which means we were all plucked out of varying degrees of anonymity to work beside the most powerful human being in the world. We won no elections, nor did we triumph in any competitive contests. We were just "chosen." As a result, most of us became minor celebrities and certainly, as LBJ put it, "marketable" to those outside the palace gates.

My time in the White House was now done. As I look back on those years, I realize they represent the only time in my life I fully set aside personal ambition. I had only one motive: to serve the president to the outermost reaches of my ability. I had only one objective: to try in my small way to help the president inject hope where none existed in the lives of so many Americans. I had only one goal: to do my job so well that it could be said that my work in the White House counted, however modestly, in raising the standard of living for all those who lived in this land.

Much earlier in my life, I had read Lord Macaulay's revelatory line, "No man is fit to govern great societies who hesitates about disobliging the few who have access to him for the sake of the many whom he will never see." Now I had come to know firsthand how accurate Macaulay was and how liberating it could be to set aside ego and ambition to help people I would never see or meet. And now I was stepping into the movie world. Oddly, I was not frightened. I figured if I could survive the brutal pit of presidential politics, I could somehow manage to navigate the brambles of Hollywood. In fact I was gravely underestimating the difficulties of the journey I was about to take.

My first meeting as chairman, president, and chief executive officer of the Motion Picture Association of America took place on May 16, 1966. We met in the boardroom of the MPAA's worldwide headquarters on the eighteenth floor of the Morgan Guaranty Bank building, 522 Fifth Avenue, at Forty-fourth Street, in New York City. In the years ahead, I was going to get to know every nook and cranny of the MPAA's offices around the world, and of the movie world itself, in Hollywood and in every foreign country with a movie industry of its own and/or theaters and television stations. I was going to embark on lifelong friendships with international actors, directors, producers, writers, and theater owners, as well as movie journalists and high government officials in just about every country on the planet.

But first I had to meet and forge relationships with the masters of the movie universe, the chiefs of the major American motion picture studios who constituted the membership of the MPAA: MCA Universal, Twentieth Century–Fox, Paramount, Columbia, Warner Bros., and MGM. My objective in this initial meeting—first impressions are often lasting—was to persuade them that I was a leader, ready to make and enact plans for the long-term benefit of these movie companies.

Assembled in that first meeting were Hollywood's reigning emperors of all they beheld, and they beheld a lot. We met in a thoroughly undistinguished, windowless conference room, around a large rectangular table surrounded by stiff-backed chairs. No pictures on the wall, nothing to herald the Hollywood connection. Within a month, I ordered the boardroom to be repainted and the long rectangular table to be replaced by an oval one and surrounded by pictures of—guess what?—movie stars. How on earth could the preeminent organization in the movie world have a boardroom that might have been designed for use by asparagus growers?

There was movie history in the room that day. At the table was the last living Warner brother, Jack, head of the storied Warner Bros. Studios. With him was his top aide, Benjamin Kalmenson, who I soon learned played "bad cop" to Jack Warner's "good cop." They could have been one helluva vaudeville act.

Darryl F. Zanuck sat with imperial assurance, the only studio head who had personally produced films. He had become head of Fox's mammoth studio when he was twenty-nine, creating smash hit films starring one of the most renowned movie stars of all time, the great German shepherd Rin Tin Tin. Zanuck produced and wrote all the great dog's movies. In later years, Lassie would challenge Rin Tin Tin for best canine actor of all time, but in his day Rin Tin Tin was top dog. Now in his sixties, as feared and as fierce as ever, Zanuck ruled

Twentieth Century–Fox like a medieval monarch. His brilliant son, Richard, who later became the production chief of Fox, proved that nepotism can indeed serve a company's best interests. Even today, Dick Zanuck is at the top of his game, along with his co-producer wife, Lili.

Across the table was Spyros Skouras, chairman of Fox (a titular position, since Darryl Zanuck called the shots), who first set foot in America from his native Greece some fifty years ago and whose picturesque accent was as unintelligible that day as it was on his first day in America.

Heading up Columbia Pictures were Abe Schneider and Leo Jaffe, successors to the late Harry Cohn, whose rough, oversize energy built a tiny, fragile company into a major enterprise that ranked with the venerable film companies that started it all. Representing Paramount were the aging but highly respected Barney Balaban and his chief aide, George Weltner. Within a year, they would be gone, replaced by one of the most charismatic figures to inhabit the movie industry, a commodity trader/conglomerate chieftain, a native of Austria who became the owner and CEO of Paramount, Charles Blühdorn.

From the MGM made famous by Louis B. Mayer as the studio that had "more stars than there are in the heavens," Bob O'Brien was in attendance. The truth is that once Mayer, the biggest of the studio titans, was toppled, MGM lost its preeminence. Within a year, O'Brien would be history. It is amazing to note that Kirk Kerkorian, the reclusive, legendary investor and biggest hotel casino owner in Las Vegas, has bought and sold MGM at least three times as of this writing. Kerkorian, a courtly, quiet, self-effacing business genius, seemed to have a divine instinct for knowing when to buy and when to sell and when to buy back and sell again. From United Artists came a powerful trio, Arthur Krim and his longtime business partner and fellow lawyer, Bob Benjamin, plus a remarkably able and wise executive, Arnold Picker. Universal Studios was represented at the table by Lew Wasserman and Milton Rackmil.

Present also was the lawyer/confidant to them all, Edwin L. Weisl. A small, somewhat rotund man, with thinning hair and a wispy brush of a mustache, Ed Weisl was the senior partner and primary rainmaker of the New York law firm of Simpson Thacher & Bartlett. Weisl was close to the most powerful business leaders in corporate and industrial America. For example, he was friend and confidant to the founder of the Hertz car rental company. He was dubbed by the financial press "the fifteenth partner" of Lehman Brothers, so intimately involved was he with its patrician chairman, Bobby Lehman. The list of his friends and clients stretched across the nation. Moreover, Ed was so close to President Johnson that LBJ forced him to become the New York State Democratic Committee chairman, purely because Ed didn't want to say no to LBJ.

Ed was the only attorney who in my long tenure in the movie industry ever represented two film companies at the same time and at the same table: Universal and Paramount. Wasserman and Paramount's Balaban and later Charles Blühdorn all had the highest regard for this amazing lawyer. If Wasserman and Blühdorn had ever had a serious quarrel, they would have asked Ed Weisl to be the binding arbitrator. Quite astonishing. Indeed, when Ed died years later, I had any number of famous industrialists, corporate barons, lawyers, and superrich investors come up to me to say how much they missed Ed, because he "was my best friend." I felt the same way.

At my first board meeting that day in May, I looked around the table at representatives from these six companies, the latter-day progeny of the Eastern European immigrants who literally invented the U.S. movie industry, and in so doing dominated world cinema. The Walt Disney Company was not at that time a member of the MPAA. (I made their entry into the association one of my highest priorities, and some five years later, I was successful in enlisting them into membership.)

As I look back on this gathering of Hollywood's titans, I count it a monument to the credibility and prestige of Wasserman and Krim that I had been chosen by the board to head the MPAA when none of them save Lew and Arthur had ever met me! I mingled with the group ahead of the meeting, trying to size them up even as I knew perfectly well they were taking my measure. The fact that I had just arrived from the White House and had the ear of the president gave me a degree of respect and power that these moguls clearly admired. Power was something they understood. And they had no hesitancy in wielding it brutally if necessary.

I wanted to demonstrate that I was no dumb-ass when it came to films, so before the meeting began, I said to Darryl Zanuck, "You made a movie I really liked. It was incredibly well done."

Darryl, his little mustache twitching in a face that I swear made him look like a squirrel about to leap on an acorn nestled somewhere in my jacket, said with some interest, "Yeah, which one was it?"

"*Wilson*," I trumpeted, naming the film produced by Zanuck about President Woodrow Wilson, played so compellingly by Alexander Knox.

With an exasperated gesture of disdain, Darryl said, "You would pick the one film that we had to arrest people to go to the theater. Disaster at the box office."

How the hell was I to know?

When finally I called the meeting to order, we went through and voted on all the technical resolutions attached to my new status. Then I launched into what I judged to be a rousing speech addressing my commitment to the movie industry in all its forms. I intended, I said, to look closely at giving parents more information about the films we exhibited so they would have an enlarged ability to guide their young children's moviegoing. This was new stuff to them, as I could see from the looks on their faces. I soared on for about ten minutes, laying claim to an ever-ascending curve of success for Hollywood, not only in this country, but around the world.

Some months later, I realized I was preaching to the most skeptical audience in the Western world. They had seen it all, heard it all, done most of it, and sometimes got it wrong. They had consorted with charlatans and dissemblers and had acted a bit of that themselves. They had tried not to be deluded by their own sometimes fatal enchantment with a script that had "dead in the toilet" written all over it. They were the captains of ships whose steering was unpredictable amid intermittent storms that threatened to capsize each of them in turn.

I concluded with a stirring (to me) declaration that I would confront problems in this country and foreign countries as well, and I would solve them. I tried to catch some sense of excitement from the group. They listened courteously, but just as they did in their daily meetings with rapacious agents, disgruntled producers, and ungrateful movie stars, they held their counsel.

Then I opened up the meeting by asking each of the moguls if he had anything to add. Jack Warner spoke up, his eyes dancing merrily above his small mustache and wide smile. (I learned later that Jack Warner was always smiling, even as he delivered a blow to your solar plexus.)

"Listen, Jack," he said, "I heard what you said about tackling the tough problems, but your biggest problem is not going to be what you think. Your biggest problem will be the people sitting around this table."

There were murmurings from the others, but curiously no voice of dissent. I looked at Wasserman and then at Krim, both of whom put their heads down so their smiles wouldn't be obvious. Then Darryl Zanuck scowled, waved his hand dismissively at Jack Warner, and growled, "What in the hell does that mean? The guy hasn't been on the job twenty-four hours, and you're already telling him he's got enemies in the room." Jack Warner let the smile ease into a subtle laugh. No one else spoke up. It was clear to me that Warner and Darryl weren't sharing moonlit dinners together anytime soon.

From that day forward, I studied each of the moguls who sat around the MPAA table, and their successors, with the concentrated scrutiny of a scientist peering through his microscope at a fascinating new species. I listened carefully. I made mental notes. I tried to discern who were the pacesetters, who could carry the room, who had creative vision, and whom I could rely on when the cannons began to fire. But most of all, I wanted to know how to deal with each of them on a daily basis.

What I learned that first day was that around the table were the viceroys of Hollywood. They were, like each generation that came after them, the most ferocious competitors ever assembled in any geographic location. Yet they were smart enough to know that they needed to work together in the best interests of their kingdom. So they listened to me as I persuaded them to collaborate on matters of great issue to the industry as a whole. They were as one in their willingness to contribute to charitable causes, especially the Motion Picture & Television Country House and Hospital. They unanimously gave me full authority to travel the world making sure that every potential territory for exhibiting movies and television programs was as open and competitive as possible.

As the meeting came to a close, Arthur Krim spoke up: "I'd like to suggest to my colleagues that we give our new leader a sincere round of applause, and let him know we are proud to follow his leadership."

Wasserman said, "I'll second that motion, Arthur," whereupon everyone at the table rose to their feet, applauding vigorously.

Then Krim said, "Jack, if it's all right with you, I'd like to move we adjourn and get to our lunch at the hotel." Good idea.

At lunch at the Algonquin Hotel, the other directors were kind and gracious, telling me they would be available to me at all times and how pleased they were I was now with them in the industry. I did feel good about it. But over the next thirty-eight-plus years, I learned that Warner's smiling prophecy was not far off the mark.

In dealing with the movie industry's strong-willed, dominating men, I soon passed the Hollywood ritual of intimidation. I learned never to cower or show fear. Not often, but a few times in my movie career I had to face down high-powered studio executives who may have been testing me, flexing the muscles that had carried the day in arguments and contests in their career.

I remember my first such collision. A few years into my tenure, I had negotiated a trade treaty in India, dealing directly with India's prime minister as well as the Indian minister of the economy. At that time, we were severely restrained by the Indian government's limits imposed on repatriating rupees earned in that country; they were allowing us to repatriate a minuscule sum each year. I thought I had achieved a minor coup by signing a new treaty with the Indians that upped handsomely the amount of dollars we could bring back to the States and also allowed us to trade rupees for dollars through a third party.

To my surprise, on my return to Washington I got a call from Taft Schreiber, second in command to Lew Wasserman at MCA Universal. He was a profoundly self-assured man, whose tenure at MCA was longer than Wasserman's, though Wasserman had become his boss. Taft was also the prime Republican at MCA, just as Wasserman was the top Democrat. I always admired this political compartmentalizing. Whichever party was in power, MCA was in friendly hands.

This was my first phone contact with Schreiber. I greeted him warmly, whereupon he fired a rhetorical missile at me, scorching the phone lines. What I heard was, "Who the goddamn hell gave you the authority to mangle an agreement with India? You screwed up the whole blocked rupee issue, which I was going to solve [Nixon was in the White House and an intimate of Schreiber's], and now you have totally destroyed my work. It's the dumbest thing I ever heard, and I am mad as hell over your stupidity."

I was caught totally off guard. I tried to explain to Taft how I had arranged a healthy compromise and that no other formula was going to be any better than what I had negotiated. "You negotiated without knowing what the hell you were doing," his voice grated over the line. "And what the hell *do* you know about negotiating with India? I had people in the State Department who have more knowledge in their left ball about India than you have in your entire body."

This was not a conversation; it was a diatribe. I tried once more to remonstrate with Schreiber, but his anger was under full sail now, and he wouldn't let up. So I waited until he took a breath, and then I said very quietly and slowly: "Taft, there is nothing in my contract that says I have to take this shit from you or anyone else. Now, if you want to carry on a civil conversation with me, that's fine, but if you insist on being hysterical and rude, I'm going to put this phone down, softly."

I surmised that the few seconds that passed in silence represented Taft's utter amazement at my reply. He erupted once more: "You are calling me hysterical? Who the hell do you think you are, when you just messed up something I was about to solve?"

I set the phone softly into its cradle. Then I picked it up again. I got Lew Wasserman on the phone and told him of my conversation with Schreiber. I said, "Lew, I am not going to take that punishment from Taft or anyone else, and if he wants the association to fire me, let him have at it. But no more crap from Schreiber. Ever again. If he calls me back, I do not intend to take the phone call. And if he wants to get rid of me, then he ought to call the MPAA board of directors into executive session."

Lew said, "Jack, do whatever you think is right." And that was it. I never found out if Lew called Taft, or if Taft called Lew, but I do know that I did not hear back from Taft Schreiber. When, about four months later, I saw him at a charity function in Los Angeles, he was sitting at an MCA table. I smiled, nodded to him, he nodded back, and that was that. Word of our exchange got around the Hollywood movie community, for I did hear from two moguls at other companies who said, in essence, "Right on."

From that time forward, I kept on course. I never provoked a fight, but I most definitely never accepted abusive behavior and was never too fearful to say, "Enough shit from you," when it needed to be said. This was a course of action taken to preserve not merely my self-respect, but my sanity as well.

Around the time of my Schreiber confrontation, I collided with another movie titan, this time Darryl Zanuck himself. After several months on the job, when I thought I had absorbed a substantial reservoir of knowledge about the foreign operations of the MPAA, I decided to see them firsthand. I called the MPAA's general counsel, Louis Nizer, and suggested that we visit Europe, particularly France and Italy.

Louis Nizer was a unique personality and at the time one of the three or four greatest courtroom attorneys in the land. He was the lead partner in one of New York's most prestigious firms, Philips, Nizer, Benjamin, Krim & Ballon. He possessed a magical memory, an asset that supertalented lawyers always have. Like Edward Bennett Williams, he could absorb, dissect, assay, and fasten in his mind huge truckloads of abstruse legal material as well as arguments he chose to make, then persuasively unloose that material to a jury without a note in front of him.

I had only one contretemps with Louis, and even that was not connected to him personally. When I was about to sign my contract with the MPAA in 1966, I was called by one of the studio chiefs. "Wouldn't it be a good idea if you and Louis Nizer could be co–chief executive officers, the two of you to run the MPAA jointly?"

My answer was swift and forthright. "No, it would not. If that is the will of the board of directors, then I decline to be involved. I am either CEO, or I withdraw from consideration of any post with the MPAA." I never heard any more from that studio boss. The matter died with that phone call. (When Louis passed away twenty years later, I spoke at his memorial service. Friends created the Louis Nizer Lecture Series and asked me to be its first speaker, which I was only too honored to do.)

So at this early stage in my tenure at the MPAA, Louis and his wife, Mildred, and my wife, Mary Margaret, and I all traveled to Paris. There, Louis and I visited with Fred Gronich, head of the MPAA's Paris office.

Fred reported to Louis and me that Darryl Zanuck wanted to see us. "Fine with me," I said. "Is he here in Paris?"

Gronich said, "Oh yes, he spends most of his time here." Odd place to run a Hollywood studio, I thought, but Darryl was a living icon, and if he wanted to rule his movie kingdom from Paris, that was okay with me.

The next day, Fred, Louis, and I appeared at the Hotel George V in Paris for our appointment with Zanuck, whom I hadn't seen since my first meeting with the MPAA board of directors. Frankly, I wasn't prepared for what I saw, though later Fred laughed and told me he hadn't wanted to spoil my surprise.

Darryl had taken what seemed to be two, maybe three, large suites and combined them into one massive piece of hotel real estate. He greeted us in a paisley robe, with crimson slippers on his small feet. He was smoking a cigar that I swear was larger than a Louisville Slugger, protruding a full zip code out of his mouth. Three very attractive secretaries bounced around in what seemed to be his office, a large desk with three phones and several chairs in front of it. He offered us drinks, but this early in the morning, we all declined.

He gave us a tour of his lodgings, including his bedroom, which was graced by a bed only slightly smaller than the Pantheon. I learned later that Darryl always kept a mistress, who was invariably an aspiring movie star. Why not aspire to movie stardom? Half the female population of the Western world seemed to be doing it. Though evidently Darryl proffered leading roles to each of them in turn, they never made the A-level cut—or, according to catty gossips, the B-level or C-level, either. But I was told that insofar as Darryl was concerned, they were Academy Award caliber.

Ah, I thought, this is what Hollywood is all about. Here I was meeting with a real-life pasha, a monarch whose kingdom circled the globe, whose every whim was indulged, and whose every command no one dared to contradict or disparage. What I didn't realize was that the Darryl Zanuck of 1966 was among the last of a dying breed. He too would fall, but his time was not quite yet.

After we had toured the bustling environment, phones ringing, secretaries scurrying, and two male assistants handing him scripts, Darryl got down to business. Like all emperors, he didn't waste time with small talk. "What the hell are you two doing in Paris? Why are you preparing to run all over Europe? Whose money are you spending?"

Well, I thought, that is one helluva fine opening shot. Louis, who knew Zanuck better than I, suppressed a smile. Once my astonishment had subsided, I decided to draw a line in the sand. "The MPAA has a lot of business in Europe. I believe it's my duty to find out firsthand what that business is all about," I said, my voice steady, though I was a bit pissed off.

"That's a lot of crap. I think it is all an excuse for some partying and seeing the countryside. It's damn expensive, and I don't like it." The cigar bobbled up and down like a rodeo cowboy on a bucking bronc.

I leaned in a bit. "Look, Darryl, if you find my presence in Europe unsuitable to you, then maybe the board of directors ought to tell me specifically if they want me to manage the MPAA sitting at a desk all day, or whether they want me to know something about the decisions I have to make by getting out to visit our offices abroad. That is what I am doing now, and that is what I will be doing when I go to Italy."

Oddly, Zanuck didn't leap to the ramparts. He blew out smoke and shifted restlessly in his chair behind his desk. "I still don't like it, but you're new on the job, so do what you think you have to do. But I think it's all a waste of money."

That was it. He got a tad friendlier as he talked about the European marketplace. He got up soon and shook our hands, signifying that the meeting was over, to my inner delight. When we got back to the lobby, Fred grinned and said, "You stood up to Darryl. Not many do that, and those who did usually had to find employment somewhere else."

Louis nodded appreciatively. He said, "Jack, don't condemn Darryl. He is who he is, a very creative, very successful, and very demanding person. I think he was impressed with you."

That night, Louis, Mildred, Fred, and his wife, Rae, Mary Margaret, and I dined at Maxim's, where the prices were higher than obscene, in order, as I put it, to bring tears to Darryl's eyes. We laughed a lot that night. But as I told Mary Margaret later, "I have no right to make sport of Darryl Zanuck. He's an icon in the movie industry, and I'm just a rookie. He has a film record few can match. He not only runs one of the top studios, he is also a producer himself. So I salute him, I really do." And I did.

I never was able to construct a lasting personal relationship with Darryl. My fault, I suspect. Yet with his son, Richard, I have had a long, loving friendship that is strong and sturdy to this day.

It gives me great pride that throughout my long tenure governing the Motion Picture Association of America, never once did I clash with the special men and women who ran the Hollywood studios and leave blood on the floor. Disagree at times over strategy, hold differing views about budgets and on the compass heading of the association's global activities? Yes, definitely. But these controversies were always resolved without lingering antagonisms or ruptured relationships. Invariably when I came away from these encounters, sometimes vindicated, sometimes giving way, I felt a renewed commitment to support these busy, enormously bright creative people who live in a perpetually tense, sometimes brutal world.

Board meetings at the MPAA in succeeding years took on the form of a Kabuki ritual. Inevitably one offhand remark ignited a rebuttal, and the furies were uncorked. Controversies among individual companies were, to my surprise, brought to the meeting table and fought out there. One day some years after I began my tenure, Sid Sheinberg, president of MCA Universal, turned on Michael Eisner, chairman of Disney, and Frank Wells, Disney's president. Sheinberg accused Disney of pilfering plans from MCA to build movie theme parks in Orlando, long the fiefdom of Disney. Eisner furiously denied the charge. Finally, I intervened to suggest that another forum would be more suitable for such arguments.

Indeed, as the years wore on it became almost a tradition for our meeting table to be a battleground. Finally, for the last decade of my tenure, I instituted what I called the "Bob Daly rule." After one of our rancorous gatherings, Bob, co-chairman of Warner Bros., said to me as we departed the room, "Jack, never call us together. We'll always be fighting." So for the rest of the years of my tenure at the MPAA, I never called another formal board meeting. We met about single issues, but never again in a general board meeting. To comply with legal regulations, I had meetings to vote on technical requirements, but the "Daly rule" stayed in effect.

How did it work? Pretty damn well. I had one committee, the finance committee, consisting of three studio heads who rotated every three or four years. This group was the central authority for preliminary approval of budgets, after which their revised version went to all the other member companies for review and approval. All other matters I took up one on one with each studio chief.

When it came to daily relationships with the Hollywood studio heads, I held firmly to a discipline from which I never diverged. I made sure to instantly answer the phone call of each studio chief. This came as second nature to me, since it was what LBJ had taught me about immediately answering the calls of senators and congressmen. If I was out of the office or traveling, my secretary was in contact with me within minutes. That call was responded to quickly. I took care to answer phone calls from top executives in California while I was in Europe. Many a time I would be calling an executive at 3:00 p.m. Los Angeles time when I was in Paris at midnight. I wanted the studio heads and other influential members of the Hollywood community to know I cared about them and gave them the respect and prompt attention they deserved. This was exactly how I handled senators and congressmen when I worked in the White House, to remarkably satisfactory results.

I never treated casually any offered counsel from the studio

CEOs. I listened carefully and courteously to what they had to say. It was not artifice on my part. The men and women who run the major studios, their selected teams as well as the lawyers and agents, and the heads of the guilds, are genuinely smart people. They thrive in a fiery competitive cauldron ruled by Darwinian principles. I learned early that such brains, intuition, and competitive fury must be listened to and respected. But I had no hesitation about offering a differing view if I felt strongly about the issue. I recognized that the studio folks knew more about production and distribution than did I, but I knew more about the unmapped terrain of Washington and of world politics.

Over the years, I had pretty much free rein to take MPAA actions and set policy. However, I was always sensitive to the corporate obligations and personal needs of the studio chiefs. I was careful to check out disparities in opinion so that I never collided with a majority of the board. I asked my colleagues at the MPAA to sound out the second and third levels of leadership at each studio and to keep trolling for information. I wanted to be well-informed on opinions and ideas rising from the bowels of each studio. I was on the phone constantly to each of the moguls, listening to their views and sometimes to their clamoring. In short, I wanted to be able to smell the wind so I would know what was ripe and what was not. Thus was the LBJ method I had absorbed put to excellent use in Hollywood.

Bookstores are laden with volumes on business leadership, tomes with endless counsel on how to be "a leader." I have my own formula, which is quite simple. It is rooted in the ability to engage in courtship, to cosset talent, to understand the human condition, and to make decisions fast. Essentially, we all want to keep our dignity intact, which means do not embarrass or patronize anyone who ranks below you. Always put yourself in the shoes of the other person. When you do, you become aware of potential missteps before you commit them.

Meanwhile, I saw how meetings with CEOs of the big studios took on a persona of their own. From this scrutiny, I came to one conclusion: In any meeting, I had to know who could carry the room at a particular sensitive moment. More often than not, it was Wasserman who pushed the lever at precisely the right time, but that varied from issue to issue. A debate would ensue. I would encourage all the moguls to express themselves so I could get a sense of where the room was heading. Wasserman would usually hold back. Then, when everyone had weighed in, he would motion to me. He would offer his judgment, usually in a low voice so that everyone had to strain to hear him. Inevitably, the meeting adjusted its heading to the course suggested by Lew.

Once, early in my MPAA years, I organized a retreat for all the MPAA board members at a hotel in Newport Beach in Southern California. We arrived on a Friday, had dinner and an enjoyable social evening, and then convened on Saturday morning to take care of business. Sitting next to me at this gathering was the outside counsel for MPAA, Edward Bennett Williams, arguably the finest courtroom lawyer in the country.

It was at this meeting that Lew Wasserman introduced me to a political weapon I had not witnessed before, not even in the White House. If the meeting didn't turn the way Wasserman chose, he would erupt into a towering, raging condemnation of all that had gone before. It was a terrifying piece of theatrics. The first time I saw this, I was taken aback. Later on, I came to appreciate the wiliness of this wiliest of all the Hollywood proconsuls. Hysteria intimidates. Intimidation softens resistance. When resistance dissolves, hysteria wins the vote. It was Lew's personal syllogism.

On the day of the meeting, we came to a vexing issue that split the board. When Lew Wasserman sensed that the board was going to decide in opposition to his view, he stood up, looked venomously at the assembly, and announced with rising anger that "this is a violation of antitrust law, and I'll have nothing to do with it in any form. It is reckless and wrong. Let the record show that I am opposed and that I am leaving the meeting in protest."

I whispered in Ed's ear, "I need you to put a finger in the dike." He nodded. I stood up to speak to Wasserman. "Please, Lew, don't leave yet. Ed Williams can speak to this antitrust issue."

I knew Lew respected Ed and trusted him. Ed said in a firm, friendly tone, "Actually, Lew, I have looked at this. I do not see any antitrust implications. Some of your other comments do make sense, and perhaps the group might want to reevaluate on the basis of some of those viewpoints."

With that peace offering from Ed Williams, Lew must have decided he could now turn the direction of things to his liking. He hesitated and then sat down. The discussion opened up again, and sure enough, Lew moved the final decision his way. At the meeting's end, Ed pulled me aside.

"Does Lew pull that hysteria bit very often?"

I said, "Not often."

Ed grinned. "Well, it was magnificent. Hell, he almost had me believing it."

Lew's command of the situation also flowed from his long tenure and extraordinary success in this crazy business. All those around the table knew that Lew was the most solidly outfitted executive in the history of the film industry. Some years ago, I presided over a labor discussion that had divided the board. Bob Daly rose to make a case for what he believed was the right course to follow. There was much nodding around the table. Lew suddenly took an opposite tack, and he made his argument compellingly.

I wanted to lance any boils quickly, so I called for the vote. To my surprise, Bob Daly, one of the wisest men at the table, changed his vote to join with Lew. Lew won the vote.

After the meeting, I grabbed Bob. "What the devil is going on? You switched your vote."

Bob put on his sweetest smile. "Jack, a man doesn't vote against his father."

Chapter 11

SETTLING IN TO RUN THE SHOW

Enjoying a jubilant laugh with one of my dearest friends, the elegant Sidney
Poitier.

In May 1966, I settled into my MPAA Washington office in the Tuckerman mansion, situated at the corner of Sixteenth and I streets. It was named after the family who first built this edifice as their home, around 1880. Across the street was St. John's Church, the church of presidents, constructed in the early years of the eighteenth century. Next door was the venerable Hay-Adams Hotel. Across H Street, which flanked the Hay-Adams Hotel, was Lafayette Square, which itself confronts the White House on Pennsylvania Avenue. The MPAA headquarters was on hallowed ground, still redolent of the founding years of the Republic, lying in the very shadow of the president's home and the Oval Office where he worked. In short, this was not a shabby neighborhood.

My office, on the second floor of the Tuckerman mansion, was small but elegant. Its choicest asset was a tiny balcony that offered me a glorious view of Lafayette Square and the White House. I was much taken with it. It was here that I sat in the first weeks of my new job, spending endless hours reading mountains of memos that came to my desk from the MPAA's New York office and its foreign offices situated in Rome, Paris, Mexico City, Rio de Janeiro, Manila, Ottawa, and Sydney. When I wasn't reading, I was on the phone or in meetings, carrying on lengthy discussions with my new colleagues in the association. I sat largely mute but alert in countless briefings conducted not only by my associates, but by key executives in the Hollywood studios. I determined that I would listen and ask questions that might be absurd but allowable, since I was a film industry neophyte.

I decided that my first business trip would be to Los Angeles. Unlike my late predecessor, Eric Johnston, I would spend more time in Hollywood than I would in Washington or New York. I began to write a speech for what would be, effectively, my inaugural appearance before my new colleagues. I arranged for a luncheon at the Beverly Hills Hotel, to which were invited various grand pooh-bahs of the town as well as my key associates in our L.A. office, executives from the studios and the creative guilds, and a number of movie stars.

When I stepped up to the podium in the elegant Crystal Ballroom of the Beverly Hills Hotel, there were some three hundred people in the audience, the vast majority of whom I had never met. This first speech had to win some hearts and minds, so I had labored over its composition, writing and rewriting. And I admit, I did have some apprehension. How would I be received? My unease was heightened when, in the very first row, I saw the internationally recognizable face and form of Bob Hope, whom I had never met or even seen in person. Hello! As I spoke, my eyes kept returning to the jutting jaw of Bob Hope, his gaze fixed on me. I finished in a rousing peroration, at least to my lights. To my amazement and delight, the first one to rise to his feet applauding was Hope. The rest of the audience took their cue from him, and I was offered a pretty good valedictory.

Bob leaped to the platform, shook my hand, and said, "Kid, that was well done. Now, remember this. Whenever you think I can help you out here, call me. I liked what you said."

Bob's endorsement gave me a shot of confidence that was sorely needed. In the years that followed, he grew to be a great friend. He even tolerated me with infinite kindness when I played golf with him, though I played with all the grace of a stricken wildebeest. I never actually asked him for specific help, but the fact that I could have if I needed to gave me confidence.

I settled into my lodgings at the Beverly Hills Hotel that day. For the next twenty years, this would be my Los Angeles home. Its fabled Polo Lounge became a watering hole for me. Its bungalows and rooms, its tennis court and Olympian-size swimming pool, were durable delights. It was the Polo Lounge that attracted the stars. To its intimate booths and tables, the brightest and the most beautiful came each evening for drinks and dinner. Mario, the all-seeing host, made sure that ex-wives and former friends were not seated in proximity to ex-husbands and former friends. Mario always had the booth facing the entrance ready for me, so I conducted my meetings in regal, and visible, splendor. For more than two decades, I pitched my tent at the Beverly Hills Hotel and the Polo Lounge, and then the sultan of Brunei bought the place and shut it down for two years for renovation.

A friend of mine suggested I try the Peninsula Hotel on Little Santa Monica, just off Wilshire Boulevard in the heart of Beverly Hills. It was a small hotel, five stories, and would be described as European in its style and ambiance. I sought out the managing director, Ali Kasikci, a gracious, wise man with a fanatical desire to make every guest feel like the sultan of Brunei. Yes, he would be happy to have me as the hotel's guest whenever I chose to be in Los Angeles.

To this hour, I am still there. Lord knows I have been a guest in all the great hostelries in Asia, Canada, Latin America, and Europe. I believe I have come to know what sets one hotel apart from the rest. It's not the décor of the rooms. All five-star hotels furnish their rooms with care, grace, and interior design of quality. It's not the restaurants, since all of them are proud of their superb kitchens, and rightly so. All of them now have superior fitness facilities. What sets apart the best of the best is the way you are treated, the way every guest is treated. At the Ritz Hotel in Paris, presided over by Frank Klein, and most assuredly at Ali Kasikci's Peninsula in Beverly Hills, you don't have to be a world-famous movie star or a Silicon Valley billionaire or some oil magnate to get "the treatment"; the only title you need is "guest."

A few weeks after I arrived in Hollywood, I got my first briefing on the international cinema world. I was mentored by one of the most well-informed of all movie executives, Eric Pleskow, the manager of United Artists' worldwide distribution apparatus. Arthur Krim had asked Eric to give me, unvarnished, all information, facts, and forecasts of the foreign distribution landscape. He sat with me in my small Washington office. He took me through a complete evaluation of the foreign managers of the film companies, complete with their strong points, their flaws, and an idea of whom I could trust to tell me facts and who would offer mostly slender reeds. In those early days, company foreign managers were like viceroys sent to the colonies on every continent. They were powerful satraps in a part of the business that over the years of my tenure as association leader was marked by an ever growing American presence as well as rising revenues and profits.

At the end of a five-hour session with Eric, I was notably better informed. On the day of this briefing, the entire American industry's world revenues were some $1.5 billion. Thirty-eight years later when I stepped down as the chief executive of the MPAA, those global revenues had spiraled upward to more than $45 billion. Moreover, the foreign sales segment had soared from some 24 percent of total revenues to 41 percent of the total. It was a seven-league leap, fortifying the global reach of the American industry's involvement in world cinema, TV programming, and home video. I confess those statistics give me no small degree of satisfaction.

At the time of my Eric Pleskow briefing, I saw quickly that our growth potential was largest in foreign territories, so I made the expansion of international markets for American films my highest priority. For more than two decades, this mandate was fixed in my sights and in my efforts. There were problems. If there had been no problems, the enlargement of international markets would have been achieved before I came on to the scene. Throughout the long rise of American cinema, there existed the notion among other countries with film industries that if those countries could somehow create barriers to the influence of American movies, their own industry would suddenly rise like Athena springing full-blown from the forehead of Zeus. This notion persisted, despite being pure myth.

For my part, I quickly became convinced that I had to establish a rapport with the world film community if I was going to expand the reach of the American movie. It was not going to be easy. It would take an exceptional commitment to traveling the world, meeting with presidents, prime ministers, ministers of culture and finance, and, of course, cinema actors, writers, directors, and producers. It meant convincing them that storytelling was key to the future, no matter the origin of the film, and that joining together was far more productive than incessant wrangling about being overwhelmed by the American movie goliath.

My ultimate goal was to make sure the American movie could move freely on all continents, compete fairly in all marketplaces, and be protected from thievery in every part of the world. The latter

objective, though I did not know it at the beginning of my movie career, was to become the prime activity of the MPAA, summed up in a
clearly stated maxim: "If you cannot protect what you own, you don't
own anything."

Within a year into my new duties, I was almost drowned by a
river of controversy I had not anticipated that tested me as nothing
before or since. While I was exploring the world cinema landscape
that I would get to know so well over the next decades, I suddenly
found myself confronting a domestic intrusion that commanded my
full attention and then some.

In the mid-1960s, American mores and customs were in turmoil.
I suppose the Vietnam War was one of the reasons. Certainly the nation was undergoing rapid social and political change that divided its
people. The campuses were in rebellion. Flower children preaching
"free love" and "Make love, not war" were growing in number. In
short, there were stirrings of insurrection at all levels of society. The
principles that had guided the country for so long had become mere
shibboleths. It was folly to think that movies, this most creative of all
art forms, could remain immune to these earth-shaking emotional
disturbances. At the same time, mainly because of the victory of a
Justice Department antitrust lawsuit against the major film studios,
the power of the Hays Code to determine what would be offensive to
the public, and to suppress it, began to erode.

I came into office at that precise confluence of political vexations
and social tumult. Film directors were straining to throw off the
shackles of the Hays office and join the riptide change in the way a
large part of the nation saw fit to conduct itself. There seemed to be a
cultural imperative to engage in the conflict over our nation's values,
whose other side could be seen in the growing discontent of public
officials. I heard rapidly mounting criticisms that movies were coarsen-
ing the nation's culture, and a good many of those public officials
were hell-bent on combating them. I myself considered the actions of
the Hays office to be blatant censorship. I didn't like the Hays Code,
and I was determined to throw it over the side, the sooner the better.
But first I had to confront what was tearing down my door.

Along came Mike Nichols's brilliant *Who's Afraid of Virginia
Woolf?* starring Elizabeth Taylor and Richard Burton. Audiences

heard language never before spoken on screen. By today's standards, the movie might be a training film for a nunnery, but in the sixties it was controversial. Because it violated all the tenets of the Hays Code, the distributor, Warner Bros., put it in the marketplace under the logo of a Warner subsidiary. I pondered what the hell to do. I was new in the job. I had not yet constructed a strategy to deal with this shift in the Hollywood arena. Creative tectonic plates were shifting. I had to act.

With Louis Nizer accompanying me, I flew to Los Angeles to meet Jack Warner and his tough-talking "consigliere," Ben Kalmenson. For some three hours in Warner's baronial office at the Warner Bros. studio, Jack, Ben, Louis, and I talked about how to handle the Nichols film. At the end of the meeting, Jack and I had agreed that we would leave in "hump the hostess" but take out three instances of "screw you" and leave one intact. Afterward, I told Louis I was thoroughly uncomfortable with the meeting. It seemed silly, even absurd, that grown men could be spending their time on such a puerile discussion. But my depression only deepened when, on the heels of *Virginia Woolf*, I was hit with another firestorm.

This time it was MGM's *Blow-Up*, starring Vanessa Redgrave and David Hemmings, from the creative palette of Michelangelo Antonioni, the famous Italian cinema titan. On screen was nudity—two female teenyboppers romping around for about fifteen seconds wearing only their earrings—to a degree never before seen in a movie distributed by a major company, although here again the film was being released under the banner of an MGM subsidiary.

Earlier, the Supreme Court had confirmed the right of cities, counties, and states to classify those films the community believed ought not to be seen by children. Indeed, Birmingham, Detroit, Dallas, Houston, Chicago, the state of Maryland, and dozens of other localities had set in place censorship boards in their communities, composed of local citizens like the widow of the local police chief, the husband of the head of the school board, or the director of the local Boy Scout troop, who were busy classifying a good many films not acceptable for children. Congressmen fulminated, child advocacy groups took up rhetorical arms, and newspaper editorials viewed the situation with alarm.

I knew I had to move swiftly, and I did. First, I junked the Hays Code; however, it became clear that throwing the Hays Code over the side and replacing it with the warning line "For Mature Audiences" was not going to cut it. It was too little and very late. So it was that after conferring with my absolutely brilliant MPAA general counsel, Barbara Scott Preiskel, I devised a plan. I ran it past Louis Nizer. Then I immediately began talks with the top brass of the theater owners association, including Sumner Redstone, who was the head of the Theater Owners of America (now the National Association of Theater Owners—NATO).

When I presented my plan to Sumner, his quick, lawyerly mind got it fast. He knew that unless we took preemptive action, we would be overwhelmed by a babel of voices, all of them unsuitable to our future. With Sumner's indispensable endorsement, I outlined a plan to the theater owners—at the time a revolutionary plan, because it ran counter to the thinking of the major studios and a good many exhibitors. The idea was to set up a voluntary movie rating system, giving advance cautionary information to parents so they could make better decisions about the movies their children went to see.

At the same time—and to me this was crucial—we had to make sure the First Amendment held sway, that filmmakers could tell any story they chose to tell without a government or an industry coercing them to make revisions. In meetings with the various directors, writers, and film actors unions, I made it plain I was determined to free the screen from anything like the Hays Code. But I also emphasized that freedom demanded responsibility. I told them that under my plan, some of their films might be restricted from viewing by children. I saw no contradiction in that. The minds of young children are not yet fully developed; therefore their rights under the First Amendment were not being violated. But adults would be at liberty to make their own movie-watching choices.

Finally, Hollywood's creative guilds signed on. But the key decision fell to the theater owners, for they would be the ones on the front lines enforcing the ratings. To my delight, they agreed to be full partners in this new voluntary movie rating system. Now, with the theater owners and creative guilds by my side, I had to campaign for acceptance from the major studios, independent producers, craft unions, religious organizations, and movie critics in print and broadcast; indeed, any time I could corral three people in a phone booth, I went into my pitch. It wasn't easy. The major studios were particularly edgy. This was something radically new, a piece of potential mischief whose implications they could not sort out. What you fear is what you don't know. I understood that.

The essence of my pitch to the studio heads was, first, that nature, politics, and the movie industry abhor vacuums. We had to fill the movie vacuum now that the Hays Code was colder than dog meat, and good riddance to it. Second, if we didn't act to self-regulate, others would do it for us through a Supreme Court decision. Third, if we wanted to keep the screen free and at the same time fulfill what I considered to be an obligation to American parents, we had to devise a simple plan that would achieve both those objectives.

The operative word in my plan was "simple." One of my heroes is William of Occam (or Ockham), a Franciscan monk who lived in England in the fourteenth century, best known for an insight freely translated from the Latin as "Entities are never to be multiplied except out of absolute necessity." Or, in plain English, "Keep it simple, stupid." I had learned from my experience with LBJ that anything hard to explain or understand turns voters off, and the same would apply to moviegoers. Simplicity is the essence of persuasion, so my design for a rating system was based on keeping the categories from expanding and making certain that the information they offered was easy to understand. No complexities allowed.

I also firmly believed that the rating system should not become an agent of social change. It could not become an arbiter of public conduct. All this would be a burden too heavy for the system to bear. All the rating should do—and could do—was give advance warning to parents with regard to language, violence, sex, and the depiction of illegal substances, so they could make their own decisions about the moviegoing of their young children. No more, no less. William of Occam is the real overseer of the movie rating system.

On November 1, 1968, after nearly a year of constant meetings, phone calls, and more meetings, the movie rating system was born. At this writing, it has lived a long, full, useful, and sometimes controversial life. It is still effective and trusted. Nothing lasts very long in

this brutal, explosive, unpredictable marketplace unless it is conferring some benefit on the people it aims to serve—in this instance, the
parents of America. By that standard, the voluntary movie rating system is getting the job done.

The rating system annually conducts a national poll through the
Opinion Research Corporation of Princeton, New Jersey, interview-
ing some 2,100 people under strict market research protocols. For
the last fifteen years, more than 70 percent of parents with children
under thirteen found the rating system "very useful" to "fairly useful"
in helping them guide their children's moviegoing. In 2006, that
parental approval rose to 80 percent. That's a pretty hefty approval
level. I daresay few publicly elected officials come close to that. I have
to admit I am mighty proud of what the movie industry, with all its
critics and supporters and all its many voices, has constructed and
kept in place.

Within the MPAA, I designed a tight organization. My concept
of leadership was to lead by precept and example. I had small
regard for new management designs wherein "facilitators" or "mod-
erators" come from the outside to explain how the "team" should be
formed and how teamwork should be fostered. Some of these designs
have merit, but many are theatrical claptrap. To my way of thinking,
a good leader builds and nourishes relationships the old-fashioned
way: He or she builds a personal rapport with colleagues based on
trust, work ethic, and loyalty.

One of the wisest visionaries I know is a soft-spoken publicity-
shy fellow named Jerry Perenchio, who bought Univision, a Spanish-
language TV and radio enterprise, guided it to unprecedented
success, and then sold it in 2006. He's been my loving friend for over
thirty-five years. Jerry offers one piece of advice that I took to heart.
He says, "Always trust your instinct and common sense. If you don't
trust them, you will regret it." To this hour, I rely on what I call my little "instinct elf" who lives somewhere between my belly and my
brain. When everyone is telling me to go that way and my little elf
says, *No, go the other way*, I go the other way. Common sense keeps
you from doing foolish things. Common sense is what often makes

ordinary voters smarter than the officials they vote for. Trusting your instinct and never ignoring common sense is one way you become a leader.

But the leader must lead. All those who worked with me quickly caught on that I never hesitated to make a decision. I never allowed anyone who worked with me to take public responsibility for any errors we made. As the leader, I both took charge when decisions were required and took responsibility when the decision turned out to be wrong. I truly believe that most people want to work alongside a leader, not someone who is reluctant to be in front of the troops when the battle begins and has a dozen reasons why he's not part of any failure.

I learned first in war and later from President Johnson that preparation (called "training" in the combat air force) is the key to survival and potential triumph. My colleagues soon got the message that I never "winged" it. They understood that before any speech, any presentation, any briefing I gave, or any meeting or staff session I attended, I spent considerable time laboring over the nature of the problem, what I was going to say, and how I would say it, always getting into the substance of whatever issue confronted us. Hour after hour, I worked until I had it sealed down in mind and memory. And when I had all the information I could possibly find and it still wasn't enough, I turned to my instincts. I was right more often than I was wrong.

I had a fanatical commitment to breaking down complex, abstruse issues so they became as simple as possible (LBJ's passion for simplicity took root in me). Whenever some of my technological gurus starting talking "technical-speak" or dealt in acronyms, I always interrupted with, "What do those letters mean?" Or, "Start over and put that in simple English sentences." I have participated in meetings where most people around the table don't want to ask a question for fear of looking as if they didn't do their homework. I took the opposite tack. If I didn't understand something, then I didn't want to leave the room until I did.

My associates quickly caught on that I worked as hard as or harder than any of them. I made them realize that hours of the day or night were no barriers to reaching me. At all times, I was ready to listen to them, to advise and counsel them, and to get down in the ditch with them if that was required.

I am an implacable enemy of bureaucracy. Because the MPAA was a small enterprise, I ruthlessly axed anything that might add a semblance of corporate complexity. We had an advantage that I meant to keep: We were nimble enough to respond quickly and flexible enough to change course, if required.

I quickly instituted an open-door policy. Each of the MPAA executives had complete freedom to enter my office at any time, and without an appointment. If my door was closed, they lightly tapped on it and entered. If it was open, they walked in. If I was on the phone or in a meeting, they would wave and come back later. I wanted all of them to know there were no barriers between them and the boss.

My highest priority was to instill in every MPAA executive—indeed, in all employees—the fact that I cared deeply about them, their personal needs, their aims, and hopes. Their dignity was never going to be diminished in any way. I never let studio executives (or anyone else) abuse my colleagues. I drew the line around them, and whenever anyone from the outside crossed it, he or she heard from me. When one studio second-level executive lashed out with an abrasive rant at one of my colleagues, I told him coldly he was no longer welcome in the MPAA offices, although his company was a full dues-paying member. I quickly phoned his superior, told him that this man was persona non grata in my office, that his phone calls would not be answered, and that any time he showed up for a meeting—which he had a right to do as an executive of a dues-paying member of the association—I would depart the room. Within twenty-four hours, the offending fellow apologized (doubtless urged by his superior) and pledged it would not happen again. Word of this development sprinted its cheery message throughout the MPAA.

Moreover, I made it clear that I wanted every man and woman who worked for the MPAA to have fun on the job. I strived to so construct the daily duties of the organization that each of us would be eager to show up for work every day. My mantra was, "Let's have fun every day as we go about doing our jobs."

During the first ten months I was on the job at the MPAA, I didn't dismiss a single executive or do any reorganizing of the enterprise.

Other than two executive secretaries, I brought in no new people. I wanted to spend time getting to know the business and test those on board, to judge their qualities, abilities, and loyalties before I went outside to bring in someone new. After that initial period of assessment, I came to know, with very few exceptions, that the men and women in executive jobs at the MPAA were top of the line. I applauded them, and complimented them, and kept them on staff.

It was, for me, a glorious decision. The MPAA flourished, with knowledgeable, experienced people who had historical memories of mistakes made once, never to be made again, people who knew what they had to do and did it. Under a new leader who took time to know them, who valued them and counted on them, they gave back more than I had hoped for. That's how morale is built and sustained.

I was so fortunate in finding three men who managed our key foreign offices in Paris, Rome, and Rio de Janiero.

Fred Gronich, heading MPAA's Paris office, was a Renaissance man. He spoke fluent French, German, and Italian and he was a walking encyclopedia of the flora and fauna, the culture and history of France, as well as of the world cinema. Early in his life, he had been a military adviser to the future prime minister of Israel, David Ben-Gurion, during Israel's 1948 war for independence. During World War II he served on General Eisenhower's personal military intelligence staff.

He knew everyone in Europe's political and film community. He started work with the MPAA immediately following the end of World War II and moved to Paris to take up his duties there in 1958. Eight years later, I came to the MPAA. I instantly found a never-ending rapport with Fred. He had a historian's eye for detail. He knew each nook and cranny of France and England. His stories about the war, European politics, and Europe's film community were never dull.

I saw him last in a hospital in Los Angeles in the late 1990s, where he had come for special treatment on his legs. He looked gaunt, worn, a shadowy frame of what used to be a vibrant body, but his face lit up when I came in the hospital room. I hugged him and kissed him. We talked for two hours.

Our talk was full of nostalgia, reshooting the scenes of earlier years when he was at the top of his game. I heard Fred's voice as once it was, beguiling, full of warmth and zest. But I could tell toward the end of our conversation, he had exhausted the strength he had so resolutely saved for my visit. I almost wept to watch him recede back into the cheerless recesses of his failing form. It was one of the saddest days of my life to see this unique, extraordinary man so near death and who two months later passed on. God, I did love him.

Marc Spiegel was in charge of our Rome office. It was a joy having Marc by my side. He is a man of intellect, a lover of movie gossip, which he relates with hearty laughter, and an ability that verges on magic: he speaks fluently six languages, Italian, French, German, Russian, Polish, and of course English. When I say "fluent," I don't mean he can order a meal or ask for directions. He can negotiate complex issues in all these languages as I observed so many times. It's an awesome, seldom-witnessed skill.

Once at the Berlin Film Festival, I hosted a dinner with famous cinema directors and actors from Germany, Italy, Great Britain, France, Poland, and the Soviet Union. Like an agile mountain goat leaping gracefully from crag to crag, Marc skipped nimbly and easily from one language to another, never missing one linguistic beat. It was a nonpareil performance. I was both respectful and terribly envious.

Marc was born in Tula, Russia, but came to America as a small child with his parents. He was a brilliant student, graduating from Harvard with an MA in linguistics, whence came in later life his miraculous gift of language. His PhD studies were interrupted by World War II. After the fall of Paris, he immediately volunteered for the U.S. Army as a private, rising rapidly in rank until he became a highly decorated lieutenant colonel at age twenty-five, serving on General Eisenhower's staff as a key intelligence officer. Eisenhower called him "Baby Colonel."

In 1966 I became president of MPAA and met Marc for the first time. For the next nearly thirty-nine years we worked closely together, as colleagues and friends. He is at this hour unslowed by age and hearty as ever in his retirement.

In Rio was Harry Stone. He was tall, with a full-blown sloping mustache, the image of a British cavalry officer, even though he was American to the core and absolutely fluent in Portugese and Spanish.

No matter who was president of Brazil, Harry was his "close friend," and even managed to get President Emilio Medici to give me a reception in Brasilia, capital of Brazil, though he had never met me. He was thoroughly charming. It was a bleak day when Harry died. He had been with the MPAA for forty years.

But the second generation moved in quickly. A brilliant, soft-spoken Chris Marcich took over from Gronich and mastered the European landscape quickly. In our new office in São Paulo, Brazil a young, vibrant Steve Solot replaced the late Harry Stone, and has been an effective leader in Latin America.

In our Washington office, Fritz Attaway, who joined me in 1975, was the master of copyright law, and Vans Stevenson and Richard Taylor were my right and left hand with state legislation and communications.

It was for me a blessed fate that allowed me to work with these exraordinary colleagues. They made me look awful good.

During the middle years, I recruited Myron Karlin from his retirement at Warner Bros., after a thirty-year career as head of Warner's international distribution. I brought him in as president of our foreign operations. He was the wisest, most experienced international expert in our industry. He was, as might be expected, a natural linguist, speaking flawlessly Spanish, Italian, French, and German. He was an inspiration to our group. When finally he retired again, I chose two co-chief operating officers, Simon Barsky, our general counsel, and Bill Murray, a born administrator. I told them that if ever they had a turf battle I would blame both of them. They never did and I never had to.

THE ACADEMY AWARDS (THE NOBEL PRIZE OF CINEMA): THE ABSURD REACH OF FAME AND MY PERSONAL MAKEOVER

As I dived into the rollicking world of film, I thought long and often about how I ought to conduct myself so that I would become effective in dealing with the Congress and with Hollywood at every level and, equally important, how I could be persuasive with high government officials on every continent. I soon came to the conclusion that if I was truly to rise to the highest levels possible in this celebrity-obsessed world, I had to construct a kind of semicelebrity status for myself. I had to develop a new public persona that would give me instant access to those whom the association had to impress. In brief, if I was going to perform in a high-profile industry, I had to become high-profile myself.

It was not a matter of ego. It was a matter of how to be successful in my new tasks. If I had thought shunning all publicity was the key to getting the job done, I would have become a recluse. In time, my initial instincts were proven right. But after almost forty years in Hollywood, I still shake my head in wonderment over the public's obsession with movie, television, music, and sports stars.

The frenzy generated by the sighting of a movie icon is bizarre. I have seen people at the Cannes Film Festival stand in the sun outside the Carlton or Majestic hotels for hours just to catch a ten-second glimpse of a star departing a hotel to climb into a limo. In Cannes in 2006, producer Brian Grazer expressed horror at public reaction when his film *The Da Vinci Code* was premiered. When Tom Hanks's limo was overrun by legions of devoted fans, Grazer described the scene this way: "People were throwing their bodies on the back of the car; they were this close to getting run over." Hundreds of people sleep several nights outside the entrance to the Academy Awards venue in Los Angeles so they can get a seat in the bleachers and ogle movies stars as they come down the red carpet. It's absolutely crazy.

Today, with television an omnipresent companion, the hunger for fame—not merely fifteen minutes, but fifteen seconds—is irresistible to almost every human being. Which may explain why people will clamor to be on the daytime talk shows and expose their most intimate experiences, even squalid personal secrets, in front of total strangers and with total abandon. When they get back to their neighborhood, their friends cluster around and say, "Hey, I saw you on TV." Ergo, you are famous.

There is another peculiarity about this kind of celebrity. Often, as I slog through an airport to catch my plane, someone will come up and say cheerfully, "I know you, what's your name?" I tell them. "Of course, I remember now. I saw you on television the other day." When I ask them what it was that I was saying, inevitably the response is, "I don't remember, but you were great." There is an immutable truth revealed in that answer. Few people can remember what they read in a magazine or newspaper or what they heard on TV. What they do remember is what they *saw*. How you looked, how you presented yourself, counts. Not your words, because words have a short shelf life in the human memory. For political candidates, this is biblical truth.

Knowing the phenomenenal power of television to fashion a personal connection with viewers, I instantly accepted whenever I was asked to appear on TV to talk about movies, politics, the impact of big media, and so on, no matter what the program. Even if it attracted a tiny audience, it was better than no audience at all. I also spent on-screen time with major network morning and evening news shows and cable programs, especially *Imus in the Morning*. Don Imus, Charles McCord, and Bernard McGuirk always treat me with great kindness. I quickly learned that the Imus show is a major audience attractor. I had finished a stint on the Imus show early one morning in New York, and as I walked back to my hotel, to my astonishment, at least six or seven people waved as they walked by, calling out, "Hey, saw you on Imus. Great show." If ever I needed empirical evidence of Don Imus's popularity, I had it now: instant fame (however fleeting)!

But the one vaulting media leap that truly lifted me out of the crowd and sent me soaring was participation in the Academy Awards. Thanks to close friends like Gil Cates, a premier film and TV producer and director who as of this writing has created some thirteen Academy Award shows, and the late Howard Koch, a kind, giving, selfless man who produced about nine Academy Award shows, my objective of achieving celebrity status was realized. Through Gil and Howard, I was transported to the Promised Land.

Both these exceptional artists gave me a presentation role in the Academy Awards. I think it is fair to say that on all of these shows I was the only "non-movie celebrity." Most of my roles were in concert with a lovely actress, presenting the Oscar to the winner of the Best Foreign Language Film, for example. Over the years, I was on some twenty Academy Award shows. My collaborators have included Jacqueline Bisset, Ann-Margret, Kristin Scott Thomas, Glenn Close, Juliette Binoche, Candice Bergen, Susan George, and Leslie Caron.

Particularly unsettling to presenters (to me, at least) are the first two or three rows of the audience, where every legendary movie star is almost sitting in your lap. These are also the rows that include all the nominees for Best and Best Supporting Actress and Actor. They gaze at you intently, some smiling, some thoughtful. During one appearance, I was about to launch into my brief remarks when I saw Jack Nicholson seated in the front row a whisper away, that leering smile fixed on me, seemingly daring me to screw up. I was almost hypnotized into muteness. Then I saw the upraised face of Julia Roberts turning toward me. For a nanosecond, I thought, What the hell am I doing here? I'm afraid more than a few members of the audience had the same question.

In all my twenty appearances on the Academy Awards, I never failed to savor the moment. Onstage is not the only glittering venue. During the show, all the presenters gather backstage in the green room, sipping tea, chatting with fellow stars, at ease (if it's possible to be at ease knowing that very shortly you will be visible to several hundred million viewers). Seldom do even the stars enjoy such a moment, when Hollywood's on-screen royalty are in the same room at the same time, with neither publicists nor bodyguards to run interference.

When the stars "go live," they are presented with a spacious life net—that is, each word they speak to announce the nominees is emblazoned on a massive teleprompter situated in the center and middle of the theater, its huge black letters on a white background. Unless you are hopelessly myopic, you ought to have no fears. As for me, I dreaded the thought that it might break down. So every time I appeared as a presenter on the awards show, I memorized my comments in advance. I was always prepared for the disaster that never happened.

But being a presenter is nowhere near as harrowing as being a nominee. The nominees—five for each category of Best Actor, Best Actress, Best Supporting Actor, Best Supporting Actress, and Best Director—strive, some with visible anxiety, to remain calm. Those who win have at the ready some rehearsed "extemporaneous" *bon mots* of gratitude, and some go on endlessly thanking their agents, lawyers, relatives, producers, physical trainers, and Jiffy Lube mechanics. If they lose, knowing the camera may descend on them, they offer a wobbly smile or studied repose to mask their disappointment. How could any artist—or anyone else—live through such a moment and not feel anxious? One nominee will triumph in a night of unforgettable glory, and the other four will lose and die a thousand deaths before hundreds of millions of viewers.

It is a ghastly piece of business. Surely there is some balm to be found in knowing that of the vast number of films produced each year, only twenty-five creative artists from the thousands that inhabit all those films are nominated in the five major individual categories. It is an extraordinary tribute. Nonetheless, to the losers, it remains a brief moment on the rack.

The day before the awards is rehearsal time. All the presenters gather onstage, just to be sure they know which part of the stage they will move from and how to exit. I was practicing one day with Juliette Binoche, the stunning French beauty. For reasons I never understood, we were supposed to enter by walking up a set of four stairs, mounted on a small plastic platform, and then descend four stairs to our appointed positions at the Plexiglas lectern. It made no dramatic sense to me. But what the hell, I'm on the show.

We moved together, her arm entwined in mine, and began our ascent. My left heel got caught on the edge of one of the stairs, and I almost stumbled forward. I righted myself and all was well, though Juliette did look at me warily. On the night of the performance itself, as Juliette and I made our way to the edge of the curtain awaiting the stage manager to give us the signal, I said cheerfully, "What would happen if my foot slips again and I latch on to you and we both go down?"

I could see that my sense of humor didn't sit well with this reigning princess of French and international cinema. After all, it is a dismaying thought to contemplate falling flat on one's ass in front of half the TV-watching world. I should have known better, because some years earlier with Jacqueline Bisset, I had made a similar foray into awkward humor as we were about to go front and center.

"Jackie, do you realize that hundreds of millions of people will be watching us and it is a one-take scene, no retake possible?"

Miss Bisset's hand clasped in mine tightened, and she said, "Why do you say such things at this moment?" Actually, her chiding was appropriate. The thought scared me as well.

But despite my occasional moments of discomfiture, these appearances were tremendously helpful. I had been having problems trying to see a high-ranking Chinese government official, a member of the politburo. One week after my second appearance on the awards show, the managing director of our Asian office called me to say that out of the blue he had received word that the Chinese official was ready to meet with me. Wonderful! In two weeks, I was in Beijing and in the official's office, striding forward to be greeted warmly by the minister, a wide smile on his face. In English came, "Ah, Mr. Valenti, I see you on Academy Awards. Verra good, verra good." Well, it damn sure must have been good to produce this kind of greeting.

The Academy Award presentations also made it possible for congressional doors to open on easy hinges. It proved, as I have repeated many times, that there is no draw comparable to celebrity, no matter how ersatz or fleeting.

I soon found out, not surprisingly, that the more I was on the awards shows, and on television generally, the more I became a semicelebrity. No one else in Washington, outside of high government circles and beyond the platform on which performed bona fide movie stars, was gaining the easy access that was lavished on me, mainly because I was "known." I was high-profile in a high-profile industry. But I never inhaled this stuff. I understood perfectly who I was, who I was not, and where I stood. I knew I was not a real celebrity. I didn't allow myself for one second to believe I was on a real stage. I was not an actor. I had no actor's skills, and thank God, I knew that. Early on in my White House and Hollywood years, I had come to learn a lot about famous people. F. Scott Fitzgerald's much heralded line "The rich are different from you and me" applies doubly to the rich *and* famous.

To be a genuinely famous movie or TV star is to find yourself elevated beyond normalcy. No one ever wants to say no to you. Everyone wants to be in your presence. No restaurant ever turns down your request for a table. No hotel anywhere will deny you the finest suite at reduced prices, sometimes even "comping" you in their eagerness to say that this famous star lodged here. Even your business associates see themselves as mere instruments of your well-being, on a lesser level no matter how powerful and influential they may be in their own insular worlds.

I saw with great frequency the narcotic effect this had on famous stars. After a while, a very short while, it becomes hard not to believe in your own godlike status. Sad are the tales of young men and women suddenly catapulted to dizzying heights of fame. It's tremendously difficult to maintain your handhold on the side of the mountain at a level where so few ever climb, where the vista is so splendid, where the air is so thin. But you can't look back or down; it's too terrifying. And all the while you are being pursued not only by the paparazzi, but by everyone who wants a piece of you for their own gain. And how long are you going to be on top? Insecurities mount. Anxieties soar. Pressures grow. Which is why drugs and alcohol are welcome temporary crutches that eventually take up full-time residency in your life. After that, the only hope is rehab.

Emerson put it all in perspective in one fifteen-word sentence: "For every gain there is a loss, and for every loss there is a gain." This applies not just to famous people, but to all people. You want to be the CEO of the big corporation. Fine, if you make it. But to do so, you had to give up time with your wife and kids when you ought to have been there, and you weren't. Emerson's rule reflects the way the world operates. Providentially, there are more than a few famous people who have made the transition from aspirant to star and still hold on to their normalcy.

So I knew I was "somebody" because of my job, a leader in the high-candlepower beam of the movie industry. But just as important, I also knew what I wasn't—an entertainer. But my visibility was an asset to the MPAA and to the movie industry. Most of the moguls knew it and appreciated what it offered in value to the association.

Dani Janssen and the Greatest Ever Post–Academy Awards Party

You don't know Dani Janssen? You should. Why? Because she is the hostess of the most unusual, most tightly controlled post–Academy

Awards party ever. In her lavish twenty-eighth-floor penthouse apartment in one of the exclusive high-rises on the Avenue of the Stars in Beverly Hills' Century City, Dani presides over her guests with generosity, affection, and sensational food, most of which she cooks herself.

Dani is a sensual, attractive woman, the widow of TV actor David Janssen. She brims over with energy, charm, and a ready, contagious laugh. There is an endearing openness to Dani, who can spot empty suits, charlatans, and hustlers several furlongs away. She exhibits a ceaseless loyalty to friends, which in Hollywood is not exactly a trait in heavy supply. To her home she invites no "civilians" (that is, non–movie industry types), only stars, top directors and writers, a few studio chiefs, and me. No more than forty or so folks at any one time are there, beginning with the twenty-five or so dinner guests who watch the awards on TV, a number to be filled out by the stars coming to Dani's following a flyby at the Governor's Ball after the awards ceremonies, most of whom arrive clutching their newly won Oscars.

Dani Janssen's 2005 and 2006 parties included the usual roundup of the famed and fabulous. At one point, I could look around the room and see Barbra Streisand and her handsome husband, Jim Brolin; Oprah Winfrey; Al Pacino; Sean Penn and his wife, Robin Wright Penn; Clint Eastwood and his wife, Dina (Clint holding his Best Director Oscar); Pierce Brosnan and his wife, Keely; Jack Nicholson; Tom Hanks and his wife, Rita Wilson; Reese Witherspoon and her then husband, Ryan Philippe; Quincy Jones; Don Rickles and his wife, Barbara; Bruce Springsteen; Michael Douglas and Catherine Zeta-Jones; Harvey Keitel and his wife, Daphna; Whoopi Goldberg; and HBO's Hollywood chief, Colin Callender, and his gorgeous wife, Elizabeth. Yeah, you're right, this is name-dropping on an epic scale, but how else can I tell you about Dani's guests? Because it is a kind of family gathering, there is a sense of ease and comfort at Dani's house that makes it special. No breathless fans or autograph seekers, no gapes of awe at being close to "a star." When damn near everyone there is a star, the scene is that much more relaxed.

There are other post-Oscar show parties. But they are more crowded with people, a majority of whom are not in the upper reaches of movie royalty. The *Vanity Fair* party is very exclusive and always a hot ticket, but even Graydon Carter, the highly visible and gifted editor of this "must read" magazine, would be hard-pressed to deny the appeal of Dani's event because of its small number of guests and the place in the movie sun occupied by them.

The other exclusive event is the Barry Diller lunch hosted by Barry and his wife, Diane von Fürstenberg, on the day before the Oscar show, at his Coldwater Canyon home in Beverly Hills. The Diller luncheon is elegantly staged (the hallmark of any Diane/Barry enterprise) on a gracefully sloping lawn, studded with tables where the stars and their entourages sit, talk, and eat. Here, in the midday warmth of a Southern California sun, one finds movie studio chieftains, writers, directors, and film icons everywhere.

A couple of years ago at the Diller luncheon, I walked up to a small, very lovely woman carrying a baby. Preoccupied with her human burden, she had dropped a water glass. I briskly picked it up and handed it back to her.

"I am glad you dropped the glass and not the baby," was my offer of conversation. "I'm Jack Valenti."

"Thanks so much," she said in a musical voice, a nice little smile on her lips. "I'm Reese Witherspoon."

Ouch! Okay, not recognizing her was a first-class blunder, but I hadn't expected Reese Witherspoon to be carrying a small child. That's not what she does in movies. Looking back on that moment I take comfort in the certain knowledge that it took up residence in my memory for a helluva lot longer than it did in hers.

When first I entered the movie world, the numero uno post-Oscar party was hosted by the diminutive, battery-powered super-agent Irving "Swifty" Lazar and his wife, Mary. I confess I did love Swifty. He was my literary agent and handled three of my books. David Wolper tells a story about Swifty that offers some insight into the man. David, the television producer who had brought *Roots*, the most viewed television program of all time, to the TV screen, wanted to make a documentary based on Theodore H. White's bestselling

The Making of the President, 1960. Swifty was White's agent. Wolper got Lazar on the phone to tell him that he wanted to film White's epic retelling of the 1960 campaign.

Swifty broke in without pleasantries. "The price is $150,000, not a cent less."

Wolper gasped. "But, Mr. Lazar, all I can afford is $25,000."

Swifty's voice came booming over the phone: "You got a deal." To Swifty, a deal was always the objective.

Swifty and his wife, Mary, gave world-class dinner parties. Mary Margaret and I were at the low end of the recognizability spectrum of the dozen or so we attended. Gore Vidal, Jimmy Stewart, Cary Grant, Jean Simmons, and Elizabeth Taylor were just a few of the glitterati seated at the Lazar dining room table.

Once, Swifty called me just as I was leaving to attend one of the Lazar dinner soirées. He said, "I know you are alone tonight, so I have a favor to ask. Would you pick up Elizabeth Taylor and escort her to the dinner?"

Well, hell, yes, why not, and fantastic. I picked up the film goddess at her home in Bel Air and we drove on to Swifty's. Elizabeth was wearing a drop-dead-gorgeous dress that I didn't need to be informed was haute couture and insanely expensive. It was a knockout. She told me this was the first time she had worn the garment; she was plainly pleased with it, and rightly so.

The dinner was a rousing success. Elizabeth sat to my right and had Ryan O'Neal to her right. Ryan and I indulged in a brisk conversation, talking around Elizabeth. I got a little wound up trying to make a point, gesticulating so energetically that I knocked over the glass of red wine in front of Elizabeth, spilling its vintage contents all over her shatteringly expensive Parisian gown. The entire table went silent, morbidly fascinated by the river of red that now adorned the dress. Elizabeth's face, that fabulous face, was ashen. I wanted to find a small hole to die in. Mary Lazar dashed to Elizabeth's side and escorted her to the bedroom, where she set about outfitting Elizabeth with some temporary clothing.

When Elizabeth returned to the table, she was so gracious, so generously forgiving, that I felt doubly unworthy. If some fool had soaked my new Giacomo Trabalza suit in indelible red wine, I would have tied the bastard to the yardarm and ordered thirty lashes. Elizabeth Taylor was classy.

In later years, the Lazar post–Academy Awards parties were sited at Spago's restaurant on the Sunset Strip. I remember one Lazar party at Spago's where I was chatting with Michael Douglas when the glorious Madonna appeared at our little table, accompanied by an odd-looking fellow attired in what seemed to be an admiral's naval uniform. She sat down with a wide smile, engaging Michael and me in conversation. As an afterthought, she turned to her companion and said, "You two do know Michael Jackson, don't you?" Well, I didn't, but Michael Douglas seemed to have met him before. Jackson mumbled something I couldn't decipher. I felt Douglas's hand squeezing my elbow as if to say "What do you think of this character?" Ambling over was Warren Beatty, who nodded to us with a wry, sly smile, fixing his gaze on the moon-walker. It struck me then that Michael Jackson was one weird fellow. It was the only time I ever talked to him, if talking can be defined as "hello" and "good-bye."

I found out later that in earlier years, Dani and David Janssen had been hosting post-Oscar parties in Hollywood while Swifty Lazar hosted his in New York City. When Lazar moved to Hollywood, he persuaded the Janssens to let him handle the L.A. event. They agreed. But when Swifty died, Dani decided to carry on. And she did. Dani's informal enterprise may be the last of the great dinner gatherings that is Hollywood to the core. The movie community is so fragmented now and surely less prone to the assembly of stars-at-dinner adventures that was the norm in the sixties and seventies.

So it is that when I settle in at Dani's on Academy Awards night, I know that this is the high plains. What other landscape could offer more?

THE BRASS RING NOT TAKEN

In jousting tournaments in the Middle Ages, knights would ride furiously aboard sturdy, fast mounts, lances at the ready, galloping toward a long pole from which hung a brass ring. The trick was, at full speed, to direct the lance tip through the ring and carry it off successfully.

That happened to me once, though at the last minute, I dipped my lance and left the brass ring untaken.

By early 1978, I had spent twelve years as CEO of the MPAA. I had literally circumnavigated the earth settling tough negotiations, had created and implemented the voluntary movie rating system, had become intimately involved in all aspects of the movie industry, and had moved easily with its movers and shakers. I felt I had done my damnedest and had won the plaudits and respect of my colleagues in Hollywood—well, most of them.

When I received a phone call from my friend Herbert Allen, I had no premonition about the subject. At that time, he was chairman and principal stockholder of Columbia Pictures, a member of the Motion Picture Association of America. "Jack," Herb said, "would you be free next Tuesday to fly to New York and have breakfast with me and several Columbia Pictures directors?"

I wanted to ask, "What's on your mind, Herb?" but I knew Herbert well enough to know he wouldn't call me for some idle breakfast chitchat. I said I'd be there. When I arrived at Herb's office—the site of the breakfast—he rose to greet me. With him was his brother-in-law, Irwin Kramer, and two other directors. We all shook hands and sat down.

Let me set the stage. Just two weeks earlier, Columbia's board of directors had struggled through a most unhappy development. David Begelman, CEO of Columbia, a tall, charming former talent agent, had gotten into a miserable situation. He had purportedly forged a check for some few thousand dollars and had been caught by the authorities. He stepped down for a time and was brought back for a time, and then it became clear he was in serious trouble. Columbia cut the ties to Begelman. He was gone for good. (Tragically, sometime later, this truly attractive man committed suicide.) Columbia was without a leader.

Herb wasted no time. "Jack, the board has met, and we have decided we want you to become the chief executive officer of Columbia, to run its studio in California and its international operations as well."

I breathed out slowly. This I hadn't expected. The plain fact was this was a job I really wanted. I yearned to run a major film studio.

I was eager to get involved in the creative excitement of making movies that audiences would clamor to see and enjoy. The idea of diving into the world of dramatic narrative roared through me like rapids on the run.

"Gentlemen, I am honored and I must confess more than a little excited. Yes, this is something I would love to do. I would like to talk to my wife and children before any final deal is struck, but Columbia is a great studio. And I believe that together we can make it greater."

Herb nodded with a smile. "Fine. We had hoped you would feel that way. We want you both because we think you will be a strong leader of Columbia and because we want someone who is known for his integrity. I ask only one thing. We need to have a final okay from you within ten days. To go longer without a CEO will not be good for the company. Would you designate someone with whom we can begin a negotiation?"

I flew back home the same day. Immediately I called Jack Trotter, my longtime Houston friend. Jack was a lawyer and CPA, but mostly he was the greatest fiscal brain I ever met or knew. In Houston whenever some wealthy investor began to try to lure other investors into his deal, the first thing he would say to his friends was, "This deal has been Trotterized." This was the gold standard. It meant that Jack Trotter had examined it and pronounced it sound and valid. Jack could have issued his own paper currency with his picture on it and Houstonians would have readily accepted it as legal tender. Trotter said he would be in touch with Herb Allen and begin negotiations on my contract with Columbia. I called Mary Margaret from the airport and told her I had some astonishingly good news to pass along. I said I was on my way home to talk with her.

The two of us sat down in our library. When I told Mary Margaret what the "good news" was, her first question was, "Will you be able to do the job out of Washington?"

I hesitated. "No, I can't. I must live in Los Angeles. I would have to run the entire worldwide operation of Columbia from there. It's the only place for me to be. Maybe from New York, but L.A. is the right place."

She folded her hands in her lap and gazed at me. "Jack, our children are fourteen, twelve, and ten. I don't want to pack them up and move across the country or to New York. I don't think it would be good for them, and I do not believe it would be good for me. We are all so comfortable here, and the children love their schools and their friends. And you know how much I love Washington."

I wasn't completely surprised by her response. But it was more firm than I had anticipated.

Then she smiled. "If this is something you really want to do, and I see that it is, why don't you spend Monday through Thursday in California and Friday through the weekend here?"

I didn't think that would work. The idea of commuting four times a month from an office a continent away had minimum allure. I had queasy feelings about sustaining a marriage in that kind of long-distance arrangement. Moreover, I didn't want to be separated from my children for the majority of a given week.

Over the next two days, Mary Margaret and I talked and talked. We brought our children into our discussions. They loved the idea of California, but as a permanent residence they weren't so sure. The fact is they made it clear that they wanted to stay in Washington. They had so many ties there.

Meanwhile, Jack Trotter called me after two days of negotiating in New York. He said, "Columbia is ready to give you just about anything you want in a long-term contract, a large salary, bonus, stock options, and perks. It'll be a hefty package. They're honest, first-rate people, and they want you."

I was in a terrible quandary. I wanted to take the job, but I knew it wouldn't work without my family. So I despaired. Finally, I talked with Trotter, who said I had to make up my mind in the next two days. "It's a rich contract, Jack, about as good as anyone can get, not only in compensation, but in stock options as well. You could become truly rich." Well, that sure as hell wasn't helpful.

I had pledged to Herbert that in ten days he would have his answer. I called him on the final day. I had to say no, and I told him why. Herbert, who has four children of his own, understood my problem. "We want you, Jack, but I know how your family feels, and they must come first."

Within a week, Herbert reached into the Securities and Exchange Commission, where one of his college classmates at Williams College was a securities lawyer. Fay Vincent had been a football hero at Williams, two years ahead of Herbert. Fay came aboard and did a first-class job as CEO of Columbia Pictures. He also became quite rich. Soon, I was caught back up in the many blessings of my own life. I became engrossed in my MPAA duties, and the sense of loss faded. I could not quarrel with my fate. I was leading an exciting life. But to be honest, I have sometimes wondered about what might have been.

Chapter 12

ICONS OF THE SILVER SCREEN

My closest friend in Hollywood, Kirk Douglas. Here I am marching in lockstep with Spartacus.

I had occupied my new MPAA chairman's office for only a few months when I got a call from Lew Wasserman. He said, "Edie and I want to give you and Mary Margaret a real Hollywood party. Tell me who you want invited."

Sure, I thought, we're part of Hollywood now; why not meet the princes and princesses of this fantasy realm? Since only the foolhardy or the clueless turn down an invitation to the Wasserman home, on the appointed evening all the inhabitants of Mt. Olympus showed up. Mary Margaret sat between Cary Grant and Gene Kelly. I sat between Angie Dickinson and Dinah Shore. Also at the two tables were Fred Astaire, Kirk and Anne Douglas, Burt Lancaster, Julie Andrews, and Barbara Stanwyck. During the evening, Mary Margaret danced in turn with Grant, Kelly, Douglas, and Astaire. When the evening was done, she said to me, "After Cary Grant, Fred Astaire, Kirk Douglas, and Gene Kelly, what else has life to offer?" Not much. Later, Mary Margaret said to me, "Isn't it awful? I can't remember what I talked about with Cary Grant and Gene Kelly. All I know is I was drowning in their charm."

Gene Kelly was especially warm to me. I told him about my visit to France (I was briefed in advance that Kelly spoke fluent French). Fred Astaire came up to shake my hand, and all I could see was that supple form gliding on the dance floor. Cary Grant said, "You and I should find some time to chat, how about that?" What would you say? Hell, I just wanted to tell people that Cary Grant wanted to spend time with me. Kirk Douglas poked me in the ribs with a big grin. "Jack, you are now a big *macher* in the movies. Think you can handle it?"

One legend who intrigued me was Alfred Hitchcock, who also

happened to be an intimate of Lew Wasserman. During his steward-ship of the MCA talent agency, for over twenty-five years, Lew had been Hitchcock's agent. It was more than an agent-artist relationship; it was an authentic friendship. Lew knew of my infatuation with Hitchcock, and when he called to say I would be dining with the Great Man, I was jubilant. It was through Lew that I was able to see the private side of Hitch, as Lew and other close friends called him.

Lew had scheduled me to join Edie and him for a dinner at Hitchcock's home in Bel Air, that enclave of winding streets and forest-covered landscapes where the movie powerful dwelled in majestic comfort. It was a rather large house but not opulent, a friendly, lived-in home. Hitchcock greeted Lew and Edie and me at the front door. He had that famously round face, that pear-shaped body, and a walk that had to be described as a "waddle." Yet the best way I can think to de-scribe him is magisterial.

It was dinner for eight, which suited me just fine, since I was seated right across the table from Hitchcock. Professionally, of course, Hitchcock was the master showman. In private, to my surprise, it was the same. His use of language was mesmerizing. He also commanded the dinner table. He encouraged others to talk, but when the discus-sion began to drift, he moved quickly to redirect it. He was a gour-mand of the first rank, wielding knowledge of food, wine, and cigars with the grace of a master fencer. According to Lew, the Hitchcock dinner table ritual called for the men to retire to Hitch's study for cigars and cognac once dessert was over. On this night, as the dessert was being served, Tony Curtis, seated at the end of my side of the table next to his beautiful wife, Janet Leigh, took out a gigantic Cuban cigar. As he moved his lighter to the cigar's end, Hitchcock spoke in that unmistakable rumble, his words carefully spaced and unhurried:

"Mr. Curtis, at this table we smoke after the dinner has been completed. And at no other time."

To his credit, Curtis swiftly extinguished the lighter, stowed the cigar, and smiled sweetly at the master. Hitchcock nodded. To be truthful, I would have reacted exactly as Curtis did. There was no suitable alternative. As the conversation resumed, Lew whispered to me, "That's how he ran a movie set." Yeah, I can believe that.

THEN THERE WAS SINATRA—THE GREATEST ENTERTAINER OF THE TWENTIETH CENTURY

The Chairman of the Board, ol' Blue Eyes, was my special favorite. There was only one word to describe Frank Sinatra: "charismatic." But even that magic word was insufficient to fully accommodate his presence. He was, simply put, the greatest entertainer of the twentieth century. Until he gained weight in his later years, he was a spindly guy, medium height, with a jutting jaw, glistening blue eyes, and a "screw you" attitude when he turned off the charm. No doubt about it: Frank did it "his way."

I was in the audience as his guest at Prince Albert Hall in London in the late sixties or early seventies; I can't remember exactly. The place was packed, the air electric with expectation. Suddenly the lights went dark, and then Sinatra came onstage with a swagger, completely in control of himself and the wound-up British audience. Holding the mike in hand, he moved with animal grace to a tall stool, on which he sat with complete insouciance.

The voice—ah, that unmistakable voice! It could only be Sinatra making love to the lyrics, enunciating every syllable. After a couple of songs, he left the stool to wander the stage, the consummate showman. All the time, the voice soared, swooped, and soothed. Sinatra wrote no songs, but he venerated those who created them: lyricists, composers, arrangers. He cared deeply about having the best of the best collaborating with him, and he invariably did. That night, England went crazy over Frank, completely jettisoning the reserve for which it was so famous. I went backstage to meet him. There were a few dozen friends there. Frank grabbed me and hugged me. "Hey, you showed up. I like that." He pressed a drink in my hand as he held court with his other guests for over an hour.

Several times, Lew and Edie Wasserman brought friends to Las Vegas when Frank was playing there in one of the casinos. We would fly to Vegas in a private jet. Lew would give all the women velvet bags full of casino chips. We would motor over to the casino, join the crap tables or roulette wheels, and then sit down for Frank's dinner show. He would have arranged a table just beneath the stage for all of us. As he sang, he gazed down at the Wasserman group, sometimes getting on his knees to send melodies on gossamer wings to Edie Wasserman, to Mary Margaret, and to the other women at the table. Heavy stuff.

After the performance, ritual called for us to go backstage to be with Frank for one or two hours, in a kind of jubilant after-the-show party. Once when he performed in Washington, D.C., in those years when his divine singing gift was beginning to fade, he sent me a personal invitation. The show ended late, and I thought, Let the guy get some rest instead of having to cope with me and fifty other people. So I went home. Bad move on my part. When next I saw him in Palm Springs, he ignored me. I learned later that he was still furious that I had not come backstage in Washington to see him. It was as if I had committed a sin beyond the possibility of expiation. And I may have.

Kirk Douglas, a friend of Sinatra's for ages, knew how to handle him. One weekend, when Mary Margaret and I were houseguests of the Douglases at their home in Palm Springs on Via Lola Street, Anne and Kirk hosted a dinner party of twenty people. Frank and Barbara Sinatra were among them. Frank was seated next to Mary Margaret. He was in a foul mood, grindingly morose despite Mary Margaret's valiant efforts to extract him from his funk. Then Kirk rose for one of his classic toasts, and this time he had clearly made it his goal to get Frank laughing again.

Kirk told the story of some years ago when Frank was headlining the Desert Inn. After the show he became unruly at the gaming tables, so disrupting the casino floor that Carl Cohen, general manager of the Desert Inn, was summoned from his apartment to handle the star who wouldn't be handled. When Cohen, a six-foot-two-inch heavyweight, arrived, Frank threw a punch at him, whereupon Cohen decked him with a massive right hook. Douglas told us that the next day, when someone asked Frank for his reaction to the fracas with Carl Cohen, Sinatra answered, "I learned never again to fight a Jew in the desert." For the first time that evening, a smile tugged at Sinatra's dour face. Then he began to laugh, as did everyone else in the dining room.

Frank was a great artist tormented by inner furies. People yearned to be near him, some of them old friends, good friends. Yet he was capable of an aloofness that was cold and frightening. I knew a couple, nice people, rich people, who so adored Sinatra that many an evening they refused all invitations, sitting alone, praying Frank would call. (He did have a habit of phoning at the last minute to suggest dinner.) So this couple, desperately anxious not to offend Frank, sat through many evenings all alone waiting for the call that so rarely came. Yet they kept on waiting. Whenever Frank did call, it came to them as the sunrise after a storm.

The first year of my White House career, the president was hosting a state dinner for a prime minister. I passed a request on to Bess Abell, Lady Bird Johnson's top assistant, to put Frank Sinatra on the guest list. To my dismay, within a day Bess was on the phone to me. "Jack, the president wants Sinatra's name off the list."

I was stunned. "Why?" was my obvious question.

Bess was noncommittal. "I suggest you ask the president," was her reply.

I did, within the hour. He looked at me sourly. "Bobby Kennedy told me it would not be suitable to have Sinatra. He has some friends who aren't the kind he ought to have, and Bobby thinks it wise to avoid him."

I was crushed. Thank God the invitations had not gone out. But I felt the sting. I never told Frank about this slight, ever, but I was well aware that Sinatra worshipped JFK. As the chairman of Kennedy's inaugural gala on January 19, 1961, Frank had succeeded in enlisting a world-class group of stars to entertain. He was at the new president's side constantly, laughing and joshing with Kennedy, having the time of his life. Frank even built an elegant bedroom addition to his Palm Springs home to be used only by Kennedy when he came to the desert. You can imagine how devastated Sinatra was when on JFK's first trip to California as president, he stayed at Bing Crosby's home.

When Sinatra died, it was as if the sky drained of song. I own just about every recording he ever made. If you love lyrics, Frank does something special to them with the languorous, sensual caress of his voice. I never tire of listening to him. I am not sure how young people regard him today, where they place him in the context of Bono, Springsteen, Tyler, McCartney, Jagger, and the rest. I do believe that Bono would have admired Frank. There was in Sinatra the same kind of almost supernatural musical gift that Bono wears so comfortably and so well.

The Towering Genius of Quincy Jones

As a little boy, Quincy Jones grew up in desperate poverty marked by the mental illness of his mother and the absence of his father, so it's a wonder funded by miracles that he ever managed to survive, much less become one of America's largest musical icons. More than that, to survive that childhood and to reach manhood with such a super-abundance of charm and grace is almost incomprehensible.

Somehow, in the rubble of this childhood the good fairies finally came to visit Quincy at age twelve. In junior high school, he learned to play the trumpet and sang in a gospel quartet. Music roared through him, set his soul on fire, and for the rest of his life those flames blazed as if fed dry tinder. A genius was born.

I am neither neutral nor objective with regard to Quincy. He's the kind of friend anyone would rejoice in. He is unfailingly there for you, no matter how poorly the fates may have treated you. I have spent almost half a century in the world of the famous—political leaders, movie/television stars, and musical legends. I have known the biggest and the best. None surpass Quincy in sheer breadth of creativity. Film producer, arranger and scorer, composer, music producer, writer, CEO of successful entertainment enterprises, collaborator with and mentor to the biggest names in entertainment: Quincy Jones truly has done it all.

I've spent many a cheerful hour with Quincy in his stunning mansion in Bel Air, a multilevel architectural masterpiece that he labored over with the designers. Q (as his friends call him) was not one to say, "Build it and tell me when I can move in." He was there poring over the renderings, changing that and revising this, to the extent that every inch of its twenty-two thousand square feet bears his personal imprint.

One day, the two of us sat at his small dining table in the library, fed by some chef who could have been a four-star celebrity on any continent.

"How about you and Sinatra?" I asked him.

"Okay," he said, "I'll tell you one story. I was flying with Frank in his plane, many years ago, on our way to Las Vegas where he was opening along with Count Basie. Frank was kicking back a stiff drink, and he turned to me and said, 'Q, it would be kind of kooky to do "Shadow of Your Smile" in the show. What do you think?' "

" 'Hey, Francis, that would be a kicker,' said Quincy.

"He smiled. 'So, Mr. Q, do you think you could fetch up a new arrangement for tomorrow night?'

" 'Francis, no problem with the arrangement, but can you learn the lyrics?'

"Frank didn't miss a beat. 'You get the music, I'll know the lyrics.' "

Quincy was grinning as he related the story. "I worked all that night and put together a new arrangement for the song, which you know was the theme in the movie *The Sandpiper*. Frank had written down the lyrics sixteen times, saying them over and again. He was mainlining his subconscious to get it tuned in. Works every time. That's what you do when you make a speech without notes, right, Jack?"

Q leaned back. "The next night, Frank was magnificent. He was so grateful to me for the arrangement. He liked it, and I liked what he did to it and to that audience. You know, what you learn when you are young is what you remember all your life."

I said, "I agree, Q. I always get a kick out of telling people that I remember the names of my first-, second-, and fifth-grade teachers. I never forgot what they taught me."

Q said, "I can still hear my daddy telling me and my brother Lloyd over and over again: 'Always do everything you do the best that you can do, and then a little more. Don't matter what kind of job, the lowest on the ladder, just do it the best ever.' Do you know how wise that is? I think that whatever success I have achieved I can trace back to my daddy's pronouncement. He was a carpenter, but he was the best damn carpenter around. He was the best."

Quincy Jones's achievements have set standards that I daresay none will ever surpass. He has won twenty-seven Grammys, plus the Grammy Living Legend Award. That's unheard of. He co-produced the Steven Spielberg–directed film *The Color Purple*. He put into the film two unknowns who had never acted before, a winsome young woman named Oprah Winfrey and another young woman who has wowed the public ever since, named Whoopi Goldberg. How's that for prescience? He has composed the music for thirty-three movies and produced *We Are the World*, the bestselling album of all time. His *Q's Jook Joint* attracted performances from the best in the world: Bono, Ray Charles, Brandy, Phil Collins, Babyface Edmonds, Gloria Estefan, Herbie Hancock, Queen Latifah, and a host of others. Why? Because they wanted what we all want: to be with and to work with Quincy.

SAM SPIEGEL, REX HARRISON, AND LE GAVROCHE

Some thirty years or so ago, Mary Margaret and I were in London, where I had movie meetings to attend. I got a call from Sam Spiegel. "Would you and Mary Margaret like to join me for dinner? The Rex Harrisons and [Rudolf] Nureyev will be there as well." Of course we would.

But first a word about who Sam Spiegel was and the immense reach of his creative imagination. His origins are vague. Sam always embellished any experience, including his provenance, but he seems to have been born in Austro-Hungary in 1911. He changed his name from time to time. Once in his movie career he was known as S. P. Eagle. George Stevens Sr., fabled film director and an old friend of Sam's, once dropped by unannounced to Sam's elegant apartment in Manhattan. The butler asked who he should say was calling on Mr. Spiegel, to which Stevens, with a casual air, said, "Tell Mr. Speigel that Mr. S. T. Evens would like to see him."

Sam lived grandly, and perhaps autocratically, but he also wrought great cinema. His body of work includes *The African Queen; The Bridge on the River Kwai; On the Waterfront; Lawrence of Arabia; Suddenly, Last Summer;* and many others. It's an astonishing list that includes four Best Picture Academy Awards. No producer has more.

We appeared at Sam's tastefully appointed apartment at Grosvenor House, one of London's superior lodgings. Sam greeted us heartily. Shortly after, the door opened to admit Rex Harrison and his then wife, actress Rachel Roberts. She was spectacularly outfitted in white, capped off by a flowing white fur hanging negligently around her bare shoulders. She was carrying a small white dog of uncertain ancestry, who nestled quietly in his mistress's arm.

Harrison in person was much like Harrison on screen: tall, slim, and brimming over with British reserve, irony, and a tinge of dignified superiority. He bowed to Mary Margaret, tipped his chin at me, and smiled beatifically at Sam. It swiftly dawned on me that Rachel was, to be honest, three-quarters smashed. She immediately knocked back a dry martini and had Sam's "man" pour her another. She sat quietly on the sofa next to Rex, nuzzling her dog and greedily irrigating her body with Sam's splendid gin. I watched her with growing admiration. How the hell could anyone maintain that pace without falling on her ass?

Rex and Sam engaged in pleasantries. Mary Margaret and I listened. Rachel got sloshed. Soon, Sam got to his feet and announced we were going to dinner at Le Gavroche, a two-star restaurant not for anyone who had to ask the cost of the entrée. It was a small, tony place much fussed about by London's upper crust. We sat at a corner rectangular table, Rachel at one end, flanked by me and the newly arrived Rudolf Nureyev, who had caused soft gasps of worship as he entered. Sam sat at the other end, with my wife on his right and Rex on his left. Drinks were ordered. Once more into the breach, Rachel ordered a double martini. The first course arrived, but Rachel pushed aside her food, calling loudly for more martinis.

I began to wonder how long she could last, and I didn't have long to wait for the answer.

Sitting next to me, now slouched against the back of the chair in which she sat, the dog lounging indolently in her lap, Rachel spoke loudly to her husband. "Rex, darling, I want you, and I want you now." We all turned to her, although Rex continued to fiddle with his fork and a slippery piece of salmon. "Rex, do you hear me? I want you . . ." And here the talk became extremely specific as she outlined what she wanted Rex to do to her and what she would do to him. The language was unambiguous and plainly pornographic. The Supreme Court itself would have confirmed it unanimously.

I began to try to slide down into my seat, and if I could have, I would have plunged under the table. Mary Margaret's usually serene complexion began to turn a truly serious shade of pale. Sam looked at Rachel sternly. "Rachel, get hold of yourself, now."

She glanced over at him and said daintily, "Piss off, Sam, I wasn't

talking to you. Rex, I need you now because . . ." This time her catalog of needs was delivered in an even louder voice. Every eye in the
restaurant was now fixed on Rachel, to which she was, of course,
smashingly oblivious.

Sam was now quite vexed, and he grabbed Rex by the forearm.
"Rex, assert yourself, handle this. Take her home. Use my car and
driver just outside."

Rex, now in full command of the salmon on his plate, looked up
for the first time at his wife. In a tone that can only be described as
"languid," he said, "My deah, please eat something. You really need
to do that, you know."

With pent-up fury, Sam said, "Rachel, Rex is right. Eat something, you're totally drunk."

Now the little dog, aroused from his nap, raised his tiny eyes and
bared his tiny fangs. But Rachel did not need Fido's support. "Fuck
off, Sam. Darling Rex, please let me . . ." And here she articulated
her desires with the precision of a scholar of Euclidian geometry.
I wanted to turn invisible, and Mary Margaret seemed to be joining
me in sliding under the table. The other diners in the room were so
absorbed by this recital of lust that every plate had grown cold.

Sam was beside himself. "Do something, Rex," he said, his voice
shaking. And then, turning to Nureyev, he said, "Help me, will you?"

I can remember the next moment as clearly as if it happened an
hour ago. Nureyev leaped nimbly to his feet, reached down, picked
up Rachel—and the dog—and in a world-class pas de deux whirled
her gracefully around two tables and floated out the door to deposit
Rachel—and Fido, the warrior dog—in Sam's limo.

By this time, Rex stirred himself into slow-motion action, calmly
following the ballet grand master and his sodden wife with unhurried
stride, paying no attention to the rabid gaze of the entire array of
diners before disappearing into the cavernous limousine. The other
diners, some of whom rose to their feet and burst into applause,
were deliciously aware that they had been eyewitnesses to a truly
once-in-a-lifetime experience.

Sam, Nureyev, Mary Margaret, and I finished our meal, but to
the chagrin of the other diners, the show was over. From that day
on, whenever Sam and I saw each other, one of us would say, "Le

Gavroche," and we would both break into unrestrained laughter, though it may have come a bit harder for Sam than it came to me.

Now to the epilogue. Some years later, in the post-Rachel era, I entered the elevator of the Waldorf Towers on Fiftieth Street off Park Avenue in New York City, where at the time I had a small apartment. To my astonishment, there in a finely cut tuxedo was Rex Harrison and a handsome tall blond lady, splendidly gowned (I later learned she was Elizabeth, his new wife). I smiled hospitably, stuck out my hand, and said, "Rex, I'm Jack Valenti. You may recall we dined once with Sam Spiegel in London, at Le Gavroche." I must have put my foot in it, because Elizabeth flashed me a look glistening with frost.

Rex looked at me glumly and muttered something like "Yes, of course." By now, Elizabeth, who doubtless had been thoroughly briefed on the previous wife's indiscretions, assumed the fierce look of an angry jaguar about to spring. The elevator seemed to take hours to go several floors as the three of us stood mired in muteness—Elizabeth glowering, Rex flummoxed, and I silently begging the elevator to please get to the thirty-fourth floor before dawn rose on the next day.

I saw Rex Harrison several times over the next years, but always from afar. If I had gotten close to him, however, I would have been careful to exile "Gavroche" from my tongue, though I would have suggested to him that Nureyev was one helluva fine fellow.

KIRK DOUGLAS AND ANNE DOUGLAS

I first met Kirk when he came to the White House in early 1964, and I liked him immediately. When I left my post at the White House to become president of the Motion Picture Association of America, we bonded, and to this hour the bonds hold fast. The fact is that my dearest friends in Hollywood are Kirk; his wife, Anne; and his son Michael. Now I include Michael's wife, the ravishingly beautiful and miraculously normal Catherine Zeta-Jones, as well as Peter and Joel, Kirk's other sons, and Peter's wife, Lisa.

Kirk is one of a kind. He has an overpowering physical presence, which is why on a large movie screen he looms over the audience like a tidal wave in full flood. Even today, after surviving two physical tragedies, his sense of humor is undiminished and his creative energy is still burning bright. Since 1946, when he filmed his first starring role with Barbara Stanwyck in *The Strange Love of Martha Ivers*, Kirk Douglas has been globally revered. He is now the last living screen legend of those who vaulted to stardom at the war's end, that special breed of movie idol instantly recognizable anywhere, whose luminous on-screen characters are forever memorable.

His wife, Anne, is so much more than the beautiful French-woman revealed at first glance. She is absolutely the most elegant woman in Hollywood. In a town where friendships often rise and fall depending on the whims and vagaries of fame and success, Anne plays to a different script. If you are sick, or if the fates have otherwise deserted you, the one person you can rely on is Anne Douglas. She will be there. A Parisian to the core, Anne is both soft-spoken and well-spoken, fluent in several languages, with a taste for beauty in its simpler forms. There is about Anne a singular grace, a strong will, and a sense of unshatterable purpose. She knows who she is, and she lives her life committed to the things she values. Great lady, this Anne Douglas.

I have in my memory box one of those evenings that you can't make up because it is too hilarious to credit with reality. Some years ago, Anne called me. She said, "Kirk is out of town. Would you take me to a party that Charlie and Mary Jane Wick are giving for President Reagan?" Charles Wick had been director of the United States Information Agency during the Reagan administration. Reagan had departed the White House the year before.

Anne and I arrived at Chasen's, *the* watering hole for a good many of Hollywood's stars, and were escorted to the private dining room at the rear. Anne had the seat of honor, between President Reagan and Bob Hope. I sat directly across, with a wide-angle view of the three of them. Now you have to understand that both Ronald Reagan and Bob Hope had many assets, but good hearing was not among them. To be candid, a fence post could have given them strong competition in a hearing contest.

Bob leaned in so he could see Reagan full face. "Ron, have you heard this one?" He proceeded to tell one of his patented stories.

When he finished, Reagan turned to Anne and said, "What did he say?" whereupon Anne repeated the story. Reagan chuckled. Then Reagan peered around Anne to say, "Bob, here's one you haven't heard," delivering a rather funny yarn. Bob turned to Anne: "What did he say?" Again, Anne dutifully repeated the joke. Hope guffawed, and Reagan beamed. Then Bob turned to Anne: "Tell Ron this one," and with a wide smile, he began his next story. Anne, now beginning to sense where the hell this was going, turned to Reagan and repeated Bob's story, with Reagan's ear almost connected to her lips. To Anne's horror, she had become trapped like Bill Murray in *Groundhog Day* for the remainder of the evening. The rest of us around the table were transfixed by the Reagan-Anne-Hope joke fest.

On the way home, an exhausted Anne Douglas said to me in hoarse tones, "I felt like a wind tunnel in there. The worst part is I didn't get some of the punch lines of those jokes."

It is a fact that Kirk Douglas has had few close friends. He has always been a maverick. Early in his career, Kirk's lawyer handled all of Kirk's money and his investments. Kirk asked no questions, since the lawyer was also Kirk's best friend. Kirk trusted him totally. Shortly after Kirk married Anne, the pragmatic Frenchwoman asked Kirk if he knew what he was worth. Kirk shrugged off the question. His money was being handled wisely. Whatever he needed, Kirk got from his lawyer, and he never wanted for anything. He was a major global star. His salaries were large and his work continuous. There was no reason to doubt that he was a very wealthy man.

To a Parisian skeptic, that was not a satisfactory answer. Anne retained an accounting firm and notified the lawyer/business manager of her decision to conduct an audit of Kirk's affairs. To her dismay and Kirk's horror, the accounting firm revealed disloyalty that bordered on sheer madness. Their report showed that the lawyer had plundered Kirk's accounts. A sizable portion of Kirk's estate had evaporated. Kirk was heartbroken. He brought no charges against the lawyer, but it affected his ability to believe in anyone again. Friends, okay, but total trust, no.

Anne once told me that she was so pleased that in me Kirk had finally found a friend he knew to be loyal. It was an emotional moment for me. I felt the same way about Kirk. To me, Kirk Douglas is a rarity. As an actor in Hollywood, he was the first to quit the studio system and form his own production company, Bryna Productions, named after his immigrant mother. He wanted to make the films he wanted to make and none other. He negotiated with the studios for financing, but the creative shape of a film was his entirely. He personally commissioned scripts and personally revised them. After he agreed with the dramatic narrative, he cast the actors and chose the director, except when he directed himself.

He made some ninety films as an actor, many of them under the Bryna banner. They included *Seven Days in May, The Vikings, Paths of Glory, Lonely Are the Brave* (Kirk's favorite of his movies and the real film debut of Walter Matthau), and *Spartacus*. It was through *Spartacus* that Kirk made his most notable contribution to the movie industry, in an act of courage that even now has resonance. It came about in an odd and unforeseen way.

The preamble to this story took place a few years earlier, in 1957, when Kirk set out to make a film he knew would be controversial. It was the true story of a mutiny in the French army during World War I. He commissioned a script and looked around for the right director. He had seen a small-budget film entitled *The Killing* by a young director still in his twenties. He was impressed with the rhythmic flow of the story, a narrative cadence that infused and illuminated the movie. He sought out the young man and settled on him as the director of his new film, *Paths of Glory*. The director's name was Stanley Kubrick.

This was Kubrick's first shot at a movie that would play throughout the world. The movie became a classic, but unfortunately, President Charles de Gaulle of France took vehement exception to this stain on French military honor. He banned the film in France. It would be some twenty-five years before *Paths of Glory* was actually screened in the theaters of France.

In 1959, Kirk read a novel by Howard Fast. It was the story of a slave in early Roman times who sought freedom so passionately that he gathered about him an army of slaves and, with an audacity that bordered on foolhardiness, rebelled against Rome and its superbly trained legions. So skillful was this warrior slave that he swept the countryside, defeating the best legions Rome could send against him. Kirk was fascinated by this tale, titled *Spartacus*.

He asked a friend, one of Hollywood's most brilliant writers, to come up with the script. There was one problem, a serious problem. The writer, Dalton Trumbo, was on the Hollywood blacklist. The blacklist was an odious registry of writers, actors, and directors who by innuendo, rumor, and mostly baseless accusations were labeled as Communists (though it is true that some of them had flirted with Communist ideas and even admired their theoretical promise). It was the worst of times. The old Hollywood moguls, all of whom were anti-Communist, were frightened by the witch hunt in Washington conducted by the House Un-American Activities Committee, headed by Senator Joe McCarthy. This committee zealously sought out Communists everywhere, in and under every bed. It was an American Inquisition.

The committee bulldozed the movie moguls into creating the blacklist: Anyone on it could not find work; their careers literally collapsed around them. Directors and actors were the hardest hit, because they couldn't hide. Writers like Trumbo could work at home and use false names on screen credits, but they were denied visible authorship. It was a Hobson's choice, but mortgages had to be paid and households had to be maintained.

When Kirk began shooting *Spartacus* in Rome, Anthony Mann, his initial choice for director, collided with Kirk. They were at odds over the creative strands that bound the film together. Mann and Kirk parted company three or four weeks into production. Kirk needed another director fast. He phoned the young director of *Paths of Glory*. Within days, Stanley Kubrick was in Rome and on the job. Kirk had chosen the best of the best to act in the movie: Laurence Olivier, Charles Laughton, Peter Ustinov, Tony Curtis, Jean Simmons, and Woody Strode, with Kirk playing the title role. It was an Olympian cast. The filming went swimmingly. When principal photography was completed and the editing almost done in 1960, Kirk, Ed Lewis, the line producer, and Kubrick gathered to solve a riddle: Whose name should go on the screen as the writer?

Kubrick said, "Put my name on as writer."

Kirk scoffed. "Come on, Stanley. You didn't write a line."

The discussion continued. Kirk finally stood up and said, "Dammit, Dalton wrote this great script. His name will go on the screen."

Ed Lewis was enthusiastically approving.

One of Kirk's colleagues on the film warned that Universal Pictures, the distributor of the film, would object.

Kirk was unmoved. "What's Universal going to do? They have millions tied up in this. I am the producer. I make these choices, no one else. I'll take my chances."

Others on the production staff were aghast. "This is madness. It will ruin your career" was the general view. A good many of his associates were convinced that Kirk had signed the death warrant to his career. But Universal was enormously pleased with the movie. They sensed big box office revenues and maybe even Academy Award nominations. When the film premiered to flattering reviews, there on the screen in large letters was the credit "Written by Dalton Trumbo." The film went on to achieve legendary success. Strangely, there was no outcry. The Hollywood moguls held their collective breath, but no retribution followed.

In one stroke, Kirk Douglas broke the back of a malicious conspiracy. The blacklist collapsed. If Dalton Trumbo's name was on the screen, how could others on the blacklist continue to work in exile? A week after the movie's opening, Kirk got a letter from Trumbo. It read: "Dear Kirk, thank you for giving me back my name, [signed] Dalton."

Some years later, the Writers Guild of America hosted a large dinner honoring Kirk. Burt Lancaster, his old friend with whom he had made seven films, came forward to award Kirk the WGA's highest medal for his courage in destroying the blacklist. I was there, sitting at Kirk's table. Burt began by saying, "Kirk will be the first to tell you he's hard to get along with. And I would be the second." Rousing laughter. Burt grew serious. "What Kirk Douglas did to reassert and preserve freedom of the screen is an act of valor that deserves the applause, approval, and admiration of everyone in this country." The dinner guests rose spontaneously, applauding with genuine passion. They knew Burt was right.

• • •

One story that Kirk tells will resonate with anyone who has encounters with top-level government officials. During the Kennedy years, Kirk had traveled on behalf of the U.S. government, specifically the State Department and the United States Information Agency. When Johnson brought in Leonard Marks as the new director of the USIA, Kirk arranged to meet him. Kirk showed up promptly and offered his name to the receptionist, who asked him to sit for a moment until Mr. Marks was ready. Kirk waited. He waited for twenty minutes past the appointed hour. Waited thirty minutes. Now, a bit vexed, he called me at my White House office.

"Jack," said Kirk, "I'm getting a little pissed. I have an appointment with Leonard Marks, but he's kept me waiting for over forty minutes."

"Kirk, get your butt over here to the White House. I'll have you met at the entrance."

Shortly thereafter, Kirk showed up. We embraced and chatted for a few minutes. I hit the presidential button on my phone console. When the president came on, I said, "Mr. President, I have Kirk Douglas with me. Do you have a free moment to visit with him?" Moments later, I entered the Oval Office with Kirk in tow.

The president came around from behind his desk to shake Kirk's hand. "Sit down here, Kirk, I'm glad to see you," he said, gesturing to the couch as he plumped himself down in his rocking chair. With a wide grin, LBJ proceeded to tell Kirk that he had seen *In Harm's Way*, a World War II film about the U.S. Navy, also starring Duke Wayne. I tactfully made no mention of the fact that LBJ usually went right to sleep as soon as any movie began screening in the White House theater. His top assistants loathed those movie nights, because when the film was over, LBJ awoke refreshed and inevitably suggested that we accompany him to the Oval Office for some work. God, those movie nights were hell.

As Kirk departed the Oval Office, he said to President Johnson, "Mr. President, this is a strange town. I can't get in to see the head of the USIA, but an hour later I am visiting the president of the United States in his office. America is a wonderful country, isn't it?"

. . .

On February 13, 1991, tragedy struck. Kirk was in the process of finishing one of some nine books he had written. One of his friends flew him by helicopter to Santa Barbara for an all-day session with his editor. When the literary work of the day had concluded, Kirk boarded the chopper for the flight back to Beverly Hills. The field was an abandoned airstrip. No tower, no radio, no nothing. Moreover, the chopper sat on the ground behind an old two-story shed that blocked their view of the rest of the field, including the dirt runway.

The chopper had risen from behind the abandoned shed to about one hundred feet when it suddenly confronted a small single-engine plane piloted by a flight instructor with his young flight student aboard. Both crafts tried valiantly to avoid each other. Both failed. The small plane rammed the chopper. Both aircraft crashed to earth. The two men aboard the small plane were killed. The chopper broke apart on the hard ground. The chopper pilot was severely injured. Kirk was unconscious.

A passerby saw the accident, and soon Kirk was in another chopper being dispatched to Mt. Sinai Hospital in Los Angeles. Anne, terrified, met the chopper and was in the ambulance with Kirk as it deposited its patient at the hospital. I was in my car in Washington when I heard the news on the radio. I was stunned. Immediately, I was on the phone to learn that Kirk was in bad shape but alive.

I got the earliest plane to Los Angeles the next morning. I raced to the hospital and was greeted by Anne. There prostrate on the bed was Kirk, being ministered to by a doctor and a nurse. They had removed the top of his hospital gown to examine his body. As I gazed down on Kirk, I could hardly credit my senses. His chest, arms, and abdomen resembled nothing so much as flesh that had been roasted too long on a spit. It was ghastly. Over the months that followed, Kirk gradually reasserted himself. He grew stronger. His vitality returned with each passing day. I was always amazed at how he never looked back. He was Kirk Douglas again. But he would never shake off the pain that stalked him.

Then came the second blow. On June 26, 1996, Kirk was leveled by a stroke. It hit him hard. He lost the ability to speak, which for an actor is the ultimate loss. The doctors told Anne that if there was no improvement within forty-eight hours, it was unlikely he would ever regain his voice. I sorrowed for him. But Kirk began a long, frustrating regimen of voice therapy, day in and day out. Weeks and months passed by. He never tired, or if he did, he never let on to Anne or anyone else. Gradually, his voice began to return. It was ragged, but he could be understood. It was really a miracle, but one born of hard, relentless labor that few would have been fit to endure.

Then came the Academy Awards of 1997. Though Kirk had been nominated for Best Actor three times—for *Champion*, *The Bad and the Beautiful*, and *Lust for Life*—he had never won. The Board of Governors of the Academy of Motion Picture Arts and Sciences awarded Kirk a special Oscar for his long film career. Michael and I urged him to receive his award, look out at the audience, and just say, "Thank you." Why chance a speech when it might go wrong? The audience and the TV viewers would understand, and they would approve. He nodded as we talked.

The night of the Oscars, Kirk's four sons, Michael, Joel, Peter, and Eric, sat beside his wife, Anne. I was in the audience as well, close to the front, praying that Kirk would follow the counsel that Michael and I had given. Kirk was smiling easily onstage, standing as erect as he could, his gaze falling on those seated in front of him. Then he gestured toward Anne and his four sons as they sat riveted, emotionally charged. He held up his Oscar in their direction and said in a rough voice, "I see my four sons up there. They are mighty proud of the old man." The audience went wild with applause. His sons' eyes glistened. Then he went on, "And I see my wife, Anne. I love her more today than I ever have before." Anne broke down in tears. The audience erupted in affection once more, rising to their feet to salute this last of the great movie legends, who had survived the threat of death and stared down the demons that had threatened to silence him. I felt an emotional tidal wave roaring through the Dorothy Chandler Pavilion in the L.A. Music Center. God, I was so proud of him.

I was even more proud of the fact that the creative juices in Kirk were never stilled. He wanted so much to make more movies. He made one film costarring his longtime friend from their struggling actor days in New York, Lauren Bacall, or "Betty" to her intimates. It was called *Diamonds*, and Kirk played an old prizefighter who had, hello, a stroke. He was funny, physically on his game. He and Betty had a rousing old time together. Then he made another film, *It Runs in the Family*. He loved this film since it included Michael playing his son, Michael's son playing his grandson, and his ex-wife, Michael's mother, Diana, playing his wife. These were roles that needed no rehearsal.

Michael Douglas

Michael Douglas attained the Hollywood pinnacle when he came on-stage in the Dorothy Chandler Pavilion with his producing partner, Saul Zaentz, to accept the 1975 Academy Award for Best Picture for *One Flew over the Cuckoo's Nest*. It was a triumph for Michael, lashing his considerable talents as producer to the wall that showcased filmdom's best.

The film had an ironic history. Kirk Douglas bought Ken Kesey's novel and staged it on Broadway with Kirk playing the leading role of McMurphy, which Jack Nicholson took on in the big-screen version. Kirk tried for seven or eight years to make a theatrical movie out of it; he wanted desperately to play that lead role on the screen. But it went nowhere. No studio wanted it. Finally, sensing that he had gone as far as he could, he turned over the book to his son. "Michael, this is now yours. You try. I can't get it done."

Michael didn't try to break down studio resistance. Instead, he persuaded Saul Zaentz to put up the funding required. They made the movie without studio involvement. I am convinced that Kirk never really got over the fact that when the film was ready to go into principal photography, he was beyond the age required of the lead role. Time had beaten him. I watched one of the earliest versions of the film, before it was distributed, with Jack Nicholson and Michael. When it was over, I turned to them and said, "If this movie isn't nominated for Best Picture, then the fix is in. It's that great." Michael and Jack both rolled their eyes as if to say "For God's sake, Jack, don't jinx this film with wild notions of Academy Award nominations." One year later, Michael stood onstage to accept his Best Picture Oscar.

Michael's movie career soared on the thermals of his extraordinary talent. It's tremendously difficult to get out from under the shadow of a famous father and find your own footing, and Kirk Douglas was an outsize figure by any standard. But Michael somehow managed to pull himself out of the orbit of Kirk Douglas the global superstar and still remain connected to Kirk Douglas the father. It was an extraordinary achievement. From the beginning, Michael was a movie maverick, much like his father. Like his dad, he wanted to compose his own career, design his own stories the way he wanted to tell them. But first he had to establish himself as an actor. Here fate and a family friend intervened, the sweet, indomitable Karl Malden. Michael took on the role of Karl's sidekick in the glossy popular TV series *Streets of San Francisco*. He made his bones in that series, and his acting career was launched.

Almost immediately, he formed his own production company. He took on films layered in risk. His film *The China Syndrome*, which he produced and starred in with Jane Fonda, premiered one week after the debacle at the nuclear plant at Three Mile Island, which is about as time relevant as a film can be. He turned next to the romantic comedy action films *Romancing the Stone* and *The Jewel of the Nile*, with Kathleen Turner. He then played a married man who made one huge emotional blunder. The film was *Fatal Attraction*, with Glenn Close and Anne Archer. It scared the hell out of every philandering married man in America. Now *that* is the definition of "influential."

Without breaking stride, he was in *Basic Instinct* with Sharon Stone, which became a paradigm for police interrogation of a sensual young woman. Then Michael took on the role of a deranged killer in *Falling Down*, not exactly the sort of role one accepts if one wants to play it safe. Then he changed narrative directions once more and took on corporate greed in *Wall Street*, exposing the avarice of these malefactors who practice treachery and deceit on a massive scale, blighting the future of employees and stockholders simply because they have the power to do so. So frighteningly real was his portrayal of Gordon Gekko that he won the Academy Award for Best Actor.

After nineteen years, he and his then wife, Diandra, decided to end their marriage. I saw Michael often in those non-married days. He was "family" to us, invariably loving to Mary Margaret and me and our children. I wondered if he would ever find some raw deep-down emotional connection that thus far had seemed to elude him.

Then at the Deauville Film Festival he met Catherine Zeta-Jones. They dined. They talked at length. This Welsh-born actress, of supernatural beauty and alluring composure, regarded him with a wary caution. But soon they were in love, and then there was their marriage.

Catherine is, to me, incapable of artifice. When she and I are conversing, I sometimes forget her glamour, her fame, and see and hear her only as a quietly normal human being, a mother who chats animatedly about her children, or talks about movies we like (never does she speak about one of her own); I find it all so comforting and rare.

In early 2006, Michael came to Washington to film *The Sentinel.* Catherine flew to Washington to be with him for a week. There oc-curred one evening a full-blown example of how so celebrity ob-sessed are the American people that even the most sophisticated are not immune.

Mary Margaret and I took Michael and Catherine to dinner at Café Milano, the must-be-seen watering hole for the movers and shakers of Federal City. It was packed. Franco, the owner, took us to the rear in as private a spot as could be found. Catherine, wearing a thin Italian shawl over a simple black dress with tiny straps, was off-the-charts gorgeous. When we finished our meal, Michael took Mary Margaret by the hand, and I was linked with Catherine. As we made our way to the front exit and passed each table, the diners rose as one, applauding as we walked by, most of them calling out sweet greet-ings. Mind you, these were not folks just off the turnip truck. They were at the highest levels of Washington power. How do you figure this? Don't try.

WARREN BEATTY

Warren is one of the most fascinating citizens of the Hollywood pan-theon of stars. He turns the stereotype of an actor on its head. He is quiet, his voice sometimes so soft that I have to strain to hear him.

He reads widely and deeply—political tomes, foreign policy magazines, plays, novels, biographies—ravaging libraries to engage the finest thinkers, and he remembers what he reads. Warren seeks out those in the Congress and the White House as well as journalists, historians, political savants, writers, and artists. He invites them to his home and engages their minds, testing their premises and jousting with their views. He has fiercely held convictions, which he brandishes with considerable passion. It's fair to say that Warren would be labeled a "liberal," but that description would be inadequate, imprecise simply because he is so open to other points of view.

Warren chooses his film stories carefully. I can think of only one debacle, the forgettable *Town & Country*. Well, actually two, when we factor in *Ishtar*. But he rides mostly an ascending curve. Take, for example, *Bonnie and Clyde*, now a modern classic, although when it first entered theatrical distribution in late 1966, it struggled to find an audience. Warner Bros., the distributor, was nonplussed. It had such potential, they had reasoned, with Beatty, Faye Dunaway, Gene Hackman, and Estelle Parsons as the stars. It was a narrative with bite and enticement. But it seemingly could not find an audience, so Warner Bros. resigned itself to taking a licking on the film and moving on. The movie was withdrawn from exhibition.

Enter Warren Beatty the firebrand. He fiercely rebutted the arguments of the Warner executives. The movie was rich in story and characters, he said. What it needed was a new marketing campaign and some reediting. Slowly, the Warner executives became convinced. They constructed a new campaign, edited the film in accordance with Beatty's skillful suggestions, and rereleased the movie, all at considerable cost. To their joy, the film took off. Audiences came and had a "must see" reaction to the movie. Today, that kind of second-chance maneuver would be unthinkable—that is, without a Warren Beatty to break through the barriers of lockstep thinking.

With *Reds*, Warren journeyed into hostile territory. The film was a controversial biography of John Reed, a handsome, intellectually curious American citizen, but a thoroughgoing Marxist, drawn to the new world of Russian communism. This was not an obvious subject for a popular American movie, to say the least, but Beatty persevered. He worked on the script, inserted himself in the movie as the star, and completed the trifecta by directing the story. He refused to make Reed a heroic figure but portrayed him as idealistic and confused. Far from being a commercial for communism, the film was an uncommon piece of cinema artistry. Warren's ultimate triumph came on Academy Awards night, when he won the Oscar for Best Director.

I first met Warren in an odd confluence of events. When I resigned my White House post as special assistant to the president to head the Motion Picture Association of America, my hometown friends in Houston were so thrilled by my new status in Hollywood that they decided to honor me with a large dinner event in the fall of 1966. The chairman of the dinner evening was Leon Jaworski, one of the most prestigious lawyers in the country, who later became world-renowned as the U.S. special prosecutor in the infamous Watergate hearings.

Leon and his committee toiled long and hard to bring off this event successfully. The committee had compiled a guest list that included just about everybody in the movie industry: actors, directors, producers, and studio executives. However, only two accepted: George Stevens Sr., a multiple Academy Award winner and one of the greatest directors in the cinema world, flew in from Los Angeles; and Warren Beatty came as well. Warren was shooting *Bonnie and Clyde* in Dallas. He and I had never met, but he persuaded the director, Arthur Penn, to allow him to depart the set early. He chartered a private plane to take him to Houston and carry him back to Dallas at the evening's end.

I never forgot what these two men did. They offered me the richest prize anyone can receive at such a time: the gift of their presence. George Stevens became a loving friend, for whom my affection and admiration continued to grow until he died, much too young. I truly loved him. I was a pallbearer at his funeral. George directed, in my opinion, the greatest western ever made, *Shane*. And as I told Warren once, there was nothing he could ever do to offend me after he agreed to join that dinner in my honor. He did it at considerable expenditure of time and energy. That can never be expunged from my memory.

In his bachelor days, Warren lived in the penthouse of the Beverly Wilshire Hotel, where his outdoor patio had a sensational, full-screen view of Beverly Hills. An extraordinary and seemingly endless parade of beautiful young women was known to pass through Warren's dwelling. I recall one evening, years ago, we were walking back to the Beverly Wilshire for an after-dinner nightcap before I returned to my own lodgings. Around 11:00 p.m. we sauntered along Wilshire Boulevard, chatting away. Suddenly, a Cadillac convertible with two gloriously beautiful young girls came into view. Their blond hair flowing, they skidded their car to a halt near the curb. "Warren, Warren!" one of them shrieked, both of them waving wildly.

We stopped in our tracks. Warren looked at me and then strode slowly to the car. He leaned over the door and engaged in what I assumed to be charming conversation with the two of them. There was laughter, the two lovelies obviously enticed. Then Warren looked over his shoulder and said to me, "Enjoyed the dinner, Jack. Let's talk tomorrow." Whereupon he leaped into the backseat, followed by the girl in the passenger seat. All three waved to me as they sped off. It was my first confirmation that in Hollywood, too, life is unfair.

Then everything changed. Warren starred in the movie *Bugsy*, the story of the glamorous gambling gangster Bugsy Siegel, who single-handedly invented Las Vegas when he built the Flamingo Hotel, first of its kind in the desert. Warren played opposite a wondrously charming, serenely beautiful young actress, Annette Bening, who hailed from the plains of Kansas. Warren had met beautiful actresses before, of course, and invariably they melted before his advances. But Annette's formidable barriers did not fall. And for Beatty, those encounters with Bening were packed with what my Sicilian forebears called "the thunderbolt." Eventually, the feeling infected Annette as well. The rest, as they say, is history. Warren was transformed from a restless lover into a thoroughly domesticated husband and father of four wonderful children.

I have always been curious about the impact of fame on those who have reached the apogee of celebrity. Once I came right out and asked Warren, "What's it like to be truly famous?"

He looked at me with that patented Beatty half grin, both quizzical and knowing. "Jack," he said, "I've been famous for over forty years." Meaning, of course, that he probably couldn't remember when he wasn't recognizable all over the world. He became famous when he was twenty-one years old, with *Splendor in the Grass*. From that moment, his career took off.

MARLON BRANDO AND TOM CRUISE

My first encounter with a living legend was—how shall I put this?—a doozy. A year into my new Hollywood life, in my office (at the time) on the corner of Beverly Boulevard and La Cienega, I received a phone call from Marlon Brando. Marlon Brando?

"Hello, this is Jack Valenti," I said.

That familiar voice entered my ear. "Jack, Marlon Brando. I would count as a big favor if you would lunch with me tomorrow at my home. I have some important things I want to talk with you about."

The next day I drove up winding Mulholland Drive, the great divide between the West Side and the San Fernando Valley. I found the Brando home, large but not opulent. The front door opened to me with a dazzling woman in a long dress greeting me with a gracious smile.

She escorted me to a library, spacious, filled with bookcases, easy chairs, and a projection screen in one corner with a 16mm projector some feet away. She departed and I sat alone waiting for my host. Ah, another dazzler stepped in, this time a willowy blond vision, who asked me what I would like to drink. Coke would be fine. As she left I prayed she would know I wanted a liquid drink and not anything else.

After a while, Brando came into the library. Here I was now alone with the man who most knowledgeable critics claim to be the greatest actor of all time. In short, a legend furlongs above all the others in their reach for legendary status.

He was, at our encounter, in his prefat years, which were yet to come. He was still lean enough and still blindingly charismatic. I was impressed. Just like a movie fan.

He shook my hand. "I'm really glad to meet you. I know about your service to the president." Then he went on, no preliminary chit chat. "I just got back from India, where I saw the most unbelievable poverty and famine. We must do something about that."

He then asked me to sit down, while some new minion, who had slipped into the room, ignited the 16mm projector. On the screen appeared scene after scene of distressed villages and villagers, a good many children with swollen bellies defined by hunger. The film ran on for at least thirty to forty minutes, with Brando doing a simultaneous commentary as I watched.

When the lights came back on, Brando moved his chair close to me. "Now, Jack, I must see the president. I must tell him what I saw and why food aid to India is absolutely vital."

I tried to explain to Marlon that the president had recently pushed through an agricultural aid measure for India. He heard me not at all. "You must get me in to see the president."

I was bearing witness to the iconic Brando in full flight of passion. Suddenly I was watching the young Brando in a skivvy undershirt, screaming, "Stella! Stella!"

We ate in some haste, Brando sitting across from me, still pressing me about the danger of not acting quickly to confront what he called "unacceptable starvation." When I left Brando's presence, I called Joe Califano, still working for LBJ in the White House. I told Joe of my visit with Brando. "I think it might be useful—and a little fun for the president—for him to meet with Brando."

Joe was hesitant, but he said he would try to get the appointment. Late the next day Joe called to say the president reluctantly agreed to see Brando, saying to Joe, "It didn't take long for Jack to go Hollywood, did it?"

Immediately I called Marlon. When he got on the phone I told him to call Joe Califano and work out the details, but the president would definitely meet with Brando. He seemed pleased.

A week later I called Califano. "Did you work out the schedule with Marlon?"

Califano said, "Hell, he never called. What am I supposed to do? What do I tell the president?"

Two good questions. I tried to reach Brando two times, but failed to connect. I left my number and the reason for my frenzied call, but as the ode goes, he never called, he never sent me a postcard, he never sent flowers. The fact is Marlon never followed up with his emotional flourish on behalf of India. The appointment with the president was never concluded. Why? Who knows.

Epilogue: A decade or more later after Brando's glistening performance as Don Corleone in *The Godfather*, I was invited by Elliott Kastner, a longtime movie producer and a close friend of Marlon's, to dine at Matteo's, a well-known Italian restaurant on the West Side. When I arrived Elliott had some six other people there. We chatted, sipped our drinks. Suddenly from a back door at the rear of the restaurant, seldom used except by a favored few, Brando appeared and pulled up a chair next to me. I could scarcely believe what I was seeing. To say he was excessively fat disconnects from reality. He made Orson Welles in his later years seem like an "after" photo ad for Jenny Craig.

Elliott was a grand host and made the conversation light, movie talk without involving anything about Marlon. Several times I thought about chiding Marlon for neglecting his White House visit, but I resisted. He never mentioned it. It was as if our lunch in his home never took place. When we all laughed at some joke offered up by one of the guests, Marlon leaned over and in "the voice" said to me, "Good to see you, Jack. I hope you'll come by again for lunch." That was it. He left early by the same private back door he entered so that few if any of Matteo's guests knew he was ever there.

Final scene. In 2001, a few weeks after 9/11, I was sitting in my Washington office when again my secretary informed me over the intercom, "Marlon Brando is on the phone."

When I came on the wire, Marlon began to talk, ceaselessly. In essence, he said he was confused by all that had transpired: the destruction of the Twin Towers, terrorists, anxieties. It was a torrential stream of consciousness, words tumbling over one another. I wasn't really sure what he was trying to convey and I missed some of what he was saying. Some of it made no sense. I tried to interject but he was not to be interrupted. Finally, he seemed to wilt over the phone.

I said, "Are you okay, Marlon?" For a few seconds, no answer. Then he said, "I must go. I must go."

That was the last of my three conversations with Marlon Brando. He died three years later. Even in repose Brando was strange. Perhaps his estrangement from what others found normal was part of the raw emotions he created in others as well as in himself. His father was remote, a failure in all things and his mother, her artistic talents lying in shadows, became a hopeless alcoholic, entangling Marlon in her hapless distress. His childhood in Omaha was a collection of ever-increasing miseries, some brutish, some dispiriting on an epic scale, and all of them indelible, harrowing memories he could not erase.

Anthony Quinn, his friend and co-star, with blinding insight sorrowfully summed up the man who had conquered audiences and colleagues with gifts seldom seen on stage and on screen: "I admire Marlon's talent, but I don't envy the pain that created it."

I'm a Tom Cruise fan.
In all my encounters with Tom, I found him a warmly gracious young man. My feelings about Tom emerge from first-hand experience. Some few years ago *McCall's* magazine was so pleased with an article Mary Margaret had written for them about famous women with strong fathers (she'd interviewed Justice Sandra Day O'Connor, Jane Fonda, Madeleine Albright, and others) that they wanted her to write another piece. This time they asked Mary Margaret to interview Nicole Kidman. Mary Margaret and I discussed the offer.

"Do you think Nicole Kidman would agree to be interviewed?" she asked me.

"I don't know, but I will get in touch with Tom Cruise and see what his advice would be," I said.

I wrote Tom for his thoughts as to whether Nicole would be receptive to a request from Mary Margaret to interview her. Tom got back to me about two weeks later. In a personal, handwritten letter to me, he said, essentially, that Nicole was in London, rehearsing for a play she was going to star in, *The Blue Room*, to be directed by Sam Mendes. He went on to say that he and Nicole were unhappy with *McCall's*.

He wrote, "Jack, you may not know our history with *McCall's*. A couple of years ago they wrote a vicious article filled with negative comments about our family." (It turned out that the magazine did apologize publicly, but Tom still felt aggrieved.)

He went on to say, "However, because this request comes from you, we both find it impossible to say no regardless of our negative history with *McCall's*. Nicole would be pleased to see Mary Margaret after the play opens. Nicole and I send you both our best wishes and look forward to seeing you soon."

I was touched by Tom's sweetly gracious letter. I had planned to be in London and Brussels a week or so after the play opened, so fortunately the timing fitted nicely with both our schedules. I got in touch with Nicole's assistant, who told me that on the evening we intended to see the play in London, Nicole would love to have us visit her backstage.

The play was at the Wharf Theater, a small venue. We sat in the very first row, almost on the stage, which, by any standard, made us intimate witnesses. Nicole played several parts in this episodic story. She was magnificent.

Afterward, we were escorted backstage to meet her. She greeted us in a long white dressing gown, immaculately simple. She was tall, slender, and absolutely radiant. We sat with her as Mary Margaret outlined what she hoped to extract from the interview. She agreed to be at the Dorchester Hotel in the late morning. "Oh yes, I'll also be on time," she said with a laugh. And she was. For over two hours she and Mary Margaret talked. According to MM, she was candid, with a lilting humor, and totally without pretense.

Meanwhile, Tom and I had drinks in the hotel foyer. He brought with him their two children, Connor and Isabella. It was quite obvious that he doted on those two kids, and they on him.

I have never forgotten Tom's and Nicole's generous response to Mary Margaret and me. Much later, when Steven Spielberg invited me to spend a half day with him on the set in Washington's Willard Hotel for a scene from *Minority Report* (starring Cruise), Tom and I reconnected. When once again I proffered my thanks to him for his letter, he brushed aside my remarks. He gave me a bear hug and said, "Friends are what count, Jack, and you are a friend."

CARY GRANT, PARAGON OF SEDUCTION

If I compiled a list of "Truly Elegant Men," at the top would be Sidney Poitier and Cary Grant. Sidney is a longtime friend, but I can be objective when I say that his poise, assurance, grace, and mellifluous voice make him one of the most elegant men in the long history of film.

The only actor who could compete with him was Cary Grant.

I first met Cary Grant at that unforgettable dinner at the Wassermans' home a few months after I came to Hollywood. Like most Americans, I was fascinated by him. The way Cary Grant carried himself, with his slim, athletic bearing, the omnipresent tan, the forest of dark hair, the chiseled face and profile, and the charm that collapsed all barriers, enchanted all who met him. He did have a dark side, I was told by some of his intimates. His tight-fisted ways were the stuff of legend. It was said that getting Cary to pick up the restaurant check was a miracle few had ever witnessed. But having started life as Archibald Leach and living his early years impoverished and often alone must have had a powerful effect on him. When he created for himself the life of Cary Grant, rich beyond measure, famous beyond comprehension, he couldn't just jettison those early memories.

Given this background, perhaps it is not so surprising that Cary Grant was one of the most astute stars in the business when it came to managing his career. He is one of the few movie legends who ever owned the copyright to films funded and distributed by the major studios. How he did that is still studied and envied to this day.

I got to know him in his later years. One night, we had dinner at a charity fund-raiser. He grabbed me and said, "Sit beside me," which I did, though the table was place-carded. But what Cary Grant wanted, he got. He chatted with me easily, even warmly, the mythical charm affecting me visibly. Both of us ignored our other dinner companions. He was in his late sixties, still handsome, the hair now white but thick, the frame still slender.

I said with some passion, "Cary, you haven't made a film since you were about fifty, or a little younger. You're in great shape, why don't you find a good script and make another movie?"

He laughed and said, "Jack, you don't understand, I'm frozen in time."

I nodded and laughed. Then later I thought about it. He was right. No one could ever imagine Cary Grant older than fifty, and most would envision him in his thirties and forties. For the rest of time, to generations yet unborn, Cary Grant remains at the top of his graceful game. On screen he is eternally handsome and elegant, an enchantment of a man unlike all others. The only star to possibly match him, I thought, might be Clark Gable, whom I never met.

KATHARINE HEPBURN

In all my years in politics and Hollywood, I have never been tongue-tied at meeting someone famous, influential, or both. After forty-plus years, I'm immune to world-renowned actors and government leaders. I know them. I mingle with them. I am not awestruck by them. Many of them are my friends, so I am easy in their company. Except for one.

Each year for the past twenty, I have gathered with good friends in Boca Grande, Florida, that charming village on the Gulf of Mexico, to play tennis over a four-day weekend. They include Jim Symington, former congressman and ambassador; Harry McPherson, former special counsel to President Johnson and law firm partner; Bill Webster, former director of the Central Intelligence Agency and former director of the FBI; the late Charles Guggenheim, four-time winner of the Academy Award for Best Documentary; John Zentay, a high-wattage intellect and greatly respected Washington lawyer; Michael Sterner, former ambassador and key State Department expert; and (sometimes) Senator Fritz Hollings. All of us are old friends. We know one another intimately. Our special angel during these get-togethers was Nina Houghton, whose late husband, Arthur, was a central figure on that private island. Nina always arranged one evening at her home for a sterling dinner with the most companionable of the island's part-time population and put us up at her guesthouse with its four bedrooms.

So on this special night at Nina's home in 1986, our little group sauntered over from across the street to Nina's spacious home over-looking the sea. We were freshly washed and clothed, our charm at the ready. Of a sudden, we were all dazzled by the sight of Nina's very special guest. It was Katharine Hepburn, her regal form, slim and elegant, right there across the room. I could swear she gave off a luminous light, but perhaps it was just a reflection of the soft fall of the moon coming through the large window fronting the sea. She was accompanied by her friend Cynthia McFadden, who would later become a successful network news anchor.

Nina is a stern dinner disciplinarian, moving guests about with the skill and firmness of a field general. To my amazement, I was billeted to the side of Miss Hepburn during the cocktail hour. She sat, back upright, a scarf around her celebrated neck, eyes fastened on me.

"So you know something about movies, don't you?" was her opening comment. I sat there mute. I nodded slowly. My fund of charm, which I had been prepared to ladle out, seemed to have sought refuge somewhere in my lower stomach.

"It's not what it used to be, is it?" she continued. I suspect she began to wonder just who this inert cretin was who sat there, seemingly unable to speak. I was numbed by her presence. My mouth felt paralyzed, as though I'd just had dental surgery. Among great actors and actresses, she was someone queenly, a superior form of being. I was truly astonished at being so physically close to her.

I finally said I was overwhelmed to meet her, and yes, they don't make pictures the way they used to, and maybe it was because Miss Hepburn was no longer doing films. Great lady that she was, she knew I was frazzled. She touched my shoulder and said in that starched New England accent, with its plummy, patrician tones, "I know who you are, but tell me more about you."

I truly, very truly, did not want to screw this up and have her depart the island chuckling over this inarticulate Texan.

"No," I said, "I want to hear you talk. I may never have this opportunity again." The words came. I was pleased. She looked at me steadily. Her eyes, so softly clear, were fastened on me. I thought: Is this the way she looked at Spencer Tracy? It was a wildly delicious thought and about a continent away from reality. But what the hell.

"I don't think much of the films today. Maybe that's because I don't see many of them. Or maybe it's because I am so connected to the past."

"No," I said, "it's because so few of the movies today match what you put up there on the screen, especially you and Spencer Tracy."

She laughed. "Mr. Valenti, you are a charming liar. But I really don't mind." She smiled heartily. "Spence was special. He really had a kind of genius. He knew characters, and he understood how stories are formed. I can't think of anyone in films today who comes close to his place in movie history." She stopped. Then she said, "Did you ever meet him?" I think she was looking right inside me. She saw my yearnings.

"No," I said, "I never met him. I always wanted to. But I am a good friend of Stanley Kramer and Sidney Poitier. I always wanted to talk to them about Spencer Tracy."

Her eyes lit up. "Oh my, I do love Stanley, he was so kind to Spence, so thoughtful. And that Sidney, such a graceful actor. I'm glad you know them. They're the best of Hollywood."

She was silent for a few seconds, then she said, "I have a splendid idea. We're going to be separated before long; I know Nina will march us into dinner and she will pair me off with someone else. Why don't you visit me in New York? We can have tea together and chat easily without the rush of time. Is that suitable to you?"

Is winning a $100 million lottery suitable to me? I nodded vigorously. She fumbled in her purse, stirring around inside, and came up with a checkbook. She ripped off the top check, then dove back into her purse again, this time coming up with a small ballpoint pen. "I'm writing down my phone number. My address is on the check. Take this and call me when you are next in New York. I promise you some refreshing hot tea." My cup runneth over.

Sure enough, Nina strode over and said, "I'm sorry, Jack, but your time is up. We're going into dinner, and Kate will have someone else sitting beside her." My night in Boca Grande with Kate Hepburn was over. But I had the check. I had in her own hand her written phone number. I had won the lottery. Now it was time to cash in.

Over the next year, I was in New York many times. Several times I drove by taxi past Kate Hepburn's home on East Forty-ninth Street.

I had the check in my jacket. But I never could summon the courage to call her and say, "Miss Hepburn, I'm here, how about tea?" Even now, I am appalled by the recollection of such timidity or, more accurately, stupidity. Why didn't I call her as she suggested? I know why. I couldn't handle the possibility of the conversation going wrong, of Miss Hepburn not being able to say to friends, "I did so like that Jack Valenti."

Later, I read about her illness. I read she had gone back to her Connecticut home, and then I read about her death. I talked to my friend Stanley Kramer, who directed her and Tracy and Poitier in *Guess Who's Coming to Dinner.*

"Tell me about her, Stanley. What was she like?" Stanley revealed no secrets, but he went on at length about her, saying all that I hoped he would say, with nary an unkind word. I recall at the Beverly Hills Hotel one afternoon, I had a drink with John Huston and asked him the same question. He essentially repeated what Kramer had said, that she was a great lady, superior in every way, and that her like was not to be found again.

I remember that check, with her name printed neatly on it, along with her address. And there splashed across that check in her whirling script is inscribed her phone number—the number I never called.

Chapter 13

MPAA ABROAD AND AT HOME

A lovely day at the Roman villa of Carlo Ponti and his spectacular wife, Sophia Loren. Languidly strolling in the gardens are Federico Fellini, Sophia, me, and Sergio Leone, famed director of the Clint Eastwood "spaghetti" westerns.

In the fall of 1966, a few months after I became president of the Motion Picture Association of America, I made my first trip abroad in that new role. I arrived in Paris with my wife and Louis Nizer, and his wife, Mildred. Fred Gronich, the head of MPAA's Paris office, dutifully met us at Charles de Gaulle Airport. I began peppering Fred with questions, one of which was, "Is it possible to visit the set of whatever film is being shot in Paris?"

Fred's face lit up. "Of course," he said without hesitation. "My friend Louis Malle is filming a movie here in Paris called *The Thief.* As a matter of fact, they're shooting tonight. Would you like to drop by this evening? Are you too tired?"

What a stroke of luck. "Not at all, we'll go tonight. Please arrange it."

That evening, Louis Nizer, his wife, and Mary Margaret went off to dine and I left with Fred to visit the Malle set. He was shooting in a section of Paris some half hour by car from our hotel, and we were fortunate to find the director taking a shooting break in a small Parisian diner. Louis greeted me as if we were old friends. It was, to my delight, the beginning of a friendship that flourished after he married Candice Bergen (with whom he had a lovely daughter, Chloe). He died some years later, much too young.

He introduced me to Jean-Paul Belmondo, the male lead. Belmondo was the reigning movie idol of France, whose rugged features and battered nose made him instantly recognizable. He was not handsome in the Hollywood sense, but he had about him a sensual tension that was arresting. He nodded, shook hands, and then ambled off. Louis, smilingly, said, "Ah, he is not comfortable with the

English language. Don't imagine you had anything to do with his disappearance." We chatted, and I asked him whom I should meet in the French film community this trip.

"One Frenchman you must meet is Henri Langlois. He runs the Cinémathèque. Actually, he rather invented it. It's a kind of sacred place for our filmmakers, especially the young ones. He is an odd sort of fellow, but his passion for film is well-known to everyone in Paris. I think you will like him. He's different." Louis jumped to his feet. "Come with me and watch this next scene." Fred and I hung close to Louis as he began to shape the scene with his actors. He moved with confidence, swiftly, but without ever seeming hurried.

The next morning, I had an appointment with André Malraux, the legendary literary giant of France. I had no inkling that over my long tenure with the MPAA, Malraux was to be the first of nineteen French ministers of culture—seventeen men and two women—with whom I would form cordial relations over countless meetings and meals and the passage of years, and sometimes confront in heated controversy. Malraux was the very first French minister of culture, and his powerful persona brought great importance to that office. From that time forward, the culture ministers presided over an ever-expanding domain, including movies, television, the literary environment, stage, radio, and of course the divine realm of art. In France, the minister of culture is a major political force.

André Malraux was also one of President de Gaulle's intimates. In his mid-thirties, he joined the Republican army in the Spanish Civil War as a combat pilot, pitting himself and his squadron in sky battles with Francisco Franco's air force. When World War II began, he joined a tank unit in the French army and was captured by the Nazis, but he escaped. He found his way into the French Resistance, was again captured, and again escaped. He was that rarity, a war hero who was also an aesthete, a writer, and a scholar.

His offices were in a richly appointed palace next to the Louvre. When Fred and I entered, he rose quickly from behind his desk and greeted me in classic French, which Fred interpreted for me. I imagine he must have known how to speak English but preferred to communicate in his mother tongue. Malraux's features were stern, with a straight, longish nose that gave the impression he had just leaped off an ancient Frankish coin. His manner was that of a man firmly in touch with himself, assured and confident. He was unsmiling, but I did not sense anything other than dignity in his demeanor.

He told me he was pleased to meet me because he believed that cinema was enlarging the visual culture of the world. He asked me what plans I had to bring the community of filmmakers in France closer to that in the United States. I told him that I cared very much about France and that as a student in Texas I read voraciously in the history and literature of France. This seemed to please him. After some ten minutes of conversation, I brought up Henri Langlois. I said I would very much like to meet him; would the minister be able to intercede for me? He pressed a buzzer on his desk, and in a few minutes his aide had arranged an appointment. I shook hands with Malraux and departed. I never saw him again, but the image of this lordly intellectual giant was forever etched in my memory.

Later that evening, I was the guest of the French film industry at the fabled Tour d'Argent, the finest (and most expensive) restaurant in Paris, close by the Cathedral of Notre Dame. During the cocktail hour, I gazed at the world-famed church sitting solemn and grand in the diminishing light of the darkening evening. At precisely 9:58, the host of the evening rose to his feet to toast me. At 10:00, as if sprung loose by unseen angels, the night lit a thousand lanterns. The entire façade of Notre Dame was enveloped by a great wave of lights, all of its spires bathed in a glistening glow of whiteness.

"This, Mr. Valenti," said the host, "is Minister Malraux's gift to you this night." I was somewhere near nirvana looking at this unforgettable tableau unfolding before me. Obviously, the minister had the requisite authority to say, "Let there be light," and Notre Dame was illuminated as if by divine intervention. It was an awesome display of Malraux's cultural reach and power.

Fred Gronich and I showed up the next day for our appointment with Henri Langlois, at number 82, rue de Courcelles. We found ourselves in a small, messy room with cans of film scattered about, the lair of a huge grizzly bear of a man. (Later, I learned that the projection theater was in a separate location, situated at the Palais de Chaillot.) When Langlois came to meet us, he filled the room. Hulking linebacker's shoulders sloped heavily to long arms and a vast circumference of unrestrained paunch. Beneath his heavy chin was a wattle of flesh. His obvious passion for film made him glow with a zealotry that was instantly appealing. I asked him how he determined what films to save.

"Hah," came the answer with a huge belly laugh. "My dear Jack, I make no such decisions. Every film should be saved. How do we mortals know what film will have meaning to those who watch it thirty years from now? No, everything should be protected, allowed to live on."

I have never forgotten that reply, conveyed with such humility and absolute conviction. How could one possibly forecast a film's place in history until it has lived long enough for the public to make the judgment? Langlois exuded that innocence found in those who love what they do so much that they are barely aware of anything else. As I departed, he put his huge arms around me and said, "I like you because you love films. I truly believe you will be good for France and for this Cinémathèque. We must stay close together."

Some months later, I read in the trade press about a falling-out between the minister of culture and Henri. Evidently, Malraux's office was upset with Langlois's cigar-box fiscal system, which he used in lieu of more formal accounting. I was stunned. But I also wanted to do something that would reach out to Henri and perhaps ease his way through what I knew would be a difficult time for him. My desire to get involved took a form I never anticipated.

On February 9, 1968, in Paris, the new administrative council created by André Malraux to monitor the Cinémathèque let it be known that Henri was out. François Truffaut, Claude Chabrol, Jean-Luc Godard, Louis Malle, Jean Renoir, Éric Rohmer, Robert Bresson, and all the rest of the great French filmmakers rose up in fiery opposition to Henri's dismissal, using the media to direct their wrath at Minister Malraux.

That day, in New York, my secretary/assistant came into my office. "Mr. Valenti, there is a man on the phone who says he is Jean-Luc Godard. He says he is calling from Paris."

I stared at her. "Jean-Luc Godard? Are you sure?" She nodded vigorously. I picked up the phone. "This is Jack Valenti."

The Gallic-accented voice said, "This is Jean-Luc Godard." (In the interest of full disclosure, I must confess I cannot to this day certify that Godard was indeed the man on the phone, though he certainly sounded like I expected Godard to sound. In Cannes on several occasions, after that call, when I was told he was in town at the festival, I pledged I would shake his hand and reconstruct our conversation to verify it. But, alas, that never happened, so all I can do is pray it was the authentic film genius himself on the wire.)

"We have a problem in Paris that demands that everyone in cinema must be engaged," he said.

I said, "Yes, I have read about Henri Langlois's firing by the culture minister."

"Yes, okay, you know. We need you, as the representative of the American film industry, to be with us in our battle to have Henri back at the Cinémathèque where he belongs, for without him there will be no more Cinémathèque. Henri says you are a friend. He needs you now."

What Godard wanted was my commitment to bring American actors, directors, writers, and executives to rally alongside the French cinema contingent. Without hesitancy, I said, "Absolutely. Count me in. I will do whatever you and Henri want me to do." Godard seemed pleased. And with that phone call, I had enlisted to lay siege to the French Ministry of Culture. A couple of hours after the phone call, I thought, I am now part of a rebellion against the French government. My God, I am helping storm the cultural Bastille!

I called several of the major studios, members of my association, to convince them that we could not stand aloof from the actions in France. I insisted we had to be engaged. Some of the studios were reluctant, fearing the wrath of the French government. But I persuaded them to let me take the bullet, and I received their grudging assent. I immediately called Fred, who told me that my decision was the right one and predicted that the government could not stand against this response from the French creative community.

I said to Fred, "Please meet with Malraux. Tell him it is urgent. Let him understand, privately, that if the decision against Langlois stands, I will not allow one meter of American film to be deposited in the Cinémathèque—ever. Do it courteously, but do it firmly."

Gronich said, "Jack, I anticipated your decision. I have already suspended all delivery of our films to the Cinémathèque." Good thinking, Fred.

He called me back the next day. Yes, he did see Malraux, who seemed to have been caught off guard by the storm of controversy that raged around his ministry. Fred had conveyed to the minister my firm resolve to stay the course on this. And on April 22, 1968, the government stood down. Henri Langlois was reinstated. Backed into a corner, Malraux simply cut his losses.

Some six years later, I was notified by the Academy of Motion Picture Arts and Sciences that Henri was to receive one of world cinema's highest laurels—a special Oscar to celebrate his tireless crusade on behalf of films, all films, from whatever source. The academy executive went on to say, "Mr. Langlois has asked that you and Gene Kelly present him with his award." I was deeply touched by Henri's act of friendship. When I saw him backstage during rehearsal, his face lit up with undisguised joy, and he wrapped his great arms around me.

"Ah, Jack, my dear friend," he said. Gene Kelly stood to embrace Henri as well.

Academy Awards night was a rousing, festive occasion, as always. Movie stars thronged the green room backstage, but Henri was the special star of the space. Hollywood's most famous crowded around him to offer their plaudits. When the time came for Gene Kelly and me to canonize Henri, I said to the audience that Henri "is the conscience of the cinema. He stood guard at the gate, all alone, when no one else was there."

Henri's remarks, translated fluently from the French by Gene Kelly, were conveyed with Henri almost weeping with joy. Afterward, Henri was exultant. It was obvious he understood how special this moment was and what it meant for film and for France. His eyes were moist as he enveloped me again, pressing me close to his goliath girth. "I am so happy, Jack," he said. "This is the best night of my life." Gene and I rejoiced with him.

I never saw him again. He died in January 1977, some three and a half years after his celebratory appearance on the Academy Awards. André Malraux had died two and a half months earlier. It was a piece of cinema drama that these two men, who ran afoul of each other but agreed most fundamentally about the importance of cinematic art, left life almost together.

BELLA ITALIA

In the fall of 1966, I paid a visit to my ancestral roots in Italy. I arrived in Rome for two events that came up unexpectedly. The first was a dinner at the villa of Gina Lollobrigida, and the second was a lunch the next day at the villa of Sophia Loren. I had never met either of these reigning Italian movie queens.

That first evening, I sat next to Gina, resplendent in a gown cut so low that it neared the latitudes of the Cape of Good Hope, with her stunning configuration (that's one way to put it) on full display. Every Italian movie star of any note was there—except Sophia. Only one queen can wear the crown at any event, as it turns out. It was a classy evening, I must confess.

At lunchtime the next day, I arrived at the villa of Sophia and her producer husband, Carlo Ponti. I arrived punctually, which meant no other guests had appeared. Sophia greeted me with warmth, as did Carlo. Their villa was filled with half a dozen paintings by a fellow named Francis Bacon. The only man I knew by that name was chancellor of England in the sixteenth century, and I knew he didn't paint.

Then the guests arrived. First was Federico Fellini. He embraced me with gusto. "Ah, Jack," he said as if we were the oldest of friends. "It's good that we have an Italian as the boss of the American cinema. You will do well, and all of Italy, most of all I, will be proud of you." I admit I was a bit in awe of this inspired movie god. Here I am being hugged and praised by him. Heaven could have little more to offer. Then in came Sergio Leone, master of the Italian western, who had elevated Clint Eastwood to movie stardom through Leone's "spaghetti western." He was followed by Alberto Moravia, the most famous of all Italian novelists. It was a gathering of creative geniuses.

We lunched at a table heaped with food, augmented by a barrel of wine. I still have a winsome photograph of Sophia, Fellini, Leone, and me strolling leisurely through the Ponti garden, like four old friends casually examining a graceful landscape. From that lunch in a lovely garden sprang a friendship with Sophia that is sweetly alive to this day.

I said to Sophia, "What do you want to do in the future?"

She looked at me for a moment, and said, "To be honest with you, Jack, I am going to learn to speak English fluently. I will work hard to do so. I will speak it so that everyone will understand me and not joke about my accent. To be an international star today, an actor must be able to speak good English."

I laughed. "Sophia, your English is very good. You don't need to fret about that."

"No, no," she insisted. "It is important. Marcello [she was referring to Italian actor Marcello Mastroianni] does not care about improving his English. He will never be an international star, though he is a great actor. It is sad. I am told that Jean-Paul Belmondo feels the same way. He does not care to speak English, only French. But to speak only French or Italian is to be subtitled in America. That is not good enough to be an international star."

She spoke firmly, without hesitation. I got my first glimpse of the steely resolve behind the commitment she had made. Everything she said to me that day came to pass. She did learn to speak English with fluency, free of the Italian accent that I heard that day in her garden. She did become an authentic international star. And she did it all with uncommon grace, wrapped in uncommon beauty.

ROBERT DE NIRO AT THE MOSCOW FILM FESTIVAL

Some years ago, before the end of the Soviet Union, Robert De Niro and I were honored guests at the Moscow Film Festival—an event that often produced some hard-to-forget moments. While it was exhilarating to be there, I must confess that you don't get a helluva lot of attention when you are on the program with Bobby De Niro.

I like De Niro so very much: He is a miraculously gifted actor who brings all of his energy to bear on whatever role he plays—villain or good guy in a tragedy or a comedy. Like Michael Caine, De Niro is a working actor who does not sit around grousing about the lousy scripts he's offered. He wants to work, because he's good at what he does. Working actors work. But providence smiles on De Niro. The great scripts seem to find him. And sometimes the scripts become infinitely better simply because he is one of the characters. Whether he's in *The Godfather* or *Goodfellas* or *Analyze Me* or *Heat*, or directing and starring in *The Good Shepherd*, his talent is explosive. And, on top of everything, he is without guile. There is a natural shyness about him, so he is not easy to get to know, but we have always liked each other and converse freely.

In any event, we were having a fine time at the Moscow Film Festival when De Niro, Marc Spiegel, and I were invited by the powerful and influential Directors' Guild to appear at their cavernous meeting hall with its massive stage and charmless décor to judge their annual beauty contest. Bobby, Marc, and I exchanged puzzled glances as we were escorted to three large chairs sitting at stage left so that we could have an excellent view of the beauties as they entered from stage right.

Bobby looked at me with a bemused smile and said under his breath, "What are we doing here? Please tell me." It was an insightful question. My answer was, "If you weren't here, we wouldn't be here." He had no rebuttal.

The head comrade of the Directors' Guild rose and with great fanfare introduced us. He then told us and the audience that the contestants came from all of the provinces of the Soviet Union to take part in this festive occasion. Then, with Russian folk music flowing from the six-piece band, the ladies walked onto the stage one by one in bathing suits. They each bowed and beamed at the judges, who greeted them with solemn courtesy. The master of ceremonies spoke briefly to each contestant in Russian—so only Marc, who was fluent, understood a thing. There were sixteen young lassies and they were doing their best to impress not only the three wise judges, but the audience as well, which whooped and applauded its favorites.

As far as we could see there was no one girl who was a standout. They were earnest, shyly jubilant, and some were brimming over with innocent wonder—and most assuredly all were well fed—but there was no standout.

Finally the time for a decision had come: A young man came out to perform some Russian songs while Bobby, Marc, and I huddled together. Marc said, "We have to make a choice." Bobby wisely held his counsel, though he did mutter, "There must be a winner."

I suddenly had an idea. "Why don't we ask the emcee to have them all come out together and walk in a circle around the stage." That sounded reasonable to De Niro and Marc. And so they came forth and this time one fair-haired Pamela Anderson–contoured young woman flashed De Niro a smile whose heat warmed the Cold War to equatorial temperatures. She almost had Bobby blushing. That was good enough for me.

As the contestants were leaving the stage, I grabbed my fellow judges by the arms and proposed the award go to the lass from Ukraine. Marc said with a grin, "You mean the one with the big . . . the big smile." "That's right," I said, "the one with the very big smile. Okay with you, Bobby?" "How can I oppose two experts?" he said, flashing a wry smile. To our amazement the audience rose to wildly applaud our judgment when the winner was announced. I have often wondered what happened to that nice young girl. She must still have a photograph of herself and Bobby De Niro among her most cherished possessions.

I daresay no other famous movie star of De Niro's caliber had the classic honor of judging a beauty contest in the U.S.S.R. Today I bet those young women would be well aware of current beauty trends and they would be, no doubt, svelte and unreasonably beautiful.

It's a head-shaking fact but true that every day of the year, there is a film festival going on somewhere in the known world. Why? Because just about everyone on this weary old planet gets goose bumps over movies and movie stars.

I have attended film festivals in Cannes, Venice, Tokyo, Toronto, Montreal, Acapulco, Mar del Plata in Argentina, Taormina in Sicily, San Sebastian in Spain, Moscow, Berlin, and in the United States, but—the most charming of festivals is, I must admit, Deauville.

This little town, in the Normandy country of France, is a marvel, the kind of locale that goes on picture postcards. Two hotels lodge all the festival visitors, the Royal and the Normandie, both on the broad boulevard that borders on the vast expanse of sea and sand.

I first came to the Deauville Film Festival in 1975. It was there I first met Anne d'Ornano, the mayor of Deauville, and later to become President of the Calvados Region of Normandy, the equivalent of being governor of a state in the U.S.

She was tall, slender, blonde, strikingly beautiful (and still is). Most astonishingly she spoke English flawlessly, barren of accent. At first, I thought she was an American married to a French aristocrat. I soon learned she was transported to America as a little girl when the war began in Europe. She stayed on until her late teens, and then returned to France. She is descended from one of France's noblest, oldest preeminent families.

Every year since 1975 Anne would host a birthday party for me in her chateau, splendidly inhabiting that graceful sloping hill with a grand visual sweep of the Deauville landscape. Each year Anne, aided by Ruda Dauphin, a delightfully attractive woman and the widow of famed French actor, Claude Dauphin, would plumb their inventive minds and come up with unusual gifts: a small vial of the sand of Omaha Beach, a charming little painting of the city, a key to the d'Ornano chateau, and so on.

Anne's traditional birthday dinner party for me was always a graceful adventure for me.

At these birthday evenings, she would have six tables of eight or ten in her dining room. Guests would include those stars visiting the festival as well as Anne's friends and mine from Deauville and Paris, including a delightful, elegant woman from Scotland, Angelika, Countess of Cawdor, as well as Anne's brother, Arnaud, and his tall, statuesque wife, Ann Marie.

At Anne's table I always sat to her right. Around the table in various years were Al Pacino, Harrison Ford, Calista Flockhart, Ashley Judd, Clint Eastwood, Anthony Hopkins, Michael and Pat York, John Frankenheimer, Ewan McGregor, Morgan Freeman, Liam Neeson, John Waters, and the list goes on. The talk was political at times, always about movies, current events, and some story telling, particularly from the movie stars. Anne at dessert time would rise to toast my birthday. I would respond. Then the evening so beguiling would come to a close. I always wanted them to last longer.

One birthday dinner evening Anne rose to toast me and present me with a gift of a key to her chateau. She said, "Over the past twenty-five years or so, I have given you just about every gift I can think of. So this year, here is the ultimate gift, a key to the front door of my home." There was laughing applause.

When I rose I said, more or less, "Dear, sweet Anne, this is not the ultimate gift. It is the penultimate gift. For while you are giving me the key to your chateau, you are not giving me the key to the gate, without which I can never enter." More laughter, with one voice, saying in French, "Right on."

Immediately, there rose Ashley Judd. This extraordinary beauty stood and looked at each of the tables in turn. Then she spoke softly, but firmly. She was, to my delight and slight embarrassment, most affectionate toward me and what I tried to do for American cinema. She floated on, the sentences parsing, the words vivid, and the humor bright and relevant. I stared at her in astonished—and admiring—disbelief. So when she stood up, without notes, speaking so easily, so generously, I knew Ashley Judd was a special kind of movie star.

There are other sweet memories of Deauville—particularly of Anne d'Ornano's two children, Catherine and Jean-Guillaime, who have become like family to me.

The granddaddy of all international film festivals is Cannes. It is younger than Venice, but not by much. It is also the nearest thing to a scene at an ancient oasis in the desert, a place where caravans from all over the world come to refresh, resupply, and trade information about goods and deals. These days, it is a market where producers and distributors from every corner of the world come to sell and buy films.

Alas, I must confess that the riotous parties and dinners that once exemplified Cannes have diminished today. Those were times when producers, studios, and independents had serious money to spend on the frivolity that gave Cannes its celebrated panache.

One evening years ago has a special place in my memory. I received a call in my lodgings at the Majestic Hotel from Dino De Laurentiis. In his thick Italian accent, he said, "Jack, I want you at a very small dinner party I am giving for Madonna. Very small. At Tetu. You'll be there, won't you?"

Tetu is the highly popular dining stop for anyone at Cannes, although it's hard to get a reservation. Its specialty is bouillabaisse, unrivaled anywhere. Madonna's new film, *Truth or Dare*, was produced by Dino, so this was a celebratory event. When I arrived, I was escorted to the end of the restaurant, where Dino's private dinner was cordoned off from the other diners. Word had gotten out that Madonna would be there, which accounted for several battalions of paparazzi, noisy, restless, and damn near unstoppable. Some of them had ladders, which they flung against the side of the restaurant to climb and film the proceedings, only to be foiled by security guards.

Dino wasn't kidding about the intimate nature of the event. I found myself seated between Madonna and Emmanuelle Seigner, a beautiful actress from one of France's well-known acting families. She was also the girlfriend (and later wife) of Roman Polanski, who was seated on the other side of Madonna.

During the day, I had pondered what the hell I would talk to Madonna about, having spent only a very little time with her at one of Swifty Lazar's parties. I asked my staff in Hollywood to send me material about Madonna. One of the faxed papers I received included a paragraph about her love of the art of Frida Kahlo, famous for her bizarre paintings as well as for being the wife of Diego Rivera, Mexico's greatest artist. Madonna was so enchanted by Kahlo's art and life, she often said she planned to make a movie about this Mexican painter. Immediately I sent out a Mayday alert, asking my staff to send me what they could find on Frida Kahlo. A few hours later, I got a thick packet of bio material on Kahlo, which I devoured. When it came time to drive to Tetu, I was ready.

At the table, besides Polanski and his lovely companion, there was Luc Besson, a highly praised French director, and his leading lady and "good friend" at the time. Dino sat across from Madonna, and next to him was Madonna's dress designer and his partner, a fellow whose name I can't remember, though he turned out to be a witty, irrepressible guest.

Madonna—and I swear I am not making this up—was wearing high black boots almost to her knees, very short black shorts clinging to her fabulous legs, and a black bra that left her flat midriff exposed. The hair atop her head was so black, it would have disappeared on a moonless night. It was one hell of an eye-popping outfit. Though I began to feel I had wandered into a place where I was not ready for prime time, I wasn't going to waste my research. I leaned toward Madonna and said in my best folksy Texas manner, "I've been told you are a great devotee of art, is that so?"

She replied, "Yes, I am. Are you as well?" What a sensual voice this extraordinary lady possessed.

"Actually," I said, "I am certainly not in your league, but I do have some passing knowledge and some painters I like." I threw out the bait. Would she bite? She did.

"That's interesting. What artists do you like?"

"I am very fond of the work of Frida Kahlo. Are you acquainted with her?" (Lord, please be gentle with me here.)

I had her full attention now, and not just because we were both of Italian descent. Before she could regain her footing, I kept going. "I wish I could have been there that night when she demanded to be taken from the hospital in a bed and transported to the art gallery where her work was being premiered. What a gutsy, uncommon woman."

Yes, Madonna said, that was a dramatic moment that she would love to see on a large movie screen. By now, my credentials had been examined and approved, and I was clearly an insightful assayer of art. Then we all joined in a game of Truth or Dare. For those of you who don't know the game, each person is posed the question "Truth or dare?" by another guest. You have a choice. If you say, "Truth," then you are obligated to answer truthfully any question put to you by the inquisitor. Or you can say, "Dare," wherein you must act out what-ever your questioner orders you to do.

As the game moved around the table, I became increasingly ap-prehensive—I mean very, very nervous. Some of the questions (well, to be honest, all the questions) were just plain sexual. When the ques-tioner across the table came to me, I prayed a tidal wave would hit the restaurant and we would all have to fight our way to shore. My ques-tion (I said, "Truth," for I sure as hell wasn't going to act out any-thing) was, "What was your most bizarre sexual encounter?" All eyes and ears were on me, a new big-shot leader in Hollywood. What to answer? I took refuge in the oldest of human responses: I lied. Said I in my most plaintive tones, "I was fifteen years old, and I was with this beautiful older woman, and all I could do was kiss her. That was all I could do."

Snickers around the table. Even Dino said, "Jack, you can do better than that."

To which I said, lying more easily now, "Well, that night I did try to do better." A few giggles. Okay, it was not one of my better moments, but at least I hadn't done too badly in the art category.

Some years later, at the Berlin Film Festival, I ran into the truly gorgeous Salma Hayek, who told me she was working on a project to produce and star in a film about Frida Kahlo. My ears perked up. I was back with my "favorite artist" again. Salma went ahead and co-produced the film *Frida*, along with Margie Perenchio. Salma played Frida, and Alfred Molina portrayed the great Diego Rivera, the master Mexican artist. Because I am a big fan of Madonna, I pray she will forgive my attempt to charm her on that never-to-be-forgotten evening at Tetu years ago. I can testify that she would have made a powerful Frida herself.

SOUTH KOREA AND A SEEMINGLY UNENDING FILM TRADE CONTROVERSY

In my long service to the movie industry, I traveled the world endlessly, meeting with chiefs of state, heads of government, and cabinet ministers on every continent. Sometimes I fought them to open up territories locked and sealed against the American movie. One of the most important battles I took on was against the South Korean distribution barrier.

The year was 1988. A powerful cartel, endorsed and supported by the Korean government, had fashioned an inventive and thoroughly disreputable scheme to profit mightily from the freeze-out of American movie distribution companies. The American studios were not allowed to open offices in Seoul, nor could they distribute their own films. They had to sell their films at a flat price, on the average less than $50,000 per film, with a top limit of $250,000, to native Korean distributors who were on the government's approved list. It was lunacy, but in Korea absolutely legal. Since American films in Korea got wide distribution through Korean channels and were very popular, Korean distributors would rack up millions of dollars in profits on our movies, leaving the Americans outside with their noses pressed against the cartel's windowpane.

Michael Williams-Jones, the energetic, bold, and very smart chief of United International Pictures (UIP), a combine of Universal, Paramount, and MGM studios, fretted under these strictures. He talked to me and urged me to take the lead in tearing down this seemingly insurmountable barricade. We both agreed that it was time to throw down a challenge to the South Koreans. We talked to the other film companies, but oddly there were a few who were not that ready to fight.

I drew up a battle plan. My first move was to meet with Clayton Yeutter, the United States trade representative in the Reagan administration. Clayton, a large, gregarious man, was receptive to my goals. He just didn't think it would be easy. The State Department and the Defense Department had special needs for Korea. They would be reluctant, if not downright unwilling, to make any moves that the Koreans might find unsuitable.

I flew to Korea to put my case before the president of Korea and his trade minister. I told them the American companies wanted to be able to open offices in Korea, just as that country was free to do in the United States. We wanted to distribute our own movies. I was treated with much courtesy but received only bland and inconclusive responses. After my meeting with the Korean president, I kept pushing the trade minister, but to no avail.

Back I went to Ambassador Yeutter. This time, I told him I believed that, based on the responses I had received, any further negotiations were unlikely to make a dent in Korea's position. We would get nowhere. I had another plan. I was ready to file a Section 301 unfair trade complaint (the designation "301" derived from the numbered section in the U.S. Trade Act). Under this procedure, the U.S. trade representative, after listening to the evidence presented by me and appraising the response of the Koreans, had the authority to declare the complaint valid. The United States could then impose sanctions on the offending country. It was, without question, the opening salvo of a trade war, if the Koreans chose to make it so.

Yeutter listened calmly but was not enthusiastic. He suggested that I reopen negotiations with the trade minister. I flew once again to Korea, and once again I tried to persuade the minister to avoid a trade conflict. He stood firm. When I got back home, after informing the studios of my intentions, I made it known I would file the 301. All hell broke loose. The South Korean ambassador asked to meet with me. He solemnly intoned that this was not the right time to disturb what he called the "superior relations between our two countries." I remonstrated that all his government had to do was grant the movie industry the same rights in Korea that all Korean companies had in the United States. "Is that not fair?"

A dismaying quiet fell over the Korean government. I pondered my next move, which was to push the 301 forward with all guns firing. But before I could produce the appropriate evidentiary papers, I got a call from Michael Deaver, former chief aide to President Reagan. He had formed his own consulting firm, and his newest client was South Korea. Deaver, charming, knowledgeable, and very well connected, suggested I meet with him and the Korean trade minister, who would be in Washington the next day.

I appeared at Deaver's elegantly appointed quarters to meet my old antagonist, Minister Hyun-chong Kim, the top trade policy authority in Korea. We met all that day and the next day, discussing each other's positions. In the late afternoon of the second day, I stood up and said, "Minister Kim, there is no more we can say that hasn't been said. I am grateful to you and Mr. Deaver for meeting with me. But it is my intention to go forward at the fastest speed possible with our unfair trade complaint. I will not withdraw that complaint. I thank you and Mr. Deaver for your time."

Mr. Kim looked at me pleadingly, but I walked out. I called Yeutter to ask him not to tolerate any more delays. "I have done all I can to persuade the Koreans. The president of Korea, the trade minister, and the rest are not persuadable by ordinary means. The 301 filing is our only alternative."

Yeutter understood. He would move the complaint forward.

Thirty-six hours after the filing of the 301, a surprise awaited me. Deaver asked me back to his office. When I arrived, Trade Minister Kim, all smiles, greeted me warmly. He said that his government would immediately grant all our requests. Our companies could open offices in Seoul. All barriers would be eliminated. Korea's market would be completely open to the American studios. It was a triumph for the American motion picture companies. And triumph is a tasty brew. I drank from it deeply that day, little imagining how quickly the brew would turn sour.

I called Michael Williams-Jones as well as the other studio international distribution chiefs. "The Korean marketplace after all these years is now open. You and the other companies can establish offices there and distribute your own films and TV programs." Williams-Jones moved with lightning speed, but he ran into a counteroffensive. At Seoul Airport, he and several aides were denied entry and forced to turn back to Hong Kong after threats were made on their lives. Michael would not be deterred, but soon after he and his aides checked into the Schilla Hotel in Seoul, the hotel was surrounded by a thousand or so protesters bused in from around the city, all of them holding placards blazing with menace and threats.

I raised hell in the press and through our government. Soon, UIP opened its offices for internal Korean distribution, but still I underestimated the hostility generated by my trade victory. UIP's first film to hit Korean theaters under its own distribution was *Fatal Attraction*, starring Michael Douglas, Glenn Close, and Anne Archer. Immediately, the life of the UIP Korean representative was threatened, his home besieged, and his family frightened out of their minds. UIP brought in two more films, *The Living Daylights*, a James Bond movie, and *The Untouchables*, starring Kevin Costner and Sean Connery. In two theaters playing UIP's films, some innovative thugs set loose live poisonous snakes in the auditoriums. As you might surmise, this had a depressing effect on attendance.

Michael Williams-Jones never flinched, nor did he exhibit any fear. He was right there in Korea, rallying his forces. He was determined to see this thing through. Finally, the protests wound down when it became clear that UIP wasn't going away and other studios were now opening their offices. The dark tide of violence receded. By the end of 1988, a wary peace settled over the marketplace.

How valuable was this solution to an unacceptable trading arrangement? American film companies were receiving some $9 million annually in combined revenues before the collapse of these barriers. Within six years after the entry of the American film companies into their own offices in South Korea, sales soared to some $177 million and continued to rise.

But my problems with South Korea were to resurface in 1998. The Korean film producers persuaded their government to install a quota system whereby theaters had to play Korean films and none other for 146 days of the year. Naturally, I found this an unpleasant prospect, and not only because of Korea. What if other countries followed suit? Once more I took to the skies, bound for Seoul. I suggested to the president of Korea that I would be willing to accept the quota if it were substantially reduced. He shook his head. He made it clear that American producers did not vote in Korean elections, and Korean producers did. As an old political hand, I understood that clearly. The president counseled me to meet with the Korean film producers personally. I did. Nearly fifty of Korea's top movie producers met with me at my hotel in Seoul and swiftly made known their opposition to fiddling around with the quota. I departed Korea empty-handed. But I did have a card up my sleeve.

I had learned that Korea was pushing the State Department for a bilateral investment treaty (BIT). On arriving in Washington, I phoned my friend Senator Jesse Helms of North Carolina, the Republican chairman of the Senate Foreign Relations Committee, through whose portals all treaties must enter so that the committee could "advise and consent." In simple terms, no committee approval, no treaty.

My friendship with Senator Helms, a gargoyle to most of Hollywood's politically active stars, came about in a thoroughly human way. I had invited about thirty senators, Democratic and Republican, to the MPAA for a simple buffet dinner and a brand-new American film to be screened in our theater. We had a full house that evening. I was the last to sit down. There was only one seat left, at a table occupied by Helms and his wife, Dot, their two grandsons, and other Republican senators and their spouses. I sat between the Helms grandsons, aged nine and eleven. I spent the dinner chatting with these two boys about movies, sports, and flying combat in the war. I ignored the senators, not deliberately, but because the little boys were seemingly absorbed by this older man spinning yarns.

The next morning, I got a call from Senator Helms. "Jack, I just want you to know that Dot and I were so pleased you spent so much time talking with our grandsons. They were impressed, saying to me, 'Grandpa, he talked to us like we were adults. We had such a good time.' So Dot and I want to say thank you. Would you agree to having lunch with me soon in the Senate dining room?" Of course. And I confess I was pleased that his grandsons thought well of me.

I have to say, the senator and I didn't agree on a lot of political issues, but we did find ourselves together on his support for Israel and his commitment to the protection of intellectual property as well as fair trade. Politics aside, though, we got along famously. I liked him very much. Many of my Hollywood friends found it dismaying that Jesse Helms and I would be good friends. My rejoinder was, "He believes in American movies getting a fair deal in world trade. He keeps his word to me and the movie industry. That's a pretty good definition of a friend."

So it was that on my return to Washington from Korea, I met with Senator Helms. I told him that the American marketplace was totally open to South Koreans. I told him I didn't think it right that the American movie industry should be subject to quotas when there were none to bar Koreans in our country. Senator Helms agreed. He said, "Jack, why don't you write me a letter that I can send to Secretary Albright. Put in it what you think I ought to say to the secretary of state about your problem."

I sat down that day to compose the draft letter. In the penultimate paragraph, I said in effect, "Unless the Motion Picture Association of America agrees with this BIT treaty, it will have an inhospitable welcome in my Committee." Stern stuff, but I figured if Chairman Helms found it too aggressive, he would make a suitable revision. When Senator Helms sent me a copy of his letter to the secretary of state, I knew how a lottery winner feels. The senator's letter to the secretary was an exact replica of my draft letter to the senator! No way a BIT treaty was going to see the light of day unless that screen quota was substantially adjusted. Candor requires me to report that Secretary Madeleine Albright, a savvy practioner of the diplomatic arts, was not fooled. She knew whose "unseen hand" was at work here, and she and I also knew there was nothing personal in all this; it was just business.

In February 2006, a year and a half after I stepped down as CEO of MPAA, I read in the press that South Korea and the United States were in the process of negotiating a BIT. But I also found out that South Korea announced it was cutting its screen quota from 146 days to 73 days—precisely at the mark that I had laid down years earlier as a suitable compromise. Press reports also indicated that the Korean producers were furious. I phoned Dan Glickman, my successor at the MPAA, to get confirmation of what I had read. Dan said it was true.

Though I was no longer in charge at the MPAA, I felt jubilant. A piece of unfinished business had come to a close. But knowing that nothing is ever finished in politics, I immediately wrote Senator Richard Lugar, chairman of the Senate Foreign Relations Committee, and ranking member Senator Joe Biden. Both had agreed to continue the "Helms doctrine" when I talked to them years before. I wanted them to know the latest movement in the quota issue, in case Korea tried to reinstate the screen quota in its original format as they negotiated a BIT with the United States.

The other good news is that the quality of Korean-produced films has taken a quantum leap. Many of their directors are now world class. Actually, the Korean movie community no longer needs a quota, since a growing number of Korean films dominate their domestic marketplace. I was quite pleased with the outcome of the entire matter.

COMMANDEUR!

On September 6, 2004, six days after I relinquished my leadership post at the MPAA, I was summoned to Paris, to the Ministry of Culture's historic office overlooking the Louvre, where I had first met

André Malraux more than thirty-five years earlier. I was informed that I was to be promoted in the Legion of Honor. (My rank, *chevalier*, was the lowest, and the next highest was *officier*.) I was, to put it mildly, delighted. When Chris Marcich, a close personal friend as well as head of MPAA's Brussels office, and I arrived, the new culture minister, Renaud de Vabres, greeted us with warmth, as did the American ambassador, Howard Leach. Outside the office, in the minister's ceremonial room, were a hundred or so invited guests, friends of mine, including Olivia de Havilland and Leslie Caron.

The minister, the ambassador, Chris, and I chatted amiably for a bit, and then the minister rose. "Come, Jack, it's time for you to become a *commandeur*." Did I hear that correctly? I thought. I knew that it was impossible for someone to leap from *chevalier* to *commandeur*, the highest honor given to nongovernment officials, bypassing *officier*, unless by the personal, special order of the president of the Republic. In the ceremonial room, the minister was lavish in his praise of me, reciting my life from my air combat duty as a pilot of a B-25 to the current moment. Then he drew me to his side and after a dramatic pause said, "The Republic of France promotes you to the rank of *commandeur* in the Society of the Légion d'Honneur."

I was speechless. To the applause of my friends and guests, he placed the scarlet-and-white medallion around my neck. My powers of speech returned, but I stayed largely with the theme of "Thank you, Mr. President; thank you, Minister." It was a surprisingly emotional moment.

That evening, I tested the power of the *commandeur* scarlet rosette, which was now nestled on a strip of white ribbon on my lapel. Chris Marcich and his young assistant, Olivier Dock, and I set off for a first-class fish restaurant in Paris to celebrate my canonization. It was a glorious evening, with a lilting soft breeze. Olivier strode ahead to talk to the maître d' for seating. He returned with a glum look on his face.

"Jack, the place is sold out. Not a table to be had. I'm so sorry."

"Don't worry, Ollie," I said. "I have an idea. Let me see if it works." With their puzzled gazes on me, I approached the maître d'.

"Monsieur, my name is Jack Valenti [I pronounced it Val-ahn-tee, the Gallic way]. I have just come from the minister of culture's office, where on the order of President Chirac he has promoted me to *commandeur* in the Légion d'Honneur." I turned my lapel toward him so he could see the little scarlet-and-white ribbon.

He threw up his hands. "Ah, Monsieur Valahntee, my most sincere congratulations to you. This is a great honor. I am so proud that you would come to me on this night." He snapped his fingers, and a waiter sped to his side. "Take Monsieur Valahntee and his guests to number fourteen."

The waiter led me and a now grinning Chris and Ollie to a table on the patio, the preferred section, where he pulled off the "Reserved" sign and beckoned us to sit down. I gestured to my friends. "If only America understood the value of this ribbon as readily as the French, Beverly Hills, New York, and Washington would be so much more congenial." The only miracle my scarlet-and-white ribbon could not perform? I had to pay for the meal.

Rebuking the Stone: Oliver and *JFK*

Early in 1992, accompanied by my lovely young daughter Alexandra, I went to a local Washington movie theater to see Oliver Stone's new film, *JFK*. As the movie unreeled, I felt a rising gorge of disbelief turning to nausea, mixed with rage. What I was watching was a piece of beguiling crap, replacing reason with a noisy lie from first scene to last. In the film, Stone elevates to sainthood Jim Garrison, a disgraced, discredited, kooky former New Orleans district attorney played by a huge star, Kevin Costner. Under Stone's direction, Costner regales the jury with an indictment of President Johnson and Chief Justice Earl Warren as evil co-conspirators, covering up the murder of President Kennedy.

I was not happy, but the ax really fell on my neck when we exited the theater and Alexandra said to me solemnly, "Daddy, I never knew it happened that way. Did you?" My anger boiled over. If Alexandra, my own daughter, was swayed by this sack of lies, what must the rest of America be thinking?

The next morning, I got on the phone with Bob Daly, my longtime friend and chairman of Warner Bros., distributors of the film. Two days later, I was in his office. Bob is now, as he was then, one of the smartest, most respected executives in all of Hollywood.

I said to him, "Bob, this film is a nest of lies from start to finish, especially the last part, which is grotesque. I aim to go public with my views. I can't let this movie go without taking on Stone."

Bob looked at me for a bit. "Jack," he said gently, "you are the leader of our industry. You have a responsibility to this industry and to the members of the MPAA. You can't go around trashing a film that is being distributed by a member company, or any other company, for that matter."

I pondered that. Bob was right, as usual. I said, "I think you have a solid point. So I am ready to call a meeting of the MPAA board of directors and resign my position. Then I will be free to make my public statement."

Bob smiled at me. "Now, Jack, you know that that's not the way to go."

We continued to talk for some time. Finally I said, "Let's try this for a solution. I'll hold my fire until all the votes are in for the Academy Awards. That way, whatever I say can't harm its chance of getting an award."

Bob nodded. The pact was sealed. I would wait for the awards voting to close, and then I would pounce. And I did. The *New York Times* gave my release prominence in an article written by Bernard Weinraub. It led with, "Jack Valenti, President of the Motion Picture Association of America and ex-aide to President Lyndon Johnson, denounced the film 'JFK' as a 'hoax,' a 'smear' that rivaled the Nazi propaganda films of Leni Riefenstahl. Mr. Valenti said that Mr. Stone's film was a monstrous charade based on the hallucinatory bleatings of a discredited former district attorney."

That was just the complimentary part of what I said, but you get the idea. Oliver Stone commented that my diatribe was off the mark, and he stood by his film, but he did say he commended my loyalty. Bob Daly stated that Warner Bros. was supporting Mr. Stone and the film. He went on to say, "As far as Jack Valenti is concerned, his loyalty to President Johnson is admirable. I can only hope that those who work for me could be that loyal. I have nothing but the highest regard for Jack." No wonder I still have such enduring affection for Bob Daly.

JACQUELINE KENNEDY ONASSIS

In the years after the nightmare assassination of President Kennedy and the awful journey from Dallas to Washington, D.C., on the afternoon of November 22, 1963, I would infrequently see Mrs. Kennedy (later Mrs. Onassis) at charity events in New York. If our gazes met for a fleeting moment, she would nod slightly to me, a mute message that I took to mean "I remember." On those occasions, I never spoke to her. The moment never seemed right, but a time did come when we were thrown together by circumstances neither of us could have imagined.

Some twenty-eight years after the Longest Day, I began drafts of a novel called *Protect and Defend*. What would happen if a vice president decided to throw down the gauntlet and enter the primaries, challenging his own president? Not since Thomas Jefferson and Aaron Burr collided in the early part of the nineteenth century had anything like this occurred. It was a fetching idea—at least to me. The title I gave it was taken from the presidential oath of office.

Over the next year, I began writing and rewriting. Helen Bartlett, godchild of President Kennedy and Jacqueline Kennedy, the closest friend of my own daughter Courtenay, and the daughter of our good friends Charley and Martha Bartlett (who first introduced Jack Kennedy to the young Jacqueline Bouvier at dinner in the Bartlett home), heard I was writing my first novel. Helen said to me, "Mr. Valenti, may I send some chapters of your new book to Mrs. Onassis? She's a senior editor at Doubleday. Maybe she would be interested."

I promptly passed along to Helen some ten chapters of my still-unfinished book. Weeks went by. Two months later, I had all but forgotten the matter. If I thought about it, I reasoned that Mrs. Onassis, gracious lady that she is, probably didn't want to give Helen bad news.

Then one Saturday morning, the kitchen phone rang. I picked it up. In an instant, I recognized the soft, feathery voice. "Jack, this is Jackie. I read the chapters of your new book, and I want to publish it."

I damn near fainted. My ears and my brain were unable to absorb that message, not to mention the fact of its messenger. I stammered, "Mrs. Onassis, that's so kind of you. Thank you so much."

Again, that voice, sweetly soft, with its agreeable edges of elite girls' school: "First, you call me Jackie, and second, I want to see you and talk with you about publishing the book. I want to be your editor."

Over the next months, my appreciation of Mrs. Onassis grew apace. We talked numerous times on the phone and in person in her office as she outlined ideas for improving the text. As we grew to know each other better, I felt increasingly comfortable in her presence. She wrote me frequently, as I did her. I still have in my possession a dozen or more handwritten letters and notes from her in her familiar schoolgirl looping script, on her pale blue personal stationery. Oddly, or maybe not so oddly, her words on paper sounded exactly like she talked, in softly expressed exclamatory sentences.

She was precise in her editing suggestions, and she understood with clarity the insecurity of first novelists (or at least this one). I remember so clearly one day when she had me to lunch at Raphael, a restaurant in Manhattan. It was 1992. She was accompanied by the editor to whom I had chatted earlier on the phone. (Irony of ironies, Shaye Areheart, Jacqueline Kennedy's assistant at Doubleday, is now the publisher and editor of this book, so many years after our lunch at Raphael.)

At that lunch we talked about my novel, with Jackie again offering me some wise suggestions about story structure. Suddenly she said, "Jack, you mentioned Mrs. Johnson." She looked at me with that mesmerizing gaze. "She and Lyndon were so dear to me. They allowed me to stay in the White House for eleven days without a single word of discontent. Such a long time, too long. I read recently that Mrs. Roosevelt was gone from her private quarters within forty-eight hours of the death of her husband." She grew silent. "Lady Bird and Lyndon treated me with such kindness, such affection. I will never forget it." Then she moved on to another subject.

On May 7, 2004, in Washington, D.C., I ran into Shaye. We were both at a book party for Kate Lehrer, wife of the celebrated PBS news anchor Jim Lehrer. Shaye's imprint had just published Kate's book. As Shaye and I chatted, I mentioned the lunch at Raphael. "Oh yes," she said, "I remember it very well. It was the first and only time I ever heard Mrs. Onassis speak about the time of the assassination."

"Funny you should say that," I said, "because others have told me that they could not remember a single time when Jackie spoke about Dallas or its aftermath." I hesitated, then said, "I so admired her, even loved her. She treated me with such kindness and attention."

Shaye smiled. "She was one of the smartest, kindest women I have ever known, and she was so fond of you, Jack. The fact that she wanted to edit your book ought to tell you that."

Shaye's remark filled me with warmth. I went home after the book party, and it was then I made a decision that I would show Shaye some chapters of my memoir before I allowed anyone else to read it. I wanted her to like it and publish it. I really wanted her to be my editor, but at that time this was just a fantasy for me.

When Jackie fell ill with cancer in 1994, I prayed for her recovery. I was in Paris on movie business when I got the news, so I picked up the phone and called Senator Edward Kennedy. "Ted," I said, "please forgive this intrusion, but I'll be back home in a couple of days. Do you think you could arrange for me to see Jackie, for just a couple of minutes?"

Ted Kennedy was understanding. "You know she is very ill. Right now just the family visits with her. Why don't you call me when you return and we'll see how she is feeling."

Two days later, I was at Charles de Gaulle Airport, in the United Airlines lounge. I stood up with a cup of coffee in my hands, watching CNN on a corner TV set. As I sipped the coffee, a line flashed across the screen: "Breaking News . . ." A somber-looking young man appeared on screen. "Sad news to report. Just a few hours ago, Mrs. Jacqueline Kennedy Onassis, widow of President Kennedy, died in her Manhattan apartment."

My cup clattered to the floor, hot coffee splashing wildly on the carpet. I stared at the screen. Then I began to weep, silently but without restraint. I didn't notice if anyone in the lounge was looking at me. I really didn't care. All I thought was how Jackie and I had shared a historic plane ride, how sweetly warm and affectionate she was, how she seemed to care so very much about my book and me. And now she was gone. A lady came to my side, and I heard her say in a soft voice, "I know how you feel. I always thought she was wonderful. Did you know her?"

I looked at her for a few seconds. I don't remember what I said. What I wanted to say, as I thought about it later, was, "Yes, I knew her, I loved her, and yes, she was wonderful." But the plain fact is, I wanted to say that to Jackie. I think she knew how I felt about her. But now I would never be able to tell her.

A year or so later, I got a call from a gentleman who said he represented a buyer of memorabilia. Did I not possess handwritten letters from Mrs. Onassis? Yes, I did. Would I be willing to talk to him about selling those letters? They would fetch a handsome sum, he promised me. No, I said, I would never sell them. Well, he said, could we talk about a price? No, I told him, you can't name a price high enough, because I will never sell them. End of conversation.

I still have those letters. Most of all, I still have my precious memories of a woman who while she lived truly owned the heart of the world. She still does mine.

Warren Buffett: The Best of the Breed

I met Warren Buffet through the intercession of another remarkable fellow named Herbert A. Allen. Herbert and I first got to know each other in 1968 when we were both partisans of Hubert Humphrey's in his race for the presidency.

Herbert was in his late twenties, and—then as now—slim-framed, handsome, self-effacing and publicity-shy, but firmly in command of his solidly held views about business, politics, and the sensible behavior of those entrusted with other people's money.

Herbert is a man who makes up his own mind, paying close attention to his instincts and personal judgments. Today he is at the apex of his powers as the head of Allen & Company, a bountifully successful investment banking firm.

Some twenty-five years ago, with great foresight, he created an annual business conference in Sun Valley, an area he has always loved. He then invited a small cadre of influential Wall Street gurus, high-tech nabobs, chiefs of entertainment, industrial and business enterprises, as well as investment bankers whose opinions he trusted.

Casual dress is the uniform, and spouses and children are welcome. Each morning, after an early breakfast, CEOs from a wide assortment of companies as well as government leaders from around the world mount a small stage to give presentations and answer questions from the audience. It is a spirited give and take—no holds barred and surprisingly candid. After lunch, everyone is free to relax and then the whole process starts again the next morning and continues in this way for four days. This is where I first met Bill and Melinda Gates and other financial and cultural titans.

At a dinner reception during the 2004 conference, two young men came up to me and introduced themselves. I was very pleased. I enjoy talking to college kids and I assumed their father or mother was the invited guest.

After a moment of idle chatter, I said, "I'm sorry, but I didn't get your names." One of them said, "I'm Larry Page and this is Sergey Brin. We're with Google." Standing next to them was a slim, very pretty woman named Anne Wojecki, who I later discovered is a Yale graduate in microbiology and a whiz kid who runs a hedge fund. After I gathered my wits, I babbled, "Good heavens, how old are you guys?" Page was thirty and Brin was twenty-nine. "And how old were you when you invented Google?" I asked. Well, the answer made me feel like a freaking failure!

But the most fascinating man I met through these conferences was Warren Buffet. He's the only businessman I know who can speak substantially and hilariously—without the benefit of notes or text—about abstruse, nearly inexplicable subjects and make them understandable and entertaining. It is an art, really, and it certainly seems magical when you are listening to this beguiling man with an impish smile on his face.

I recall one talk he gave at lunch, shortly before the high-tech bubble burst. There was a herd of young bulls there from the investment community just dying to cross horns with this icon and bring him down. One of them rose and chided Warren, saying, "Mr. Buffet, you have studiously avoided investing in the high-tech industry.

You've missed out on the grandest investment opportunities in years. How come?"

"Well, you may be right," Warren replied, giving the young man a winning smile, "but it has always been my policy never to invest in a business I don't understand and whose assets I cannot find." When the bubble burst and the dotcoms came crashing down, guess who wasn't affected by the fall?

On another day at Allen's conference Warren was asked about his early career and how he got started. "Actually," he said, "when I was a very young I wanted to be an insurance actuary"—pause for dramatic effect—"but I didn't have enough charisma for the job." I was one of the many who nearly fell out of our seats laughing. When asked how he picks companies to invest in, he said, "I always look for companies so well managed that even an idiot can run them"—again the pause—"because sooner or later one will."

For several years Warren and I have indulged in a fiercely competitive golf games on the Wednesday afternoon of the conference. We play for a dollar, but the loser—in a solemn ceremony on the eighteenth hole—must prostrate himself before the winner and hand over the one-spot. On one beautiful afternoon, we were riding in a golf cart while an hour of Warren's time was being auctioned off on eBay to benefit his late wife Susie's favorite charity. As we rode along, he was getting the results of the auction over his cell phone. Midway on the back nine I asked him, "What's the price so far?"

"Over six hundred thousand," he replied with a grin.

"Do you think it's going higher?"

He smiled widely. "You planning to bid?"

All I could think of was how damn lucky I was to be spending four hours with Warren at no charge, while some super-rich hedge-fund manager was offering serious money to have this man's attention during lunch. Hey, isn't that what the American dream is all about?

THE GREAT SCREENER CONFLAGRATION

For those not familiar with Hollywood patois, there may be some confusion about what the term *screener* means. Several months or so before the deadline for Academy Award nominations, the studios would distribute copies of films they hoped might be nominated in the various award shows that preceded the grandest prize in all of the cinema world: the Academy Awards. These copies were called "screeners." Copies were typically sent to all academy members, to the special nominating committees of the Screen Actors Guild (SAG), the Directors Guild of America (DGA), the Writers Guild of America (WGA), the Hollywood Foreign Press Association (the Golden Globes), the British Academy of Film and Television Arts (BAFTA), independent filmmakers, movie critics, and so on. In time, as you might surmise, the flow of these screeners into thousands of homes became a pattern, then a ritual, then a given, and finally a right.

The onset of the digital age in the late eighties and early nineties fostered the wholesale theft of brand-new movies, taken down from the Internet and circulated illegitimately around the globe. So it was that in August 2003, my antipiracy department executives sent me a report that of the sixty-eight titles delivered as screeners to the homes of cinema people in 2002, about half were already being sold as illegal DVDs in places like Russia, Europe, and Latin America. I was deeply upset by this report. I studied it and talked to my antipiracy experts, who felt this was an unacceptable rate of theft. I did, too.

In September, I began a series of meetings, in person and on the phone, with the heads of the film studios. Some of them were appalled. All were angry. I told them I thought we ought to ban screeners for the coming year and then examine the marketplace carefully to find out if this ban had reduced theft of our valuable creative works. I began to assemble a chorus of approvals from the studios.

Then I took a step that would come back to haunt me. The action I took violated the essential political rule I had learned from LBJ: Never surprise your friends and allies. Always consult quietly. Explain. Listen. Then decide. None of this demands the loss of decision-making authority, and it damn sure allows you to locate, and if possible remove, land mines. For reasons that even at this writing are unclear to me, I ignored this rule I knew so well. One factor was time. I had waited too long to deal with the issue. I should have confronted this piracy report in early August and canceled my vacation.

Now either I had to let the screeners go out—it takes time to send thousands of screeners to various constituencies—or I had to enlist the studios to stop them now. I chose the latter.

In mid-September, the MPAA issued a press release in my name declaring the new policy of the studios: No more screeners. The news exploded like a thousand hand grenades. If I had been accused of strangling children in their cradles, it would have generated a smaller outcry. At the height of the imbroglio, Lynda Obst, a highly successful film producer with a crisp sense of humor, wrote a letter to *Variety* discussing screeners and ended with the comment "We do love our swag." It was said in fun, but it was also true.

Each day, opposition grew more heated. Nothing in my long years in Hollywood had so inflamed the film community. On October 10, 2003, an ad appeared in the trade press. It was titled "To Jack Valenti and the Motion Picture Association of America." It had over one hundred names endorsing its message, which essentially denounced the cruelty and arrogance of the screener ban. Too many signatures on that letter belonged to good friends of mine—longtime friends, actors, directors, writers, and producers, including Robert Redford, Robert Altman, Norman Jewison, Martin Scorsese, Pedro Almodóvar, Paul Thomas Anderson, Bernardo Bertolucci, the Coen brothers, Bill Condon, Francis Ford Coppola, Nora Ephron, Jodie Foster, Ang Lee, Mike Leigh, Barry Levinson, Sidney Lumet, David Lynch, David Mamet, Arthur Penn, Sydney Pollack, Tim Robbins, Jim Sheridan, Julie Taymor, John Turturro, and on and on.

To say I was pained is to undershoot the mark. Actually, I was sick at heart. I pondered the alternatives long and hard. Then Frank Pierson, president of the Academy of Motion Picture Arts and Sciences, called me. Frank, winner of the Academy Award for Best Screenplay for *Dog Day Afternoon*, is a wise, serious, thoughtful man who is highly respected in our industry. I trusted him. So when he presented me with his idea, I listened. We worked on it together. When we were done, I believed we had indeed found a viable middle ground. Screeners would be sent only to the 5,800 members of the academy. I knew that this would not please everyone, but it was a sensible alternative to sending out no screeners or going back to the

2002 design, which encouraged piracy. Why the academy? Because the Academy of Motion Picture Arts and Sciences is the only organization whose members cut across the entire movie industry, including all those who work before and behind the camera.

Pierson also agreed to stringent rules of the game. He would send out a document to all academy members. If they sent back the document with their signature on it, they would be (1) authorizing the academy to send their name and address to the studios; (2) pledging they would not allow any screeners to leave their home; (3) aware that the studios were reserving the right to identify/watermark screeners; (4) confirming that they understood if a pirated screener was traced back to a screener sent to that member, he or she would be expelled from the academy (that was a severe penalty).

I called a meeting of the studio chiefs. I explained the proposed academy plan, and I told them that we would still face tremendous opposition. Independent filmmakers claimed that without screeners their small-budget movies would lack resources to attract favorable attention as well as reviews; members of the Hollywood Foreign Press Association, which stages the increasingly popular Golden Globe Awards, would strenuously object; the Screen Actors Guild, with its two-thousand-member nominating committee, would be vexed, as would the British Academy of Film and Television Arts, the British equivalent of the academy.

The MPAA's member companies decided to go along. This decision applied equally to all subsidiary companies of the studios. Moreover, the studios would expand and make available special screenings for films, large and small, in New York and Los Angeles. It would be a one-year experiment. I received a bundle of responses, some laudatory and some not. But Frank and I believed it was necessary to put in print the thought process we had journeyed through. I wanted to explain to all of Hollywood what the academy plan was all about and why it was reasonable and right. So I published a brief article in *Variety*, trying to explain our compromise.

I still had one nagging worry: lawsuits. I summoned the entire board of directors of the MPAA, the heads of the Hollywood studios, to a conference call with our outside counsel, Richard Cooper, former Supreme Court law clerk and now a senior partner at Williams

& Connolly, one of the nation's premier law firms, to air out the academy plan. It was a full turnout. We traversed the field, going over every aspect of the noisy conflict. But foremost in our minds was the growing threat of the theft of our movies.

I asked Richard to assess the possibility of a lawsuit and what the likely outcome would be if one was filed. He answered forthrightly: "If a lawsuit is filed, I would expect us to win. But I caution you that no prediction comes with a guarantee. A lot depends on which federal judge presides. To repeat: I think we will win, but there is no guarantee of victory."

I agreed with Richard. I was comforted by the fact that we ought to win since our motives had to do with survival of an industry, but I could not get rid of my instinctive concern that no lawsuit is a slam dunk. The meeting ended. We would go forward with our pact with the academy. But the furor raged on.

I made public my desire to meet with any group that wanted to suggest alternative courses, as long as they included an effort to control thievery. The result was a day-long series of meetings I held in my lodgings at the Peninsula Hotel in Beverly Hills. I sat down first with Lorenzo Soria, president of the Hollywood Foreign Press Association, founders and producers of the Golden Globes, sometimes a harbinger of the Academy Award winners. The old Golden Globes had been replaced by a new show, and the investment was paying off. TV ratings increased, and the show was reaching impressive new heights. Lorenzo is a cultured, civilized man, soft-spoken but nonetheless firm in his views, which he valiantly explained to me. He was reasonable, and I gauged some of his remarks to be on target. I pledged to him I would try to work it out.

I met next with representatives of the independent film production community. There assembled that day a group of very serious and gifted people: Dawn Hudson, spokeswoman for the group; Bill Condon, a first-class writer, director, and producer; and Sean Penn, in my judgment one of the four or five greatest living actors performing on the screen. I confess that Condon and Penn made a persuasive case. Their principal argument was that many small-budget independent films didn't have sufficient funds to advertise. The screeners that flowed not only to academy members but also to critics as well as the

Golden Globe, SAG, and DGA members were essential to giving them a presence, without which they would be overlooked. I had to admit that it made sense.

I also met with the Los Angeles Film Critics Association. As you may surmise, these gifted writers spoke with some passion. Their case was similar to that of the actors and producers. Again I squirmed, because again the arguments made sense.

Frankly, it was a very long day.

Alas, the furor roared on, and my anxieties grew. I was admonished by several independents that I had left them with no alternative but to sue. Moreover, even the major studio subsidiaries that bought, produced, and distributed independent low-budget films were stirring restlessly. Stories appeared in the press citing unnamed subsidiary presidents who were openly challenging the decision of their bosses.

I got a phone call from Harvey Weinstein of Miramax, owned by the Walt Disney Company. Harvey, a large, rumpled human volcano possessed of uncanny creative and marketing instincts, had elevated the small-budget film to Academy Award heights, snatching Best Picture Awards from the majors. I remember the 1999 Academy Awards ceremony, when to my amazement *Shakespeare in Love* triumphed over Steven Spielberg's *Saving Private Ryan* as Best Picture of 1998. I was sitting two seats away from Jeffrey Katzenberg, who headed DreamWorks, producer of *Saving Private Ryan*. When the Best Picture Award envelope was opened and Miramax's film won the Oscar, Katzenberg had a dazed look on his face (as did I). I considered Spielberg's movie the greatest war epic ever filmed. But Harvey blew it away in the voting with his "little" movie.

Harvey was on the phone with two presidents of major studio subsidiaries, Michael Barker, co-president of Sony Picture Classics, and James Schamus, president of Universal's Focus Films. Both Barker and Schamus were first-class movie producers. Harvey allowed Jim and Michael to do most of the talking, which consisted of bombarding me with reasons why my decisions were crazy. I told them I was still searching for alternatives, but I pledged them to confidentiality. Enough rumors were being trumpeted, and we surely didn't need any more. We talked for some time, though no specific alternatives were aired beyond summarily repealing the ban on screeners. After one more reminder from me that we had pledged to honor the privacy of our conversation, the call ended.

The next morning, the *New York Times* ran a damn near verbatim account of the phone call. I was furious as I punched up Harvey's number. When he came on the line, I attacked before he could say a word. "Dammit, Harvey, you guys told me that call was off the record, and now it's all over the *Times*." Perhaps it was because I had launched the first strike (usually he is the one to first squeeze the flamethrower trigger), but Harvey was oddly conciliatory. He never leaked anything, he said, implying that someone else might have done so. But I had vented my spleen. The harm was done. And Harvey had won again.

I held no grudge. Besides, there was no denying Harvey's marketing genius. For example, he used the movie rating system as both a trampoline and a punching bag. He got thousands of dollars of free advertising by condemning the rating system as censorship. The press gorged on his diatribes. Little films that would have died on the publicity vine now were getting major airtime. It was a mixture of baloney and brilliance. Harvey booked one of my favorite actresses—and a good friend—Helen Mirren, on one of the network morning shows. Helen's take on the evil power of ratings was a prize performance. She almost persuaded me! I was ready to take to the barricades to denounce Jack Valenti when I came to my senses. Harvey had struck again, and the luminous Helen Mirren was his instrument.

I slept fitfully the next several nights. I remembered Richard Cooper's legal forecast that no lawsuit's outcome can be guaranteed. I began to wonder how many more screeners we would have to send out to stave off a lawsuit. Only a handful would be required to satisfy the independents, about eighty or so for the Golden Globes, and another two thousand to service the nominating committee of the Screen Actors Guild. I admitted the SAG number was large, but I would try to negotiate it down. Add in the Directors Guild and the Writers Guild, plus sixty to seventy for the movie critics, and we would have a manageable number. Unhappily, I didn't see how we could accommodate BAFTA (the British academy), but maybe I could work out something there. All in all, it would amount to 25 percent or so more than we were prepared to send to the academy members. Moreover, I would try to impose the same stern requirements we had placed on the academy—that is, loss of membership if any pirated screeners could be traced back to the screener recipient. I thought, This is a solid case for compromise and change. I felt better.

I called one last meeting of the studio chiefs in November. The decision would be taken this day, for we were running out of time. Once more, I had a full house on the meeting call. All the studios were represented. The debate was lively, very lively, with remarks both strident and thoughtful. I went over my new plan, with its screener arithmetic in detail. I felt I had to put the choice firmly, clearly. I also had Richard Cooper reiterate his prediction that if we were sued, we would not be able to predict the outcome, though the lawyers believed we would win. I sensed I had a chance to win the final vote.

But some reasonable rebuttals were made by a number of the studio executives. We would look silly doing a 180-degree turn now, was one response. If the suppression of piracy was our central objective, why cave in to noisy opposition? was another. We were in the right. Protecting valuable creative property in the long run was as important to those who opposed us as it was to the studios.

I went back again with the core reasons why this turnabout was necessary. The additional screeners would be a small price to pay for ending once and for all this controversy that was devouring our industry. But, when questioned, I could not say with certainty that we would not be sued. Then again, if we were sued, I could not say we would lose the lawsuit. Therefore, went the counterarguments, why retreat without some strong guarantees? Alas, uncertainty is too blunt a sword to carry into combat.

The meeting ended. I did not command the votes I needed. We would go forward as per our earlier meetings. I felt I had made my case as forcefully and clearly as I could. What was missing? Where was my argument deficient? In hindsight, my colleagues' belief in my instinct was outweighed by my lack of certainty as to what would happen.

We were indeed sued. We went into federal court in New York, presided over by a grim-faced federal district judge, Michael P. Mukasey. Oddly, as I watched the legal proceedings in the judge's court-room, I saw no evidence that the judge had any concern about the essence of the case—that is, the protection of highly valuable creative property. When I testified, the judge never once looked at me. He was constantly hunched over his computer, which was offering him something, but I never could figure out what the hell that something was. Maybe free cable TV? This wasn't the way things worked in *Law & Order* or even *Perry Mason*. The judge always looked at the witness, didn't he?

Richard Cooper was masterful in my judgment. He and the MPAA's brilliant general counsel, Simon Barsky, did their best to counter what I began to see as a foregone conclusion once we got in front of Judge Mukasey. We lost the case.

Henceforth, the MPAA could not gather the studios in any policy that hinted at antitrust activities. I put out a press statement: "From Day One, the screener policy has been about one thing, preserving the future of our industry for filmmakers of all sizes by curtailing piracy. We know, without dispute, that in the past screeners have been sources for pirated goods both domestically and overseas. . . ." What else could be said?

Oh yes, we did have some screener theft. The academy kept its word. They expelled one of their members when it was proven he had used his screener to foster illegal distribution. To me, the whole enterprise was a sad piece of business. The only good news was that I was damn glad it was over. It was a bitch.

THE ANATOMY OF AN EPIC BATTLE ROYAL: THE NATIONAL TV NETWORKS VS. TELEVISION PROGRAM PRODUCERS

Did you ever hear or read about the Financial Interest and Syndication Rules? Before your eyes glaze over, let me explain how that abstruse controversy ignited a titanic war, pitting the three national networks, NBC, CBS, and ABC, against the motion picture studios and their television arms, independent TV producers, stars, directors, and writers. In the entertainment industry, it was a world war that shook the creative landscape in this country.

Put simply, the Fin-Syn Rules said that no television network could demand a financial interest in any TV program owned wholly or in part by an outside producer. Nor could they syndicate that program—that is, sell it to individual TV stations once the program had ended its carriage on prime time. Why was this important? Because the three national networks decided which TV programs got on prime time. The major television production studios, along with independent producers and actors, TV directors and writers, fervently believed that the repeal of the rules would forever destroy the entrepreneurial future of non-network producers of TV programs. The networks would own all the programs by coercing the producers to do their bidding. Everyone would be a contract employee. It was not a pleasant thought. Actually, it was a horrible thought.

The Fin-Syn Rules had been in effect since 1971. Twelve years later, Mark Fowler was chairman of the Federal Communications Commission, and his top priority was deregulation. Thus, on August 12, 1983, Fowler pulled the trigger and announced hearings to repeal the Fin-Syn Rules. The entire Hollywood TV production community erupted in dismay mixed with raw fear. Everyone was ready to go to battle stations, but first there had to be a central command in place to take charge.

At that time, Mary Margaret and I were vacationing in Hawaii at Kapalua Bay, with our close friends Ann and Lloyd Hand. At breakfast time in Hawaii, the phone rang. It was Sid Sheinberg, president of MCA Universal, headed by Lew Wasserman. "Jack," he said without small talk, "we have a huge problem. The FCC has just announced it's going to have hearings to repeal Fin-Syn."

"What's the play, Sid?" I asked.

"You need to get back to L.A. as fast as possible. Lew, Barry Diller, Bob Daly, and others are calling a meeting at my home tomorrow morning. You must be there at eight a.m. You have to take command. We can't allow this guy Fowler to win. We have to turn the FCC around."

I looked at my watch. "Okay, Sid. I'll get airline reservations today, as quick as I can. I'll be at your place tomorrow morning."

I arrived in L.A. in the evening, and at 8:00 the next morning, I was at breakfast with Lew, Barry, Bob, and Sid. It was pretty simple.

I knew and insisted the others understand that "turning the FCC around" was no leisurely walk in the park. It would be difficult, to say the least. It must be a massive, round-the-clock effort, enlisting every ally we could find and with all the political clout we could muster.

We adjourned our meeting before noon. I was on my way to Washington to summon my troops. Our opposition would be the powerful national TV networks, and they would not be an easy mark. Bob Daly had contacted the independent TV producers, who pledged an alliance with us. I retained Joel Jankowsky, a key partner of Bob Strauss's law firm, Akin, Gump, Strauss (and a lot of other names), to lead the lobbying warriors we intended to assemble. Joel was a young and attractive lawyer with heavyweight political savvy who had been the chief legislative assistant to Speaker of the House Carl Albert in an earlier lifetime. He knew the congressional jungle very well. He would be my consigliere, which meant I had a trusted, top-of-the-line field commander.

Meanwhile, Washington lawyer Mickey Gardner had previously rounded up a solid group of independent TV producers operating under the name of the Committee for Prudent Deregulation. I thought this was a lousy name. Later on, we merged the groups under the banner Committee Against Network Monopoly. I had a great affection for the word *Monopoly* as our battering ram.

I enlisted some ten or more other lobbyists, including first-class professionals who worked for the MPAA member companies in Washington, like Jay Berman and Mike Berman (no relation), so that when we added congressional commandos from the creative guilds, actors, writers, directors, and independent producers like Leonard Hill, I had an army. At our first meeting on the weekend, we designed our strategic plan. We were not dealing with ordinary workdays or workweeks. This was going to be a battle waged with calendars, not clocks.

Our plan was simple. First, we had to be all over the FCC, commissioners and staff, with a carefully plotted presentation that was easy to understand. It went like this: The networks were grabbing monopoly (much emphasis on the word *monopoly*) power to the long-term detriment of an open marketplace. They would own every program in prime time because they had the power to do so. They would shut out the independent producer. Creativity in TV would shrink. The networks would command all creative sources, not as individual programmers, but as serfs to the networks, no longer running their own production companies, but operating as employees of the networks. Just three individuals, the heads of the networks' programming, would stamp their imprint on television. Hundreds of other voices would go mute because they would no longer have a rostrum from which to program.

The second phase of our plan was to inundate the Congress with our presentation. We would bring into congressional offices high-profile stars, actors, producers, and directors, as well as independent TV producers who knew the subject in detail. Norman Lear, at that time the most famous TV producer, came in, as did Henry Winkler, who was "the Fonz" on *Happy Days*, and Kirk Douglas, a megastar who was solid on the facts and details. I urged the major studios to stay in the background. I would put front and center the Davids of independent TV production arrayed against the Goliath networks. This was going to be a battle between the little guys and the leviathans. I wanted to keep my leviathans in the closet.

Third, we had to enlist the White House, so that the administration supported our position. Ronald Reagan, a former actor, was president. Some might say that Reagan had a millimeter's depth of understanding about the crucial issues of the day. But none could make those assertions about the Fin-Syn issue. After all, he reigned for seven years as president of the Screen Actors Guild. Reagan knew this issue cold.

We packaged our presentation in simple form, brief, compact, to the point. Keep it simple, I urged our troops. Make what you say memorable so that the gist of our arguments can be stated in five minutes. For the next two weeks, we drowned the Congress in visits, phone calls, memos, more visits, and more meetings with staff and members of Congress. Three times a week, we met in the morning at 8:00 a.m. At times, we had twenty to twenty-five men and women around that table. These were the very best of the best lobbyists who had fought a hundred battles in both Houses and lived to triumph in most of them.

In a visit with Senator Bob Packwood, chairman of the Senate Commerce Committee, I said, "Mr. Chairman, a suggestion. Instead of hearing me and my colleagues tell you why we are right, and then the next day have the networks tell you why they are right, why not have me sit across the table from you with a network representative alongside me. That way you can hear us both, and then question us and have each of us challenge the other's facts and prophecies."

The chairman liked the idea. Some four days later, a top-scale representative from one of the networks (alas, I can't remember his name) and I sat in front of Packwood. We went at it full tilt. I have to confess I loved it. Later, Senator Packwood reported to me that he found the exercise to be useful. Packwood commented that if an advocate couldn't defend his position against an on-the-spot rebuttal by an opponent, that position might not be worth defending. Right on, Mr. Chairman.

I kept to myself, even from my closest allies, two phone calls. The first was to Lew Wasserman. Lew had been Reagan's agent for over twenty years. He knew him intimately, and I knew that Reagan knew he owed his last role as host of *General Electric Theater* to Wasserman. If we could persuade the president to have his administration offer support of our cause, it would be very valuable. The president cannot interfere with independent agencies. We knew that, which was why all we desired was administration backing.

My second call was to Charlton Heston. Chuck was also a former president of the Screen Actors Guild. He and his wife, Lydia, were close friends with Mary Margaret and me for long wonderful years and still are. I asked Lew and Chuck to speak to President Reagan. Both agreed to do so. I never called them back to check on the calls, nor did they call me. If I was asked, "Did either Lew Wasserman or Charlton Heston talk to President Reagan?" I wanted to be able to answer forthrightly, "I don't know." It's what the CIA calls "deniability."

An odd and most pleasant irony occurred. In 1980, one of my good friends in Congress, Bob Carr from Michigan, a member of the Appropriations Committee, was defeated for reelection. I sorrowed for Bob. The day after his defeat, I called to tell him how terrible it was and that I wanted to help him in any way I could. At that time, all of Washington, including me, believed that Bob's political career was over. But I liked Bob as a friend. He had been receptive to my pleading for my movie causes. I admired him greatly.

"Jack," he said, "you're the first and so far the only one who's called me. I'm not getting many phone calls. In Washington, when a member gets beat, most folks take his name off their phone list. So I really thank you." Over the next months, I tried to interest some associations in employing Bob Carr. I thought Bob's tenure in Washington politics was over. To everyone's surprise, Bob took on his successor in the next election and won! He was now back in Congress, retrieving his seat and his seniority on the Appropriations Committee.

During my battle with FCC chairman Mark Fowler, the networks were as energetic as we were. In the midst of this furious struggle, a cadre of network lawyers and executives visited the newly reelected Bob Carr. (This encounter was described to me by an old friend, who happened to be on the networks' team.) As they neared the end of their presentation, Carr broke in to say to them, "I think you're making a pretty good case, and I want to hear more, but tell me, who is on the other side?"

The networks' persuaders reported that TV producers and the MPAA and its studios were their chief adversaries. Carr asked them if that meant Jack Valenti was on the other side. The answer came back, "Yes, he's leading the charge."

Upon hearing this, Bob Carr stood up and said, "Gentlemen, I'm sorry, I really am, but I don't think I need to hear any more. If Jack Valenti is on the other side, I'm going to support him. You see, when I was defeated and thrown over the side, I received one call some days after the election. It was Jack. He wanted to help me at a time when no one figured I would be back in this chair to help him or anyone else. No offense, but I didn't get any phone calls from you. Thanks for coming by."

Then came the hammer blow to the networks. On November 2, Senator Pete Wilson, testifying before the Senate Commerce Committee, read a letter from presidential counselor Edwin Meese wherein Meese reported the White House's support for a two-year moratorium on repeal of the rules. Witnesses from the Departments of Commerce and Justice confirmed their support for a two-year moratorium. In other words, the White House was signaling its position.

It was now clear to Fowler that his cause, for the time being, was withering. But rather than have the entire Congress have to vote, Fowler agreed to something other than utter defeat for him. Our final solution took place on November 16, when Fowler said there would be no repeal but urged the parties to negotiate and come back in May 1984 to report.

It was over. We had pulled off a political miracle. I offered my gratitude to all my allies. The negotiations began. At times, they resembled a Three Stooges comedy, all flailing tugs and pulls, artificial anger and outrage, charge and countercharge. They devolved into the long negotiations over several years, with Bob Daly now as our chief negotiator. Daly was exquisitely dexterous in his every move. He never made a misstep. He was masterful in his leadership and in guiding a restless room of angry TV networks on one side and fearful TV producers on the other.

We started those negotiations in 1984. But it wasn't until August 29, 1995, that the FCC finally rang down the curtain. Fin-Syn was repealed. We had kept the rules in place for twenty-four years! But a new era had intervened. The major studios, once the implacable foes of the national networks, had themselves become national TV networks. Nothing lasts. Everything changes.

THE 2004 REPUBLICAN AND DEMOCRATIC CONVENTIONS

By some crazy coincidence, the Republican and Democratic conventions both asked me to participate in their events in 2004.

Some two months before the Republican convention, I received a phone call from Gordon Smith, Republican senator from Oregon. I had met Gordon early in his campaign and was attracted to his intellect, his warm personal manner, and his devotion to his family, including his radiantly beautiful wife, Sharon, and their children. When Gordon called me, I was delighted to hear from him, but I was surprised by what he had to say. "Jack," he said, "we want to honor you for all your service to your country as well as for being the chief leader of the American film industry. We are going to do just that in New York City at the Republican convention."

I have never tried to hide my political lineage. I was an LBJ Democrat. I was proud of my service to President Johnson. But I always felt good about being nonpartisan in my movie job, because I considered the movie industry to be a national asset, not beholden to either party. Gordon went on to say, "We have reserved the Rainbow Room for Thursday, the last day of the convention. We will toast you, celebrate you, and cheer you on."

I told Gordon that I was not going to resist that kind offer—indeed, I would accept it with gratitude. I arrived in New York a day and a half before that event to attend a huge lunch in honor of the Speaker of the House, Dennis Hastert. I came into a cavernous room, and as I circled the premises, I saw not more than three feet from me the world-famous leader of U2, which happens to be my favorite rock group. It was Bono. Some six months earlier, I had become the part-time president of Friends of the Global Fight Against AIDS, Tuberculosis & Malaria. Naturally, I knew that Bono was the first among equals in battling to cope with these three pandemics, so I stepped up to him, put out my hand, and said, "Bono, I'm Jack Valenti. You don't know me, but I am very anxious to help you in what you are doing."

To my surprise, he grasped my hand and said in that friendly Irish lilt, "But I do know you and what you and the Friends of the Global Fight are doing to help the Global Fund. I am so grateful to you."

Curious, I asked him, "What are earth are you doing here at the Republican convention?"

He laughed. "I'm here because I am trying to persuade the Speaker and others for the American funding that is absolutely essential if we are going to keep Africa from collapsing from disease and poverty. That's why I came to New York. And you can be a big asset, Jack. You are greatly needed in this fight, and I will be calling you for help."

Since then, I have come to know Bono much better. Here is a multimillionaire global rock star, but instead of doing what a good many civic-minded celebrities do—that is, add their names to a benefit, send a check, and do a public announcement—Bono shows up. He is there in person. He personally tugs at the lapels of public officials whose advocacy and power are necessary to flesh out the programs into which Bono invests his time, his energy, and his presence. Moreover, he is a walking encyclopedia. He knows what he is talking about. He doesn't need aides around him whispering facts in his ear or passing him talking points. He is just amazing.

At the appointed hour on Thursday, I came to the Rainbow Room. A crowd of roughly two hundred merrymakers, including my successor, Dan Glickman, were collected there in this famous room. Senator Smith; his wife, Sharon; and his two gorgeous children greeted me with open affection. He mounted the platform to introduce me. He was overly generous, but I must confess that I inhaled everything as if it were true. And before I could respond, California governor Arnold Schwarzenegger, who had delayed his departure from New York to be present, stepped up.

I have known Arnold for more than twenty years. I have known his dazzling wife, Maria Shriver, since she was nine years old. So my connection with the governor and Maria is neither casual nor short-lived. Arnold, with his actor's skill and star's aura, had the audience rapt, and me as well, particularly when, as we say in Texas, he "bragged on" me. When he departed the rostrum, he gave me a bear hug, waved to the crowd, and was off. I count Arnold to be a new kind of political leader, who is learning each day how to be the kind of governor he wants to be. I support him. Win or lose, I support him.

My few remarks, offered in gratitude, were anticlimactic, but I was pleased beyond measure to have been honored by this extraordinary event.

A month earlier, I had been asked by the Democratic National Committee to preside over a special morning event at the Democratic convention in Boston. I was to be the chairman and emcee for a salute to veterans at the Bunker Hill Memorial. I began to wonder which saint was guiding my new prosperity, as I considered the fullness of the month. Truly, my cup runneth over.

At the appointed hour, punctually, I was on the rostrum at the Bunker Hill Memorial. The day was warmed by spangles of New England sun as some six hundred people, men, women, and some children, filled the chairs set up at the memorial. It was my duty to introduce a number of veterans of World War II, Korea, and Vietnam, which I did with mounting pride. I introduced General Wesley Clark, wounded three times in Vietnam, winner of two Silver Stars for his bravery in the field. When I came to Senator Max Cleland of Georgia, I asked the audience how this country could ever repay the selflessness of a warrior like Max Cleland. "How do you respond to a man who left two legs and one arm on a bloody battlefield in Vietnam and who never whined or felt sorry for himself?"

Then, what was the climax for me: my introduction of Senator Daniel Inouye of Hawaii. In 1945, he was a twenty-one-year-old first lieutenant in the 442nd Regimental Combat Team, operating in Italy. The 442nd was composed entirely of Japanese Americans, most of whose families were put in internment camps by the U.S. government. This unit was to end the war with the highest ratio of casualties and more medals for valor won on the battlefield than any other unit in the entire American armed services in World War II.

I told the story of Dan Inouye, how, just nine days before the war ended, this young officer was given the deadly task of rooting out and destroying three German machine-gun nests on an Italian hillside that were systematically butchering all who came near. Inouye gathered his platoon and ran into a withering hail of machine-gun fire that cut down most of his men. He was hit in the leg. Limping and bleeding, he kept going. Then he was hit again, this time in the stomach. Gasping in pain, he kept going. By some miracle, two of the machine-gun nests were destroyed. Inouye exhorted his troops to follow him up the hill to take out the final gun emplacement. His right hand gripped his last grenade. As he prepared to pull the pin, a Nazi rifle grenade severed his right arm from his body. Nearly unconscious, Inouye somehow reached with his left hand to snatch the grenade from his lifeless right hand. His teeth gripped the pin and pulled it out, and with his left hand he hurled the grenade into the remaining machine-gun embankment, scoring a direct hit, killing all inside, and silencing the guns. Inouye collapsed to the ground, bleeding heavily and in terrible pain, and passed out.

For this extraordinary feat of personal bravery above and beyond the call of duty, Daniel Inouye was awarded the Congressional Medal of Honor, the highest accolade our nation offers to men who have lifted the bar of courage to extraordinary heights. When I approached the end of my introduction, my voice cracked. I was close to breaking down. As a former combat pilot, I understood the fear that swallows a man in war, that stops his heart and invades every pore; yet the combat warrior does his duty, does what he is trained to do despite the terror in his veins. I suppose that was what young Dan Inouye felt. But I was uncertain whether I could have challenged death as he did, which was why, my voice cracking, I could not go on in my introduction of former lieutenant Daniel Inouye.

He came forward, smiling, the right sleeve of his coat jacket hanging freshly pressed but empty. As he came to the mike, I embraced him and whispered in his ear, "I love you, Dan." He gripped my back with his left hand, a hard, loving embrace. He knew how I felt.

That evening, the first night of the Democratic convention, I sat with Jill Abramson and Maureen Dowd, munching on sandwiches as the three of us watched the TV screen.

I count Jill and Maureen to be treasured friends, as well as Olympian journalism professionals. Maureen, in my judgment, is the premiere newspaper columnist in the country. Her prose is saucy, nimble-footed, sometimes dipped in venom, and on paper the equivalent of a heat-seeking missile fastened on whatever target she chooses. To be candid, I am mesmerized by Dowd's language and deeply grateful I am not in her sights. I might add her good friend, Kirk Douglas, and I both agree she is one sensually attractive lady.

Jill is a no-nonsense managing editor whose integrity is always visible in her duties at the *New York Times*. At one time she was one of the best writers at the *Wall Street Journal*. She speaks with the patois of soft, honeyed southern vowels in which others, including me, find wondrous wisdom.

As the convention events unfolded, Maureen scribbled notes (she was working), Jill focused on the screen, and suddenly there was

Bill Clinton, center stage with charm and ease sprinkling stardust over the audience. He proceeded to grab every viewer by the sleeve and turn them into speech groupies.

I remarked to Maureen, "Do you remember that column you wrote during Al Gore's campaign for the presidency [the Gore people had stuffed Clinton in the attic, keeping him off public platforms] and you wrote a column addressed to Gore, leading off with the line, 'Al, let the big dog run!' Remember that?"

She grinned. "Yes, I remember."

"Well," I said, "the Big Dog is running tonight."

Chapter 14

THE DEATH OF LEW WASSERMAN AND HOLLYWOOD'S GENERATIONAL LEADERSHIP CHANGE

The fabled Barry Diller, who headed Paramount Studios and then Fox Studios, and is now a reigning prince of the Internet.

On June 3, 2002, Lew Wasserman died. It was a black day for me. This man, who next to Lyndon Johnson had been the most important influence on my life, was now gone. At least once a week for more than three decades, we had talked on the phone, or had met for lunch in the Universal commissary, or had seen each other in a meeting.

His death was not a surprise. For the last year or so, Lew's body, seemingly invulnerable to mortal ills, began a slow descent, his formidable energy draining away. I often thought that the day Lew sold his company, something inside him began to withdraw. I don't know if that is so, but I believed it. I grieved when MCA was no longer Lew's company, even though he stayed on as chief executive. When the Japanese sold MCA to the Bronfman family, father and son paid him homage by naming the black tower the Lew Wasserman Building; still, it wasn't the same, nor would it ever be again.

Edie Wasserman, a power in Hollywood with or without her husband, asked me to be one of the speakers at Lew's memorial. It was held on July 15, 2002, in the Universal Amphitheater, with some five thousand in attendance. Other speakers included Sid Sheinberg, Lew's longtime right-hand man; Barry Diller, who had such large respect for Lew; Jeffrey Katzenberg, who like so many of the best and the brazen chose Lew as a model; Suzanne Pleshette; and Bill Clinton. Al Gore sat in the audience. I listened to them all, held in thrall by the memories they invoked. Suzie was hilarious, as always she is. Barry, Sid, and Jeffrey recounted their stories about Lew, and of course, Clinton was Clinton, the unsurpassed orator.

As for me, it was a hard day. No one on that stage owed more to Lew than I did. Without his insistence to the MPAA board of directors that I be made president, I would never have been an intimate participant in the events of Hollywood for almost thirty-nine years. I tried to explain to that memorial audience what Lew meant to me and to the film industry to which he devoted his adult life. I summoned all my strength not to get emotional when the reality of his gone-ness hit me.

I finished off my remarks with a story of the time I sat next to a burly official of the Teamsters union. I asked him what it was like to negotiate labor contracts with Lew. "Well," said the thickset man, "he was the toughest sumbitch I ever faced, a hard-fisted man. But when the negotiation was done and Lew stood up to shake my hand, I didn't need any lawyer memo to make sure what was agreed. In all my years, not once did Lew ever try to call off or renege on an agreement. You know something, that's what folks call integrity. I call it trusting a man to keep his word. Lew always kept his word."

As I look back, it became apparent to me that when Lew sold MCA Universal, an irrevocable change had taken place. He was still Lew Wasserman, whose shoes would never be filled by anyone, whose knowledge and experience in the movie and television world ranged far beyond that of any other. But the muscular influence that flowed from being in active command of a major Hollywood movie/TV giant had been reduced, and he knew it.

In those latter days, I made it a point to lunch with Lew at least once every two weeks. In the black tower that now bore his name; at the same table in the commissary that he occupied for years, with the same waitress taking his same lunch order of tuna salad; sitting in his office at his same antique English desk, its top polished to a sunlit shine with nary a paper to disturb its burnished glow—Lew carried on as he had for fifty-five-plus years. As Lew and I ate together in the Universal commissary, studio employees, stars, directors, agents, and others who were lunching there that noon would come by the table to pay respects. He was Lew Wasserman, legend, myth, king of a cinema empire. And yet, and yet, it was unreal because it was ending. I grieved even then. I never told him what I felt, that it was a colossal mistake to sell his company.

My wife and I continue to hold fast to his wife, Edie. Feisty, candid, perceptive, protective of her husband and his legacy, Edie is unique. She is wondrously generous. She and Lew have given many millions to provide full scholarships each year to more than a hundred students at several universities and many more millions to the Motion Picture & Television Country House and Hospital, which takes care of sick, needy former artists and employees of the industry. I'm happy to report that Casey Wasserman, Lew and Edie's grandson, carries on the family philanthropic tradition. Casey, who refused to enter the world of Hollywood so dominated by his grandfather, has carved out his own highly successful career as the founder of Wasserman Media, specializing in the marketing and representation of sports stars. With two children of his own, he and his wife, Laura, are nurturing a new generation of Wassermans. If heredity means anything, those kids have the right stuff.

HOLLYWOOD'S GENERATIONAL CHANGE OF LEADERSHIP

Within several weeks of my accession to the presidency of the MPAA, I received two calls. One was from the office of Walt Disney and the other was from the secretary to Sam Goldwyn, the man who produced the very first Hollywood film. Both of these founding fathers asked me to visit them.

I showed up first at the Disney studio lot. I was ushered into the simply furnished office of the grandest genius of all cinema history: Walt Disney. He rose from behind his desk, shook my hand, and introduced me to his brother, Roy, and two of his young assistants. He motioned me to a chair.

Walt Disney was rather gaunt, his cheekbones prominent in a face that was not memorable. But I do remember his eyes. They fastened on me with intensity. Walt remarked on the content of live-action films. A growing number of these films, he commented, were not in his judgment suitable for American families. By inference, he intended me to know that the Disney concept was just the opposite. He urged me to visit his animation artists, who he allowed were the best in the world. None of the others in the room said anything, they just listened to their leader. After some twenty minutes or so, the meeting was over.

Walt told me again how glad he was to meet me. He hoped that

I would take leadership in holding fast to the moral precepts of America. A staunch conservative Republican, Walt knew of my White House background with President Johnson. I daresay he was not ready to endorse Lyndon Johnson's version of the Great Society. He was, however, courteous enough to steer the conversation to other spheres. He accompanied me to the door and with genuine friendliness bade me on my way.

A few months later, Walt Disney died. I was always grateful that I had that rare opportunity to be in his presence. It is difficult to overestimate the influence of Walt Disney not just on Hollywood, but on the entire world of visual entertainment. Without his innovative mind, the future would have been far different from the one later generations were to enjoy.

Some few weeks later, I accepted Mr. Sam Goldwyn's invitation to lunch with him. My lunch with Mr. Goldwyn took place at his sumptuous Beverly Hills home, adorned with priceless art and furnishings. As I sat before him, just the two of us, served by his butler on the veranda overlooking an exquisite garden, I was more than a bit awestruck. Here was the original pioneer of the movie industry. He had been present at its dawning, with the premiere of his first major film, *The Squaw Man*, directed by Cecil B. DeMille in the early part of the twentieth century. And here I was, sitting with him, talking with him, a guest in his home.

I plied him with questions. He seemed pleased that I was so keenly interested in the history that he could describe so uniquely because he had both lived it and created it. He took me through the years, commenting on Hollywood legends, those who fought him as well as those with whom he made peace. I can report that he didn't spare the rod on a number of his former peers.

How fortunate I was, for within a month I had met and talked with two of the greatest pioneers in all of world cinema.

I catalog in my memory those who literally invented Hollywood: Sam Goldwyn, L. B. Mayer, Harry Cohn, Carl Laemmle, Adolph Zukor (I met Mr. Zukor on the occasion of his one hundredth birthday party), the Schenck brothers, and Irving Thalberg. I was lucky enough to get to know all of the second generation of Hollywood leaders. Lew Wasserman of MCA Universal and Arthur Krim of

United Artists were first among equals. They were the first two movie leaders I met who from time to time actually based decisions not on what was good for their company, but on what was in the long-term best interest of the industry.

Krim died much too early. Wasserman prevailed long enough to mingle with the third generation, which included some splendidly creative, awesomely smart men and women. But to my view, the sale of MCA to Matsushita Electric was a watershed moment for Hollywood. The third and fourth generations now took over.

Since my first meeting with the movie moguls in New York City in mid-1966, cataclysmic change had taken place. The glory years of Warner Bros.' Jack Warner and Fox's Darryl Zanuck ended. The studios, formerly little kingdoms presided over by absolute monarchs, were no longer sovereign states. In the mid-1970s, the contract system that bound movie stars, directors, writers, and producers to studios in roles of indentured serfs was buried in Forest Lawn Cemetery. The movie community had become a fragmented, rapidly evolving landscape. Now the Hollywood studios were divisions of giant multinational corporations, their revenues part of an immense spreadsheet where they represented a minor percentage of worldwide sales and profits. Reporting earnings every quarter, these large film/TV/home video corporations were infected with global anxieties: mounting demands for higher profits to pacify security analysts, the dismaying expense of film production, pressure on studio executives to repeat blockbuster hits and banish failures.

The changing DNA of the movie industry became glaringly obvious when the Bronfman family, headed by Edgar Bronfman Jr., soon purchased the majority share of MCA from Matsushita. Edgar's first move was a brilliant one: He brought in Ron Meyer, a founding partner of Creative Artists Agency, one of the most powerful talent agencies in Hollywood, whose other founders included Michael Ovitz and Bill Haber, among others.

Ovitz was aloof, sometimes stern, attracted to ancient Asian doctrines of war and management. Ron Meyer was different; he was invariably warm and a shrewd observer of the human condition, so that he understood artists and their real and imagined personal anxieties. He handled all these with a steadying hand. The plain fact is you liked to be near Ron. He also had a feel for talent and good story-telling.

MCA Universal is now NBC Universal, and its commander, Bob Wright, understood Ron's assets. Wright chose Meyer to stay on as head of the studio, which to my mind bodes well for NBC Universal's future. I must confess my affection for Ron. He early on told me, "Jack, whenever you need me I'll be there, no matter what." And he was. Often when an issue was being hotly debated among the MPAA member companies, he would say to me, "How do you feel about this? If you were in my shoes, what would you do?" He always trusted my judgment. It's hard not to feel warm toward that kind of colleague and friend. And if in the end your career is judged by your company's success at the box office and on the TV screen, that works for Ron, as well.

I was present at the birth of the new Disney company. I was at the home of Frank Wells in early 1984 when he and Michael Eisner were quietly discussing the offer made by the Bass brothers of Texas, who had just purchased a large percentage of Disney stock. Also present that evening was Al Checchi, one of the fiscal boy wonders trained at Harvard Business School, who was then working for the Bass family. Sid Bass had first sought to appoint Wells as chairman/CEO and to bring in Eisner as president. But Eisner demurred. He would come aboard only if he was the CEO. To everyone's astonishment, Wells had no objection.

Frank Wells was as physically attractive as any movie star. He was superbly educated, a first-class lawyer with a class-A intellect and charm to match. He and Eisner were a made-to-order pair—Eisner the volatile creative type and Wells the conciliator. It was a magical team. Wells was also a fearless adventurer. Before the Disney experience, he took a year off from his duties at Warner Bros. to climb the seven highest peaks in the world and then wrote a book about it.

It was on that evening at Wells's home (I am still not sure why they asked me to be present) that Michael and Frank began to shape their plans. They brought in the best people they could summon, Jeffrey Katzenberg and Rich Frank and Dick Cook. They all threw themselves into seven-day workweeks. They resuscitated Disney classics lying inert in the archives. They widened Disney's viewer reach. And with unmatched intensity, they sent Disney soaring upward. It was an amazing resurrection of a legendary studio, once languishing and now on corporate steroids.

Eisner continued on after Frank Wells's death in a tragic helicopter crash. Shortly after, at the Herbert Allen conference in Sun Valley, Eisner suffered a mild heart attack and was flown to Los Angeles for surgery. This was followed by a rift between Eisner and the tireless, driven Katzenberg. Then Eisner hired Michael Ovitz, setting in motion a saga that even now reads like a bad novel made into a bad movie. It was all so depressing.

Nevertheless, anyone who had purchased $10,000 of Disney stock when Eisner took over the company and held on to it would have earned some $300,000 twenty years later. Not a bad return. It's what Wall Street describes as "stockholder value." For twenty years, Eisner guided Disney to unprecedented profits and growth in market value. Eisner rode that mighty wave with an all-consuming pride that the Disney company was being reborn under his command. In fact it was.

Bob Iger, tall, handsome, quietly effective, had a stormy time when Michael Ovitz arrived at Disney via the hand of Eisner. Iger's principal chore was giving mouth-to-mouth resuscitation to the ABC television network. Iger persevered with no outward signs of discontent. Meanwhile, ABC, in the doldrums, suddenly came alive on Iger's watch. Two new TV shows went on stream—*Desperate Housewives* and *Lost*—and viewers flocked to watch them. Iger became Sir Lancelot, and rightly so. As the new CEO of Disney, he brings to the table long, successful creative experience in a madly unpredictable arena and an easy, unpretentious manner. He understands with clarity what Disney needs to do. I have little doubt he will do it.

When Jeffrey Katzenberg departed Disney, he engineered something with two close friends, Steven Spielberg and David Geffen, that had not been done in a generation: They started a brand-new top-of-the-line movie studio from scratch, called DreamWorks. Katzenberg's creative command of animated films was something to behold. DreamWorks spun off its highly successful animation sector into a separate company headed by Katzenberg, and in 2005 DreamWorks itself was sold to Viacom (Paramount Studios).

ry Semel's prime assets were a relentless energy and total
.ce in his own judgments, which time and again were magically
.l. The movie/TV world is so riven with the fear of making a
.ake that anyone who exudes assurance without the corrosive
. of arrogance has momentum. Semel had it. He and Daly
.amless team. They both resigned at the same time. Bob went
.n the Los Angeles Dodgers and later Save the Children.
.ry parachuted into what was, for him, the virgin territory of
.alley, Sunnyvale, California. He purchased a huge block of
.stock and became CEO. At that time, Yahoo! was stumbling.
.ave Yahoo! a new direction. He kept asking questions and de-
.g answers. Mainly he kept asking, "Why are we giving away
.ing we do? Have we ever thought about charging for some
.Hey, not a lousy question. He so stirred up that high-tech
.losing firm that it soared to merry new vistas of profitability.
. canny quick-study habits surprised the hell out of Wall Street
.o! stock prices hit the stratosphere. If anyone doubted Semel's
.rm visionary gaze in the movie business, his rousing success at
.dismantled those critics.
.t the stability at Warner continued. Barry Meyer, who signed
.he beginning of the Daly regime, became CEO, with Alan
.s president. The transition to Barry Meyer as chairman and
.vas swift, with neither creative bumps nor fiscal potholes.
. central personal prize is his long confirmed sense of integrity,
.vith his self-effacing, anti-publicity-seeking comportment. He
.ed, respected, and admired by employees, by competitors, by
.eriors at Time Warner's headquarters in New York. It's as sim-
.hat. He is far more often right than wrong, which makes him
.date for most valuable player in any league.
.n Horn, Harvard MBA, became president. Horn got his early
.s as a relentless, hard-driving youngster with the incredibly
.ful TV programming team of Norman Lear, Jerry Perenchio,
.d Yorkin. This trio created such titanic hits as *All in the Family*,
. and many more. Horn learned well on a very fast creative
.Ie has a deserved reputation for caring deeply about the art of
.naking, which favorably impresses the talent, storytellers who
. do business with Warner Bros.—and with Alan Horn. There

Steven Spielberg, as everyone over t
greatest cinematic storyteller of this gei
his films, *ET*, *Schindler's List*, and *Saving
movies, each so different from the oth
Spielberg's cinematic genius. At the age o
Sid Sheinberg, then president of MCA U
a resolve to direct his first TV movie bef
did. The TV film was *Duel*, a scary thrill
visible driver. Hard on its heels came his fi
land Express, starring Goldie Hawn. The S
rainbow rising.

David Geffen is the exemplar of th
story. He started out all alone as the mana
through a faultless facility for spotting ta
and genius for the business side of a merd
supernatural sense of timing, he rose to
world with his own label, Geffen Recor
agreed to be a billionaire and then some.
It is far more valuable to have David Ge
enemy. He never deserts his friends. He
I count David as a friend, which pleases m

Warner Bros. can claim the longest-l
ment team, reaching back almost thirty y
agent–turned–studio boss just at the end o
founding Warner brothers, with Jack Wai
Over the last sixty years, only four men ha
Jack Warner on the Warner Bros. lot—W
Bob Daly, and now Barry Meyer. That's sta
in Bob Daly, who had been successful as he

When Daly took command of Warner
agement style and team that for two dec
ahead of the curve and resisted mistakes. Se
Daly executed a masterstroke. He design
chairman and co-CEO. It is rare in U.S. bu
out pressure from the outside, to share ulti
colleague. It bespeaks a confidence, inner
Daly's part.

Te
confide
success
big mis
elemen
were a
on to r

Te
Silicon
Yahoo!
Semel
mandir
everytl
of it?"
money
Semel'
as Yah
long-t
Yahoo

B
on in
Horn
CEO
Barry'
along
is trus
his su
ple as
a cand

A
tutori
succes
and B
Maud
track.
movie
want

is about Alan a genuine warmth toward those who work for him and with him that is very soothing to actors, directors, and writers. These qualities are talismans of immense worth in Hollywood.

Time Warner was commanded by Richard Parsons, a tall man who was invariably gracious to all who worked for him. Everyone called him a great diplomat, but when the occasion required, he could be tough but fair.

Fox, now owned by Rupert Murdoch, began its long ascent into the future when Barry Diller, representing the third generation of leadership, came aboard. Diller was a college dropout who was so smart, it was at times quite scary. When he came to Fox (then owned by the late massive Marvin Davis, billionaire Denver oilman), Diller made a decision at which the rest of Hollywood hooted derisively: He was going to construct a brand-new fourth television network. What one soon learns is never to underestimate Diller.

According to what we call "reliable sources," Barry was a rough, tough boss, ripping the paint off the wall with some of his scorching responses to what he judged to be foul-ups and jerk-offs from overpaid associates. He never let up. Slowly, inevitably, Diller exacted from his colleagues a round-the-clock assault on the television landscape. Fox grew its station complement and began to create programs with strong audience appeal. The TV critics dismissed them as meager fare. Critics may rail, but audiences are what count. The Fox network and station population grew. Fox TV prospered. Diller had won.

When Diller departed Fox, instead of moving to another studio, as he could have done, he took almost a year off, wandering in his car through the country, making special stops in Silicon Valley and Seattle, home to Microsoft. He bought the complexities of a new technological tool (for him), a Mac PowerBook computer. Like some curious explorer in a strange new land, he saw in the digital landscape the blossoming of a whole new world that he intended to enter, reshape to his own design, and master. And he did just that. With his digital company, InterActiveCorp, Barry Diller now stands astride the world that has transformed the way we communicate, are informed, and buy products. Diller got inside early. He always does.

A Diller story: Some years ago, Barry called me to have lunch with him in his office in his then role as CEO of Fox. When we gathered, I sat across from him at his desk. He was in a festive mood. "Jack," he said, "I would like you to come over here with me. I'd like you to resign from the MPAA, join me at Fox. What do you think about that?"

I was, of course, surprised. I yield to no man in my admiration for Barry, with his considerable assets of mind and prophetic vision and his always fertile seedbed of inventive ideas. I feel for Diller a genuine rapport, the sort of affection you feel for a kindred spirit and for someone whose soaring skills enlist your boundless admiration.

Without thinking too long, I said, "Barry, what would I do here?"

He said, "We'll figure that out when you get here. We'll have some fun, and we'll get a lot done."

I leaned forward. "You know how I feel about you as a friend. Right now our relationship is like this—" I spread my hands in front of me, both of them level with the other. "But if I come here to work at Fox, our relationship will be like this—" Here I put my left hand down about an inch or two below my right hand. I went on, "Barry, I love you, you know that, but I don't want to work for you."

He laughed merrily and put his head back on his chair. "Well, okay, then." The laugh relaxed into a wide grin. "Let's have lunch." He got up, put an arm around my shoulder, and marched me into the next room, where lunch was set. We had, as usual, an invigorating conversation.

The fourth generation of leadership at Fox came forward in the person of Peter Chernin, president and chief operating officer of News Corp. under chairman Rupert Murdoch. News Corp. is truly an empire, with TV stations, TV network, film studio, direct satellite delivery, publishing, foreign entertainment, and news delivery systems in the United States, a number of EU countries, and Asia. When you try to make sense of the Murdoch empire, you need a Rand McNally world map.

Rupert Murdoch is soft-spoken, a quiet man, courteous, not at all intrusive. Yet somehow the genes inside him took shape in a rare architecture that provided him qualities of long-range prophetic vision and the resolve to implement what he wanted to create, a combination few possess. His father, Sir Keith Murdoch, was a valorous journalist who first broke the story of the abysmal failure in distant

Gallipoli, wherein brave Australian soldiers were needlessly cut down in World War I. When his father died, Rupert inherited a tiny newspaper in Adelaide, Australia. That was it. From that small publication grew one of the mightiest media empires in history. It is one of those fantasy stories come true that business historians itch to tell. One of Murdoch's prime assets is the ability to pick the right men and women to man the ramparts of News Corp. He confirmed his superior judgment of leaders when he chose Peter Chernin to be his right arm, the right man at the very right place.

In November 2005, I presented Peter with an award from the Museum of Television and Radio for his extraordinary achievements in our industry. What follows is part of what I said in introducing him. It's a summary of a man comfortable in his own skin, ready to challenge the future:

> "There are three secrets to Peter Chernin's success. The first is that he has what Mr. Churchill called 'the seeing eye.' Peter sees, as Churchill so melodiously phrased it, 'beneath the surface of things, he knows what is on the other side of the brick wall, he follows the hunt three fields before the throng.' He clearly sees what others see only dimly, if at all. Peter owns this asset of measureless worth, the gift of vision.
>
> "The second secret is that Peter is one of the very few who operate a large business enterprise whose personal whole life experience has been bound up intimately in creative storytelling. That is, he is possessed of a thorough understanding of the alchemy of dramatic narrative, as well as being comfortable and confident in the fiscal mysteries of spreadsheets. That's a pretty good combination for business success in the wild, improbable media world.
>
> "The third secret is this: In a crisis, he is the ultimate cool, unflappable leader, imperturbable, in control. The entire world could fall upon him and you would find him there standing in the ruins, undismayed, which is why no difficulty can overcome his central will or rupture his sense of purpose."

In addition to these qualities, Peter has had the good sense to surround himself at Fox with two fast-moving creative executives who gave new vigor to the studio—Jim Gianopulos and Tom Rothman, who share authority for running a successful film enterprise.

Toward the end of my MPAA tenure, when John Calley, one of Hollywood's creative giants, moved on, Sony Pictures' U.S. commander, Sir Howard Stringer, made a surprising choice to replace him. From global book publisher Penguin, he plucked their chief, Michael Lynton, to become Sony Pictures' CEO. I liked Michael immediately. He was neither flamboyant nor a kinetic presence, but you always knew he was there and not for show. He is more intellectual than a mere fiscal baron. He was a top Harvard Business School graduate, the second of the HBS breed to rule a studio. (Alan Horn, president of Warner Bros., is the other. To my way of thinking, which may be a little biased, if you have an MBA from Harvard, you can't be all bad.)

Alan Horn, Michael, and I were a threesome on a panel, part of a day-long "Harvard in Hollywood" conference bringing together executives, directors, actors, and writers who graduated from Harvard to talk about their craft and adventures in Lotus-Land. I was mighty proud of both Michael and Alan. They were funny, absolutely without ego, and they had the audience mesmerized as they spoke with brevity and wit about the travails of a movie studio decision maker—Alan from his years in the creative arena and Michael from his storytelling background in print.

When Michael heard I was writing this book, he called me to meet with him. In his office, he gave me a tutorial in marketing books. "Spend time with the booksellers. They will do more to increase your book sales than anyone else because they know more than anyone about what readers want to read. If they like you and your book, you're on your way to the bestseller list," he told me. It is a piece of advice I do not intend to ignore. I am grateful to him.

One formidable Hollywood titan was Sherry Lansing, the first woman to head production at a major studio (Fox). She became a seriously successful independent producer, and then she became president of Paramount. She also became the heroine of every woman in Hollywood, including my daughter Courtenay, an executive at Warner Bros. Courtenay said to me, "Daddy, in Hollywood every young and not-so-young woman wants to be Sherry Lansing." A model and actress in her twenties, Sherry Lansing is so charming that when she turns down a producer's project, relations remain cordial. She's married to celebrated director Bill Friedkin, who brought to life two of the greatest stories of all time, *The Exorcist* and *The French Connection*.

Sherry and Jon Dolgen were also a remarkably successful professional team for over a decade at Paramount, with Sherry president of the studio and Dolgen its chairman and CEO. Dolgen, famed for his aggressive (some would say combative) management style, had some mystic force that made him a very able executive. I admired him greatly.

Sumner Redstone could have been one of the nation's finest antitrust lawyers when he graduated from Harvard Law School, but instead he took over the family theater business, a string of some hundred movie theaters, a good many of which were drive-ins. From that modest beginning he built a huge media kingdom that stretched around the world, including Paramount Studios, CBS, MTV, children's cable programs, etc. It was an astonishing accomplishment that few businessmen in America can match.

When Sumner Redstone decided to split his empire into two entities, with Viacom retaining the cable and movie divisions and CBS taking over TV and radio, the latter division was commanded by Les Moonves, arguably one of the two or three wisest, toughest, most successful TV executives living today. In the new Viacom setup, Tom Freston ascended to the chairman's role. Freston, who spearheaded MTV's dominance of the youth market, has the smarts and vision to embellish Paramount's future. He selected Barry Grey, a first-class producer and manager, to run Paramount. Grey came to that post having established a winning record in the hottest competitive tar pit in the country. At this writing, Tom Freston is no longer . CEO of Viacom. His departure is just another indication of the movie industry's unpredictability.

As Hollywood moves forward under the leadership of this new generation of leaders, I find myself filled with optimism for the future. This is an impressive group of visionary executives who see beyond the present, and are superbly equipped to run massive, complex, creative businesses in a brutally competitive, extremely volatile global environment. I count myself fortunate to have had up-close and intimate relationships with the best brains in the industry. I learned from them. I enjoyed being around them. I believe they trusted my judgment. These are grades as high as I could hope to give and to receive.

PART IV

RACING
TO THE
FUTURE

$$Chapter\ 15$$

STEPPING DOWN AND SUMMING UP

My gorgeous family. *Front row:* my younger daughter, Alexandra; my oldest child, Courtenay; and my fabulous granddaughter, Lola Lorraine. *Second row:* my perfect grandson, Wiley; my beautiful wife of forty-four years, Mary Margaret; and my movie-star-handsome son-in-law, Patrick Roberts, husband to Courtenay. *Upper row:* me and my only son, John.

It was in mid-May 2002, as I took stock of what was then thirty-six years in Hollywood, that I began to think for the first time about stepping down as the MPAA's leader. I wasn't tired, mentally or physically. I believe I was in the best physical shape of my life. My memory was never better, and my energy was robust. I loved what I was doing. I still sprang out of bed every morning eager to face the day. The long hours I devoted to the job, the furious travel to all the continents, the commuting to and from the West Coast, the ceaseless preparations to understand and master the issues, and my speeches, the interactions with my colleagues—none of this was work at all; it was sheer fun. I enjoyed, even loved, the challenges, contesting with the best and the toughest, debating with adversaries of the moment, thrust and counterthrust. I wasn't afraid of what lay ahead. I rejoiced as I dashed toward the future.

Yet I knew I should make my move to step down, and soon. Stirring inside me was LBJ's oft-stated admonition "Always leave at the height of a party." He used to say, "When they want you to keep on speaking, that's the time to stop, instead of twenty minutes later hearing them say, 'When is that old goat going to shut up?'"

I knew the studio bosses wouldn't want me to leave now. I knew them well enough to know they were more than satisfied that the MPAA operated at a high-velocity level of energy, efficiency, initiative, and success both in this country and around the world. I was immodest enough to believe they had both faith and pride in my leadership. I truly believed they trusted my judgment. I had no anxieties about my place in Hollywood, none at all. What did nag at me was the certainty that nothing lasts. I had seen too many high-profile people in Hollywood and Washington who hung on too long, deluded into believing it would go on forever. What I did not want to face, if I stayed in place for three or four more years, were murmurings from the studio enclaves, "When is that old bastard going to leave?"

In early 2003, I took aside my onetime MPAA colleague Matt Gerson, a wise, thoughtful lawyer and leader, for a bit of lunch. I valued Matt's counsel. I told him of my departure thoughts, and my plan to set the stage for my successor. Matt, a first-class lawyer with superior judgment, a rising star in Washington, was at that time the head of Universal Studios' government affairs office. He knew all the players in the MPAA. He listened intently and asked only one question: "Is this something you really want to do?" Good question. But it was one I had already answered to myself. Yes.

When I explained to Matt my reasoning, he understood. He even laughed when I mentioned to him that if I stepped down this year, 2003, my tenure would be coincident with the terms of eight presidents. I would have served the equivalent of six and a half terms as a senator and nineteen terms as a member of the House. He commented, "Well, I have to admit you never were seriously challenged in the primaries or the general election."

I knew I wanted to depart on my schedule, my timing. In short, I wanted to write my own departure script.

In July and August 2003, I held private, one-on-one meetings in Los Angeles with each of the studio commanders. I told them confidentially that I wanted to confer with them about a successor, with the hope of having that successor on board by the first of the New Year 2004. They all expressed surprise at my decision, and asked me to reconsider. But I made it clear that the time had come. Now I had to find my successor.

I called a meeting of the MPAA board, the first of several that led to the decision to offer the job to Congressman Billy Tauzin, Republican chairman of the House Commerce Committee, though it was a close thing between Tauzin and Senator John Breaux, who, like Tauzin, had announced his retirement from the Congress. Tauzin was a skilled general in the House who lost no battles and whose merry humor masked a tough resolve. It was a toss-up, but finally the studios gave Tauzin's candidacy the nod. I immediately called Billy. He was most definitely interested. I dispatched to him three weighty thick black binders—the latest business plan, a huge stack of material relating to issues facing us here and abroad, and the MPAA budget.

Billy and I sat in my library at my home on a Saturday. He had an impish grin on his face. "Hey, Jack," he said, "this job ought to be handled by three people, not just one. I got dizzy going through these binders." We both had a nice laugh, and Billy made it clear he was ready to get specific. Beginning the next day, I met with his designated lawyer and we began to negotiate a contract. I agreed to pretty much everything the lawyer requested.

A contract was drawn up, vetted by the member companies and sent on to Tauzin's lawyer. All that was needed was Billy Tauzin's signature and the deal was done. My successor would have been chosen. A couple of days later, in early 2004, Billy called me. His voice was contrite. "Jack, this is a hard call for me to make. But I am going to have to pass on the job offer."

I was more than a little astonished. "Can you tell me more, Billy?"

"Well," he said, "I have been offered a position by another group which I have to say is much heftier in compensation than the MPAA's offer, which I know was a generous one. I'm sorry, Jack, I do hope you'll understand. You and I have been friends for over twenty years. I want to keep that friendship."

Oddly, I did understand. I probably would have reached the same conclusion if our positions had been reversed. Billy was a longtime friend and still is. Through the grapevine, which in Washington is the most active plant on the planet, I learned that the pharmaceutical industry had been pursuing him. He is at this moment the president and CEO of Pharma, the giant association that represents the U.S. pharmaceutical industry in this country and around the world.

I understood. I always remembered Barry Diller's classic line, one of the most compact, compelling responses to adversity I ever heard. When his battle with Sumner Redstone over the purchase of Paramount Pictures reached the very serious money level and aimed to go higher, Barry simply departed the field, saying in language only he could have composed, "We lost. They won. Next." What a brilliant valedictory! That's exactly what I was thinking: "Next."

But now I had a problem. I immediately called Senator Breaux.

"Thanks, Jack," he said, "but I have some fixed plans in place, which means I have to say no. But I'm grateful for the call." More conference calls with the studios. Peter Chernin suggested we go the headhunter route, so we asked Spencer Stuart and that firm's high-quality search executive, Jim Citrin, to take over the selection process. Jim and his stellar crew of associates quickly put forward some twenty-five names, with full dossiers on each. All were high caliber. This list was winnowed down to four. We went through them deliberately, but I knew that the best candidate was Dan Glickman.

I had known Dan for many years. He was a congressman from Wichita, Kansas, serving some eighteen years. To be elected and re-elected as a Democrat—and Jewish—from that most conservative part of the country meant you had to have superior qualities of leadership and powers of persuasion. Dan also served as secretary of agriculture in the cabinet of President Bill Clinton. So he was outfitted with a gold-standard background rich in real-life experience. When one of my Hollywood friends questioned the worth of being secretary of agriculture as an experience needed in the MPAA job, I quickly informed him, "Remember, the secretary of agriculture knows a lot about manure."

Dan's most alluring quality is his fluent sense of humor; he sees a bit of fun in situations where others see only gloom. I have often remarked that I count dullness to be the one sin for which there is no expiation. Glickman is never dull. I had total confidence that Dan would be a superior leader of the MPAA, and to my delight, I didn't have to "lobby" my colleagues. They saw as I did that Glickman had the skills to take the MPAA into a successful, ascendant future. I've always believed that a departing leader has to be measured by how wise he is in picking his successor. Gratefully, as of this writing, I can say that wisdom has been completely borne out.

With the MPAA board ready to hire Dan, there occurred a strange intrusion. I had heard and read about the so-called K Street Project. It was reputed to be the brainchild of Tom DeLay, Republican House majority leader, and some of his House colleagues and Republican lobbyists. It was, according to the rumor mill, a concentrated effort by the House Republican leadership to thwart the choice of Democrats to fill important trade association jobs or corporate government affairs offices in Washington. If an opening for a new chairman or president of an influential association appeared, heavy pressure was applied to its board of directors to make sure a certified, loyal Republican got the job. Most associations caved.

I had always considered this kind of political hardball odious, but it had bypassed the MPAA. Then, two weeks before I planned to announce Dan Glickman as my successor, I got the phone call. It was a friend of mine, a Republican lobbyist of some repute. My lobbyist friend said, "Now, Jack, please understand I am just a messenger."

"All right," I said, "what message do you have and from whom?"

"I have been asked to tell you that if the MPAA chooses a Democrat for your job, Tom DeLay and the House leadership will not take this kindly."

My spine began to stiffen. So the K Street Project was not some phantom. It was real. And it was here right in my face. Trying to keep the rasp out of my voice, I said, "I understand, and this is my response. First, I tried to hire a Republican and he turned me down. But I sought Billy Tauzin not because he was a Republican, but because I thought he was best fitted for the job. Second, this job is nonpartisan. I have run it so for more than thirty years. I have as many Republican friends in Congress as I have Democrats. That policy will continue. Third, this job will go to whomever my colleagues and I believe to be the best person to lead the MPAA. What political party he belongs to will have no value. Fourth, and hear me clearly, you tell Mr. DeLay and the House leadership that I don't take kindly to anyone who puts this kind of pressure on me and the MPAA. Understood?"

The lobbyist tried to be pleasant. "I told you, Jack, I am only carrying a message. Yes, I understand, and I will pass on what you said."

I decided not to disclose this distasteful conversation to anyone. I wanted to present Glickman as my successor with no distractions. Disclosing this unfortunate phone conversation from the clawhammer K Street Project would set off a noisy debate in the press. That I didn't want. Or need.

On July 1, 2004, at 12:30 p.m. Washington time at the Hay-Adams Hotel, I stood on a rostrum with Dan Glickman by my side to announce the succession of leadership at the MPAA. I heard no more from the K Street Project. But, alas, after Glickman took over officially, there were press reports from unnamed sources about how the MPAA would suffer politically as a result of Dan's accession to the job because he was a Democrat. Petty stuff, I thought, and nasty as well.

On September 1, 2004, it was over. Thirty-eight years and four months ago, I departed the White House to enter my Hollywood life. That is a long time by any gauge—far longer than I ever thought I would spend. I was on the job through five decades, from the sixties to the first decade of the new century.

My active day-to-day management of the MPAA had indeed ended. But I had the warm satisfaction that comes to anyone who has lashed his whole person to a belief in something that has heft and substance. How deep an impact I made in the movie world over those long years will be decided by those final arbiters time and retrospection. But I feel good knowing I gave it all I had for a long, long time.

The studios were more than generous with farewell gifts I never expected. First, there was the ceremony on December 6, 2004, when, before several hundred studio executives, actors, writers, directors, and friends, I planted my feet and hands in concrete at Grauman's Chinese Theater in the center of Hollywood, joining some 250 other men and women of old and modern Hollywood. Just across from Grauman's is the venerable Hollywood Roosevelt Hotel. In front of the hotel, inserted in the sidewalk, is my "star" on Hollywood Boulevard. It's the one place I don't mind having folks walking all over me.

At the reception following my concrete mixing at Grauman's, Peter Chernin, speaking on behalf of the other studio chiefs, astonished me by announcing that the MPAA building in Washington would bear my name on its entrance. And then, in mid-2005, at the MPAA office on the corner of Sixteenth and I streets, one block from the White House, a very special celebration was held. To that morning event presided over by Dan Glickman, the new CEO of the MPAA, came a crowd of friends, members of Congress, and the heads of the six studio members of the MPAA: Peter Chernin of Fox, Barry Meyer of Warner Bros., Ron Meyer of NBC Universal, Brad Grey of Paramount, Michael Eisner and Bob Iger of Disney, and Michael Lynton of Sony Pictures. Speaking generous words about me were Senator Ted Stevens, Republican from Alaska; Senator Daniel Inouye, Democrat from Hawaii; Congressman John Dingell, Democrat from Michigan; and Congressman Henry Hyde, Republican from Illinois.

The event commemorated the new name of the MPAA building in Washington, the Jack Valenti Building. I had some mighty fine emotions rolling through me on that day. My comment was, "How good it is to hear eulogies about yourself and at the same time have a building named for you while you are still alive!"

But stepping down is not retirement. Retirement to me is a synonym for decay. The idea of just knocking about, playing golf or whatever, is so unattractive to me that I would rather be nibbled to death by ducks. So long as I am doing what I choose to do and love to do, work is not work but total fun.

So it was especially fortuitous when, about six months before I relinquished the CEO job at the MPAA, I was visited by a good friend and high-achieving business consultant, Adam Waldman. With him was Ed Scott, an unpretentious, highly successful high-tech company founder who sold his business creation for a ton of money and was now devoted to philanthropy. They wanted me to take on the task of being a part-time president of Friends of the Global Fight Against AIDS, Tuberculosis & Malaria.

The prime motivation of the Friends organization is, first, to rouse the American public to the horrors inflicted on millions of people by these three pandemics and, second, to nourish and support the Global Fund, situated in Geneva, Switzerland, funded and founded in 2001 by the G8 countries. The more I listened to Adam and Ed, the more I digested the material they offered me, the more I came to believe this was work I wanted to do.

Why? Working in the White House was the only time in my restless life that I was free from all personal ambition. Working for LBJ and being part—even a tiny part—of his battle to remove forever the ills, barriers, and hopelessness that had plagued many millions of Americans for too long was so gratifying to me. I judged my new work at the Friends organization would stir once more some selfless motivations within me. And it most assuredly has.

The Global Fund's sole mission is to combat on all continents the scourging pandemics of AIDS, malaria, and TB. Its record of achievement is manifest in the strides it has made in holding back the huge tide of death. The fund operates at this date in 132 countries. Its daily aim is to keep a lot of sick people from dying and to cure those who have a chance for survival. It's the kind of labor that gives me good reason to rise each morning with new zest for the onrushing day.

The Friends of the Global Fight is a vital enterprise. We have a first-class executive director, Natasha Bilimoria, a woman of considerable talents with steely resolve, and a board of prestigious, energetic men and women. I am proud to be playing a small role in what has to be the world's most important task—ridding the world of three pandemics that slaughter too many people, especially too many little children. Maddening frustration comes with the knowledge that 6 million people die each year from one of these pandemics—3 million from AIDS, 2 million from malaria (mostly children), and 1 million from TB. This is the equivalent of forty-three 747 jumbo jets, fully loaded, crashing every day—or the equivalent of New York City entirely populated by orphans.

Not since the Black Death, which almost depopulated Europe during the Middle Ages, has this planet borne witness to such horrors. In 2006, on behalf of the Global Fund, I visited the KwaZulu Natal province in southern South Africa. What ripped my heart apart was the little children whose entire extended families have died from disease. The children are so starved for affection they cling to a visitor's legs, unwilling to let go. When you look into their eyes, it's hard not to weep. When they wake in the night, crying out for someone to come to them, no one does. How do we live with that? How?

In 2005, the Gates Foundation surveyed the Friends of the Global Fight. From that assessment came a grant from the most extraordinary of all philanthropic enterprises, the Bill and Melinda Gates Foundation, which has helped our efforts immeasurably.

Meanwhile I still pay close attention to physical fitness. I don't need any medical exhortations to know that if your body is not instantly responsive to your commands, your brain is going to grow slack as well. I am, as the cliché goes, doing just fine.

The future is where the fun will be and that's why I'm racing there as fast as I can.

But more than that, it's a time for me to rejoice in my family.

I confess that I was gone away from home too much when my children were younger and in school. I was traveling the world and this country on behalf of the movie industry, commuting three times a month to Los Angeles, soaring off to Asia, Latin America, Europe, and Africa. I was not there sometimes when I should have been there to help Mary Margaret with our kids. Once, having dinner last year with my son, John, I said, "Son, I want to use this moment to apologize to you for missing too many of your baseball games when you were on St. Alban's team. I missed a key game when St. Alban's won the title and you were selected for the all-city team in your league. I am so very, very sorry."

John smiled. "Dad, you were there when you could be. I have always been so proud of you, so you never have to apologize to me for anything." But I knew I did.

My children have grown up with their heads on straight, all good citizens, owing to the firm and loving, "being there" hand and steady guidance of Mary Margaret. I'm no child behavior expert, but I am a confirmed believer in the notion that at least one parent "being there" is absolutely necessary, being there especially when children so searchingly want and need a parent to help them, to soothe their fears, being there for their games and concerts, making them know they are wanted and loved. There is enough unforeseen messiness in later life to guarantee employment to psychiatrists without adding to the bill absent parents and nonexistent parental love. Mary Margaret was always there. Her presence became priceless, given my absences.

My firstborn, Courtenay, took her first ride on an airplane before she was one year old—it was on Air Force One. Our shelves are bulging with hundreds of photos taken of her with President Johnson in the White House. She became quite a famous young lady from the array of "LBJ and Courtenay" photos published in newspapers and on TV. When LBJ departed the presidency, I told Courtenay, "Sweetheart, we all fall from power sooner or later, but at the age of five!"

Courtenay, beautiful, serenely organized, a Tufts graduate, a staunch support base for her two siblings, now has a superior position with the Warner Bros. movie studio in Hollywood. As of this writing, she is executive vice president of Warner's film production division.

What pleases me—no, "pleases" is not right; "makes my heart sing" is a better phrase—is when young talent agents come up to me and say, "I know who you are, you're Courtenay Valenti's father." Yeah, I love that.

And when stars like Michael Douglas, George Clooney, Robert Redford, Rita Wilson and Tom Hanks, Charlize Theron, and others report how much they respect her judgment, her story sense, and her always joyful rapport with and support of the talented stars, producers, writers, and directors who work with her, it's hard to describe a father's reaction. They also report that she sticks to business. She knows what she believes in, and she will fight hard for a story she thinks ought to be told on the screen. She has another trait that in a high-voltage arena like Hollywood is wondrously rare: She is self-effacing almost to a fault. She is closemouthed about what she does at Warner Bros. She never mentions in social conversation the movie stars she works with and knows well. She devotes herself with single-minded force to her daily tasks. To Warner Bros. and its top executives, she is totally loyal. Quite a remarkable person, this Courtenay daughter of mine.

She married a tall, handsome-gifted artist, Patrick Roberts, who is an omnivorous reader, a loving husband, and a wonderful devoted father to my absolutely perfect grandchildren, Wiley and Lola Lorraine, now aged five and two and a half. It is rather odd to me that I am totally besotted with Wiley and Lola. I never really expected my reaction. Grandparenting was new to me; I had no idea how being a grandparent would affect me. I was surprised by the passions and the spread of love, unalloyed and unfenced, that roared about inside me. It is quite amazing.

I get my kicks talking to my son-in-law. Pat is movie-star handsome, but he has zero interest in what others think about his good looks because that is not what he is about. He's a loving, caring husband and father who adores his children and his wife. What I am most intrigued about is that he is the most antibullshit fellow I know. He tells you what he thinks and, most important, why he thinks it, because whatever the subject, the issue, or the controversy, he has read and digested its molecular composition. You may not agree with him, but that's your problem.

John, my Stanford graduate son, came into this world garlanded with a president as his godfather. John was born July 30, 1966, a short time after my entry into Hollywood. When he was a few months old, we asked President Johnson if he would agree to be John's godfather. The president thought that was a fine idea. And so did Mary Margaret and I.

We gathered at the Venezuelan embassy. Ambassador Enrique Tejera-Paris and his wife, Pepita, had a son, Gonzalo, born ten days earlier than John. Florence Mahoney, our dear friend whose husband once was editor in chief of all the Cox newspapers, would be godmother. Presiding over Gonzalo's and John's christenings was none other than the papal nuncio, the highest-ranking Catholic prelate in the United States since he was the personal emissary of the pope. Pretty heavy stuff for me, at least.

Naturally, the press was there in a big way. Not every day does a president of the United States show up at a foreign embassy with the papal nuncio, and for a christening of all things. The *Washington Post* carried a three-column photo of Mary Margaret, the president, and little John in my arms. Kind of nifty. I whispered in John's tiny little ear, "Son, take in as much of this as you can while you can. It doesn't get any better."

John has several traits his old father counts as having measureless value. He is loyal to friends and colleagues. He is energy in motion. He works without any clock to complete his chores. He is totally involved in whatever challenge he takes on. He has a joyous, inventive brain. From his earliest beginnings, he has been a reader, an excitement that to him is still alive. What he reads, he comprehends and remembers, which I find to be uncommon. He has an entrepreneurial streak in him. He is enriched by the prospect of building an enterprise from ground zero. With a partner, he has done that twice, only the last time the rise of his company collided with the high-tech bubble bust. It fazed him not at all. John has one last matchless quality—he has a mimic's flawless skill and a wit of sizable impact. The fact is people like to be around him and his always-available spirit-lifting magic.

The birth of Alexandra on October 9, 1968, was a day that caused me immense personal guilt. Mary Margaret had gone into

George Washington Hospital, but with sufficient forecasts on the part of her doctor that the birth would be several days away. I had to fly to Los Angeles on some urgent Hollywood business, but I felt confident I could complete my meetings and be back on the plane in plenty of time. Alas, when the plane set down in Washington, the airport sound system brayed loudly, "Mr. Valenti, please pick up the airport courtesy phone." Not too promising, I thought, and I was right. It was the hospital calling, telling me that Mary Margaret had just given birth to a fine healthy girl. I raced to the hospital, seething with the damnable knowledge that I should have stayed home to be present when the child was born. Mary Margaret was so full of a mother's pride that she forgave my absence. At least that's what she said.

Alexandra, my youngest, still remains a dauntless free spirit. Dark-haired beauty that she is, in contrast with my wife's blond fairness, she is casual about her loveliness. While it is part of her, she treats it with small regard. She came alive in middle school, devouring books and learning with ceaseless joy. To our delight, she was accepted at the University of California at Berkeley, where her intellectual curiosity blossomed. When I visited her on campus, I was taken aback because she was reading and quoting authors I never heard of. She has in the later years become fascinated by the camera, not being in front of it, but working behind it. She has directed a ten-minute short film featuring her good friends Minnie Driver and Sam Rockwell and is deeply involved in creating and directing music videos in Austin's thriving music-film landscape. She is blessed with a creative gift that she nourishes and expands. One of the nicer connections in her life is that her godparents are Anne and Kirk Douglas.

As for me, I can't wait for the future to present itself. New challenges, new problems, new summits to reach, and to possibly hear the sweet melodies of triumph. I know that everything changes. Nothing lasts. All things are forever in a state of flux. What is up will soon go down, and what is down will eventually go up. Change irrigates the landscape of politics—and life. In politics, twenty-four hours is an eternity.

Yet most of us resist change, except those who have little and expect even less. It is an ageless contradiction that we strive to keep what we have but wish that some change would gain entry into our lives. The British have tried the hardest to split that riddle. Anthony Bailey wrote that the queen is "an agent of change and a reminder of permanence," which may be the chief reason why the monarchy in Britain survives. But the British are ingenious. One observer of that sceptered isle wrote that "the English, not being a very religious people, invented cricket to give themselves a sense of eternity."

Nonetheless, there is one time that has not lost its hold on me. As I look back on my life, I am still tormented by that day in Dallas that stood witness to the murder of a young president. It haunts me to this hour. When that memory is triggered, it is as if all the grotesque horrors of tragedy come abruptly back to life. Every minute of that dismal mental tape flashes across my brain, blotting out everything else. Some four decades after the assassination, I was reminded of the power of those memories when I returned to that same bend of the street on Dealey Plaza.

I had been encouraged by the city manager of Dallas to visit the museum situated on the sixth floor of the Texas School Book Depository. Mary Suhm, a strikingly attractive woman, tall and imposing and accounted to be one of the most successful and effective of all city managers in the nation, said to me, "You of all people ought to visit that sixth-floor museum. After all, you were there when it all happened on Dealey Plaza just below the window on the sixth floor."

I came onto the sixth floor of the Texas School Book Depository with some foreboding. It is impaneled with photographs of that long-ago day, including a huge blowup of Lyndon Johnson being sworn in as the thirty-sixth president of the United States. I looked closely at this picture, LBJ with his right hand raised, and in the lower left corner was my own face, fastened intently on Johnson. As I stood looking at this photograph, my eyes unable to turn away, I was trapped in a cage of memory.

Then I moved on toward the sixth-floor window through which four decades ago Lee Harvey Oswald peered, aiming his bolt-action Mannlicher rifle. When I gazed out the window, I saw for the first time how terribly close the depository was to the traffic that swung around the bend onto Dealey Plaza. I could have thrown a baseball and hit a car moving below. I imagined a motorcade, cars moving slowly at eight miles an hour, and Oswald, a marine skilled with a Mannlicher rifle, at the ready on the windowsill. I thrust my hands together as if I were holding a rifle, aiming at the cars below. Then my hands began to tremble. Angry lizards started crawling over my flesh. A marksman would have no trouble in sighting and shooting, the target was so close.

Suddenly the scales fell from my eyes. It was November 22, 1963. For a brief harrowing moment, I was in the motorcade, traveling that strip of concrete. Six cars ahead was President John F. Kennedy and his wife, all smiles and jubilance. I stepped back from the window. But I have never been able to step back from that reality.

I know that I want to continue speaking before students to help them understand the inexpressible joy of serving this country. I tell them that no free, democratic nation can lay claim to greatness unless it constructs a moral compact that guides the daily conduct of the society, that inspires its people to believe in and nourish civic trust. This moral imperative is not connected to any religious denomination. Rather, it is a code of conduct that instructs people how their behavior toward others is a measure of the worth of their life.

The moral compact is shaped by what William Faulkner called "the old verities," the short words, the strong words, the ancient words (I even add a few more words of my own), words that define what this free and loving land is all about. To put it another way, these words give heft to the value of our values. Values are necessary to the fitness of any lasting society. I am not referring to the so-called values that animated the 2004 presidential election. Abortion and gay marriage are not values; they are social and political issues, which are subjects for debate.

The real values of this land are the "old verities": "duty, honor, service, valor, pity, pride, compassion, sacrifice." These are the great words to live by and die for. These are words that give birth to civic virtues that illuminate this nation's largeness of spirit, free and unhobbled, which is the mark of this democratic society. I tell high school and university students that if they treat these words casually, if they find them "uncool," if they regard them as mere play-words observed and honored only by the rubes and the rabble, the unlearned and the dumb-asses, then they will in time bear personal witness to the slow undoing of the greatness of America.

On December 10, 1950, on a stage in Stockholm, Sweden, the world was treated to an expression of belief so deeply felt and so strongly built that scarcely anything written can compare with its nobility. It is William Faulkner's speech when he accepted the Nobel Prize for Literature. I have read this speech many times. I have committed to memory some passages that give me solace and hope. One such passage becomes, in my mind, the true testament of the grandeur of this collection of states and peoples whose dreams and hopes might sometimes seem to lie scattered and in disarray, but in reality are bound up in the worth of our remarkable experiment in democracy.

Listen to this excerpt from Faulkner's speech:

"I decline to accept the end of man. It is easy enough to say that man is immortal simply because he will endure: that when the last ding-dong of doom has clanged and faded from the last worthless rock hanging tideless in the last red and dying evening, that even then there will still be one more sound: that of man's puny inexhaustible voice, still talking. I refuse to accept this. I believe that man will not merely endure: he will prevail. He is immortal, not because he alone among creatures has an inexhaustible voice, but because he has a soul, a spirit capable of compassion and sacrifice and endurance."

Few write with a pen as divine as Faulkner's, but all can read his words and know they speak directly to each individual heart. Since no one can lay exclusive claim to the ownership of truth, those words of truth are ours, for each of us to keep, to hold, to honor for ourselves as individuals, for our families, and for generations of Americans yet to be born.

That is the great secret of this country, for which so many have died for the long-term benefit of all who were born here, came here, and live here. My father, who at age twenty-four volunteered to go to France to fight with General Douglas MacArthur's Forty-second Rainbow Division during World War I, would endorse those words.

So would my immigrant grandfather, a semiliterate peasant from Sicily, who became a passionate American patriot who adored this country with a fervor that could not be measured. They had no doubts about this free and loving land.

Neither do I.

ACKNOWLEDGMENTS

A special brand of gratitude must go to Shaye Areheart, whose early embrace of this book now brings it to readers' eyes. For writers who sometimes believe they are singing uncertain melodies, to have a publisher want to make your book come alive is to truly feel a unique emotion. We share unforgettable memories for I first met Shaye when she was an editor working closely with Jacqueline Kennedy Onassis, who became the editor of my first novel. Lovely memories.

I must say "Thank you, thank you" to Peter Guzzardi, whose wise, always tolerant, and sensitive editing skills gave this book added value. Also, to Laura Ratchford, his colleague, who attended to my anxieties with graceful encouragements, I say "thank you" as well.

To the artisans and craftspeople at Harmony Books, my deep appreciation for giving this book what I judge to be an elegant and beautiful design.

I also wish to thank Jenny Frost, the president and publisher of the Crown Publishing Group, who believed in me and my book from day one.

Much grateful affection to my indispensable colleague, Judy Dickie, for her ceaseless attention to and labors on the countless details of completing a manuscript.

I pay special tribute to the LBJ Presidential Library in Austin, Texas, whose first-class researchers preside over an enterprise of openness and ever-ready assistance. Claudia Anderson was so wonderful in helping me dredge up remembrances of long-ago days.

My thanks also to Dr. Betty Sue Flowers, who oversees the LBJ Library with such effectiveness.

My gratitude to Bob Barnett, my lawyer and literary counselor, for his guidance and support.

Of course, my wife, Mary Margaret, was there beside me during this book journey, filling in those empty places where my memory flagged with her own intimate knowledge of LBJ's ceaseless attacks on the ills which besieged the nation. She was indispensable.

And finally I thank all my loving friends in the movie industry, those behind as well as in front of the camera. Special affection must be paid to the heads of the major studios over the long years, and to the Directors Guild of America, and its leaders, Michael Apted, Gil Cates, and Jay Roth for selecting me as one of only fourteen persons in the Hollywood community to become Honorary Life Members of the DGA since its founding in 1936. For all of the above who made every day of my almost thirty-nine years of my wondrous Hollywood adventure, full of laughter, excitement, some (momentarily) despairing moments, as well as the sweetness of some triumphs, I embrace them warmly. It was, for me, one helluva run.

INDEX

Note: **Boldfaced** page references indicate photographs.

Steven Spielberg, as everyone over the age of five knows, is the greatest cinematic storyteller of this generation. Just pick three of his films, *ET, Schindler's List,* and *Saving Private Ryan.* These three movies, each so different from the others, are a confirmation of Spielberg's cinematic genius. At the age of twenty, he sold himself to Sid Sheinberg, then president of MCA Universal, as a director, with a resolve to direct his first TV movie before he was twenty-one. He did. The TV film was *Duel,* a scary thriller of a killer truck with no visible driver. Hard on its heels came his first theatrical movie, *Sugarland Express,* starring Goldie Hawn. The Spielberg saga had begun its rainbow rising.

David Geffen is the exemplar of the classic American success story. He started out all alone as the manager of one musical star, and through a faultless facility for spotting talent, an intense interest in and genius for the business side of a mercurial creative arena, and a supernatural sense of timing, he rose to the summit of the music world with his own label, Geffen Records. Today, he is generally agreed to be a billionaire and then some. I will posit the following: It is far more valuable to have David Geffen as a friend than as an enemy. He never deserts his friends. He never forgets his enemies. I count David as a friend, which pleases me greatly.

Warner Bros. can claim the longest-lived, most stable management team, reaching back almost thirty years to Ted Ashley, talent agent–turned–studio boss just at the end of the lengthy reign of the founding Warner brothers, with Jack Warner the last of the breed. Over the last sixty years, only four men have ever sat in the office of Jack Warner on the Warner Bros. lot—Warner himself, Ted Ashley, Bob Daly, and now Barry Meyer. That's stability. Ted Ashley brought in Bob Daly, who had been successful as head of CBS.

When Daly took command of Warner Bros., he designed a management style and team that for two decades stayed continuously ahead of the curve and resisted mistakes. Some years into his tenure, Daly executed a masterstroke. He designated Terry Semel as cochairman and co-CEO. It is rare in U.S. business for any CEO, without pressure from the outside, to share ultimate power with a chosen colleague. It bespeaks a confidence, inner security, and vision on Daly's part.

Terry Semel's prime assets were a relentless energy and total confidence in his own judgments, which time and again were magically successful. The movie/TV world is so riven with the fear of making a big mistake that anyone who exudes assurance without the corrosive element of arrogance has momentum. Semel had it. He and Daly were a seamless team. They both resigned at the same time. Bob went on to run the Los Angeles Dodgers and later Save the Children.

Terry parachuted into what was, for him, the virgin territory of Silicon Valley, Sunnyvale, California. He purchased a huge block of Yahoo! stock and became CEO. At that time, Yahoo! was stumbling. Semel gave Yahoo! a new direction. He kept asking questions and demanding answers. Mainly he kept asking, "Why are we giving away everything we do? Have we ever thought about charging for some of it?" Hey, not a lousy question. He so stirred up that high-tech money-losing firm that it soared to merry new vistas of profitability. Semel's canny quick-study habits surprised the hell out of Wall Street as Yahoo! stock prices hit the stratosphere. If anyone doubted Semel's long-term visionary gaze in the movie business, his rousing success at Yahoo! dismantled those critics.

But the stability at Warner continued. Barry Meyer, who signed on in the beginning of the Daly regime, became CEO, with Alan Horn as president. The transition to Barry Meyer as chairman and CEO was swift, with neither creative bumps nor fiscal potholes. Barry's central personal prize is his long confirmed sense of integrity, along with his self-effacing, anti-publicity-seeking comportment. He is trusted, respected, and admired by employees, by competitors, by his superiors at Time Warner's headquarters in New York. It's as simple as that. He is far more often right than wrong, which makes him a candidate for most valuable player in any league.

Alan Horn, Harvard MBA, became president. Horn got his early tutorials as a relentless, hard-driving youngster with the incredibly successful TV programming team of Norman Lear, Jerry Perenchio, and Bud Yorkin. This trio created such titanic hits as *All in the Family*, *Maude*, and many more. Horn learned well on a very fast creative track. He has a deserved reputation for caring deeply about the art of moviemaking, which favorably impresses the talent, storytellers who want to do business with Warner Bros.—and with Alan Horn. There